PETER MATTHIESSEN, naturalist, explorer and novelist, was born in New York City in 1927 and graduated from Yale University in 1950. He also attended the Sorbonne and, in the 1950s, co-founded the *Paris Review*. His many expeditions to the wilderness areas of the world have taken him to Alaska, Asia, Australia, Oceania, South America, Africa, and Nepal – all of these journeys memorably described in such books as *The Cloud Forest, Under the Mountain Wall, The Snow Leopard, Tigers in the Snow* and in the three works reproduced in this volume. He has collaborated with some of the world's greatest wildlife photographers, including Hugo van Lawick in the original edition of *Sand Rivers*, and Eliot Porter in an edition of *The Tree where Man Was Born*. Matthiessen has also written eloquently of the fate of the North American Indians in *Indian Country* and *In the Spirit of Crazy Horse*; and he is the author of many works of fiction, including *At Play in the Fields of the Lord, Far Tortuga*, the short story collection *On the River Styx* and the critically acclaimed Watson trilogy.

" . . . an irresistible and effortless mix of natural history, anthropology, reflection and travelogue [and] a learned, poetic and profoundly moving portrait of the region . . . Even now, years after I first read it, *The Tree where Man Was Born* seems imbued with a precious vision"

JEREMY SEAL, *Sunday Times*

"*The Tree where Man Was Born* [is] the best travel book ever written about East Africa" BRIAN JACKMAN, *The Times*

"*African Silences* is a considerable achievement, an entertaining and disturbing expedition into the heart of ecological darkness"

AODHAN MADDEN, *Irish Times*

"Matthiessen is a talented writer, an imaginative traveller and a man of true originality" FRANK MCLYNN, *Independent*

"Our greatest modern writer in the lyrical tradition" *New York Times*

"One of our best writers" DON DELILLO

PETER MATTHIESSEN

An African Trilogy

The Tree where Man Was Born
African Silences · Sand Rivers

THE HARVILL PRESS
LONDON

This revised edition first published in 2000 by
The Harvill Press
2 Aztec Row
Berners Road
London N1 0PW

www.harvill.com

1 3 5 7 9 8 6 4 2

A CIP catalogue record for this book
is available from the British Library

ISBN 1 86046 788 1

Designed and typeset in Stone Print by
Libanus Press, Marlborough, Wiltshire
Printed and bound by Biddles Ltd,
Guildford and Kings Lynn

Contents

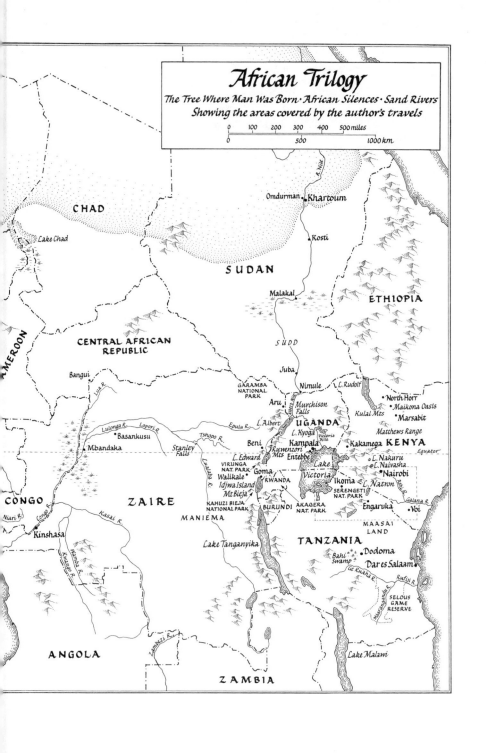

African Trilogy

The Tree Where Man Was Born · African Silences · Sand Rivers

Showing the areas covered by the author's travels

0   100   200   300   400   500 miles

0   500   1000 km

CHAD

Lake Chad

Omdurman · Khartoum

Kosti

SUDAN

Malakal

ETHIOPIA

CENTRAL AFRICAN
REPUBLIC

SUDD

Juba

Bangui

GARAMBA
NATIONAL
PARK

Nimule   L. Rudolf

Aru   Murchison
Falls

North Horr
Maikona Oasis
Kulal Mts   Marsabit

CAMEROON

Lulonga R.   Lopori R.

Epulu R.   L. Albert

UGANDA   L. Kyoga

Victoria
Nile

Matthews Range

Basankusu

Tshopo R.

Beni   Kampala   Kakamega KENYA

Mbandaka

Stanley
Falls

L. Edward   Ruwenzori   Entebbe   Equator
Mts

L. Nakuru
L. Naivasha

Lya R.

VIRUNGA
NAT. PARK Goma   Lake

Nairobi

Walikale

RWANDA   Victoria

Ikoma   L. Natron

CONGO   ZAIRE

Lualaba R.

Idjwa Island
Mt Bieja

SERENGETI
NAT. PARK

Galana R.

Kasai R.

KAHUZI BIEJA
NATIONAL PARK   BURUNDI

AKAGERA
NAT. PARK

Engaruka   Voi

Niari R.   Congo R.

MANIEMA

MAASAI
LAND

Kinshasa

Lake Tanganyika

TANZANIA

Kwango R.

Bahi
Swamp   Dodoma

Dar es Salaam

Wamba R.

Gt Ruaha R.

Rufiji R.

Mavagunga R.

SELOUS
GAME
RESERVE

ANGOLA

Zambezi R.

Lake Malawi

ZAMBIA

Introduction

In early 1961, on the way around the world to join an anthropological expedition into New Guinea, I journeyed from Cairo south up the Nile Valley, wishing to see Egypt's great temple at Abu Simbel (at that time threatened by the Aswan Dam), the warrior herdsmen of the South Sudan (fighting the Islamic government in Khartoum in the civil war that still continues four decades later), and the great animal herds of the Serengeti Plain, all of which, in 1961, seemed on the point of disappearance.

By steamer, train, and truck, I finally arrived in Uganda and Kenya traveling as far south as the Ngorongoro Crater, in the country still known then as Tanganyika (now Tanzania). A few days later, the Sunday air charter from Nairobi permitted a day's visit to the Serengeti, where I saw the first leopard of my life, and on the homeward journey, the plane surveyed the endless companies of plains game that is the greatest wildlife spectacle left on earth. However, I had no sense of having truly experienced the Serengeti, and when, in 1968, I was invited to return there by John Owen, director of the Tanzania National Parks, I fairly leapt at the opportunity. I would be provided with a small house at the edge of the Plain and my own Land Rover, research assistance from the park wardens and the field biologists of the Serengeti Research Institute and the freedom to explore on foot (so long as I did this out of sight of tourists and parks visitors).

These first travels in the Sudan and East Africa, continued over several years, were recounted in *The Tree where Man Was Born*. In the decade that followed, I returned regularly to Tanzania on visits to my wife's family in the Southern Highlands and southwestern Tanzania; I also visited Botswana and Namibia as a field guide for a wildlife safari company operating out of Austin, Texas.

In the winter of 1978 I reached West Africa, accompanying a primatologist, Dr Gilbert Boese, to Senegal-Gambia and Cote d'Ivoire on an informal survey of what was left of West African wildlife, from the dry savanna woodlands near the Sahara to the Guinea forests of the coasts. From there I continued eastward to the lakes and mountains of the great Rift Valley on the Zaire–Rwanda border, where I had a look at the rare mountain gorillas. Eight years later, in the winter of 1986, I returned to Central Africa, accompanying ecologist David Western (at that time director of the NY Zoological Society's research program, Wildlife Conservation International, and later director of Kenya's national parks) on a light plane survey of wilderness regions of Central African Republic, Gabon and Zaire. The primary purpose of our cross-Africa expedition – what turned out to be a very hazardous foray in a small light plane – was to determine the status of the small forest elephant, whose slender tusks were beginning to replace the larger ivory of the bush or savanna elephants on the world market; we also hoped to shed some light on the elusive and mysterious "pygmy elephant", which had been reported from these forests for nearly a century. On the way west, in Haut-Zaire, we would have a look at the small group of northern white rhino that had managed to survive the wars and poaching in their native range; in the region of the Sangha River where C.A.R., Gabon, and Cameroon come together in what is now the Dzanga-Sangha International Reserve, we would research the forest elephants; and on our return, we would join an okapi research project in Zaire's Ituri Forest and go hunting with the Mbuti Pygmies, perhaps the last large group of hunter-gatherers left on earth.

The two Central African journeys, are described in the second section, excerpted from *African Silences*.

Between these two journeys, in the winter of 1980, I accompanied the photographer Hugo van Lawick on safari to the remote southern regions of the Selous Game Reserve, in Tanzania, a region of 22,000 square miles – by far the largest wildlife sanctuary in East Africa, and also the least accessible and the least known; this "last safari into the last wilderness", as its sponsor, Tom Arnold, a young British MP had described it, was led by Brian Nicholson, the Selous' former warden, who had served there for more than twenty years and knew it better than anyone alive. Our vehicles proceeded to the end of the rough tracks at a beautiful confluence of rivers, where the warden and I forded the Mbarangandu not far above where it meets the Luwegu and continued southward on a foot safari, following the dry sand rivers and old elephant trails through the savannas and wooded hills. This foot safari is described in the third section, excerpted from *Sand Rivers*.

After each return from Africa – most recently, last winter (1998) – I think, well, that should do. But the longing for Africa, once contracted, is an incurable condition which, like malaria, recurs again and again. It is not so much the need to see wild creatures – though their multitudes and sounds, their forms and colors, are endlessly exhilarating – as the need for our own renewal of that precious glimpse of the earth's morning that stirred me so profoundly years ago.

Under the sky of the Sudan, the stillness in this ancient continent where our kind was born had made me restless, the echo of so much earthly life that had come and gone, the imminence of mystery withheld on the waiting air, eternal and yet present in each moment. Here in Africa, where whole landscapes seem alert, a sense of purity and danger is reawakened, of origins and time and mystery, as if some marvelous childhood faculty had been restored.

PART 1

The Tree where Man Was Born

In Memoriam

DEBORAH
LOVE
MATTHIESSEN

in love
and
gratitude

1 The Tree where Man Was Born

In the time when Dendid created all things,
He created the sun,
And the sun is born, and dies, and comes again.
He created the moon,
And the moon is born, and dies, and comes again;
He created the stars,
And the stars are born, and die, and come again;
He created man,
And man is born, and dies, and does not come again.
  Old Dinka Song[1]

The tree where man was born, according to the Nuer, still stood within man's memory in the west part of the south Sudan, and I imagine a great baobab thrust up like an old root of life in those wild grasses that blow forever to the horizons, and wild man in naked silhouette against the first blue sky. That bodeful man of silence and the past is everywhere in Africa. One hears the silence, hears one's step, and stops . . . and he is there, in the near distance. I see him still: a spear point glitters in the sun.

In the south Sudan, man is tall and gaunt, and black as the burnt skeleton of a tree: Dinka, who carves his scars in shallow v's, and Shilluk with his raised beads of skin in a string curling down toward the ear, and Nuer with six jagged welts, temple to temple – his terrible brows and filed front teeth, jutting like fangs, give Nuer a fixed death's head grin that is not to be mistaken for a smile. In 1961, a few still wandered as far north as Khartoum, where I first saw them. In mission shorts, they stalked the Arab bazaars of Omdurman, dwarfing the scurrying traders of the suq. Others crossed the Khartoum bridge near the confluence of the Blue Nile and the White. Oblivious of bridge and rivers, ignoring the horn blare and exhaust stink and shrill shouting of despised beings who owned no cattle, the entranced figures forded the twentieth-century traffic in the single file that would wind southward nearly a thousand miles across desert and river into Equatoria.

To most of the tribesmen, the Sudan government is a foreign power, having come into existence (in 1955) without the agreement or even the knowledge of many of its inhabitants: the desert north is a part of the Arab world while the south, a thousand miles away, lies in black Africa. In 1961, when I traveled south through Egypt and the Sudan into East Africa, these southern provinces – Upper Nile, Bahr el Ghazal, and Equatoria – had been made "closed territories", since the tribesmen would not heed their Moslem government. No foreigner could pass through without a permit, and no photographs of the naked peoples were permitted. Nor was the journey overland an easy one, for there was no road across the desert, which extends for several hundred miles south of Khartoum. In the absence of scheduled transport, I rode upon the cargo of an old trading truck sent south during the dry season by the merchants of Omdurman, and my bed of potatoes, wire tubing, tinware, and iron doors was shared with two whites met in Omdurman – a young student bound home for South Africa and a bearded American veteran of the Israeli wars with a hidden sheath knife, beret, dark glasses, and gold earring – as well as sixteen mission tribesmen, mostly Dinka and Shilluk, with a pair of Nuer. No matter how we arranged ourselves, we were never in close physical contact with less than five companions, and in the long wait and great heat, morale was low when at twilight the truck started up and set off through streets which even in the poorest towns of the north Sudan are swept clean daily by twig brooms; on a minaret, against a clear pink sky, a muezzin called the faithful to the prayers of evening.

Night had fallen by the time the truck had cleared the city, and a spray of stars froze on a blue-black sky. The vague track wandered south into a soft emptiness of cooling sand haired over thinly, here and there, by bitter thorns of drought. In the headlight's jogging beam danced ghostly gerbils, hopping and fluttering on tiptoe, like stricken birds. And farther onward, close to midnight, where the sands relented, came the birds of night – the African owl, and nightjars, and pale Senegal stone curlews whirling straight up into the dark like souls departing.

As the night passed, the way grew less distinct. Random tracks leading off into the void were followed faithfully by the driver, who was no Bedouin and knew nothing of the stars. Once the truck halted, and the Moslem cabal in the cab got out their prayer rugs, washed their feet, and in the beam of the headlights, touched their foreheads to the ground. Presumably they were pointed east, toward Mecca, but this did not appear to mean that they knew which way was south, for the truck soon halted once again, having traveled for some time in rude circles; shortly thereafter it was driven remorselessly into a ditch. The passengers leapt from the tilted cargo and stood in a long respectful line while the driver spun his wheels into the earth. When the axles touched at last, he left the truck and joined the line, contemplating the work of Allah with every evidence of satisfaction. Then everybody but the two Americans, who had none, got out blankets and lay down upon the desert.

The cold of the desert night, toward four, was the cold of the dark universe descended. Dawn came at last, and an hour later, a faint warmth; nourished by dusty dates and cold sardines, we dug the truck out of the desert. Solitary figures, white shrouds blowing, wandered the landscape; the brown lumps of their habitations merged with a stony rise a mile away. Near the ditch grew a thin grass, but elsewhere, as far as the eye could see in all directions, stretched sere distances burned off to gravel.

In the old millenniums of rain during the Pleistocene and after, much of this waste had been well-watered grassland. Years later, flying at dawn from Rabat on the Atlantic coast and drifting southeast over endless red infernal reaches of gravel, windspun sand, and smoky sky, I would see the ancient rivers of the Ice Age, like fossil tracings in the sands of the Sahara. Hunters had once wandered there, and left red drawings on those rocks, but now there was no sign of life, no track. Seven millenniums ago, when men of Asia brought wheat and barley, sheep and goats, to the lower Nile, the desert was already spreading, and the work of drought was rapidly advanced by the goats of man, which ate the thorn that had sewn tight a land that soon unraveled into sand.

The Stone Age hunters found by the Asians are known as the Tasarians and Bedarians, and the Afro-Asiatics born of these encounters raised villages on the flood plains of the Nile that would become the dynasties of Egypt. Until now, Africa had known no agriculture, nor any domestic animal except possibly the dog. But in the next one thousand years native plants were domesticated in West Africa, and certain millets in the highlands of Ethiopia. By 3500 BC, domestic stock appears to have passed into the hands of the West African Negroid peoples, perhaps by way of traders from the Mediterranean who were already opening up the great north-south caravan routes across the Sahara. Advanced cultures had rapidly developed in West Africa – the Nok culture is thought to have begun well before 2000 BC – but although some trade no doubt continued, the peoples of Bilad al-Sudan – Land of the Blacks – were little affected by the surge of Mediterranean civilizations. Domestic animals and a few plants had been acquired, but the age of bronze went by without their knowledge. Even the use of iron that had reached the Cush kingdom of Meröe, not far north of Khartoum, by 300 BC, took another thousand years to reach the tribesmen of the south Sudan, for the desert between the Nile and the mountains of Ethiopia was all but impassable, and travel on the river was impeded by the vast riverain swamp known as the Sudd, which prevented the extension of Egyptian splendors into the south and marked the southern limits of the Roman Empire. The Romans were still able to graze animals on what are now the sands of Libya, and Alexandrian ivory traders, mentioned in Ptolemy, brought back reports of the great central lakes and what are thought to be the snow-capped Ruwenzoris, the Mountains of the Moon, but few Mediterranean invaders got farther than that part of the Sahara called the Nubian Desert, an hallucinatory void burned by bright winds. What was left of the North African pastures was destroyed by hordes of Bedouins who swept through the northern continent ten centuries ago; today a few Arabs and sad donkeys cling to dim sand-strangled outposts, and a rare caravan of camels navigates by the lone railroad track that comes to Khartoum across the waste from Wadi Halfa.

As the day went on, the camels vanished from the sand horizons. Close to the Nile, the desolation was offset by a haze of grass behind the river banks, but this is a land of bare subsistence where the threat of drought is made worse by the desert locust. Today the sun had become fierce, and the bare land a reflector: distant huts turned eerily in a melted sun, like igneous lumps in the lava seas of a volcano. At the huts where the truck stopped to trade and cool its tires were hordes of a non-biting fly that seeks out moisture at the eyes and mouth. The flies formed black rings on the eyes of the small children, giving them a haunted appearance, but only the very smallest fretted, the rest having learned the resignation to discomfort that was so noticeable in the tribesmen on the truck. The "Europeans", as whites are known in Africa, were much less stoic. The damp touch of the flies, in company with heat and filth and a cumulative fatigue, brought on a half-delirium of thirst and soreness. We fashioned poor turbans out of rags, but the light refracted from the burnished land seared our faces to masks of leather. The Sudanese went bare-headed without complaint, but the Israeli veteran turned a dangerous color: with his dark glasses and rag-tattered head, he glared out over the land like some sort of mad avenger. And the South African boy, the only white to demonstrate with the African students in London after the notorious Sharpeville Massacre in his own country – he spent three weeks in jail for his pains – whose nerves, giving way in the press and stench of his multi-colored kind, brought forth the very phrase of the colonials that he had quoted earlier in contempt: "These bloody niggers, they're just down out of the trees!" He laughed at himself, close to tears, so shocked was he by his own outburst, and so relieved that these tribesmen spoke no English. Yet the Africans, who had learned that he came from the country of apartheid and were by no means blind to his ambivalence, plainly preferred him to the soldier, who was truly democratic in a way that few whites are, and recommended himself, besides, by an overt hatred for the Arabs in the cab, whom these tribesmen hated also: the Arab trade in slaves, which devastated the south Sudan in the nineteenth century, has never been forgotten or forgiven. But the soldier was beyond their ken, not the beret and beard and earring but because he kept no tribal distance, observed no protocol. Intensely conservative, fearful especially of the bizarre, the Africans glowered at the pantomimes and clowning that he offered as a means of communication. Caught up by the anti-white fever sweeping Africa, they felt patronized or even threatened, and were forever on the watch for foreign attempts to encroach upon native territories from the imperialist enclave set up just behind the cab, out of the desert wind. But the soldier tried and tried again, refusing to see that his friendliness gave offense, that these carved masks might have been just as suspicious, perhaps more so, of his black friends in America, who were also westerners, with a makeshift western sense of life and death.

Gradually the square huts of mud-brick were replaced by the African beehive hut, a cylinder of mud and sticks topped with straw thatch bound tight into a cone. In mid-afternoon, the truck reached Kosti, where we sat waiting in the suq for the sun to die. Kosti has what might be called a sewing-machine economy; ancient specimens of these instruments, in the smaller villages, are ordinarily the sole evidence of the machine age. We ate strange local sheep off doubtful ware, drank the black tea of the desert, and in the late twilight, started off again, traveling onward intermittently until after midnight, when once again we lay down upon the ground. The night was warmer, warm enough for the mosquitoes, and it came to an end at last. During the night, the hippos bellowed from the Nile, a distant sound, the first murmurings out of the heart of Africa.

The first light shone on a new land of long grass and small acacia, with occasional great solitary baobab. The feather-leaved, sweet-scented acacias or thorn trees, in their great variety, are the dominant vegetation in dry country south to the Cape, but the tree of Africa is the baobab, with its gigantesque bulk and primitive appearance; it is thought to reach the age of twenty-five hundred years, and may be the oldest living thing on earth. The grassland danced with antelope and birds – tropical hawks, doves, pigeons, guinea fowl and francolins, bee-eaters, rollers, hornbills, and myriad weavers, including the quelea or Sudan dioch, which breeds and travels in dense clouds and rivals the locust as an agent of destruction. At the edge of a slough stood two hundred crested cranes and a solitary ostrich, like a warder; where trees gathered in a wood were the white faces of the vervet monkey. In the afternoon, the savanna opened out on a great plain where gazelles fled to the horizons, and naked herdsmen, spear blades gleaming, observed the passage of the truck through the rushing grass with the alert languor of egrets. All the world was blue and gold, with far islands of acacia and ceremonial half-circles of human huts. Toward dusk, the truck arrived at Malakal, where it would turn to go back into the north.

* * *

The two days passed in Malakal, awaiting a ride south, I spent mostly on a long peninsula which cut off a swamp along the Nile edge. There was a footpath to a point on the peninsula where a Shilluk tended a weir; from here, in crude dugout canoes, the tribesmen crossed the river to a large village in a grove of palms. Respecting crocodiles, I did not press to be taken across, for the north wind which blows from November to March was sweeping up the river, and the canoes were desperately overcrowded; instead I watched the people come and go and listened to the singsong of their voices. Shilluk women who passed along the path bore cargoes on their heads, swaying like cobras through the blowing grass, and bands of girls, straight-backed, high-breasted, flirted and waved. The men were painted in a gray ash or red ocher, and the oldest had several rows of beads raised on their foreheads, but scarification, which is performed at a boy's initiation into the tribe, is dying out, for few younger men had more than a single row, and some were not scarred at all.

From the village across the river, on the wind, came a chant and a thump of drums. On the peninsula, bent figures hoed small gardens, and in the swamp behind, two naked fishers, laughing and arguing, handled a cast net. Cisticolas flitted through fierce reeds, and a snake slid out across some rotted sedge into the water, and trees of the river danced with turquoise rollers. In such a setting, in the expectant sunrise, the naked men seemed archetypal: here were dark figures of prehistory. A few centuries ago, the Shilluk lived as far north as Khartoum, and perhaps these glistening fishers were descended from some of the earliest known Negroids, a community of Middle Stone Age fishermen who inhabited the Khartoum region at least seven thousand years ago. (It has been suggested that the Khartoum fishermen invented pottery, possibly through the accidental burning of the mud-lined baskets that are still in use.[2]) The early Negroids appear to have been scattered and few; perhaps they were sedentary fishermen whose modern dominance of the African population came about with the development of agriculture. Possibly they evolved in the central lakes region, and only later came to occupy those regions southwest and west of the Sahara which are now associated with the "true Negro", whoever that may be: a skull contemporaneous with the skulls found at Khartoum has been dug up northeast of Timbuktu, in a land which had not yet turned to desert, and other remains of ancient Negroids have been found in Nigeria and on Lake Edward.

That so little is known of Negroid origins is one of the enigmas of inner Africa, where history must be deduced from chipped stones, clay sherds, rock paintings, and the bones of man and prey. It is presently assumed that Bushmanoid, Pygmoid, and Negroid are races of an ancestral African who adapted over the millenniums to differing environments – the open grasslands, the equatorial forests, the river basins – and would later share his continent with Caucasoids* out of the north, and that a confluence of Negroid and Caucasoid produced the long-headed, small-faced race called the Nilotes or Nilotic peoples, represented by these tall Shilluk casting their nets upon the Nile.

One morning on the Nile peninsula, in a large company of tribesmen, I met two Shilluk who had ridden on the truck. Dressed as they were in mission pants, their pagan scars and fierce filed teeth could only seem grotesque. The two candidates for civilization were glad to see me, for my acquaintance was an evidence of their worldliness. "*Ezzay-yek, ezzay-yek!*" they greeted me in Arabic – another attainment – and offered a passive rubber handshake. And staring after these new Africans as they moved off toward the river, I felt a terrific sadness. The Shilluk believe that when God set out to create man, he used light-colored clay, but toward the end his hands became dirty, and that the dark peoples were less favored than the light in such attainments as guns and a written language.[3]

There is a Nuer song that may have come from the Arab slaving raids of the last century . . .

> The wind blows *wirawira*.
> Where does it blow?
> It blows to the river . . .
> This land is overrun by strangers
> Who throw our ornaments into the river
> And draw their water from its bank.
> Blackhair my sister,
> I am bewildered.
> Blackhair my sister, I am bewildered.
> We are perplexed;
> We gaze at the stars of God.[4]

We left Malakal in the cab of a small pickup truck whose driver was called Gabriel Babili. A cable ferry took us across the Sobat River, where a group of Dinka washed

---

* The term "Caucasoid" is used loosely here to signify peoples with Eurasian blood who have mixed with Africans to varying degrees over the centuries. The Caucasoids include the Hamitic-speaking Berber, Tuareg, Egyptians, and Ethiopians of northern Africa as well as more recent Semitic invaders such as the Arabs and Somali; the northern Sudanese today are a mixture of Arab, Hamite, and Negro. Since racial and linguistic groupings are still disputed by authorities, so that no two books on Africa are consistent, I have confined myself where possible to the names of the main language families (cf. Nilotic, Hamitic, Semitic) and avoided more precise and less dependable terms such as Nilo-Hamitic, Cushitic, Sudanic, Afro-Asiatic, etc. The selected references-bibliography at the end of the text will indicate where full discussion of such questions may be found.

themselves, slowly and gracefully, beside a stranded metal whaleboat, a sister craft of the British boat in the museum of the Mahdi wars, at Omdurman. In the windblown grass along the track, men of the Nuer carried paired spears of the style used by the Dervishes, which, together with hoes, fish-hooks, and ornaments, are gotten in exchange for hides. The truck stopped everywhere to trade. Once the way was blocked by a great herd of the archaic cattle of Egyptian art, their huge horns curved inward at the tip. The herdsmen were coated from face to foot with ash; the mouths and eyes in the gray masks looked moist and hideous. Some were heedless of the truck, not understanding it, and others, panicked by the horn, fled for their lives. "Across the dry plains to the east ran a road to Abyss-in-i-a," said Gabriel Babili, who had a bad smell, mission English, and an enchanted smile.

Christian missions were established in the south Sudan as early as AD 540, at the time of the Axumite Christianity in Ethiopia, and the Nubian kingdoms that resulted held out against the tide of Islam until the fourteenth century. But modern missions set up at the turn of this century in what had become the Anglo-Egyptian Sudan do not appear to have made a deep impression. The people are beautiful, the women modest, and the girls saucily turned out in head feathers, beads, copper bracelets, and cowries, but away from the towns the men go naked – from a narrow point of view, that is, for often those parts of their persons of no interest to moralists are superbly decorated with beads and clay – and this freedom from shame is a source of distress to missionary and Mussulman alike.

In terms of material culture, the Nilotes of the south Sudan have remained among the most primitive people in Africa, and moral disapproval of their condition dates back at least as far as the 1860s, when the august Sir Samuel Baker, barging upriver with Mrs Baker and a sedate avalanche of baggage in search of the headwaters of the Nile, concluded that the Dinka had less character than dogs (perhaps Sir Samuel had stern British dogs in mind) due less to this abominable nudity than to what Sir Samuel perceived as an unconscionable absence of rules and regulations in their society or for that matter of any society at all that could be recognized as such by a subject of Her Britannic Majesty. But, in fact, the Nilotic societies are based on a very elaborate set of laws and customs, including the practice among Dinka and Shilluk of their own form of ancient Egyptian divine kingship, with its custom of putting to death the failing chief. Among the Dinka, the Master of the Fishing Spear indicates by a sign of the hand that he is now to be buried alive "to avoid admitting . . . the involuntary death which is the lot of ordinary men and beasts".[5]

The Nuer and Dinka subsist chiefly on milk, cheese, and blood drawn by arrow from their animals' necks. In the rainy season, they grow millet, and in the dry season, when the cattle are herded to the rivers, they eat fish. They are poor farmers and poor hunters, which accounts for the abundance of wild creatures in their land. In effect, their dependence on cattle is total. Besides blood and milk (meat is rarely eaten except when a beast dies of its own accord) the herds furnish dung for fuel and plastering, hides for decorative leather articles, tail hairs for tassels, bones for armlets and utensils, horns for spoons and fishing spears, and scrota for pouches. The ashes of burnt dung supply hair dye and hair straightener – the hair of the Nilotes is markedly longer than that of the Bantu peoples farther south – as well as mouthwash, and the urine is valued not only for tanning but for churning and cheese-making and for bathing the face and hands. Inevitably, intertribal wars are fought over cattle and cattle land, the aggressors being the Nuer and the victims the Dinka. Originally, God gave an old cow and a calf to Dinka and to Nuer, his two sons, but Dinka stole the calf of Nuer under cover of darkness. God, enraged, ordered Nuer to seize Dinka's cow, and the Nuer have done so ever since. It remains the tradition of both tribes that the Nuer takes openly what the Dinka takes by stealth, and the Nuer adhere to an ancient custom of raiding and killing Dinka, who are resigned to their inferior role and offer small resistance; instead they prey upon the Bari, who live mostly on the islands of the Nile and, as a defense against mosquitoes, are said to array themselves each night in a coat of mud. The Nuer rarely war on the more sedentary Shilluk, who have few cattle and subsist mostly on maize meal, eked out by small animals speared in the night and by trapped birds. Alone of the three tribes, they have developed a crude snare, but they remain poor hunters, and are often hungry. The Nuer say[6] that formerly Stomach lived apart from Man, off in the bush, an unobtrusive creature glad of a few roasted insects from the bush fires. Then Man permitted it to join his body, and it has tormented him ever since. But in most tribes in the Sudan and elsewhere, hunger and all human afflictions came about with God's departure from the world. Once the sky pressed so close to the earth that the first man took care when he lifted spears or tools, lest he strike God. In those times, so the Dinka say, God had given the first man and woman one grain of millet every day, and this was plenty, until the woman took more than her share and, using a longer pestle, struck the sky. Then the sky and God withdrew out of man's reach, and ever since man has had to work hard for his food, and has been visited by pain and death, for God is remote, and rarely hears him.[7]

The savanna was still gold, still blowing. Toward sunset, the grass turned silver, and in a strange light a cheetah slipped across the track, its small head carried low. The plain changed gradually to woodland – acacias, fig, baobab, euphorbia, and palms. Soon vegetation crowded to the road, which was crossed at dusk by a band of bush-pig, neat-footed and burly, neck bristles erect, as if intent on punching holes right through the truck. They churned into the scrub. Gabriel, dire in all his thoughts, spoke darkly of encounters with night elephants, and blinded himself by keeping the lights on inside the cab "so other car not hit we", although no other car had been seen that day. He was also fearful of rebellious tribesmen, who were raiding the government posts and whose attitudes toward drivers, most of them Arab, were not to be depended on. In this district alone, he said, seven warriors had been shot down in the past month.

The road edge glittered with night eyes – jackals, a porcupine, mongoose, a squirrel, small cats, gazelles, and the small woodland antelope known as duiker. I kept an eye out for an antelope known as Mrs Gray's lechwe, but this intriguing creature remained hidden. Toward nine, the truck surprised a pair of lionesses in the track; two males crouched down into the grass off to one side. These first wild lion I had ever seen were stirring, turning their heads without haste to regard the lights, then vanishing in matched bounds into the dark, one to each side. I stared at the dusty grass where they had gone, but the night was still. Perhaps the cats had been stalking a tiang, for moments later a band of these large blue-flanked antelope (the East African race is called the topi) fled past, eyes flashing. Panicked by the truck, they seemed at the same time drawn to it, rushing the headlights, one by one, before veering away.

That night was spent on the floor of a Dinka hut, with bats chirping in the thatch above and the rhythm of chants and tom-toms in the distance. Toward four, we resumed the journey south. In a rainy mist, at dawn, a giraffe crossed the track and moved off westward toward the Sudd, pausing after a time to peer over its long shoulder. By midday, the track had come to Equatoria, the southernmost province of the Sudan, and late that afternoon it arrived at Juba, where we said good-bye to Gabriel Babili.

At Juba, the sweet smells of rot on the soft air, the tin ring and squawk of radios across the bare dirt yards of open-air cafés, the insect din, the mango trees in silhouette against the southern stars, evoke all tropics of the world. In the river, a few hippos rise and sink, and a lone ostrich, property of the governor, skirts pools in the mud street, and lepers come and go like the brown kites, tattered and scavenging. In early February, 1961, it was a refuge for displaced Belgians from the Congo, who occupied every bed at the hotel, and in a lot nearby the cars abandoned by refugees already fled to Europe were gathering red dust. The hostel of sorts to which we were sent had been commandeered by fleas, and we slept outside upon the ground, departing Juba without regret the following day. Through the border town of Nimule, the Sudanese assured us, passed all manner of transport into Uganda, for was not Nimule the frontier city of the largest country in all Africa, with vehicles arriving from all corners of the world?

Our truck climbed all afternoon toward the plateaus of central Africa. But thanks to a dispute with the Arab driver incited by the soldier, who had risked our lives on more than one occasion by saluting the Moslems with hurled spit, we were thrown off in the dead of night at a silent crossroads known as Mangara. The culprit, who would clown in hell, ran after the truck down the road. "Hey, fellas, *wait* a minute! Like, there are *lions* here!" A kind citizen, attracted by his outcry, soon stood beside us in the darkness, and opened a room of the crossroads store for us to sleep in, and toward noon of the next day another truck picked us up and took us on to Nimule. There the border guards admitted that no machine of any kind had challenged their barrier in many days, though they, too, expressed confidence that Nimule was the crossroads of the world.

Nimule is little more than a gathering of huts to which women carried water on their heads a mile or more uphill from the river, and the fried fish, bananas, papaws, and a scrawny pullet scavenged in the village would not be enough to see us through the long hot days. But we did not know this in the beginning, and at dawn on the second day, before any vehicles that might take us south could arrive from Juba, the South African and I walked a few miles downriver, where a small tract has been set aside for wildlife.

Nimule is the only national park in the Sudan, and in the number and variety of animals to be seen in a small area, it is one of the best in Africa. It is also one of the most beautiful, a natural park between the mountains and a bend in the Albert Nile. To the south and west, early one morning, the mountains of Uganda brought the sky of Africa full circle. Somewhere in those mountains, down to the southeast, lived a light, small people called the Ik who until recently used pebble tools of the sort made in the Old Stone Age; in the Congo's Ituri Forest, to the west, lived Pygmies who still carried fire rather than make it.

Soft hills inset with outcrops of elephant-coloured boulders rose beyond a bright stretch of blue river, and elephants climbed to a sunrise ridge from a world that was still in shadow. More than a hundred moved slowly toward the sun; the landscape stirred. The small boat manned by two askaris – rangers in khaki shirts and shorts, rakish safari hats, and long puttees – pushed through reeds and scudding nympheas to the open water.

On the west bank, the askaris shook small bags of a fine dust to gauge the direction of the wind. We moved inland. Very soon there arose out of a copse a herd of buffalo, with its coterie of cattle egrets rising and settling once again on the twitching, dusty backs. To judge from the rapidity with which the askaris cocked their rifles, we were too close; the beasts took a few steps forward. Wet nostrils elevated to the wind, they wore an aggrieved, lowering expression. There were no handy trees to climb, and I wondered how to enter most promptly and least painfully the large thornbush close at hand. But the buffalo panicked before I did, wheeling away in dark commotion, leaving the white birds dangling above the dust.

To the south, on a rise that overlooks the Albert Nile where it bends away into Uganda, a herd of kob antelope stepped along the hill – some sixty female kobs and calves led by a single male with sweeping horns and fine black forelegs – and the delicate oribi, bright rufous with brief straight horns, scampered away in twos and threes, tails switching. A gray duiker, more like a fat hare than an antelope, gathered its legs beneath it in low flight, and a sow wart hog with five hoglets, new sun glinting on the manes and the inelegant raised tails, rushed off in a single file at the scent of man. Here and there a stately waterbuck regarded us, alert.

Kob and waterbuck would be large animals elsewhere in the world, but here they seemed almost incidental, for to the east of them, the entire hillside surged with elephant, nearly two hundred now, including a few tuskers of enormous size. And to the north, on a small hillock, stood four rhinoceros, one of these a calf. The askaris approached the rhino gradually, keeping downwind – not always a simple matter, as the light wind was variable – and eventually brought us within stoning distance of the animals; they were astonished that we had no cameras, but simply wished to *see*. The rhinos were of the rare "white" (*weit*, or wide-mouthed) species, a grazing animal that lacks the long upper lip of the black rhino, which is a browser; mud-crusted, with their double horn, their ugliness was protean. The cow and calf having moved off, two males were left, and these, aware of an intrusion but unable to detect it, moved suspiciously toward each other, stopping short at the last second as if to contemplate the risks of battle, then retreating simultaneously. Having just come to Africa, I did not know that the white rhino is gentle and rarely makes a charge; buffalo in herds are also inoffensive, and no doubt the askaris were teasing as well as pleasing us, though they kept their laughter to themselves.

Beyond the rhino, dry trees rose toward the dusty mountains, and beyond the hills hung the blue haze of Africa, and everywhere were birds – stonechats and silver birds, cordon bleus and flycatchers, shrikes, kingfishers, and sunbirds. Overhead sailed vultures and strange eagles and the brown kite of Africa and South Asia, which had followed me overland two thousand miles from Cairo, up the Nile. Here in Equatoria, in the heart of Africa, with Ethiopia to the east, Uganda and the Congo to the south, Lake Chad and the new states of what was once French Africa to the west, one sensed what this continent must have been, when the white rhinoceros was not confined to a few pockets but wandered everywhere, like the kites, from the plains of Libya south to the Cape of Good Hope. Today Libya is a desert, and the wild things disappear. The ragged kite, with its affinity for man and carrion, will be the last to go.

2 White Highlands

In a low and sad voice (Moga wa Kebiro) said that strangers would come to Gikuyuland from out of the big water, the colour of their body would resemble that of a small light-coloured frog (kiengere) which lives in water, their dress would resemble the wings of butterflies; that these strangers would carry magical sticks which would produce fire.... The strangers, he said, would later bring an iron snake with as many legs as monyongoro (centipede), that this iron snake would spit fires and would stretch from the big water in the east to another big water in the west of the Gikuyu country. Further, he said that a big famine would come and this would be the sign to show that the strangers with iron snake were near at hand. . . . That the nations would mingle with a merciless attitude towards each other, and the result would seem as though they were eating one another.... Many moons afterwards ... the strangers dressed in clothes resembling the wings of butterflies started to arrive in small groups; this was expected, for prior to their arrival a terrible disease had broken out and destroyed a great number of Gikuyu cattle as well as those of the neighbouring tribes, the Masai and Wakamba. The incident was followed by a great famine, which also devastated thousands of the tribesmen.
Jomo Kenyatta, *Facing Mt Kenya*

Those days at Nimule I recall as the longest in my life. There was no point in trying to cross the border, as the nearest town was far away across an arid plain. For fear of missing the stray vehicle that might pass through, we waited forever at the guard post, and during this period – though we never knew the reason for the crisis until days later, when finally we got away into Uganda – Patrice Lumumba, the firebrand of the new Africa, was murdered at Katanga in the Congo.

Overnight, the friendly Sudanese became bitterly hostile. Guards and villagers gathered in swarms, their pointing and muttering interspersed with shouts and gestures. We could not understand what was being said, but it seemed clear that our crime was being white – so far as we knew, there were no members of our race closer than Juba, a hundred miles away – and that our fate was being decided. (Numbers of whites were killed that year in Africa; a thousand died in Angola alone.[1]) Until now, the people of Nimule had been gentle and hospitable. The schoolmaster had offered us his hut, and even his own cot, and when our food ran out, the border guards shared their calabash of green murk and tripes into which three dirty white hands and seven or eight black ones dipped gray mucilaginous hunks of manioc, a low vegetable that, like maize, was brought to Africa from the Americas at the time of the Atlantic slave trade.

After a day and night of dread, peremptorily, we were summoned once more to eat from the communal bowl. Doubtless the schoolteacher had interceded for us, though he had been at pains to seem as hostile as the rest. I knew we must accept the food to avoid discourtesy, and the South African agreed; bravely he gagged down his tripe, retiring immediately behind a hut to puke it up again. But my countryman refused to feed, declaring that if he ate he would die anyway; he ignored our pleas and curses. The Africans took baleful note, and muttered, but did nothing; like the tribesmen on the truck south from Khartoum, they feared this hairy avatar, who sat inscrutable behind dark glasses, making strange ceremonial dipping motions with his hand.

In Uganda, parting company with my companions, I made my way southwest to Murchison Falls, where the upper Nile, descending from the high plateaus of the central continent, bursts through a narrow gorge. From there I went to Queen Elizabeth National Park, across Lake Edward from the Congo, which has a prospect of the Mountains of the Moon, and from there to Kampala, north of Lake Victoria. This wet and fertile country of the central lakes is a great kingdom of the Bantu peoples, who form the mass of the population throughout east, central, and south Africa. The Bantu – their own word for "people", used by scholars to describe a language family rather than an ethnic group – are made up of many tribes in many countries, most of them tillers of the soil. Banana fronds and smoke-plumed villages fill a landscape of wild sunlit colors set against purple clouds. Graceful people in white shirts and bright kangas walk everywhere along red roads to flowering markets, and the umbrella, jitney bus, and bicycle are ubiquitous – an African of Kenya tells[2] of seeing a Ugandan with a whole stove mounted on his bicycle, upon which he prepared and cooked and ate his meal while pedaling along.

For all its life, there is something about this domesticated country of rank greens and imminent rain that I found oppressive. In East Africa, most of the limited land suited to agriculture lies in the weather of great lakes and mountains, in country of heavy humid leaves and bruised thick skies, and the small farms or shambas, each with its corn patch, thatch hut, and roosters, differ little from those to be seen in tropics all around the world – this was not the East Africa of my imaginings, a remote region shut away until a century ago by deserts and mountains of north Africa, the rain forests of the Congo, the gray thorn nyika and unnavigable rivers of the Indian Ocean coast, a land of wild beasts, silence, and immensities where man was a lone herdsman with a spear or a small aborigine with bow and arrow. Also I felt ambivalent among the Bantu, or at least among acculturated Bantu, whose adoption of western dress and aspirations had been accompanied almost everywhere by rejection of western rule. Patrice Lumumba, whose murder had involved us so abruptly in the chaos of anti-colonialism, had been a Bantu, and these people share much with the black American or West Indian whose ancestors were transported out of Africa in Anglo-Saxon ships, and whose anger and unrest and hope lashes the white conscience in the cities of the West. The Bantu is the new African who is met with in Kampala and Nairobi, in streets and offices, shops, customs, roadsides, markets. I shook his hand, said, "Jambo, Bwana!" and smiled warmly. In shirt and tie, speaking good English, he seemed deceptively familiar, and only several journeys later did I see that in my ignorance and lack of curiosity I had failed to perceive him at all. Yet it is these people, not the gentle hunters, the fierce herdsmen, whose history is the most remarkable on the southern continent, these Bantu-speakers who overcame the stupefying obstacles of tropical climate and disease, tribal warfare and wild animals, to move and expand and found cities and kingdoms far in the interior of what the western world, until a century ago, had dismissed as Darkest Africa.

In January, 1961 – perhaps during the days that I spent at Nimule – Patrice Lumumba wrote a last letter to his wife.

I am writing these words not knowing whether they will reach you, when they will reach you, and whether I shall still be alive when you read them. . . . History will one day have its say, but it will not be the history that is taught in Brussels, Paris, Washington or in the United Nations. . . . Africa will write her own history, and to the north and south of the Sahara, it will be a glorious and dignified history. . . . Do not weep for me, my dear wife. . . . Long live the Congo! Long live Africa! [3]

The earliest record [4] of East Africa, from an Alexandrian trading voyage of the first century AD, makes no mention of any black men, and it is probable that none were there; east and south Africa were still the province of Bushmanoid hunter-gatherers and the Caucasoid herdsmen who were drifting down the continent along the grassy high plateaus of the interior. Derived from the Caucasoids, it appears, were the "Azanians" found along the coast of "Zinj" – tall bearded men, "red" in color, a piratical tribe of fishers who traded tortoise shell, soft ivory, and aromatic gums for iron blades and beads and cloth. Perhaps by this time the Azanians had mixed with those early Indonesians who brought the out-rigger canoe and the marimba to the Indian Ocean coast and were to colonize Madagascar. Then, in the first centuries of the Christian era, waves of black peoples appeared out of the interior, bearing iron tools and weapons of their own.

The knowledge of iron that had spread from Meröe on the Nile, traveling to West Africa, perhaps, by way of old trade routes to Lake Chad, then south and east again through equatorial forest that metal tools and domestic plants had made less formidable, had encouraged a surge in population. Among the peoples set in motion were the ancestors of the Bantu-speakers, who are thought to derive from Negroid stocks in the Cameroon Highlands region of the Niger River. Wherever they came from, it appears that the great Bantu increase that impelled a geographic spread took place in middle Africa, in the Katanga region between the headwaters of the Congo and Zambezi, where an advanced and very wealthy civilization that mined and traded in copper had developed at Lake Kisale by the eighth century. By that time, Bantu peoples had occupied both coasts and settled the fertile lands around Lake Victoria, and within a few centuries, with remarkably small divergence in the Bantu tongue, they had spread throughout the subcontinent as far south as the Cape, then north again into present-day East Africa, and along the coast to the Juba River and Somalia. From the Caucasoids, perhaps, they acquired the Ethiopian millets and domestic animals that permitted them to settle the dry countries of south Africa, where many became herdsmen. On the southeast coast, they had access to such tropical Asian crops as the banana, yam, and taro, the coconut and mango. The implement of Bantu pros-perity was the iron blade, in ax and hoe and spear, which insured their dominance and the adoption of their language almost everywhere. Older Negroid stocks found living along the rivers as well as certain herdsmen and hunter-gatherers were absorbed – hence the variety of Bantu physical types, which are mostly lighter and less prognathous than the Negroids of West Africa. Even today, as far south as Natal, non-Negroid features are discernible in certain Zulu who interbred with the Xam Bushmen, and adopted a Khoisan language, whereas the Pygmies of the Congo and the pygmoid Twa of the central lakes are clearly of the Old People in origin, despite their adoption of Bantu speech.

In most of East Africa, the Middle Stone Age gave way abruptly to the Iron Age, without that intervening stage of New Stone Age settlement that came about elsewhere with the domestication of plants and animals. Yet here and there the remains of Neolithic earthworks, terraces, dams, wells, and irrigation ditches have been found, together with stone "hut circles" or pit dwellings dug into wet hill regions suitable for farming. These are thought to be the work of northern peoples, the Caucasoid "Proto-Hamites", precursors of the modern Hamites of north Kenya and Ethiopia. The great kingdoms of the interior – the mining civilization at Katanga, the stone city of Great Zimbabwe in Rhodesia, the lake kingdoms of Uganda and Ruanda-Urundi – were all Bantu domains, but Zimbabwe, at least, may have been influenced in its construction by the northerners, who are known to have worked in stone.

On the east coast, the Azanians soon vanished among the eastern Mediterraneans and the Asians – Persians, Indians, Chinese – whose brown sails, on the winds of the monsoon, were drawn like kites to a growing trade in tortoiseshell, gold, ivory, amber, leopard skins, myrrh, frankincense, and slaves. Traditionally the Bajun fishers that one sees today at Lamu, on the Kenya coast, are descended in part from the Persians. By the tenth century Moslem Arabs were dominant, and long before medieval times the trading forts that have since become the small cities of the coast had been established. Meanwhile, the Bantu were beset by waves of Nilotic and Hamitic peoples moving south, and their political systems disrupted everywhere by feverish tribal wars set loose by the slave trade, which was intensified, in the sixteenth century, by the arrival on the east coast of Portuguese navigators, first among the Europeans. Though they established trade with the people of the Zimbabwe region, the Portuguese knew nothing of the interior. The slaving caravans not run by local tribes – for the tribes were encouraged to prey upon one another – were managed by Arabs or Swahili Bantu, a coastal people that intermixed with the Arabs (could the Swahili have derived from the Azanians?) and whose tongue, with its elements of Arabic, was to become the trading language of East Africa.

In South Africa, at the Cape, the Dutch East India Company established a supply port for its fleet in the seventeenth century, and later the Dutch South Africans known as the Boers, trekking inland, helped to set off a great northward expansion of Ngoni Zulu, who were to overrun Zimbabwe and settle finally in the region of Lakes Nyasa and Tanganyika. Elsewhere the Europeans had no territorial ambitions nor even curiosity about the hinterland, with its fierce heat, tsetse fly, beasts, spears, disease, and pillage. Such missionary-explorers as David Livingstone who penetrated into central Africa in the mid-nineteenth century were astonished to find elaborate civilizations based on concepts that apparently had filtered southward by way of Meröe and the Sudanic civilizations, and certain baroque and cruel customs of these kingdoms laid a firm base for the belief in African barbarism that has been used ever since to excuse the more refined atrocities of the pale peoples from the north, but much of this despotism arose out of the anarchy brought by the slave trade and the advent of firearms. It may be that at the time of the white man's coming the great Bantu kingdoms were already in decline, leaving few traces of the past, for in the tropics, a city of thatch and timber – not necessarily more primitive than one of stone – would subside into the earth with the turn of seasons.

In the late nineteenth century, for political reasons having little to do with Africa, the nations of Europe had embarked on colonial conquest. Less than twenty-five years after Speke and Grant had discovered the Nile headwaters, in 1864, East Africa had been divided into British and German spheres of influence, and by the turn of the century, a railroad had been built from Mombasa, on the Kenya coast, into Uganda. In the next decades, plantations of cotton, coffee, tea, pyrethrum, sisal, and pineapple drew more and more white settlers to East Africa, and modern medicine, like the iron hoe two thousand years before, brought on a renewed increase in the African population. Now, however, there was nowhere left for these Africans to go.

The Kikuyu of Kenya who occupied the highland forests when the first Europeans appeared in the late nineteenth century had not been there for more than a few centuries. Tradition and the evidence agree that they came from Juba Land, north of the Tana River, toward the coast, having been displaced in the fifteenth or sixteenth centuries by invasions of Galla nomads from the Horn of Africa, who had been displaced in their turn by waves of Somali crossing the Red Sea from Arabia. At the headwaters of the Tana on Mt Kenya and the Aberdares, the Kikuyu came upon a small, pit-dwelling people known as the Gumba who presently vanished into hiding places underground and failed to reappear. Broken pots of a people presumed to be Gumba have been found high in the Aberdares, on the cold moors to which the remnant aborigines retreated. Jomo Kenyatta, who in the thirties won a degree in anthropology as a student of the eminent Malinowski, at the University of London, suggests that these Old People absorbed the first Kikuyu wanderers into the region, and made hunters of them, and that the resultant race was that hunting tribe of obscure origin whose remnants are known today as the Dorobo: "There is strong reason to support the latter theory, for soon after the Gumba had disappeared as a race, there came into being another race of hunters known as the Ndorobo or Aathi, who seemed to have grown like mushrooms in the forests. Unlike their predecessors they were not short in stature, but something between the Gumba and the Gikuyu." In any case, the Kikuyu interbred extensively with other peoples, for at the turn of the twentieth century, at least, certain Kikuyu clans claimed blood relationship with tribes as various as the Maasai, Kamba, and Dorobo, as well as the Chagga of Kilimanjaro.[5]*

* "Masai" is properly "Maasai" and "Kikuyu" is more accurately "Gikuyu", but in the latter case I have retained the "literary" spelling, which is now favored by the tribe; also, I have dropped the Wa– prefix (signifying "people"), which is used so inconsistently throughout the literature (one finds Wakamba but not Wakikuyu, Wandorobo but not Wamaasai).

From the beginning, the aboriginal hunters, small and few, and the primitive herdsmen, who drifted with the seasons and remained isolated in their own customs, were more agreeable to Europeans than the Bantu cultivators, who were not only ambitious but occupied the most desirable land. A prejudice that still continues was set down as early as 1883, in the region of what is now Nairobi:

At Ngongo we had reached the southern boundary of the country of Kikuyu, the natives of which have the reputation of being the most trouble-some and intractable in this region. No caravan has yet been able to penetrate into the heart of the country, so dense are the forests, and so murderous and thievish are its inhabitants. They are anxious for coast ornaments and cloth, and yet defeat their own desires by their utter inability to resist stealing, or the fun of planting a poisoned arrow in the traders. These things they can do with impunity, sheltered as they are by their forests, which are impenetrable to all but themselves.[6]

But within a few years another explorer had perceived that this tribe "was destined to play an important part in the future of East Africa",[7] and the young engineer who became famous for killing the man-eaters of Tsavo, two great maneless lions that terrorized the railroad construction crews for months, considered the Kikuyu intelligent and industrious.[8] So did an official of the Imperial British East Africa Company – later Lord Lugard, greatest of all African administrators – who had to fight them at what is now the Nairobi suburb of Dagoretti. "Kikuyu promised to be the most progressive station between the coast and the lake," Lugard wrote in *The Rise of Our East African Empire*. "The natives were very friendly, and even enlisted as porters to go to the coast, but these good relations received a disastrous check. Owing largely to the want of discipline in the passing caravans, whose men robbed the crops and otherwise made themselves troublesome, the people became estranged, and presently murdered several porters." The East Africa Company, obsessed with the promise of Uganda, was inefficient and undercapitalized in Kenya, and its agents ravaged the villages of both the Kamba and Kikuyu in an effort to make the Machakos and Dagoretti stations self-supporting. As the British Commissioner at Zanzibar had written to his wife in 1893, "By refusing to pay for things, by raiding, looting, swashbuckling, and shooting natives, the Company have turned the whole country against the white man."[9]

In the first years of the twentieth century the Maasai herdsmen still engaged in cattle raids across the country, and Arab-Swahili caravans continued a murder-ous slaving trade throughout the hinterlands. In western Kenya the Nandi fought the railroad, tearing up rails and spearing Europeans. A railroad trader named

John Boyes, "King of the Kikuyu", was the only white settler in the region of
Nairobi, which as late as 1907 was little more than a tent city and rail depot called
Mile 326, near the swampy springs known to the Maasai as N'erobi, "place of
cold waters", at the south end of the fertile Kikuyu hills. These hills, well watered
and free of tsetse fly, already supported a prosperous Kikuyu population, and to
help justify the immense expense of the Uganda railroad, land schemes were
developed to encourage settlement by Britons. Plagued by strange soils and a
violent climate, dangerous animals, sullen natives, and disease, these first settlers
earned every bit of the progress they had made by World War I, and not unnatu-
rally, they tended to resist the League of Nations mandate, reaffirmed by the
British government in 1923, that African economic welfare and advancement took
precedence over their own. As their control of the colonial legislature increased,
so did their resistance to the historical and moral truth behind "the sacred trust
of civilization" that their development of Africa was supposed to represent: hadn't
they already done enough, in bringing "the native" medicines and peace? (And it
is true that white rule was accompanied by an enforced peace among the tribes,
without which transition to the modern world, not to speak of independence,
would have been impossible.) The coming of white women to the colonies had
led to a strict separation of the races, and meanwhile, the British government,
proceeding stolidly with the "betterment of the native", succeeded mainly in
increasing his population and dissatisfaction. In the Nairobi region, the numerous
and accessible Kikuyu were encouraged to emulate the white man in his values
and religion, to serve him and advance his commerce as apprentice Europeans,
but their reward was increasing servitude and contempt. The hunter or herdsman,
off in the bush, might be considered picturesque – at the least, he retained a certain
dignity – whereas the mission African, ill-smelling in his single set of cast-off
clothes, was a parody of the white man. Judged by values that were not his own,
he was much patronized and derided, even as his own resentment grew.

The assumption of knowing the African's mind has been very often heard
in the usual phraseology: "I have lived for many years amongst the Africans
and I know them very well." Yet this is far from the actual fact, for there is
a great difference between "living" among a people and "knowing" them.
While a European can learn something of the externals of African life,
its system of kinship and classification, its peculiar arts and picturesque
ceremonial, he may still have not yet reached the heart of the problem. . . .
With his preconceived ideas, mingled with prejudices, he fails to achieve a
more sympathetic and imaginative knowledge; a more human and inward
appreciation of the living people, the pupils he teaches, the people he meets

on the roads and watches in the gardens. In a word he fails to understand the African with his instinctive tendencies (no doubt very like his own), but trained from his earliest days to habitual ideas, inhibitions and forms of self-expression which have been handed down from one generation to another and which are foreign, if not absurd, to the European in Africa.[10]

Jomo Kenyatta's *Facing Mt Kenya*, written in the 1930s, is essential to an understanding of the conflicts that were to give rise to the Mau-Mau Rebellion, 1952–1956; though never a terrorist himself, Kenyatta spent seven years in a detention camp as an early advocate of land reform and a symbol of Kikuyu resistance. A great source of Kikuyu bitterness was the conviction that the tribe had been tricked out of its land, for every foot of Kikuyu land was owned by individual tribesmen, not only the pieces for which token sums were paid but also the fallow land that was appropriated by the government, then dispensed to the colonials on the grounds that African farming techniques would be the ruin of it. Much high-minded legislation for the benefit of whites was bullied through by Hugh Cholmondeley, Lord Delamere, whose memorial was an order of the British Crown, in 1939, that no African or Asian was permitted to own land in what had already become known as the White Highlands. Four-fifths of this best land in Kenya was now the province of perhaps four thousand whites; a million Kikuyu were to make do with the one-fifth set aside as the Kikuyu Reserves. The tribe's exposure to missions and clinics had led to a fatal population increase, and their growing poverty and frustration were all the more onerous for the education that numerous Kikuyu had struggled to obtain. Those who had fought in the British Army in Burma, then returned to inferior status in their own land, had an additional cause for bitterness, and many of these soldiers joined the Land Freedom Army movement, which was armed mostly with the cane-cutting machete called the panga. A half century of resentment was set aflame by the winds of pan-Africanism sweeping the continent, and the rebellion fell into the hands not of men like Kenyatta but of fanatic malcontents such as Dedan Kimathi, who made the name Mau-Mau, as the colonials called the movement, a symbol of the alleged barbarism, bestialities, and black magic that gave its oathing ceremonies such evil repute. But in the opinion of most Africans, Kimathi has been much maligned and the Mau-Mau atrocities exaggerated to excuse the savagery of the repression, and veterans of the Kenya Regiment acknowledge that atrocities were committed by both sides.

Until recent years, most Africans clung to the hope of a fair accommodation with the white man, and Mau-Mau received only limited support from other tribes. The last of the guerrillas, led by the strange Kimathi, retreated into the high Aberdares, and at the end they wore animal skins, like the vanished Gumba who had fled there from the Kikuyu centuries before. In the dense forests of bamboo, on the moorlands of black trees and tussock from which torrents plunge into the stagnant clouds in the ravines, one can envision the human figures in their scraps of reeking hide, the remnant aborigines and the Kikuyu outlaws, hunched at their covert fires. At Gura Falls, red gladioli shiver in the mountain wind, and far below, in the greening mist, three bushbuck, kin of those whose meat and skins sustained life in the fugitives, stand listening to the rush of rains off Kingankop.

In Nairobi, in 1961, Mau-Mau was still fresh in people's minds, and in the streets and pubs, a colonial tone of voice prevailed. Yet Independence was already under-way in Kenya, and change everywhere seemed imminent, even in South Africa, where the student who had come south with me from Khartoum had gone to warn his parents to flee that medieval region before the inevitable uprising. The Mau-Mau Rebellion, though defeated, had led within a very few years to victory, and Jomo Kenyatta, released from prison a few months after my arrival, was to become Kenya's first president. The Old Man or Mzee, as he is known to black and white alike, decreed that the past must be put aside in the interests of Kenya's future, and even appointed the police officer who had led the hunt for Kimathi as his private bodyguard. Those whites who would not work with blacks left quickly, and others left, too, who despaired of their prospects and security. "I reckon I'll go south," one man told me. "Rhodesia, or South Africa." He shook his head. "I was raised in the White Highlands, you know. We never thought we'd lose it. Never."

A number of remarkable civil servants stayed on in Kenya (and Uganda and Tanzania) to help the new country get a start, although a main purpose of their jobs was the training of Africans to replace them. For their part, most black Kenyans shared their president's good-humored attitude: there is still a "Lord Delamere Room" at the Hotel Norfolk and few of the visitors walking Kimathi Street in front of the New Stanley know or care that it was named in memory of the desperate Mau-Mau leader who was hung.

With the collapse of colonial governments, the destruction of wildlife by rampag-ing Africans had been widely predicted, and a glimpse of the last great companies of wild animals on earth was the main object of my trip to Africa in 1961. Since then (though their future remains uncertain) the East African parks and game reserves have actually increased in size and numbers. Even the Congo's great Albert Park (now Kivu National Park), for which the worst had been foreseen, escaped serious damage. The one park destroyed by political unrest is the beautiful small park at Nimule, where civil rebellions, already begun when I passed through, have broken down all order. Blaming the revolt of the Nilotic tribesmen on mission efforts to discourage Moslem influence and resurrect the bitter memories of the slave trade, the Sudanese government has expelled the missionaries, and it is feared that the repression of the wild peoples has neared the stage of systematic genocide. A large shipment of ivory and white rhino horn that turned up in Mombasa a few years ago was apparently intended to buy arms for the desperate tribesmen, and almost certainly it came from Nimule. John Owen, a District Commissioner in that region of the former Anglo-Egyptian Sudan who later became director of the Tanzania National Parks, flew over Nimule in a light plane in 1969. "A careful search," he told me, "produced nothing but one buffalo." Very likely the vanishing white rhino is gone forever from the Sudan.

Mr Owen had invited me to return that year to Africa, and I came by way of Entebbe, in Uganda, flying out of the raining reaches of Lake Victoria into western Kenya. A clearing sky laid bare the high plateaus that extend southward the entire length of eastern Africa; the plane's shadow crossed the Nandi hills, the Mau Range, and Maasai Land. Soon the circles of beehive huts, like scars on the crusty skin of the Rift Valley, drew together in the tin-roofed Kikuyu accumulations that surround Nairobi.

In 1961, Nairobi was still a frontier town where travelers to wilder parts were served and outfitted. Gazelle and zebra crossed the road at Embakasi Airport, and the Aathi Plain and the Ngong Hills, bringing Maasai Land to the very edges of the city, made it credible that the first six people to be buried in Nairobi's cemetery had been killed by lions.[11] The National Museum was still called the Coryndon, the British Director of the National Parks wore a monocle, and the Norfolk and New Stanley were the only presentable hotels. Eight years later, hotels of international pretensions soared out of the polyglot byways of Nairobi, Delamere Avenue had become Kenyatta Avenue, and processional boulevards with names like Uhuru (Independence) and Harambee (All Together–!) carried visitors too rapidly from one end of this small city to the other. But beneath an enlarged and shining surface, Nairobi was the same hot curry of bazaars and colonial architecture, curio shops, mosques, noise, and reeking slums, where crippled beggars were the envy of the swarms of unemployed. Once I had acquired the sunburn and old Land Rover that permitted me to be taken for a settler, I was beset by young Kenyans in the street who were anxious to find work of any kind.

Unemployment, not to speak of street theft and corruption, permits diehard colonials to point at the inefficiency of the Kikuyu, who are too able and ambitious to be borne: "They all have degrees, these bloody Kyukes, but they can't do a bloody thing." But it would be more fair to say, ". . . but there isn't a bloody thing for them to do," for the new nation has few places for all these aspirant accountants, pharmacists, lawyers, and white collar workers, and few people trained in the skilled labor – carpentry, mechanics, and the like – that was formerly done by Asians. Even more so than the whites, the Asians were resented: the common man feels he was exploited by the shopkeepers, while the educated speak of an Asian practice of sending their money out of the country. Those who have lost their jobs seek desperately to emigrate almost anywhere, but they are quiet, and their plight, wherever possible, has been ignored. In an Asian shop on Hardinge Street (now Kimathi Street), African help has replaced the sallow children who were so cheap and efficient, and a pair of strong safari shorts, tailored for pennies in a few hours in 1961, cannot be copied in inferior material at three times the price in less than fifteen days.

Whites are needed but not wanted – hence the undercurrent of rudeness beneath the precarious civilities. A black man abusing his authority, less in malice than in lack of confidence, is a daily trial for those not shepherded past such hazards by the tour companies (though one is startled just as often by a magical courtesy and gentleness). I remember one day in the Highlands, when the car had broken down. An African who yelled, "What's wrong!" from the back of a passing truck was showing off his English, not expressing concern, and perhaps he was jeering – the red-faced settler beside me was quick to assume so. "Mind your bloody business!" this man fumed, under his breath. For the new African, such confrontation is a way of forcing the white to look at him at last, to perceive him as a man, an individual, on equal terms and face to face. Or so I assume, without much confidence; the episode occurred in 1970, when after several stays in Africa, having read much and heard more, I knew less than ever about the essential nature of the African.

> The discovery of Bantu philosophy must trouble those of us who are concerned with the education of Africans. … we have thought we were educating children, "big children", and this seemed an easy task. But now, suddenly, we see that we are dealing with a humanity that is adult, conscious of its own wisdom, penetrated by its own universalist philosophy. And we feel the ground slipping from beneath our feet.[12]

The first night of my return was spent at the New Stanley, since the old-fashioned Norfolk was full. After dark there was a light failure for two hours, most of which I passed contented in a huge white colonial tub, watching weird flickers of faraway torches in the bathroom airshaft and listening to the cries of the staff below, the sound of breakage and feet pounding. In front of the hotel, next day, African guests from the new nations were mingling with travelers of all tongues; tourists of limited income are now common in Nairobi, and the old dark green safari wagons make way for zebra-striped tour buses in herds. Inside at the Long Bar, the settlers in town from the White Highlands, from Nyeri and Eldoret and Rumuruti, exchanged gossip, news, and exasperation with the African that before Independence would certainly have been expressed in the hearing of the barman. The Long Bar is a last redoubt of the old-style wardens and white hunters – now called "professional hunters" – and the talk turned inevitably to the great days when the native knew his place. But others present understood that Independence had to come. As one such man remarked to me after a game warden had decried the "bloody Kyukes", "the end of the game", and all the rest, "Those old boys oughtn't to take on like that – after all, they had the best of it."

Much has been written of the colorful decades when the Kenya Colony could be spoken of as "white man's country", and there seems no point in adding to it here. I wasn't there, and anyway, the patterns of colonialism do not differ very much from one place to another. For me, the least fascinating aspect of East Africa is the period of technocracy and politics that began under white rule, which lasted little more than half a century among the millenniums that man has been in Africa. Jomo Kenyatta, born Kamau wa Ngengi, whose lifetime easily spans the entire colonial period, never laid eyes on a white at all, so it is said, until after the turn of the century, when he was already ten. And one of Livingstone's bearers was still living in the 1930s, when Karen Blixen, in her splendid *Out of Africa*, began the lament for the end of the great days. In 1970 I chanced to meet the Kikuyu hero of that book, her servant "Kamante". Kamande Gatora is a contained person with the watchfulness of the near-blind; he had taken the Mau-Mau oath, and been imprisoned, in the years after his mistress had gone home to Denmark, despite "the kind deeds I was receiving from her untold and the old life we stayed with her, like black and white keys of a piano how they are played and produce melodious verses."[13] It was idle to address him, and I stood silent, for my words could not be understood, and my face was but a blur in his blind eyes, though the eyes were cold and clear.

> It is not easy to get to know the Natives. They were quick of hearing and evanescent; if you frightened them, they could withdraw into a world of their own, in a second, like the wild animals which at an abrupt move-ment from you are gone – simply not there.... When we really did break into the Natives' existence, they behaved like ants, when you poke a stick into their ant-hill; they wiped out the damage with unwearied energy, swiftly and silently – as if obliterating an unseemly action.[14]

In a letter dictated a few years ago, Kamande gave a "description of my mind concerning the old life and the new. Simply I can see just like the same. We were enjoying what we had, and until now we are enjoying what we have, so I don't see any different. And the times were not so old for the history begins in our lifetimes. When Baroness leave for England the Mr Matthew Wellington leave in Mombasa. Mr Wellington help carried Dead Bwana Livingstone to the sea, so the history is now."[15]

A half century after he had come to work for the "everlasting dear Baroness", as a sickly boy responsible for her dogs, Kamande stood there in the Langata dusk in the last light from the Ngong Hills and the Maasai Plain. In this old African's remote unsqueamish gaze one saw that reasons were beside the point, that such events as Mau-Mau and the passage of his mistress had causes not apprehended by the stranger, who must fail in a logical comprehension of the African, yet may hope to intuit his more mysterious, more universal sense of existence. Life begins before a soul is born and commences once again with the act of dying, and as in the Afro-Asian symbol of the snake of eternity swallowing its tail, all is in flux, all comes full circle, with no beginning and no end.

3 Northwest Frontier

Somewhere the Sky touches the Earth,
and the name of that place is the End.
  – *Wa Kamba saying*[1]

Of all roads in East Africa, the road north from Nairobi toward Mt Kenya will hold most associations for the traveler with any acquaintance with the brief history of the region. One soon comes to Thika and the Blue Post Hotel, a relic of the days not long after the turn of the century when the first planters of coffee and flax and pyrethrum were clearing Kikuyu Land, and continues to Nyeri, named in 1903 by Colonel Richard Meinertzhagen, the hero of the Nandi wars, who witnessed a procession of some seven hundred elephant through its village street. Crossing the equator at Nanyuki, the high road begins a slow descent over the ranching country west of Mt Kenya – Kere-Nyaga, named for Nyaga or Ngai, which is the Maasai word for God used also by the Kamba and Kikuyu – a formidable mountain, dark and looming, jagged and malign, rising to snow fields that the Africans avoided, for the bright whiteness was a kingdom of Ngai.

Before World War I, when Elspeth Huxley was a child on a Thika farm, a few Dorobo still wandered in these highlands:

A brown furry figure stepped forth into a shaft of sunlight, which awoke in his fur pelt a rich, rufous glow, and twinkled on his copper ornaments.

He was a small man: not a dwarf exactly, or a pygmy, but one who stood about half-way between a pygmy and an ordinary human. His limbs were light in colour and he wore a cloak of bushbuck skin, a little leather cap, and ear-rings, and carried a long bow and a quiver of arrows. He stood stock-still and looked at me just as the dikdik had done, and I wondered whether he, too, would vanish if I moved.... I knew him for a Dorobo, one of that race of hunters living in the forest on game they trapped or shot with poisoned arrows. They did not cultivate, they existed on meat and roots and wild honey, and were the relics of an old, old people who had once had sole possession of all these lands – the true aborigines. Then had come others like the Kikuyu and Masai, and the Dorobo had taken refuge in the forests. Now they lived in peace, or at least neutrality, with the herdsmen and cultivators, and sometimes bartered skins and honey for beads, and for spears and knives made by native smiths. They knew all the ways of the forest animals, even of the bongo, the shyest and most beautiful, and their greatest delight was to feast for three days upon a raw elephant.[2]

Like the Bushmen of South Africa, who were hunted down or driven into swamps and deserts by black men and white alike when they struck at domestic stock that threatened their hunting lands, the Dorobo were threatened by the clearing of their forests, and doubtless there were skirmishes and killings before they attached themselves to the Nandi and Maasai as rainmakers and tricksters, circumcisers and attendants of the dead. Probably it is too late to discover the true origins of this outcast people, who have lost their own language and whose name (from the Maasai il-torrobo, meaning "poor man", or "person without cattle" – thus, any hunter-gatherer) is now used to describe almost any man who has reverted to subsistence in the bush, or "turned Dorobo". Still, it interests me that the Muisi Dorobo who once inhabited Mt Kenya's bamboo forests were said[3] to have been very small, and that one of the two main clans of the Dorobo was known as the Agumba – the other was the Okiek – who lived in covered pits and were said to have gone away toward the region of Kismayu after failing to stop the clearing of their forests by the Kikuyu; I like to think that the Agumba and the vanished Gumba may be one. Perhaps the Dorobo are related to such remnant hunting groups as the Ik of northeastern Uganda, who were also hunters until recent years, and are also described as lighter-skinned and smaller than their neighbors, and conceivably both groups may derive from the same ancestral stock as the larger Khoisan or click-speaking peoples (such as the modern Bushman relatives known as the Khoi or Hottentots) whose traces have been found as far north as the Blue Nile and Ethiopia. (Both Bushman and Pygmy, where unmixed with other groups, are slight and small and yellow-brown in color, and while differences in other physical character appear to justify a racial separation, their Bantu-speaking neighbors, from Uganda to South Africa, know both groups as the Small People – the Abatwa or Twa.)

In Africa, for all its space and emptiness, there is no place any longer for the Small People, most of whom have been described by those who found them as gentle and quiet, in harmony with the land and the changing seasons, with none of the aggressiveness and greed that the domestication of plants and animals, with its illusion of security and permanence, brought to mankind. In former times, the Bushmen say, wild animals spoke with men, and all were friends. They had a reverence for the life and death of the animals they hunted – what the Nandi, in reference to the wilderness instinct of the Dorobo, call *comiet*, "affinity"[4] – and their legends have the ring of all creation. The Small People, the Old People, still quick with instinct, knew the secret of the silence, and I wanted a glimpse of the vanishing hunters above all.

In Nairobi one heard of bands of hunters that were said to derive from the Old People, including one group "somewhere" in the hills east of Mt Kenya that were described as a remnant of the Gumba, but those for whom good information was available had long since adopted both language and ways of the stronger tribes around them (even the Ovajimba of southwest Africa, the last tribe known that makes and uses crude stone tools, have adopted the speech of the Herero Bantu who pass through their country). The only hunter-gatherers in Kenya said to be living more or less as they had always done were a few primitive fishermen of Lake Rudolf, the El Molo, considered by some authorities[5] to be a relict group of the Dorobo.

In June, 1970, I accompanied the photographer Eliot Porter, his two sons, and a daughter-in-law on a journey to Lake Rudolf by way of Mt Marsabit, a well-organized safari into remote country with scant water that I could not attempt alone in my old Land Rover. Until recently, this Northern Frontier, or NFD, a waste of desert and near-desert scrub and thorn extending north and east to Ethiopia and Somalia, has been closed to travel, being under control of Somali shifta who claim it for their country. Shifta, or "wanderer", is a name for tribesmen without property, but the term has come to signify guerrillas or bandits; the Somali guerrillas and the true bandits, who may be Somali or Boran, are lumped together under this same term. The Boran are also the chief victims of the shifta operations; their villages are burned and livestock stolen by bandits of all persuasions, and those left standing may be reduced to rubble by Kenya's security police, who often conclude that those Boran settlements not actually composed of shifta give shelter to the raiders. In consequence, numbers of Boran must turn to banditry in order to survive, and others subsist as refugees at Isiolo, where they mix with Somali traders, Bantu laborers from the south, and a few Samburu and Turkana.

Beyond the sentry barrier at Isiolo, the road disintegrates to dirt, and fences end. Traditionally this frontier region between the highlands and the NFD has been a province of the Samburu, and a tract of high plains by the Uaso Nyiro River has been set aside as a game reserve named in their honor. Here the safari truck had set up camp in a grove of umbrella thorn with a westward prospect of the Laikipia Plateau; the Uaso Nyiro comes down out of Laikipia and dies eventually in the Lorian Swamp, east of Mado Gashi. With water so close, it came as a surprise, each day at daylight, to see a flight of white egrets undulating southward over the dry scrub, bound for waters unknown under Mt Kenya.

The plains and hills that surround the Uaso Nyiro are inhabited by striking animals such as the reticulated giraffe and Grevy's zebra (seen in mixed herds with the more common Burchell's zebra) that are absent farther south; the fringe-eared oryx and the blue-legged Somali ostrich have replaced the more southerly races of their species, and the gerenuk is the most conspicuous of the gazelles. This extraordinary creature, stylized even to the carved eyeline and the bronzy gloss that gives its form the look of well-oiled wood, browses habitually on its hind legs, tail switching, fan ears batting, delicate hooves propped on the swaying branches. When I came to Samburu previously, in winter, the long-necked animals had been nibbling on florets of a gum acacia that filled the air with its sweet scent, but now the long dry season had begun, and the high plains had reverted to near-desert.

Samburu has been a game reserve since 1966, but most of its life it has been closed due to the shifta; bandits on a poaching raid killed two of its African game scouts only this year. Such tracks, fords, dams, and bridges as it can claim are largely the work of Terence Adamson, who in February was living in a thatched banda of his own construction by the river, and had been kind enough to lend me the only complete map of Samburu's tracks. A strong old man with a white head, in floppy hat, huge floppy shorts, and heavy shoes, Mr Adamson is a bachelor and hardened recluse who in the seven years he was stationed at Marsabit, one hundred miles off to the north, went to Nairobi just once, for a bad toothache; he loathes Nairobi and what it represents of the change in Africa, and will never go again if he can help it.

Although a veteran of shifta raids on Isiolo, where an African district commissioner has been assassinated, Adamson is sympathetic with the guerrillas. "Why should these Somali be under Kenya? Somalis don't think of themselves as African at all, and of course they're right." He sighed. "They have odd ways, granted, like all Arabs, but they stick to their word, and they stick to their code, like it or not – once I saw half a Samburu in the fork of a tree here; he'd been dragged up by a leopard after the Somali had caught up to him for cattle stealing."

In the old days – for Mr Adamson's generation, their own youth and the great days of the Kenya Colony are the same – Adamson used to sleep outside on the ground wherever he went. "Rhinos could be a nuisance sometimes – just as blind at night as they are in the day. Chough, chough, chough," he said, making a rhino face. "Never two or four snorts, always three." He shook his heavy head. "In ten years the game will be up in Kenya. I just hate to think what will happen when the Old Man goes – I just hope they let me see it out."

Winds of the southeast monsoon blew up from the hot nyika, and a haze of desert dust obscured the mountains. But the Uaso Nyiro flows all year, and along its green banks the seasons are the same. A dark lioness with a shining coat lay on a rise, intent on the place where game came down to water. At a shady bend, on sunlit sand bars, baboon and elephant consorted, and a small crocodile, gray-green and gleaming at the edge of the thick river, evoked a childhood dream of darkest Africa. Alone on the plain, waiting for his time to come full circle, stood an ancient elephant, tusks broken and worn, hairs fallen from his tail; over his monumental brow, poised for the insects started up by the great trunk, a lilac-breasted roller hung suspended, spinning turquoise lights in the dry air.

On a plateau that climbs in steps from the south bank of the river, three stone pools in a grove of doum palms form an oasis in the elephant-twisted thorn scrub and dry stone. The lower spring, where the water spreads into a swampy stream, has a margin of high reeds and sedge; here the birds and animals come to water. One afternoon I swam in the steep-sided middle pool, which had been, in winter, as clear as the desert wind; now the huge gangs building the road north to Ethiopia were washing here with detergent soaps that bred a heavy film, and I soon got out, letting the sun dry me. A turtle's shadow vanished between ledges of the pool, and dragonflies, one fire-colored and the other cobalt blue, zipped dry-winged through the heat. Despite the wind, there was a stillness in the air, expectancy: at the lower spring a pair of spurwing plover stood immobile, watching man grow older.

In the dusty flat west of the spring, ears alert, oryx and zebra waited. Perhaps one had been killed the night before, for jackals came and went in their hangdog way east of the springs and vultures sat like huge galls in the trees. With a shift in the wind, a cloud across the sun, the rush of fronds in the dry palms took on an imminence. Beyond the springs oryx were moving at full run, kicking up dust as they streamed onto the upper plateau. Nagged by the wind, I put my clothes on and set off for camp.

Climbing from the springs onto the plain, I crossed a stone ridge where, in winter, a fine lion had made way for my Land Rover; I stared about me. In every distance the plain was sparse and bare. Strange pale shimmers were far oryx and gazelle, and an eagle crossed the sky, and a giraffe walked by itself under the mountains. A Grevy's zebra stallion (why not "gray" and "common" zebra?) charged with a harsh barking, veered away, then circled me, unreconciled, for the next two miles, unable to place a man on foot in its long brain.

Northward, over pinnacles and desert buttes, the sky was clear, but directly ahead as I walked south, dark rain arose over Mt Kenya, fifty miles away. Coming fast, the weather cast a storm light on the plain, illuminating the white shells of perished land snails, a lone white flower, the white skull and vertebrae of a killed oryx.

I wanted to look at the species of larks that had the dry plain to themselves, but the sun, overtaken by the clouds, was sinking rapidly toward the Laikipia Plateau, and there were still four miles to go through country increasingly wooded; I hurried on. Awareness of animals brought with it an awareness of details – a shard of rose quartz, a candy-colored pierid butterfly, white with red trim, the gleam of a scarlet-chested sunbird in the black lace of an acacia. Set against the sun at dawn or evening, its hanging weaver nests like sun-scorched fruit, its myriad points etched on the sky, there is nothing so black in Africa as the thorn tree.

In the open wood all senses were attuned to lion, hyenas, elephant and especially elephant, as in the unlikely event of trouble there is little to be done about lion or hyenas besides climb a tree. The antelope were very shy, yet at one point a string of impala passed close at full speed, bouncing high; I hoped that no lion, having missed its kill, now sat disgruntled by the trail. At the edge of the woodland, fresh elephant spoor was everywhere, and inevitably there came the *crack* of a split tree that is often the first sign of elephant presence. None was in sight, however, and I hurried past. The red sun, in a narrow band of sky between clouds and mountains, had set fire to spider webs in the grass that while the sun was high had been invisible; where I had come from, flights of sand grouse were sailing down to the Buffalo Springs for their evening water. Then the sun was gone, and across the world, a full moon rose to take its place.

The earth was still, in twilight shape and shadow. In the wake of the wind came the low hooting of a dove, and one solitary bell note of a boubou. I met no animals but the giraffe, a herd of eleven set about a glade, waiting for night. The giraffe were alert to my intrusion but in their polite way gave no sign that they had been disturbed.

* * *

Night had come to camp before me. Already the Africans had built a fire and set lanterns before each tent; they formed a line and murmured in astonishment as I came in alone out of the trees. These men are Kamba from the dry thorn scrub on the east slope of the highlands; they are more accustomed to the bush than the Kikuyu, and more willing to sleep upon the ground. The name Kamba means "traveler", for they were always ivory traders, and participated in the slave trade, journeying south beyond Kilimanjaro and as far north as Samburu. As bush people who held little land that was coveted by settlers – except in the region of Machakos, their arable land is marginal – they are considered more dependable than the Kikuyu, who are said to be "spoiled" by their exposure to the missions and civilizing influences of Nairobi. In Kenya, most safari staff are Kamba, who are noted for filed teeth, dancing, hunting, and a frank, open character.

In the days of the raiding Maasai, the Kamba gave a better account of themselves than most, being more expert at bush craft than the gaunt herdsmen and defending themselves skillfully with poisoned arrows. As early as 1889, they were warring successfully against both Maasai and Galla, and even made cattle raids on their old enemies; the Kamba bow, used with good effect on elephant, was strong enough to drive an arrow through the buffalo-hide shield of a Maasai, killing the man behind it.[6] More recently, the Kamba have resisted the ravages of bush-clearing (for tsetse control) by lying down in front of bulldozers. Wilderness people, they speak softly, even among themselves; the white man, in the presence of such people, lowers his voice.

The Land Rovers, driven by Jock Anderson and Adrian Luckhurst, had not yet returned with the Porter family from the north bank of the river; Adrian's wife had also gone along. I would have liked to talk to the Africans, but I spoke no Kamba and very poor Swahili, and even if my Swahili had been excellent, there was no reason to talk that they would understand: I was full of good will but had nothing at all to say. Feeling above all impolite, I sat down by the fire with a drink, and listened to crickets and soft African voices and the hum of the kerosene lamp, there was a moon in the acacias and a dying wind. Even in camp, wild things were going on about their business – tiny red pepper ticks with bites that itch for days, and a small scorpion, stepping edgily, pincers extended, over the bark bits by the camp table, and ant lions (the larvae of the lacewing fly) with their countersunk traps like big rain pocks in the fire ash and sandy soil. Unable to find footing in these soft holes, the ant slides down into the crater where the buried ant lion awaits. A faint flurry is visible – the ant lion is whisking sand from beneath the ant to hurry it along – and then the victim, seized by its hidden host, is dragged inexorably into the earth.

* * *

This morning the sun rising in the thorns looked silver and wintry in a haze and wind that made black rooks shift restlessly on the dead limbs. The silver sun was where the moon had been, in eerie light of day. The coarse bark of a grey zebra woke the plain, and the egrets went undulating southward, and oryx fled in all directions, cold dust blowing.

To the wood edge along the track where I had walked, a white-haired man had come the night before. He sat in a canvas chair beside his Land Rover, facing west over the Samburu Plain; an old black man, twenty yards away, sat on his heels against a tree trunk, facing south. There was a camp cot but no sign of a tent. Both figures were motionless, transfixed. Adrian recognized George Adamson, who for many years had been senior game warden of the NFD: "Has to be somebody like Adamson who knows what he's doing in the bush, I reckon, sleeping out like that, without a tent." I thought of this man's brother who had slept upon the ground, and the old days gone, and the future unforgiven: "I do hope they let me see it out here – forty years, that's a long time, you know. They say Botswana – Bechuanaland, really – is all right, but I don't know."*

The Adamson brothers have worked in wild parts of East Africa for nearly a half century, and with Louis and Mary Leakey, who continue their monumental excavations at Olduvai Gorge, are among the last of their generation still active in the bush. Other veterans of the great days such as the white hunter J. A. Hunter, and C. P. J. Ionides, "old Iodine", of Tanzania, the acerbic ivory poacher turned game warden turned herpetologist, and Colonel Ewart Grogan, who made a famous walk from the Cape to Cairo at the turn of the century, and "T. B.", Major Lyn Temple-Boreham, game warden of the Maasai Mara and one of the few white men the Maasai have ever been able to respect (T. B. once remarked to Adrian, "The Maasai care for nothing but cattle, water, and women, in that order") had all died since Independence came.

Adrian waved to the figure in the chair, who did not wave back; white man and black, at right angles to each other, remained motionless, as if cast in stone. Like old buffalo, these old men like their solitude, gazing out over the Africa that was.

At Archer's Post, the new road crosses the Uaso Nyiro and runs north toward Ethiopia. One day it may actually arrive at Addis Ababa, but as yet it has not reached Marsabit, and none of it is surfaced. The work crews are mostly Kamba and Kikuyu, brought up from the south, with a few Turkana mixed among them. The Samburu

---

* I have since been told that the African was Stanley, Mr Adamson's camp cook of many years, who was seized not long thereafter by an adopted lion known as Boy. Hearing a scream, Mr Adamson came running and killed Boy, but the old man died.

herdsmen will not work upon the roads. They share the attitudes of true Maasai, whose lands in Laikipia they occupied after the great Maasai civil wars of the 1880s, and to whom they are so similar that they are often called northern Maasai: the Samburu call themselves il-oikop – "the fierce ones", but to the Maasai are known as il-sampurrum pur (literally, the white butterflies often found around sheep and goat dung) due to their constant movement in search of water.[7] "Our customs are the same as theirs," says an old Samburu picked up along the way. The Samburu and the road laborers gaze at one another, mutually distrustful and contemptuous.

The herdsmen are driving their cattle north, humped Asian zebu with a few long-horned Ankole, and each carries his short sword and club and two leaf-bladed spears of the style used by the Maasai until this century, when the javelin-bladed spear came into fashion; also, a leather water bottle and a small leather pouch. One has an elegant wood headrest, bartered, perhaps, from a Turkana. As a morani, or young warrior, he is painted in red ocher, and his greased braids are pulled up from the nape of his neck, jutting out over his forehead like the bill of a cap. The Samburu regard themselves as "the world's top people",[8] and certainly they are more handsome and aristocratic than most other beings, but perhaps because their territories are surrounded by fierce nomads such as the Boran and the Turkana, the Samburu are not so arrogant as the Maasai.

To the north, odd pyramids and balanced rocks take form in the blue dust haze of the desert. Low thorn scrub is interspersed with toothbrush bush, combretum,* and the desert rose (*Adenium*), with its pink fleshy flowers, rubber limbs, and poison sap, a source of arrow poison. Eliot is struck by desert patterns and details, and we stop here and there to record them. From under a bush darts an elephant shrew; it sits on a dry leaf, twitches, sniffs, and vanishes with a dry scatter. At a hole in the red desert is a ring of grain chaff several inches deep; harvester ants gather kernels from the thin grasses and discard the husks. Farther on, where dark ramparts of the Matthews Range rise in the west, the isolated bushes shelter pairs of dik-dik from the heat: this is Guenther's dik-dik, grayer, larger, and longer in the nose than the common or Kirk's dik-dik, which is found south of the Uaso Nyiro. (As with the zebras, "common" and "gray" dik-dik seems much simpler: Messrs Kirk and Guenther, with Burchell, Grevy, and the estimable Mrs Gray of Mrs Gray's lechwe, should be confined to the taxonomic nomenclature, cf. *Equus*

---

* Because few plants in Africa have common names (except in the language of the local tribes – these names should eventually be given preference over European ones), generic names such as "acacia" (*Acacia ssp.*) and "euphorbia" (*Euphorbia ssp.*) are used ordinarily instead; I have extended this unscientific but inevitable practice to other prominent genera, cf. Commiphora, Grewia, Dombeya, Terminalia, Combretum, and the like, to avoid burdening the text with italics and capital letters.

Burchelli, where they belong. And for that matter, why should these ancient rocks of Africa commemorate the unmemorable General Matthews? Why not restore the Samburu name, Ol Doinyo Lenkiyio?)

From the mountains, which are said to shelter a few Dorobo, comes the Merille River. Samburu are digging water points in the dry river bed, and huge leather bottles, some of them three or four feet high, stand like amphoras near the holes. Other tribesmen squat beneath a big tree on the bank. The young boys, naked but for thin beads and earrings of river shell, have a scalp lock of hair on their plucked heads; the girls wear calfskin aprons and a cotton cloth tied at one shoulder that parts their pretty breasts. Unmarried girls are painted red, and some have lines of raised tattoos on their fair bellies; an infant in a sling wears a small necklace of green beads. The married women carry a heavy collar of doum palm fiber decorated with large dark red beads, and arm coils of silver steel and golden copper, the gold on the lower arm and the silver above, or the reverse. Men or women may wear metal anklets, bead headbands, copper earrings; one morani has ivory ear plugs and a string of beads that runs beneath his lip and back over his ears. At a little distance, he leans carelessly upon his spear, ankles crossed in a stance that is emblematic among warrior herdsmen from the Sudan south into Maasai Land.

North of the Merille the first dromedaries appear, a small herd in the shelter of the thorns; their keeper is nowhere to be seen. Far cones jut out of the desert, and a group of peaks has a shark-fin appearance, as if swept back by ancient winds off the High Semien, in Ethiopia. This is called the Kaisut Desert, but in June, just after the rains, the black outcroppings of lava are bedded in a haze of green.

Tin shacks of the road gangs gleam in the merciless sun at Loku-loko, in compounds enclosed by high barbed wire. Outside are the dung huts of parasitic Samburu attracted to the settlement, and a few cowled Somali women come and go. Some of the huts have rusty tin sheets stuck onto the roof, in emulation of the tin ovens of the workers; the traditional Samburu village compound is reduced here to a litter of loose hovels. Nowhere on the wind-whipped ground is there a tree or a blade of grass; the thorn scrub has been bulldozed into piles. Dust, rusting oil drums, blowing papers, black requiem birds, a scent of human poverty: in temperate climates, poverty smells sour, but in hot regions it is sickeningly sweet.

Mt Marsabit rises from the desert haze like a discolored cloud. Grassy foothills climb in steps toward isolated cones, and the air cools. In a meadow, like a lump from the volcanoes, stands a bull elephant with great lopsided tusks curved in upon each other, the ivory burnished bronze with age like a stone font worn smooth by human hands. This high oasis far from the old trade routes and new tourist tracks, and cut off in recent years by shifta raids, is the realm of the last company of great-tusked elephants in Africa. Many have tusks of a hundred pounds or better on each side, and those of a bull known as Ahmed are estimated at 150 and 170 pounds, and may soon cross, as in the extinct mammoth.

Marsabit in June: great elephants and volcanoes, lark song and bright butterflies, and far below, pale desert wastes that vanish in the sands. On Marsabit are fields of flowers, nodding in the copper-colored grass: blue thistle, acanth, madder, morning glory, vetch and pea, and a magnificent insect-simulating verbena, its flowers fashioned like blue butterflies, even to the long curling antennae. The blossoms of the different families are all of mountain blue, as if born of the same mountain minerals, mountain rain. One cow pea has a large curled blossom, and to each blossom comes a gold-banded black beetle that consumes the petals, and each beetle is attended by one or more black ants that seem to nip at its hind legs, as if to speed the produce of its thorax. Next day I came back to investigate more closely, but the flowering was over and the beetles gone.

The roads of Marsabit are patrolled by the Kenya Rifles, there to protect the tribesmen from the shifta, and also an anti-poaching force whose quarry is often the same. They waved us to a halt. A vast elephant had been located not far from the road; they imagined it was Ahmed, who had not been seen for several weeks. All was invisible but a granite dome that rose out of the bush, and black men and white ones, creeping up, stood in a line before the gray eminence as before an oracle, awaiting enlightenment. Eventually the dome stirred, a curled trunk appeared, and modest tusks were elevated from the foliage that brought a jeer from the disappointed Africans, though they laughed gleefully at their own mistake.

Ahmed eluded us, as did the greater kudu. In size, this striped antelope is only exceeded by the eland, but the animals are not easily seen, having retreated into the retreating forest, restricted now to high Mt Marsabit. "*Moja moja tu,*" said the Boran ranger who led us to its haunts – one sees one here and there. The Samburu crowd them with their herds, and so do the Galla – the Boran, Gabbra, and Rendille. (The Galla tribes, found mostly in Ethiopia, are modem Hamites, related to the Egyptians, desert Tuareg, and Berbers of the north.) Boran men wear the Moslem dress of the Somali, though most are pagan; the women dress also like Somali, but their faces lack the oriental cast that make the Somali what some consider the most beautiful women on this continent.

Three of the dead volcanoes on Mt Marsabit contain crater lakes, of which the largest is Gof Bongole. From the high rim of Bongole, looking south, one sees the shark-fin mountains of Losai; eastward, the desert stretches away into Somalia. Of late, it was said, the mighty Ahmed, formerly unassailable in his serenity, had become vexed by the attentions of mankind, and perhaps he was bothered also by the roar of the machines that were bringing the new road from the south, for now he remained mostly in these forests behind Bongole, where he came to water. I awaited him one morning by an olive tree, sheltered from the monsoon wind by the crater rim. From the desert all around came a great silence, as on an island where the sea has fallen still. An amethyst sunbird pierced my eye, and a butterfly breathed upon my arm; I smelled wild jasmine, heard the grass seeds fall. From the crater lake hundreds of feet below rose the pipe of coots, and the scattering slap of their runs across the surface. But no great elephant came down the animal trails on the crater side, only a buffalo that plodded from the crater woods at noon and subsided in a shower of white egrets into the shallows.

Sun and grass: in my shelter, the air was hot. Mosque swallows, swifts, a hawk, two vultures coursed the crater thermals, and from overhead came a small boom, like the sound of a stooping falcon. But the bird hurtling around the crater rim was a large long-tailed swift of a uniform dull brown. This bird, described as "extremely uncommon and local … a highlands species which flies high, seen only when thunderstorms or clouds force them to fly lower than usual"[9] is the scarce swift. Though not the first record at Marsabit, the sighting of a bird called the scarce swift gave me great pleasure.

Our camp was in the mountain forest, a true forest of great holy trees – the African olive, with its silver gray-green shimmering leaves and hoary twisted trunk – of wildflowers and shafts of light, cool shadows and deep humus smells, moss, ferns, glades, and the ring of unseen birds from the green clerestories. Lying back against one tree, staring up into another, I could watch the olive pigeon and the olive thrush share the black fruit for which neither bird is named; to a forest stream nearby came the paradise flycatcher, perhaps the most striking of all birds in East Africa. Few forests are so beautiful, so silent, and here the silence is intensified by the apprehended presence of wild beasts – buffalo and elephant, rhino, lion, leopard. Because these creatures are so scarce and shy, the forest paths can be walked in peace; the only fierce animal I saw was a small squirrel pinned to a dead log by a shaft of sun, feet wide, defiant, twitching its tail in time to thin pure squeakings.

The Game Department people say that we should not travel beyond Marsabit without armed escort, but to carry more people is not possible: the two Land Rovers and the truck are full. We drove out from beneath the mountain clouds, descending the north side of Marsabit into the Dida Gilgalu Desert, where a raven flapped along a famished gully and pocked lava spread like a black crust across the waste.

Ahead, volcanic cones rose from the sand haze like peaks out of low clouds; the day was overcast with heavy heat. Larks and ground squirrels, camel flies and ticks; the camel fly is so flat and rubbery that it flies off after a hard slap. Occasional dry dongas support bunch grass and the nests of weavers; in this landscape, the red rump of the white-headed buffalo weaver is the only color. Though animals other than snakes are not a problem here, a lone traveler had made a small thorn shelter at the side of the road, to ward off the great emptiness. Round lava boulders, shined by manganese and iron oxides, and burnished by wind and sand, looked greased in the dry light – a country of dragons.

To the north, the Huri Mountains rose and fell away again into Ethiopia. We took a poor track westward. In the wall of an old river bed was a cave of swifts and small brown bats where man had lived, and from the dust of the cave floor I dug an ancient digging stick with a hacked point. Not far away, on the bare rock of a ridge, were tattered habitations of dung and straw where silhouettes of goats and man came together in a knot to watch us pass. Here where nothing grows, these primitive Gabbra subsist on blood and milk, in a way that cannot be very different from the way of the first pastoralists who came here many centuries ago.

The Gabbra mission at the Maikona oasis is a litter of huts patched with tin and paper, on a barren ground stalked by rooks and curs. Here children gnaw on the thin bitter skins of borassus palm nuts from the foul oasis. The nuts lie mixed with withered livestock turds around the huts, and they will be here when man has gone; such nuts are found in Old Stone Age sites that are fifty-five thousand years old. The people go barefoot on the stones, rags blowing, and they are idle, all but the smith, who pumped his fires with twin bellows made of goat skin: from scavenged car springs and an angle iron, he was beating a lean spear. As in all the Galla tribes, the smith has been despised and feared since the advent of the Iron Age brought this strange element to man, yet he seemed more cheerful than the aristocratic idlers who stared away over the desert.

Maikona lies at the south end of a black lava field that stretches north a hundred miles into Ethiopia; the lava ends in an abrupt wall where the wave of stone, thirty feet high, came to a stop. The lava flow forms the north wall of an ancient lake bed called the Chalbi Desert, a vast reach of ash and dead white soda that gives off the heat waves of mirage: for fifty miles, brown columns of dust pursued our caravan westward. Gazelle in quest of salt moved slow as ghosts across white fields of alkali, and a jackal overtaken by the heat lay with sick calm in the ash and watched men pass. The sun turned orange in a tawny sky, then luminous in the strange way of desert suns; it melted the Bura Galadi Hills on the horizon.

At dark, in the northwest corner of the desert, the cars reached the oasis at North Horr, where a police post protects the Gabbra of the region from shifta and from bands of nomad raiders out of Ethiopia. The women here have strong desert faces in black shrouds, metal arm coils and cobra-head bracelets, piled trading beads hand-fashioned from aluminum, ancient amulets; one necklace has a Victoria coin, worn thin by intent hands across a century of desert cooking fires. Perhaps it had come from the Sudan, snatched from the torn pockets of dead English at Khartoum.

Children come, with fireflies in their tight hair; the lights dance through the blowing palms. Far from the world, they play at being airplanes, which they know only from the lights that pass over in the dark, north out of Africa. Tonight there were no airplanes, but an earth satellite of unknown origin arched over the Southern Cross, followed toward midnight by a shooting star that died in a shower of ethereal blue light over the High Semien, in Ethiopia.

I slept under the desert stars, content to be somewhere called North Horr, between the Chalbi Desert and the Bura Galadi Hills: the lean sinister names evoked medieval legends, desert bandits, and the fierce grotesque old Coptic kingdoms of Abyssinia.

By morning the wind was blowing up in sandstorms. Flights of sand grouse, seeking water, hurtled back and forth over the cracking palms, and a train of camels etched a slow crack into the desert to the south.

Beyond North Horr, the track is too poor for the truck, which lacks four-wheel drive; it would meet us some days hence at the El Molo village, Loiyengalani, near the south end of Lake Rudolph. The eight white people in the party, with the Kamba cook, Kimunginye, would travel light in the two Land Rovers, since the plan was to arrive that night at Richard Leakey's archeological camp at Koobi Fora, some one hundred ten miles beyond North Horr. We carried our own food and bedding, and Richard, who expected us, would furnish the gasoline and water that would carry us back south again to Loiyengalani.

In the gravel beds of a dead river one car, towing a small trailer, had to be unhitched and pushed: beyond the river, the track made by Leakey's annual caravan was indistinct. The region is less hostile than the deserts farther east, and less monotonous. Dry river beds intersect broad dry grass plains broken here and there by sand dunes, brimstone outcrops, and ridges of dark volcanic rock scattered with bits of chert and gypsum, and the animals are tame and common, for there is no one here to hunt them. But farther on all creatures vanish, and the arid plain under a gray blowing sky seems more oppressive than bare desert, as if life had been here and had gone. In this wind is the echo of cataclysm: this is how the world will look when man brings all life to an end.

The land east of Lake Rudolf appears to have been a main migration route of early peoples, for here and there upon the landscape are strange stone heaps four or five feet high, ten feet across, encircled at the base by a ring of larger stones that gives them form. Some of these cairns or graves, most common near the water points to which the old track winds, have been identified as Galla. Others, like the tracks themselves, may be thousands of years old, growing gently in size from pebbles cast on them out of respect by passing nomads. In such silence one still hears the echo of those pebbles, tinkling to rest on the side of the mute heap.

African prehistory is an edifice of probabilities, and its dates are continually set back as new archeological sites emerge: it is now thought that Caucasoid wanderers came south into East Africa at least as early as ten thousand years ago, perhaps much earlier,[10] when all men on earth were still hunters and gatherers. These "Kenya Capsians" or "Proto-Hamites" whose remains have been found near the Rift Valley lakes used obsidian tools for working wood, bone, and hides, and were among the first people known to have possessed the bow and arrow, but essentially they were sedentary fishermen, like their contemporaries, the Negroid fishermen of Khartoum. Strangely, although one group was clearly Negroid and the other Caucasoid, both had the same barbed bone harpoons and curved arrowheads called lunates, made open pottery incised with wavy lines, and removed the two central incisors from the lower jaw, as all peoples of Nilotic origin, including the Samburu and Maasai, do to this day. A later people living near Lake Elmenteita[11] used two-edged stone blades and more symmetrical lunates, and made fine pottery before the Egyptians had learned to do so, but there is still no real evidence of a Neolithic culture based on domestic plants and animals before 1000 BC, at least a millennium after the red cattle people of the rock paintings had left their traces in the Sahara.

South of the Sahara, Neolithic civilization was confined to certain hillsides of East Africa, and the evidence suggests that its peoples brought their animals and cereals out of southwest Ethiopia. Although the stone bowls and pestles that symbolize their culture might have been used for the grinding of red ocher and wild cereals, the Proto-Hamites surely had domestic grains as well. Meanwhile related peoples, discovering that they could live on milk and blood, were moving into a nomadic cattle culture of the sort still seen today; a Greco-Roman account of 200 BC tells of herdsmen south of the Sahara who worshipped their cattle, fed on blood and milk, practiced circumcision, and buried their dead in a contracted position "to the accompaniment of laughter".[12] (The "worship" of the cattle by the herdsmen, then as now, is better understood as deep affection – expressed in odes and lullabies, pet names and the like – for a life-giving force that is seen as the people's special gift from God; in the same way, the Pygmies sing to the forest and the Bushmen to the desert that gives them sustenance, not in worship but in gratitude. The nomad herdsmen, like the Bedouin Arabs who would later sweep across the northern continent, were the true barbarians of Africa, preying on others and ravaging the land. Very likely they obtained their animals and

spears from the tillers they came to despise, but the prestige attached to the ownership of the precious animals that came south under their sticks was everywhere
extended to their customs, which still survive in the great cattle kingdoms from
the Sudan south into Tanzania, and are imitated by many tilling tribes as well.

The descendants of these "Proto-Hamites" have persisted into recent times.
The Meru (Bantu) of Mt Kenya have a tradition of a cattle people called the
Mwoko with whom they warred only a few centuries ago, and who buried their
dead in a contracted position under stone cairns, as the Galla do today. Farther
south, the Gogo (Bantu) know of cattle keepers who preceded the Maasai onto
the steppes of Tanzania.[13] This people dug wells and built reservoirs, carved holes
in the rocks for the game of bao, built clay-lined huts that were fired like pottery
and were red and white in color, suggesting the use of clays: probably red ocher
can account for the color of the mysterious Azanians and the "red people" of
the Saharan rock paintings, as well.

Ruins left by the Neolithic tillers are found almost invariably in hill country
suitable to terracing and irrigation, and eventually these hills were surrounded
and absorbed by the successive waves of Bantu-speakers who came after. Then, in
the late Middle Ages, the black pastoral Nilotes came down out of the Sudan, while
to the eastward, the so-called "Nilo-Hamites" – the Karomojong tribes, the
Nandi peoples, the Maasai – swept southward from a region beyond Lake Rudolf.
Traditionally, these people have been considered hybrid between the Nilotes and
the Hamites, but some of their words are neither Nilotic nor Hamitic, and recently
it has been suggested[14] that their Hamitic strain, at least, derives from a separate
ancestral stock entirely. The term "Nilo-Hamitic" might be useful in distinguishing
these brown, thin-featured herders from the darker Nilotes farther west, but even
here it is not dependable: the Turkana, a tribe of the Karomojong, are coarse-
featured and black. In Africa, after millenniums of human migrations, random
physical traits are poor evidence of racial origin, and language is not always very
much better. Most of these people are more Nilote than not in both language and
customs but the southernmost tribes, the Nandi and Maasai, have such distinctive
Hamite practices as circumcision and clitoridectomy in initiation rites, the age-
grade system of young warriors, despised clans of blacksmiths, and a taboo against
fish. Conceivably all these practices were acquired from the Galla, who are known
to have wandered the region north of Lake Rudolf in the fifteenth and sixteenth
centuries, but more likely they are the heritage of earlier Hamites absorbed in the
southward migrations, who may be responsible for the lighter skin as well. These
vanished peoples left their traces in the terracing and irrigation techniques of the
Negroids, both Bantu and Nilote, who cultivate those hillsides where their remains
have been found, and who have adopted – in these regions but nowhere else – all

the Hamite customs noted above.[15] The Galla tribes are the only modern Hamites in East Africa, but four hundred miles to the south, in the region of the Crater Highlands of Tanzania, peoples persist whose origins appear to be Hamitic. If so, they derive not from the Galla but from older stocks that have been isolated for many centuries, perhaps since the time of the earliest invaders out of the north.

Lake Rudolf glimmered in the west, a silver sliver down among dark mountains. Still fifteen miles inland from Allia Bay, the track turned north toward Koobi Fora. This cauterized region, in wetter climates of the Pleistocene, attracted huge companies of animals, including early hominids whose stone tools, dated at 2.6 million years, are the oldest known. Last year near Ileret, a frontier post just south of the Ethiopian border, Leakey's expedition found a skull of *Australopithecus boisei* which he believes to be 850,000 years older than the celebrated cranium of this man-ape uncovered by his parents at Olduvai Gorge. In Richard's opinion, this land east of Lake Rudolf is the world's most important archeological site, not excluding Olduvai, though others say that finds of comparable significance are being made by a French expedition to the Omo River, at the north end of the lake, in Ethiopia, which has come upon remains of *Homo sapiens* that have been dated at two hundred thousand years, or about twice the age of former estimate.

At twilight the track passed an oasis of borassus palms known as Derati that was the water source for Leakey's base camp at Allia Bay in 1968 and 1969. Beyond Derati, gray zebra and oryx clattered across stone ridges, and a black-bellied bustard rose in courtship, collapsing its wings on the twilight sky like a great cinder in the wind. Then a striped hyena rose out of the rock, a spirit of the gaunt mountain: it turned its head to fix us with its eye before it withdrew into the shadows. This maned animal of the night, with its cadaverous flanks and hungry head, is the werewolf of legend come to life.

The striped hyena is less uncommon than unseen. Even Jock Anderson, who was born in Kenya and has traveled the bush country all his life, had only glimpsed one once before, at Amboseli. But the pleasure we took in it was shadowed by the knowledge that the estimated distance to Koobi Fora was long past, with dark upon us. We stopped for a conference. At midday, I had felt uneasy about travel in desert country with two gallons of water for nine people – what would happen in the event of an engine breakdown, a wrong turning, one car separated from the other? But Leakey had made things sound so simple that Anderson had not anticipated the slightest trouble. Not that we were in trouble now, but we were down to two quarts of water and a ration of beer and fruit juice, and could not be sure that the eight gallons of spare gasoline would carry both vehicles back to North Horr, much less Loiyengalani, even if we turned around right on the spot.

Presumably we were close to the Koobi Fora track, but side tracks are no more than shadows on this stony ground, and if the search failed, our only course was to go north to Ileret and radio for help. "We'd have to get in contact with somebody," Jock said shortly. "Assuming we make it," Adrian added, "past the bloody shifta." In the frustrating knowledge that Richard's camp was within fifteen miles of where we stood, it was decided to make camp at Derati and retreat to North Horr or Loiyengalani the next day.

Jock Anderson was grim and quiet; he is a man who dislikes turning back. But Jock had more to worry about than gas and water. We had been warned at Marsabit that an armed escort was desirable in this country, and at North Horr the police had described a gun battle that had taken place in the past month at Derati, where Leakey's supply caravan, with its armed guard, had come upon camped shifta, and five shifta had been killed. For the moment, Jock spared the party this ominous news. He was amazed at Leakey's claim that he had traveled from Marsabit to Koobi Fora in a single day, and annoyed that Richard had been so casual in his directions.

In the dark, at Derati, lacking a decent lantern, we could find no water, only foul-smelling pits of algal murk under the roots of the borassus. We rationed out the beer. Everyone was hot and dirty, and Eliot Porter cut his leg badly in the darkness, and nobody looked happy. There was more discomfort than emergency, but trouble, once started, has a way of unraveling until it is out of control, and when Stephen Porter said, "It's not a game, we could die of thirst out here," his wife told him to hush up, but nobody contradicted him.

Derati is a gloomy place in the shadow of a mountain, and the one bright element in that evening there was the old Kamba cook, Kimunginye, who made supper without benefit of lamp or pot. With a panga he cut neat sticks by shearing palm sections from the central stalk of a fallen frond, and these he laid crossways on paired logs to make a grill; in the wood ash, deftly, one by one, he laid potatoes. Strips of meat were broiled upon the sticks and a can of string beans heated in the fire. For lack of liquid we ate lightly, but the food was good. Kimunginye is a calm old African who at midday had not asked for water, even in the hundred-degree heat: the Kamba are tough – tough as the hyena's sinew, as the Maasai say. Perhaps Kimunginye recalled how, in his parents' time, these "red people", ugly as raw meat, had caused the great locust famine by running a railroad through his country (the man-eaters of Tsavo were seen by the Kamba as the spirits of dead chiefs protesting the encroachment on Kamba Land) and brought an end to the ivory trade by forbidding the Kamba to hunt elephant. If so, he gave no sign. This day was no different from another, and he went on about his work, as one felt certain that he would even if the next day were his last, his movements slow and gentle because so sure, without waste motion. The Kamba know that man dies "like the roots of the aloe", and dying was serious enough, so said his manner, without putting oneself to extra trouble over it. Kimunginye was the embodiment of what the Samburu call *nkanyit*,[16] or "sense of respect" – that quiet that comes from true awareness of the world around, with all its transience and strange significations. And I was filled with admiration, knowing, too, that Kimunginye was not exceptional, that his qualities are shared by many Africans who, seeing no need to emulate the white man, have remained in touch with the old ways.

Overhead, the crashing palms lashed wildly at the stars. In this bleak land the wind seems constant, with gusts that come as suddenly as avalanche. Grimy from a long day in the heat, we put our cots down in the fire smoke to discourage lions and mosquitoes; we would travel after midnight, to avoid the desert heat of day and its demands upon the water. Wind, discomfort, apprehension made sleep difficult for everyone except Adrian, who was so tired from the long day's drive that he went to sleep without his supper. Jock and I scarcely slept at all. He had confided to me the news of shifta, and my mind kept turning on the fact that there were two women to look out for in the event of trouble.

The wind still blew at 3.30 a.m. when we rose and broke camp and drove southward without breakfast. No water could be spared for tea, but if anyone was thirsty, he did not say so. Progress on the stony track was very slow, and it was near daylight when we passed the track down to Allia Bay, barely discernible in the cinder waste. From a visit by air last year to Allia Bay, Anderson knew of a rock pool inland, at the head of a rocky gorge; here, just after sunrise, we found water. In celebration, washing and drinking, we remained at the place two hours, then went on southeastward toward North Horr. The lonely sea, still silver, still remote, vanished behind its somber walls. Twenty-five miles from North Horr, just past the well called Hurran Hurra, a track turned off toward Loiyengalani, and as the spare gasoline was still intact, we took it; it was better to walk the last miles into Loiyengalani and send the truck back to the Land Rovers with fuel than to be stuck indefinitely at North Horr, where no fuel was available, nor transport out. The track went south along the Bura Galadi Hills, then west again, and at mid-afternoon Lake Rudolf reappeared, some seventy miles south of where we had last seen it.

Lake Rudolf, one hundred and fifty miles in length, was once connected to the Nile, and still contains the great Nile perch, two hundred pounds or better, as well as Kenya's last significant population of the Nile crocodile. Today the brackish lake is six hundred feet below the former channel to the Nile, and still subsiding, its only important source being the Omo River, which flows in the Rift fracture that crosses Ethiopia from the Red Sea. The prevailing winds of the southeast monsoon drive waves onto the west shore, in Turkana Land, twenty-three thousand square miles of near-desert wilderness extending west to the Uganda Escarpment, which forms the divide between the Rift Valley and the Valley of the Nile.

In the western light, the lake was a sea blue, choppy with wind. The foreshore was littered with water birds – flamingos, pelicans, cormorant, geese, ducks, sand-pipers and plover, gulls and terns, ibis, egrets, and the Goliath heron, largest of all wading birds in Africa. Behind them ran herds of feral ass, big-headed and wild as any zebra. At one time, the Turkana say, this shore had wild animals and good grassland, but generations of domestic stock have eaten it down to thorny stubble.

The first human beings seen since leaving North Horr were Turkana nomads, camped in a dry stream bed. To the south rose a forest of borassus palms that was sign of a large oasis; the two vehicles rolled into Loiyengalani with three gallons of gasoline between them. Word had come by radio to the police post that a truck from Koobi Fora had been shot at the day before in the region of Derati, and neither the North Horr police post nor the people at Koobi Fora had any idea where we might be. Subsequently Leakey told me that the killing of five shifta had occurred, not at Derati, but at the spring a few miles south where we had found water.

Loiyengalani is composed of a police post and a small Asian duka that serves the nomad herdsmen and El Molo; often these Indian shopkeepers were the first to penetrate unsettled regions, and few urban Africans with the training to replace them would care for the loneliness of their life. At the source of the spring, not far away, a safari lodge had been constructed, but in 1965 three men were killed here by the shifta, including the lodge manager and a priest who had come here to set up a mission. Since then, a mission has been established, but the Loiyengalani lodge subsides into the weeds. An old African sweeps the fading paths in the hope of a future, and hastened to fill the swimming pool in honor of our arrival. One of his tasks, as he conceives it, is to keep the lodge grounds clear of Samburu, Turkana, and Rendille, whose grass huts, like clusters of small haystacks, litter the oasis. None of these people of bare open spaces takes shelter from the sun and wind among the trees, preferring to build their thatch ovens on the round black stones between the oasis and the shore. The region abounds with a small venomous snake known as the carpet viper, and palm fronds left lying even for a day or two are sure to harbor one – hence the preference for the bare stones. Anyway, as one man says, the wind keeps the huts cool enough, and with one hand, one can make a window anywhere one likes.

The man who said this was an El Molo, or, more precisely, in their own pronunciation, Llo-molo; the name, he said, came from the Samburu Loo Molo Osinkirri,[17] the People Who Eat Fish. The main village of the Llo-molo, perhaps twenty huts in all, is situated still farther from the oasis than the huts of the herdsmen, on a bare black gravel slope above the lake. Stuck onto the rocks like swallows' nests, the huts have triangular mouths protected from the heavy wind by a screen of palm fronds. The black gravel all around is littered with tattered fronds and livestock dung, fish bones, old hearths, bits of rope and netting, rags. Fish dry on the thatch roofs, and on the rocks above wait rooks and gulls. Below, a smaller village stands outlined on the inland sea.

The Llo-molo, who pride themselves on honesty and hospitality, accommodate the nomads in their village even though they do not like them. The Samburu and Turkana here are forever pilfering and fighting, and a few may linger for weeks at a time as guests of the Llo-molo, who have plenty of fish and cannot bear to eat with all these strangers hanging around looking so hungry. Other tribes, the Llo-molo say, know how to eat fish better than they know how to catch them, although the Turkana fishermen on the west shore, who use set nets and fishing baskets, would dispute this. "We have to feed them," one Llo-molo says, "so that they will feel strong enough to go away."

The Llo-molo are mostly smaller than the Samburu, and many have bow legs, apparently as a result of rickets caused by their specialized diet. The men have white earrings carved from the vertebrae of cattle or Nile perch, and the women wear skirts of braided doum-palm fiber under the red trading cloth, but otherwise they imitate the Samburu, to whom they claim relationship: their moran are indistinguishable from the Samburu moran who joined them in a dance to honor the strangers. The faces of both were outlined in red masks of livid ocher, the dress and ornamentation were identical, and both carried paired spears with cowhide sheaths on the honed edges.

The dance, essentially similar in all the cattle tribes, was joined by a few Turkana warriors and women; no other women danced. Alone in East Africa, the women of the Turkana are treated as individuals worthy of respect. Though less elegant than the Samburu women, they have a bold stride and gay manner, and great character in dark, strong faces set off by beadwork and thick metal earrings. Turkana men wear black grease in their hair instead of red, and the hair is balled up in a wad of blue clay into which black ostrich feathers are inserted, and they are not circumcised. Between 1909 and 1926, the Turkana, who trade cattle into Ethiopia for rifles and to this day stage cattle raids against other Karomojong, resisted the combined authority of Kenya, Uganda, and the Sudan. But repression was less damaging to the Turkana than the drought and overgrazing in their arid lands, and today the tribe sends its men southward, seeking work.

The dancers pack together in a phalanx. As the dance begins, the moran, spears upright, step out whooping one by one, in the long, leaping Maasai trot that in time of war and cattle raids carried the herdsmen three hundred miles or more over the plains. (Adrian remarks that the Giriama of the coast, most of whom have never laid eyes on a Maasai, say to this day that there is no sense fleeing a Maasai, they have legs that can run forever.) The dancers tremble. Now two or three step out at once, and those in the main body begin to leap straight up and down, spears glinting in the sun; they shoot the chin out as they rise and stamp with the right foot as they touch the ground, and on each rise the upright spears and clubs, or rungus, are twirled all the way around. Some dancers make shrill whoops, patting their mouths; other clap hands in rhythm: "N-ga-AY!" The chant is heavy and guttural, repetitive, but one man sings a litany in counterpoint, and another orates fiercely in the background as the dance accumulates its force. The young women and old men become excited, swaying and laughing; an infant in a necklace of tiny dik-dik bones is bouncing on a girl's bare shoulders. At first these onlookers had teased the dancers but now they are caught up by the dance, eyes shining: "UM-ba-AY-uhl AH-yea-AY-y!" The old women, sullen, sit in the hot shadows of the huts, weaving palm fronds into skirts and nets and harpoon line. Perhaps they sense a condescension in the visitors, or wonder if the village will be paid.

The dance grows ever more excited, more complex, the greased red faces glistening with sweat. The moran chant in circles and then circles within circles, leaping, twirling, spears and metal arm coils shooting light, and always the chant and whooping, mournful and harmonious, the voice of man crying out to the ascending sky in exaltation and unutterable loss.

When, in 1885, Count Teleki's party reached the summit of the mountains at the south end of the lake, then made their way down to the shore, they were as stunned by the wind and sandstorms of this "valley of death"[18] as they were by its fierce beauty. At that time, the near-naked Llo-molo were all living on small islands out of fear of stronger tribes, and especially the Turkana, who made frequent raids against the Rendille of Mt Kulal. One island village still exists and can be seen from shore, but the huts are so low and amorphous that from afar, in the sun and black sand and hard light, they look more like boulders than human habitations. The small bare island, known to the Llo-molo as Lorian, is composed of two small rises with a flat saddle in between, and the huts on the saddle are outlined on the blue mountains of Turkana Land. The Turkana say that there were formerly Llo-molo on the great South Island, far offshore, but that over the years the fires there had died out one by one.

With colonial pacification of the nomads, some Llo-molo moved to the mainland at Loiyengalani, the Place of Many Trees, and acquired a few cattle by trading fish to the herdsmen who passed through; the twenty-odd Llo-molo who still cling to Lorian have only goats. The two villages at Loiyengalani, with the remnant huts on Lorian, contain all known Llo-molo, who are scarcely more numerous today than they were in the time of Count Teleki. Their health has improved with the addition to their diet of milk and blood, meat, berries, borassus nuts, and ugali or maize meal, but the Llo-molo, being thought of as inferior, take no wives from outside the tribe, while their own young girls may be sold off to other people for a bride price.

Nguya, whose brother Nanyaluka will be next chief of the Llo-molo, says that the people who lived on Lorian subsisted entirely upon fish, which are everywhere plentiful; all the tilapia the people need can be netted a few feet away from the legs of the scrawny cattle that browse among the water weeds for want of fodder on the shore. But the fishermen of Loiyengalani go to a sand spit opposite Lorian to catch and dry fish for the village. They plant their spears in the black sand to warn off raiders, and build a fire by spinning a stick in a cleft of softer wood over a tuft of dung, taking turns with this ancient fire drill until the wood dust glows. Then more dung is laid over the spark, and the whole lifted in both hands to the wind until smoke appears and fire is created.

Lines, ropes, and nets are woven of the fiber of the doum palm. Gill nets, carried looped over the shoulder, are spiked to the lake bottom with an oryx horn, the free end being loosely overlapped with the next man's net. This process is repeated according to the number of fishermen, and meanwhile the lower mesh line is treaded into the mud, to keep the fish from fleeing out beneath. Now a boy splashes through the shallows, scaring fish into the net. The tilapia, one or two pounds each, are picked out and carried ashore, where a man squatting on his heels strips off the operculum, then draws the guts gently through the gill cavity, after which he uses the hard operculum to scale the fish. All is done deftly, without haste, and in moments the sparkling meat is rinsed off in the lake. Some of the fish are boiled and eaten, but most are split and spread onto palm matting to dry; every little while the fishermen pause to hone soft-iron knives on the glinting stones.

One morning a young man of Lorian came to the mainland on a small raft of two palm logs stabilized by log outriggers and propelled by a short pole used like a kayak paddle. On his raft, for trading purposes, he carried a black goat. After renewing his red ocher and having his hair adjusted by the fishermen, he set off with his goat for Loiyengalani.

In the old days, both crocodile and hippopotamus were taken here, and the Llo-molo harpoon, virtually identical in its design to harpoons still used in the salt waters of the world for ocean fish such as swordfish and tuna, may be a separate invention of these people. A long, straight shaft is carved from the hard root of a thorn tree, then greased and bent straight in the fire and the sun; a barbed harpoon point formerly of bone but now of iron is fastened to the harpoon line, pulling free of the shaft when the quarry has been struck. There is a light harpoon for heavy fish, a heavy one for crocodile, and for hippo the long horn of an oryx; the animal is killed by multiple spearings. For hippo, the Llo-molo must now go north to Allia Bay, where they remain a month or more eating the meat. Sometimes they dry a little to bring back for the women and children. Crocodiles, too, are hunted in the north, although some still occur near Loiyengalani.

This morning the head of a very large crocodile – "*Mkubwa sena mamba!*" – is spotted in the water off the point, a mile away. Through binoculars the surfaced snout and eyes can scarcely be made out; the fishermen cannot have seen the crocodile, only a rock that has no place along a shore that has been memorized for generations. The brute sinks slowly out of sight, to reappear some minutes later farther off; it raises the whole length of its ridged tail clear of the water before sinking away again. Everywhere else, including the Omo River, this Nile crocodile is very dangerous to man, but here it seems to be quite inoffensive. Lake Rudolf crocodiles can leap clear out of the water, and have no difficulty catching fish; mostly they hunt at night, in the lake shallows. But they also have an excellent sense of smell, and will travel a long way overland for carrion. It is said[19] that these ancient animals are unable to resist the call *im-im-im*, of a weird nasality attained by closing off one nostril of the caller, but I found no chance to put this predilection to the test.

Sometimes tilapia and Nile perch are taken with the spear, in clear water off the black stone shore south of the settlement. The fish schools are shadows in the water, and the men stalk them along the shore, moving ever more quietly until they are poised, spear shaft balanced in the left hand, butt cupped in the right, line dangling in a neat coil, the harpoon point with its hard glitter in the sun like the bill of a taut heron. Nguya and his brothers squat, knees cocked, black wet legs gleaming, until they are balanced, centered, and in time with all around them; the earth is poised, all breathe as one and hurl at the same moment. Later, Ngwinye, fishing alone, pierces a one-pound fish at least fifteen feet from shore. The stalk, the squat, the wait and rise and throw is a dance more stirring than the spear dance of the moran, which had been taken from another culture. Here was the Llo-molo hunter, the aboriginal man of Africa whose old ways fade among the colors of the people who came after; it was only a glimpse, for I was here too late. Today the three fishers wore mission shorts who only a few years ago had worn fish skins or gone naked.

Hundreds of feet above the lake is a strange old rock with two parallel lines of thirteen holes in its flat surface, carved for the ancient pebble game called bao: the land beneath the rock, eroding, is tilting it gradually into a gully. Forms of bao are still played by primitive people all over Africa, for the game comes down out of the Stone Age. Each stone represents an animal, and each hole a stock corral or boma; the point of the game, like the point of pastoral life, is to acquire more stock than one's opponent.[20] The bao rock may have lain beside a vanished stream, but more likely it lay by the old shore of the lake, which was markedly higher even in the time of Count Teleki. The gaming rock, perhaps thousands of years old, passed the time of those dim figures whose passage here is marked by the silent cairns.

On the old shore there is no sign of life, no bird, only gray shell and dusty rock and small concretions that hold fossils. All is dead but for a solitary toothbrush bush, mswaki, drawing a magic green from the spent stone. Then out of the emptiness flies a hare with a gaunt jackal in pursuit. The animals whisk back and forth and circle rises; the hare dives into the lone bush, the jackal close behind. A rigid silence is pierced by a small shriek. Soon the jackal reappears, hare in its jaws, and reverting to its furtive gait, makes off with its quarry down a gully. The rocks are still.

Inland, black boulders climb to far-off ridges that rise in turn to the Kulal Mountains, in Rendille Land. The Kulal is forested, but between the forest and the lake is desert; the only soft note in this landscape is the voice of the crested lark. Down the desert hills, early one morning, came herds of sheep and goats, like far white specks, and by midday the herds were watering at the lake shore, attended by four lithe girls bare to the waist, in red bead necklaces and golden bracelets. Leather pouches swung from their slim shoulders and in the wind their skirts wound gracefully around long legs. These Rendille were wild creatures from the eastern deserts, and when approached they ran.

The Rendille men resemble the Samburu in dress and comportment, but here they mix little with other tribes, perhaps because these despised folk eat fish. A Galla people, they wander the near-desert between Mt Kulal and Marsabit, and others live between Lorian Swamp and the border of Somaliland. Probably they came originally from Somalia, driven out by the Somali expansion that seventy years ago carried all the way west to Mt Kenya. The Rendille are desert nomads, and mostly they herd camels instead of cattle: when a man dies, the Rendille say, his brother mourns him with one eye and counts his camels with the others.[21]

Chewing hard twigs of mswaki, the Rendille stand like herons on one leg to contemplate our ways. One man presents himself before me: "*Kabala Rendille*," he announces: I am of the Rendille. This is all the Swahili that he knows. He has a thorn encased in a foot that is swollen hard, and looks on with a cold smile as Eliot Porter tries in vain to remove it with a pocket knife. "He wouldn't flinch if you cut his foot in half," Adrian said, with that headshake, part condescension, part respect, that white East Africans reserve for the nomad's stoicism and endurance.

Days on this shore, though very hot, are bearable because the heat is dry, and because the wind is never still for more than a few hours. Each evening it comes howling down out of the Kulal Mountains to crash into the palms. Mounting in wild fits until after midnight, it causes the ballooning tents to lunge on their doubled moorings, and banishes all hope of sleep. Toward dawn, the winds abate, and by mid-morning may subside in vague light airs, or die with the same suddenness with which they came. The desert waits. Soon the palm fronds twitch again, and by mid-afternoon the wind is gathering toward the tumult of the night. In other seasons, said to be far worse, man takes shelter from the sandstorms in his hut, waiting dully for the months to pass.

June had turned into July; one morning we headed south. The winds and days were much the same, yet the lake has turned from a clear blue to jade, and we turned a last time to observe it from the southern mountains. From above, the inland sea is seen at its most beautiful, flowing north between two ramparts of dark mountains into the lost centuries of Abyssinia: on the desert horizon, in a desert light, the lake falls off the world into the sky. And seeing such splendor as he saw it, one regrets that Teleki named so strange a place after a Hapsburg princeling.* Before Teleki it was a lake of legend called "Samburu"[22] but a better name still might be Anam, Great Water, a name used by the Turkana.

There is no road around the south end of the lake, only the foot trails of the few Turkana who pick their way over the lava flows to Loiyengalani. A bad track climbs out of the Rift and heads for South Horr across a region of black boulders, cairns, and strange stone circles in the sand, tracing the way of the ancient nomads toward Baragoi, and Maralal on the Laikipia Plateau, and the high savannas of East Africa.

4 Siringet

The Dorobo know the spoor of all the animals, and they like to see the animals. The animals are not bad, for we and they all dwell in the forest together. The intelligence of animals is not like that of people, but it is not very different, for animals also are intelligent. All animals of the forest are alike, though we eat some and not others, because we the Dorobo and they the animals all live side by side in the forest.

an anonymous Dorobo[1]

One winter dawn of 1961, looking westward from the Olbalbal Escarpment, I saw the first rays of morning sun fall on the Serengeti Plain, in the country that was

* In early 1971, the name was debased still further when two thousand miles of this region were set aside as the "East Rudolph" National Park.

still known then as Tanganyika. Eight years later, when I stood in the same place, in Tanzania, the mighty landscape had not stirred. No road was visible, nor any sign of man, only a vast westward prospect spreading away to the clouds of Lake Victoria. Off to the north rose the Gol Mountains, in Maasai Land; in the near distance, scattered trees converged in the dark shadow of Olduvai Gorge. Beyond the shadow, spreading away in a haze of sand and golden grass, sun rays and cloud shadow, lay lion-colored plains that have changed little in millions of years.

Occupation by man's ancestors of the Olduvai region at the edge of the great grassland has probably been continuous or nearly so since hominid creatures first emerged from the forests of central Africa. Like the modern baboon, man's ancestors were primarily vegetarians that turned to small game and carrion when berries and roots were scarce, and evolved gradually as scavengers and hunters when the stones used for splitting hides and seeds and bones were flaked into hand-axes and missiles. The earliest hominid found at Olduvai is the man-ape *Australopithecus*, heavy of brow and small of brain; he is thought to have been slight and swift, with an arm fit for slinging rocks and sticks.

In the early Pleistocene, perhaps three million years ago, crocodiles floated in the shallow lake at Olduvai where *Australopithecus* left his remains, and ever since, in response to variations in the radiation of the sun, or cyclical variations of the earth's axis, that lake has died and come again and died many times over in the long rhythms of rain and drought that characterized the Ice Age. In Africa, where these oscillations were less violent than on other continents, many great animals still survive, but tool-users such as *Homo erectus* and his contemporaries, who were large creatures themselves, hunted mastodons, gorilla-sized baboons, wild saber-tusked pigs the size of hippopotami, and wild sheep as large as buffalo, as well as such animals as the white rhinoceros, once common on these plains. Possibly the white rhino, which is twice the weight of the black, is a giant form that has persisted into the present; although confined to the west bank of the Nile in the south Sudan and adjacent regions of Uganda and the Congo, it was once more common than its relative throughout the continent.

In the Pleistocene, the volcanoes of the Crater Highlands were still forming, and campsites of the early men who stared at the smoke-filled sky have been located beneath layers of volcanic tuff. The west foothills of the highlands, under Lemagrut Volcano, are steps made by tilting and faulting of the earth's surface that only took place some fifty thousand years ago, in the time when the Rift Valley was created. In this wet period of the Middle Stone Age, the use of fire had already spread throughout the continent, and remains found recently at the Omo River in Ethiopia together with a smooth-browed skull found earlier at Kanjera, in west Kenya, are evidence that modern man (*Homo sapiens sapiens*) existed at the time of these great tectonic movements, sharing the earth with more primitive men whose end he doubtless helped to bring about. Man the hunter had long since lost his body hair and developed sweat glands to dispel the tropic heat, and no doubt he also produced pigmentation to protect his bare skin from the tropic sun. In the next millenniums, while the heavy-browed *Homo sapiens Rhodesiensis* subsided slowly into the earth, his smooth-browed cousin modified his tools and developed language, learned to daub himself with ferruginous red clay, and suffered the first stirrings of religious consciousness, represented by the burial of his dead. *Homo sapiens sapiens*, the chimpanzee, and the gorilla are the sole survivors among the host of African apes, man-apes, and men that once competed for existence, and the gorilla, like the white rhinoceros, may soon follow the defeated ones into oblivion.

Little is known of man's evolution between the bone shards of a generalized *Homo* who used hand-axes a half-million years ago and the Kanjera skull of fifty thousand years ago, and there is a like absence of prehistory between Kanjera Man and the remains of the Negroid fishermen of Khartoum and their contemporaries, the so-called Proto-Hamites, who were the earliest invaders of East Africa from the north, some seventy centuries ago, and whose remains are the most recent found at Olduvai. Furthermore, no line of descent between these men and today's Africans has been clearly established, although many authorities see Bushmanoid characters in the Kanjera skull, and at least one[2] has suggested that the Irakw peoples of the south part of these highlands, who speak in a strange archaic tongue, may actually derive from Proto-Hamite hunters rather than from the Neolithic herdsmen and tillers who came after. In any case, hunter-gatherers have wandered this region since man evolved. The Bushmen have retreated into inhospitable parts of southern Africa, and such groups as the Gumba are entirely gone, but Dorobo hunters still turn up in the vicinity of Loliondo, trading honey and ivory to the Maasai whose ways they have adopted, and in the arid hills near Lake Eyasi to the south, where Rhodesioid Man left his remains, a few bands of Old People still persist, living much like Stone Age Man of forty thousand years ago.

The vast open space known to the Maasai as "siringet" is bordered in the east by the Crater Highlands, in the west by hills and a broken woodland that thickens as it nears the rain belt of Lake Victoria. Northward beyond Loliondo, in Maasai Land, it touches the Loita Hills and the plateaus of the Maasai Mara, in Kenya; to the south, it dies away in the arid thorn scrub west of Lake Eyasi. This eastern region of the plain lies in the rain shadow of the Crater Highlands, and is very dry. In winter, Serengeti days are made by the prevailing southeast winds, which lose their precipitation when they strike the east wall of the Highlands; even regional storms that come up over Oldeani and Endulen, on the south slope of the volcanic massif, fade at the Olbalbal Plains – hence the near-desert dust, black rock, and thorn of Olduvai Gorge, which is dry almost all the year. From Olduvai, the plain stretches west for thirty miles across short-grass prairie and long-grass plain to the riverain forests of the Seronera River, where weather from Lake Victoria becomes a factor.

The sun going north after the equinox causes a northeast monsoon, and the meeting of northeast and southeast monsoons produces rain; the winds, colliding, are driven upward, and in the cooler atmosphere, discharge their water. In summer a hard southeast monsoon comes from cool latitudes of open ocean east of Madagascar, and because the meeting of monsoons takes place over the south Sudan and Ethiopia, rain is scarce in the Crater Highlands. But distant anvil clouds and cumulo-nimbus herald the separate weathers of the lake basin, and by late spring the plains animals are already moving down the drainage lines that flow west toward the woodlands. In November, when the northeast monsoon swings southward and the Pleiades appear, white clouds rise on the eastern sky. Then the short rains fall, and the great herds, drawn by the first flush of new grass, return to the open plain in the annual movement, known as the "migration", that serves as pasture rotation for the wild animals.

In the winter of 1961, when I first visited the Serengeti, the greatest drought in memory was in progress. The short rains had failed entirely and the cow gnu or wildebeest, lacking milk, abandoned many of the calves; the following year there were no calves at all. But herd animals are adapted to calamities, and by the winter of 1969, when I returned to Seronera, their numbers had already been restored.* That January, the wildebeest were still moving eastward. The endless companies of animals, filling the sullen air with sullen blarting, are divided into cow-and-calf herds and herds of bulls; the bull gnus, especially, are wildebeests in their behavior, leaping, kicking, scampering, bucking, exploding crazy-legged in all directions as if in search of stones on which to dash their itching brains.

Often the wildebeest are accompanied by zebra. The striped horses, which foal all year instead of in a single seasonal avalanche, have less young to look out for and more intelligence to look out with; it is rare to see a zebra foal lost from its family band of stallion and mares. But among the gnu, the bony-legged calves are hard put to it to keep pace with their foolish mothers, and are often lost among the milling animals. Once separated, they are doomed, and fall to the predators in short order. The very plenty of their numbers in the few weeks of the calving may help preserve the species: the predators are too glutted to take advantage of all the opportunities, and many calves survive to blart another day.

Many wildebeest, streaming toward the highlands, cross the south end of Lake

* Droughts appear to fall in ten-year cycles: another serious drought occurred in 1971.

Lagarja, the headwaters of the Olduvai stream that cut the famous gorge; like almost all lakes of this volcanic region, it is a shallow magadi or soda lake of natron – native sodium carbonate in solution. In the low woods by the donga that drains the plateau to the west, a family of five cheetah lived that winter in the airy shadow of umbrella thorn, and greater and lesser flamingos, drawn to the soda lake's rich algal broth, rose in pink waves between the dark files of animals crossing the water. Since gnu are ever willing to stampede, the crossing is a hazard for the calves, and one morning of early winter more than six hundred drowned. Death passed among them like a windstorm, and its wake was awesome, yet the carcasses littered along the lake shore were but a third of one per cent of this antelope's annual regeneration in the Serengeti. Bloated calves had been dragged ashore by lions and hyenas, and others floated, snagged on mud reefs in the foamy shallows. In the thick heat of central Africa a stench so terrible clings to the throat; death had settled in the windless air like a foul mist. Among the carcasses, probing and sweeping, stepped elegant avocets and stilts, ignoring the taint in the stained water, and vulture and marabou in thousands had cleared the skies to accumulate at the feast. These legions of great greedy-beaked birds could soon drive off any intruder, but they are satisfied to squabble filthily among themselves; the vulture worms its long naked neck deep into the putrescence, and comes up, dripping, to drive off its kin with awful hisses. The marabou stork, waiting its turn, sulks to one side, the great black teardrop of its back the very essence of morbidity distilled. With George Schaller of the Serengeti Research Institute I made a count of the dead calves; and the vultures gave ground unwillingly, moving sideways. Vultures run like gimpy thieves, making off over the ground in cantering hops, half-turned, with a cringing air, as if clutching something shameful to the stiff stale feathers of their breast. The marabou, with its raw skull and pallid legs, is more ill-favored still: it takes to the air with a hollow wing thrash, like a blowing shroud, and a horrid hollow clacking of the great bill that can punch through tough hide and lay open carcasses that resist the hooks of the hunched vultures. Vultures fly with a more pounding beat, and the cacophony of both, departing carrion, is an ancient sound of Africa, and an inspiring reminder of mortality.

Dr Schaller, a lean, intent young man whose work on the mountain gorilla had already made his reputation, was studying the carnivores of the Serengeti. In the winter of 1969, he spent as much time as possible in the field, and often he was kind enough to take me with him. Usually we were underway before the light, when small nocturnal animals were still abroad – the spring-hares, like enormous gerbils, and the small cats and genets. The eyes of nocturnal animals have a topetum membrane that reflects ambient light, and in the headlights of the Land

Rover the eyes of the topi were an eerie silver, and lion eyes were red or green or white, depending on the angle of the light. The night gaze of most animals is red, like a coal-red beacon that we once saw high in the branches of a fever tree over the Seronera River; the single cinder, shooting an impossible distance from one branch to another, was the eye of the lesser gallego, or bushbaby, a primitive small primate which may or may not resemble the arboreal creature from which mankind evolved.

In a silver dawn giraffes swayed in the feathery limbs of tall acacias, and a file of wart hog trotted away into the early shadows. Where a fork of the river crossed the road, a yellow reedbuck and a waterbuck stood juxtaposed. With its white rump and coarse gray hair, the waterbuck looks like a deer, but deer do not occur in Africa south of the Sahara; like the wildebeest, gazelles, and other deer-like ruminants, from the tiny dik-dik to the great cowlike eland, the reedbuck and waterbuck are antelope, bearing not antlers but hollow horns: the family name, Antilopinae, means "bright eyed". All antelope share the long ears, large nostrils, and protruding eyes that together with speed help protect them against predators, but non-migratory species such as topi, waterbuck, and kongoni seem more vigilant than the herd species of the green plain.[3]

At Naabi Hill, the wildebeest were moving east after the rains. In their search for new growth, wildebeest are often seen trooping steadfastly over arid country toward distant thunderstorms, which bring a flush of green to the parched land-scapes. Some two hundred thousand were in sight at once, with myriad zebra and the small Thomson's gazelle. Eight wild dogs were hunting new gazelle left hidden by their mothers in the tussocks; one snatched a calf out of the grass only yards from the tires of the Land Rover, and with the two nearest dogs tore it to bits. The death of new calves is quick; they are rended and gone. But one calf older than the rest sprang away before the dog and made a brave run across the plain in stiff-legged long bounces, known as "pronking", in which all four hooves strike the ground at once. Like the electric flickering of the flank stripe, pronking is thought to be a signal of alarm. Though its endurance was astonishing, it lasted so long because most of the dogs were gorged and failed to cooperate. While the lead dog snapped vainly at the flying heels, the rest loitered and gamboled, picking up another calf that one of them ran over in the grass.

The Land Rover, dodging humps and burrows, followed the chase across the plain. Schaller clocked the young gazelle, which dodged back and forth for two and a half miles on the car's gauge and more than three in actuality; it never ran in a straight line. (The zigzag is less an evasion tactic than a way of seeing out of eyes set back on the sides of the head; in a herd, pursued animals usually run straight out.) The calf's spirit tempted us to intervene but we did not, since it was doomed whatever happened; separated from its milk when the chase began, it would have gone hungry while awaiting the first of the many beasts and giant birds that would come for it on sight. Finally, two dogs moved up to flank the leader, and in moments, the chase was over. The calf, still bouncing desperately, veered back and forth across the paths of the spurting dogs, and the dog to the eastward snatched it from the air; the other two were on it as it struck the ground.

One day, by a depression that holds water in the rains, I found a chipped flake of obsidian, much used by primitive man for his edged tools. There is no obsidian on the plain; the chip had been brought here long before. I wondered about the men who brought it – what size and color were they? Were they in hides or naked? What cries did they utter? Staring at the sun, the sky, were they aware of their own being, and if so, what did they think?

Doubtless the primitive hominids whose remains have been found at Olduvai were drawn to the edge of the great plain by the legions of grazing animals, and doubtless they were glad of a bit of carrion. The hunter Frederick Selous, in the 1870s, was appalled to see natives eat meat of an elephant eight days dead – "Truly some tribes of Kafirs and Bushmen are fouler feeders than either vultures or hyenas"[4] – but accounts of life on rafts and in prison camps, in plague and famine, make clear that the most civilized man will eat both carrion and his own kind when survival is at stake, as it must have been each day for low-browed figures who lacked true weapons and perhaps language, despite the physical capacity to speak. (Perhaps the earliest *Homo sapiens* of the Old Stone Age had no fire, and the gift of flame from the supreme Creator, recognized by almost all African tribes, was an earth-shaking event that is still remembered in the myths.)[5]

Traditional theories of the social life of earliest man are based on the behavior of non-human primates, although the apes are essentially vegetarians, and have lived very differently from man for more than a million years. Social systems, which often differ greatly among closely related creatures, tend to evolve in response to ecological conditions, and George Schaller felt that much might be guessed about early man from a comparative study of the social carnivores,[6] which also pursued game in open country. While unable to run down his prey in the way of the wild dog or hyena, or even rush it swiftly as the lion does, man would have used such lion tactics as driving, ambush, and encirclement, and come upwind to the quarry, as lions have never learned to do. And as with the carnivores, a successful kill would inevitably depend on the social group that would share the food.

To judge from remains of predators found at his sites, early man was an increasingly effective creature who drove such unaggressive daylight hunters as the cheetah and the wild dog from their kills. In the dark, he was at a disadvantage and took shelter, leaving the hunt to leopard, lion, and hyena, but in the day, confronted with his sticks and stones, strange upright stance, and the shrieks, scowls, and manic jumps of primate threat display, these more dignified creatures probably gave way.

To learn how hunter-scavengers might fare, we sometimes walked some fifty yards apart for two hours or more over the plain. On most of the hunts gazelle calves were plentiful – with throwing sticks, four or five could have been killed, and with bolus stones (found at Olduvai) still more – and it was almost always possible to locate food by watching vultures in the distance. One day we came upon a Thomson's gazelle, dead of disease, that the carrion-eaters had not yet located, and also a young Grant's gazelle that must have been taken by the two huge lappet-faced vultures that we drove away, for the kill was fresh and no predators were anywhere about. Another day, when Schaller was elsewhere, I saw from a distance the white belly of a female Thomson's gazelle, fresh dead. As I approached, the first vulture, a big lappet-face, came careening in and took a swipe at her white flank. The vulture was instantly driven off by a second female gazelle; the great bird, flop-winged, chased its assailant but did not renew its assault on the dead animal.

The gazelle was still warm, and I slit open the belly to see if she had died in calving. She had milk but no calf; the wet newborn thing crouched in the grass some twenty yards away. A half hour later, her companion was still on guard, but more vultures were gathering, and finally the body was abandoned to a motley horde of griffons, white-backs, and hooded vultures that stripped it to the bones in a few minutes.

Jackals, vultures, and hyenas are alert for the defenseless moment when a new calf is born; often hyenas will attend the birth. But one day there was a mass calving of wildebeest in a shallow valley like an amphitheater between the isles of rocks, and it may or may not be significant – I simply record it – that the calving took place in the very middle of the day, when the sun was high and hot and the plain still. There was no predator in sight for miles around, nor a single vulture in the sky. Cow wildebeest were down all over the place, and a number of tottery calves less than an hour old swayed and collapsed and climbed again to their new feet. By late afternoon, when the predators become restless, raising their heads out of the grass to sniff the wind, these calves would already be running. (Wildebeest calves can usually run within ten minutes of their birth, but even this may be too slow; I have seen a lioness, still matted red from a feed elsewhere and too full to eat, walk up and swat a newborn to the ground without bothering to charge, and lie down on it without biting.)

For fear of scattering the cows, I restrained a desire to go close, for the calves will imprint on the nearest moving thing and are not to be deterred. One day, I was followed from a grazing herd by a young calf, and my efforts to head it back to safety finally resulted in putting the herd to flight. The calf did not follow, and the herd forsook it; nor would it permit itself to be caught. Finally I too left it behind. A mile away I could still see it – I can still see it to this day – a thin still thing come to a halt at last on the silent plain.

The unseasonal rains of late January continued into February, falling mostly in late afternoon and in the night; many days had a high windy sun. In this hard light I walked barefoot on the plain, to feel the warm hide of Africa next to my skin, and aware of my steps, I was also aware of the red oat and red flowers of indigofera, the skulls with their encrusted horns (which are devoured like everything else: a moth lays its eggs up on the horns, and the pupae, encased in crust, feed on the keratin), the lairs of wolf spiders and the white and yellow pierid butterflies, like blowing petals, the larks and wheatears (Olde English for white-arse), the elliptical hole of the pandanus scorpion and the round hole of the mole cricket, whose mighty song attracts its females from a mile away, the white turd of the bone-eating hyena, and the pyriform egg of a crowned plover in water-colored camouflage that blends the rain and earth and air and grass.

Bright flowers blowing, and small islets of manure; to the manure come shiny scarabs, beloved of Ra (god of the Sun, son of the Sky). The dung beetles, churning in over the grass, collide with the deposits of manure, or attach themselves to the slack ungulate stomachs full of half-digested grass that the carnivores have slung aside. They roll neat spheres of ordure larger than themselves and hurry them off over the plain. Here dung beetles fill the role of earthworms: the seasonal droppings of hundreds of thousands of animals, most of which is buried by the beetles, ensures that the soil will be aerated as well as fertilized.

By morning the ground is soaked again and the tracks muddy. Frogs have sprung from fleeting pools, and the trills of several species chorus in the rush to breed. Companies of storks, nowhere in evidence the day before, come down in slow spirals from the towers of the sky to eat frogs, grass-mice, and other lowlife that the rains have flooded from the earthen world under the mud-flecked flowers.

The grassland soil is built of ash blown westward from the volcanoes of the Highlands. Beyond the ash plain, in the vicinity of Seronera, the soil is derived from granitic rock and supports an open woodland vegetation. This is some of the oldest rock on earth – certain granites here are two to three billion years old – and on the plain the bone of Africa emerges in magnificent outcrops or kopjes, known to geologists as inselbergs, rising like stone gardens as the land around them settles, and topped sometimes by huge perched blocks, shaped by the wearing away of ages. The kopjes serve as water catchments, and in the clefts, where aeolian soil has mixed with eroded rock, tree seeds take root that are unable to survive the alternate soaking and desiccation on the savanna, so that from afar the outcrops rise like islands on the grass horizons. In their shadows and still compositions, the harmonious stones give this world form.

When the sun has risen and the morning's hunt has slowed, the cats may resort to the rock islands. Perhaps they seek shade, or the vantage point of higher elevation – for the leopard its kopje is a hideout between raids – or perhaps, like myself, they like their back to something, for especially in summer, when the herds have withdrawn into the western woodlands and a dry wind blows in the dry grass, the granite heads are a refuge from the great emptiness of the plain. Kopjes occur in isolated companies, like archipelagoes – one group may be ten miles from the next – but most groups are related to a rising spine of rocks that emerges more or less gradually from the ash plain, from the low Gol Kopjes in the east to the majestic Morus at the edge of the western woodlands. Highest of all is Soit Naado Murt (in Maasai, the Long-necked Stone), nicknamed Big Simba Kopje, which juts straight up a hundred feet or more near the center of the spine, just off the main road from Olduvai to Seronera.

The lonely Gols are kopjes of the short-grass prairie, lying off to the north of the Olduvai-Seronera road. The shy cheetah is a creature of the Gols, its gaunt gait and sere pale coat well suited to these wind-withered stones, and one day I saw a glowing leopard stretched full length on a rim of rock, in the flickering sun shade of a fig; seeing man, it gathered itself without stirring, and flattened into the stone as it slid from view. It is said that a leopard will lie silent even when struck by stones hurled at its hiding place – an act that would bring on a charge from any lion – but should its burning gaze be met, and it realizes that it has been seen, it will charge at once. A big leopard is small by comparison to a lion, or to most men, for that matter, but its hind claws, raking downward, can gut its prey even as the jaws lock on the throat, and it strikes fast. It is one of the rare creatures besides man known to kill for the sake of killing, and cornered, can be as dangerous as any animal in Africa. Rural tribes have trouble in the night with leopards that steal into their huts to seize children by the throat and carry them off undetected – a testimony to the sleeping powers of the African as well as to the great stealth of this cat. Ordinarily, the unwounded leopard is not a menace to adults, but this past winter, a night leopard killed an African receptionist, Feragoni Kamunyere, outside his quarters at Paraa, Murchison Falls, and dragged the body, bigger than itself, a half-mile or more into the bush, presumably to feed its waiting cubs. The strength of leopards is intense: I have seen one descend the trunk of a tall tree head first, a full-grown gazelle between its jaws.

There are few trees in the Gols, which are low and barren, yet in their way as stirring as the Morus, which rise like monuments in a parkland of twenty-five square miles, and have a heavy vegetation. Impala, buffalo, and elephant are attracted to the Morus from the western woods, and the elephants, which are celebrated climbers, attain the crests of the steep kopjes, to judge from the evidence heaped upon the rock. One day at noon, from this elephant crest, a leopard could be seen on the stone face of the kopje to the south, crossing the skeletal shadows of a huge candelabra euphorbia. In the stillness that attended the cat's passage, the only sound was a rattling of termites in the leaf litter beneath my feet.

Here near the woods the long grass is avoided by the herds. Lone topi and kongoni wander among these towers, and an acacia is ringed by a bright circlet of zebras, tails swishing, heavy heads alert. The wild horses are not alarmed by man, not yet; all face in another direction. Somewhere upwind, in the tawny grass, there is a lion.

I spent one February day on a small kopje, gazing out over the plain. The kopje overlooks a swampy korongo – not a true stream but a drainage line – that holds water in this season, and is bordered by dense thicket. On this rock, in recent days, I had seen a lioness and cubs swatting around the dried carcass of a gazelle that must have been scavenged from a leopard. I circled the place and studied it before committing myself, and climbing the rock, I clapped my hands to scare off dangerous inhabitants. In daylight, lions will ordinarily give way to man, and snakes are always an exaggerated danger, but care must be taken with the hands, for adders, cobras, mambas all reside here.

The hand claps echoed in a great stillness all around; the intrusion had drawn the attention of the plain. A stink of carrion mingled queerly with the perfume of wild jasmine on the rock. The birds fell still, and lizards ceased their scuttering. Then the early sun was creased by clouds. Standing in gray wind on the bare rock, I had a bad moment of apprehension – the sense of Africa that I sought through solitude seemed romantic here, unworthy. At my feet lay the reality, a litter of big lion droppings and a spat-up hair ball.

I looked and listened. From the fig tree came a whining of the flies. The sun returned, and from the sun came the soft wing snap or flappeting of the flappet lark, and the life of the plain went on again, bearing me with it.

Already the granite was growing warm, and leaves of a wild cucumber strayed on its surface. Squatted by a pool of rain that baboons had not yet found and fouled, I studied my surroundings. By the korongo spurfowl nodded through rank grass inset with a blue spiderwort, crimson hibiscus, a bindweed flower the color of bamboo. Soon a reedbuck, crouched near the stream edge until the intruder should depart, sprang away like an arrow as its nerves released it, scattering the water with high bounding silver splashes. Where it had lain, golden-backed weavers swayed and dangled from long stalks of purple amaranth. A frog chorus rose and died, and a bush shrike, chestnut-winged, climbed about in the low bushes.

A mile away to the northwest stood the great kopje that the Maasai call Soit Naado Murt. In the southern distance, toward the Morus, zebra and wildebeest passed along the ridges, and where the unseen carnivores were finishing a kill, the vultures were a black pox on the sky. To the east, under a soaring sun, ostriches ran down the grass horizon, five thousand feet above the sea. There came a start of exhilaration, as if everything had rounded into place.

Now it was man who sat completely still. In the shade of the great fig, a soft hooting of a dove – coo, co-co, co-co. The dove, too, had been waiting for me to go, blinking its dark liquid eye and shifting its pretty feet on the cool bark. Now it had calmed, and gave its quiet call. Bushes at the kopje base began to twitch where mousebirds and bee-eaters stilled by the hush were going on about their bright-eyed business, and agama lizards, stone eyes glittering, materialized upon the rock. The males were a brilliant blue and orange, heads swollen to a turgid orange-pink (kopje agamas have been so long isolated on their rock islands that color variations have evolved; those at Lemuta Kopjes, in arid country, are mostly a pale apricot), and they were doing the quick press-ups of agitation that are thought to be territorial threat display. Perhaps man lay across the courtship routes, for they seemed thwarted and leapt straight up and down, whereas the females, stone-colored, skirted the big lump that did not concern them.

As if mistrustful of the silence, a kongoni climbed to the crest of a red termite mound to look about; I focused my binoculars to observe it only to learn that it was observing me. The long-faced antelope averted its gaze first. "The kongoni has a foolish face," an African child has said, "but he is very polite."[7] Not far away, a Thomson's gazelle was walking slowly, cocking its head every little way as if to shake a burr out of its ear. It was marking out its territory by dipping its eye toward a stiff prominent blade of grass, the tip of which penetrates a gland that is visible under the eye as a black spot; the gland leaves a waxy black deposit on the grass tip, and the gazelle moves on a little way before making another sign. Once one knows it is done, the grass-dipping ceremony, performed also by the dik-dik, is readily observed, but one sees why it passed unnoticed until only a few years ago.

In the still heat that precedes rain, a skink, striped brown, raised its head out of the rock as if to sniff the flowers and putrefaction. A variable sunbird, iridescent, sipped from a fire-colored leonotis, blurred wings a tiny shadow on the sky; it vanished, and the plain lay still.

*   *   *

A big weather wind from the southeast came up in the late morning, and by noon it was shifting to the east, turning the dark clouds on the Crater Highlands. Once again, the herds were moving. To see the animals in storm, I abandoned my rock and went over to Soit Naado Murt, and climbed the broad open boulders on the south side, away from the road.

Soaring thunderheads, unholy light: at the summit of the rock the wind flung black leaves of twining fig trees flat against the sky, and black ravens blew among them. I straightened, taking a deep breath. From its aerie, a dog baboon reviled me with fear and fury. Puffs of cold air and a high far silent lightning; thunder rolled up and down the sky. Everywhere westward, the zebra legions fled across the plain. But dark was coming, and soon I hurried down off the high places. At the base of the rock, the suspense, the malevolence in the heavy air was shattered by a crash in the brush behind, and I whirled toward the two tawny forms that hurtled outward in a bad late light, sure that this split second was my last. But the lion-sized and lion-colored animals were a pair of reedbuck, as frightened as myself, that veered away toward the dense cover of the korongo. I stood still for a long time, staring after them as darkness fell, aware of a strange screaming in my ears. Then I came to, and moved away from the shadows of the rock. A pale band in the west, under mountains of black rain, was the last light, and against this light, on the rock pinnacles, rose the hostile cliff tribe of baboons. In silhouette they looked like early hominids, hurling wild manic howlings at my head.

5 In Maasai Land

The primal ancestor of the Masai was one Kidenoi, who lived at Donyo Egere (Mount Kenia), was hairy, and had a tail. Filled with the spirit of exploration, he left his home and wandered south. The people of the country, seeing him shaking something in a calabash, were so struck with admiration at the wonderful performance that they brought him women as a present. By these he had children who, strangely enough, were not hairy, and had no tails, and these were the progenitors of the Masai.

Joseph Thomson, *Through Masai Land*

Like many white men that one comes across in Africa, Myles Turner is a solitary whose job as park warden of the Serengeti keeps him in touch with mankind more than he would like, but one day he got away on a short safari, and was kind enough to take me with him. We would go to the Gol Mountains, in Maasai Land, and from there attempt to reach by Land Rover that part of the Rift Escarpment that stands opposite a remote volcano known to the Maasai as *ol doinyo le eng ai*, the Mountain of the God, called commonly Lengai.

The eighth of February was a day of low still clouds, waxy gray with the weight of rain. On the plain, the herd animals were restless, and the gnu, crazy-tailed, fled to the four winds, maddened by life. At Naabi Hill, the eastern portal of the Serengeti Park, three lionesses lay torpid on a zebra. Vultures nodded in the low acacias, and the hyenas, wet hair matted like filth on their sagging bellies, dragged themselves, tails tight between their legs, from the rain wallows in the road.

We turned off north toward Loliondo, then east again under Lemuta Hill. Between Lemuta and the Gols is a dry valley, in the rain shadow of the Crater Highlands; here the hollow calls of sand grouse resound in the still air, and an echo of wind from the stoop of a bateleur eagle. Where we had come from and where we were going, a pale green softened the short grass, but in the shadow of the rain, despite massed clouds in all the distances, the flicked hoof of a gazelle raised the soil in a spiral of thin dust.

On the far side of the desert valley is the Gol – the "Hard Country" of the Maasai – a badlands of arid thorny hills and high cold wind. The Gol is crossed by a canyon two miles wide, Ngata Kiti, that climbs gradually in a kind of arch and descends again into the Salei Plain. Ngata Kiti is the eastern range of the migrant herds, and theoretically connects the Serengeti populations with those of the Crater Highlands, but in 1959 this "Eastern Serengeti", which included Ngorongoro Crater, was returned to the Maasai. In addition, the government attempted to close off Ngata Kiti, where a few nomad Maasai kept a few cattle. Heavy posts linked with seven strands of wire were planted straight across the valley mouth. The wildebeest, faced with this fence, were undeterred; the wire held, but the whole fence went over. "Tried to interfere with what thousands of animals had done for thousands of years," said Myles, a slight wiry man with weary eyes in a weathered face and a wild shock of sandy red hair. He glared at the old fence line with satisfaction. "It's marvelous the way those animals smashed it flat. I use the posts for firewood now, out on safari."

At the mouth of Ngata Kiti is Ol Doinyo Rabi – the Cold Mountain – named for the chill wind that sweeps the Gol in summertime, when the herds have gone west to the woods, and the land is empty. This day there were small companies of wildebeest and zebra, and a secretary bird, that long-limbed aberrant eagle that stalks the open ground, but the true habitants of the Gol are the gazelles, which are the first to reach Ngata Kiti and the last to leave it. Probably the thin grass is sweet, since this soil has been enriched by the volcanoes, but here in the rain shadow it is stunted for lack of water. The vehicle seemed small and lost between the walls of Ngata Kiti, winding slowly up the valley toward Naisera, the Striped Mountain, named for black streaks of blue-green algae that have formed on its granite face. Halfway up, big fig trees burst from ledges and crevasses, the bare roots feeling their way down to sustenance one hundred feet below. Behind Naisera we made camp in a grove of umbrella thorn and wildflowers; I remember a delicate apricot hibiscus. At Naisera there are highland birds: the ant-eater chat and the bronzy sunbird, crombecs, tits . . .

Myles's Land Rover was packed with gear of all descriptions, and a truck carried tents for each of us and two tents for the staff, as well as stoves, stores, and water. Like most British East Africans, Myles is extremely thorough in his safari preparations, and saw nothing strange at all in having seven pairs of hands to help us through a short trip of three days – what was strange to him was my discomfort. Not that I let it bother me for long. While the tents went up, I watched white clouds cross the black thunderhead behind Naisera; lightning came, and a drum of rain on the hard ground across the valley. On the taut skin of Africa rain can be heard two miles away. Bird calls rang against Naisera's walls, which on the north are painted white by high nests of hawk and raven. At the summit, in the changing light the swifts and kestrels swooped and curved, and an Egyptian vulture gathered light in its white wings. Then the sky rumbled and the white bird sailed on its shaft of sun into the thunder.

The storm arrived in early afternoon. I lay content beneath the raining canvas, head propped upon my kit, and gazed through the tent flap down past Naisera into the dry valley below Lemuta where no rain fell. In the thunder, wildebeest were running. When the rain eased, I crossed the grove to a cave in Naisera's wall that had a small boma of thorn brush at the mouth, and a neat dry hearth. In a similar cave in the Moru Kopjes, shields, elephants, and abstract lines are painted on the walls in the colors that are seen on Maasai shields; the white and yellow come from clays, the black from ash of a wild caper, and the red ocher is clay mixed with juice from the wild nightshade. Presumably the artists were a band of young warriors, moran, who wander for several years as lovers, cattle thieves, and meat-eaters before settling down to a wife, responsibilities, and a diet based on milk and cattle blood. According to Leite, a young Maasai ranger, this cave in the Gol Mountains was also a place of meat-eating, which is forbidden in the villages, and which no woman is allowed to watch. Those women who see it are flogged, he told Myles, who nodded in approval. Leite is tall and brown, with a stretched ear lobe looped into a knot; he gazed about him with an open smile, happy to be here in Maasai Land.

Leite's people were part of the last wave of lean herdsmen to descend upon East Africa from the north. Perhaps five centuries ago the present-day Nandi tribes invaded western Kenya, driving earlier herdsmen known as the Tatog south from the region of Mt Elgon; the Maasai tribes were farther to the east, in the grasslands and surrounding plateaus of the Rift Valley, and they, too, appear to have displaced an earlier people, known to the Dorobo as the Mokwan,[1] who had long hair and enormous herds of long-horned cattle, and who may be the same herdsmen as the Mwoko, recorded by the Meru Bantu of Mt Kenya.

In regard to the coming of the Maasai, the Dorobo say[2] that a Dorobo hunter at the Narok River saw great companies of people coming down out of the north, and hid; he was caught by the Maasai, and guided them to water for their cattle. The Maasai are thought to have reached Nakuru and the Ngong Hills near Nairobi in the seventeenth century, and their heaven-born first laibon or medicine man was found as a youth in the Ngong at a time thought to have been about 1640. Subsequently they continued south along the Rift, and in the vicinity of the Crater Highlands held great battles with a people that their tradition calls *il Adoru*[3] – conceivably the Barabaig, a tribe of the Tatog so fierce that they are known to present-day Maasai as *il Ma-'nati* or "Mangati", the Enemy, a name reserved, so it is said, for a worthy foe.

Otherwise, the Maasai met with small resistance. By the nineteenth century, they had driven the Galla tribes northeast across the Tana, and Maasai Land extended east and west one hundred and fifty miles and five hundred miles north and south, from the region of Maralal on the Laikipia Plateau to the south end of the Maasai Steppe in Tanzania. Their raids, which spread from Ikuria Land on Lake Victoria to the Indian Ocean coast, were feared by Bantu, Arab, and European alike, so much so that Maasai Land remained unexplored until less than a century ago. Avoided by the great slave routes and trails of exploration into the interior, it was the last terra incognita in East Africa.

Linguistically the Maasai are closest to the Bari of the Sudan,[4] and the many customs that they share with other tribes of Nilotic origin include male nudity, the shaving of females, the extraction of two middle teeth from the lower jaw, the one-legged heron stance, the belief that the souls of important men turn into snakes, and the copious use of spit in benediction. Like the Nuer, the Maasai believe that all cattle on earth belong to them, and that taking cattle from others is their right. Originally it was God's intent to give all cattle to the Dorobo, but the great Maasai ancestor Le-eyo tricked the Dorobo, and God into the bargain, receiving the cattle in their place. Hence the Dorobo must live by hunting and gathering, which the Maasai despise. Eland and buffalo may be eaten by Maasai, since these are thought of as wild cattle, but no other animal, or fish or fowl, is ever hunted except for decorative or ceremonial purposes – ostrich head plumes, monkey-skin anklets, ivory ear plugs, and the great helmets of lion mane that once identified a proven warrior. (An exception, the rhino, is poached for its horn, which is bought from the Maasai by Asian traders and sold in the East as an aphrodisiac; this commerce is at least as old as the *Periplus of the Erythraean Sea*, an account of a trading voyage to the east coast in the first century AD. In a six-month period of 1961, the Leakeys found over fifty speared rhino in the Olduvai region alone, each stripped of a horn that may be worth a few shillings a pound to the Maasai but far more to the trader. A recent increase in the trade has threatened the black rhino with extinction, all to no purpose, since despite its shape and dynamic angle, the horn – not true horn at all, but hard-packed hair – can do nothing to spur the love-bent oriental, who may pay as much as two hundred dollars per pound to ingest it as a powder.

Like the Dinka, the Maasai have a moon legend of the origin of death, which was formerly unknown among mankind, and is still thought of as unnatural: Naiteru, a deity residing on Mt Kenya, instructed the patriarch Le-eyo that if a child of the tribe should die, he must cast away the body with the words, "Man dies, and returns again; the moon dies and remains away." But since the first child to die was not his own, Le-eyo did not bother to obey, and ever since then, man has died and the moon has been reborn. Eventually Le-eyo called his sons to his own deathbed to ask what they wished as an inheritance. The greedy elder son, who became the ancestor of all Bantu, wanted part of everything on earth; the younger said he would be content with some small remembrance of his father. This modesty was rewarded with great cattle wealth, whereas the Bantu son was given a little bit of everything, and ever since has been eking out his days with his wretched agriculture.

Within the tribes, certain Maasai became smiths, and fashioned the spear blades and the short sword known as the simi; as in Hamitic tribes, such people were inferior. When the white man appeared in the late nineteenth century, he was called l'Ojuju, the Hairy One, and lacking cattle, was despised with all the rest.

> I have tried to produce an impression on the Maasai by means of forest fires, by fiery rockets, and even by a total eclipse of the sun . . . but I have found, after all, that the one thing that would make an impression on these wild sons of the Steppe was a bullet . . . and then only when employed in emphatic relation to their own bodies.[5]

At the time this was written by Karl Peters, whose perfidious treaties with unsuspecting chiefs laid the groundwork for Germany's seizure of Tanganyika, the power of the Maasai was already waning due to drought and disease and a growing resistance from such victims as the Nandi and the Kamba, as well as incessant war between their own marauding tribes; cheered on by their women, they staged great civil wars on the open plain, one consequence of which was the utter disruption of the Laikipiak Maasai, whose lands were taken over by the Samburu. In 1869, the Samburu had infected the Maasai with cholera, which raged through the tribe in epidemic, and just before the Europeans appeared in force in the 1880s, they were swept by smallpox, and their beasts struck down by waves of rinderpest, or pleuropneumonia, a cattle plague from Asia that also affects certain antelope (rinderpest is thought to have eliminated the greater kudu from wide areas of its former range). Kikuyu and Kamba herds, in Kenya, were also afflicted, bearing out an old Kikuyu prophecy that great famine and disaster would precede the fatal coming of pale strangers. Like the Kamba, the Maasai believe that a comet foretells the coming of disaster, and they say that a comet crossed the sky just before the appearance of l'Ojuju: the great laibon Mbatien had also prophesied the advent of the white man in a vision brought on by honey wine. On his death-bed, Mbatien bequeathed his title and attainments to his son Lenana, much to the annoyance of the elder son Sendeyo, who had reason to believe that Lenana had cheated him out of his heritage. Once again the Maasai split into hostile factions more or less separated by the boundary between what had become, in 1895, British and German East Africa. But after twelve years of rinderpest, small-pox, famine, and German harassment in the region of Kilimanjaro, Sendeyo forgave Lenana, and the Maasai were reunited. Already Lenana had made peace with the British; so weakened were the Maasai, in fact, that they needed European protection from their enemies. Because of their great misfortunes, made so much worse by their delight in fighting one another, they were unable to resist the Hairy Ones – unlike the Nandi, farther west, who were not pacified until 1905, and the Turkana, in the north, who held out for another twenty years. The Maasai wanted very much to fight against the Germans in World War I, which brought Tanganyika under British administration, but the British thought it unwise to give them arms.

In the Serengeti, according to their own tradition, the Maasai were most numer-ous near Lake Lagarja and in the south part of the plain, but until 1959, when their herds were banished, they lived intermittently at Moru Kopjes and elsewhere in the park, and signs of their long stay include mints and peas that thrive in the wake of overgrazing by domestic herds. Some of the kopjes have been stripped of trees, and at others the vegetation seems induced by man – certain acanths and morning glories that accompany the disruption of the soil, and thorny nightshades (*Solanum*), and an introduced legume whose spiny fruits are thought to have stuck to the old Army greatcoats gotten in trade at the Asian dukas after the last war. Today these greatcoats, regardless of temperature, are a favored article of dress throughout East Africa, though most Maasai wear the shuka or toga of broadcloth, dyed in red ocher, that is knotted on the right shoulder.

Maasai herds are still seen intermittently along the eastern boundaries of the park, and a few moran may turn up at the settlement at Seronera. One-legged or ankles crossed, leaning on their spears, they gaze impassively at the less aristocratic Africans in the service areas. Ostensibly they have put aside their warlike ways, but not long ago a dead morani was discovered on the plain – speared to death, apparently, since no predators were near. As yet, only vultures had found him. A passing Maasai might pluck some grass, which as cattle food is a symbol of good will and peace, and spit on it in benediction, and place the grass upon the skull, to protect himself from evil, but the body would be left untouched on the great siringet, under the African sky.

When the rain stopped, I climbed Naisera. Leite came with me, bringing along his muzzle-loading musket, taken from a poacher. This gun was long since defunct – it had not worked for the poacher, either. Even in the time of Livingstone, such muskets were very common in the interior – it was firearms that persuaded the Arab traders to venture inland – and with the advent of the breech-loading rifle, then the repeater, late in the nineteenth century, great numbers of muskets were inherited by the Africans. In Tanzania, thousands of muzzle-loaders are still registered, and guns of the mid-nineteenth century are still carried for purposes of prestige.

Three klipspringer stood outlined on the rock's crest; by the time we reached the top, they had disappeared. We crouched in the wind and gazed up and down Ngata Kiti. To the eastward, far beyond the far end of the valley, the Mountain of God rose for a long moment in the swirling clouds, then vanished. The Maasai say that Lengai or Ngai moved to this place in the sky after a Dorobo hunter shot an arrow at him, and most of the day for most of the year his realm is hidden; now Ngai is remote, beyond their reach, and they are visited by death and famine. Leite took delight in my elation at the sight of the holy mountain. Later he exclaimed to Myles, "Lengai must be the Mountain of God – it is so extreme!" In 1967, this last active volcano of the Crater Highlands erupted, shrouding its slopes and all the country around with fine gray ash.

I spoke no Maasai and Leite no English; we communicated with hand signs and good will. Leite cautioned against touching a certain euphorbia whose milk was hurtful to the eyes, and showed me a small plant, ol-umigumi, taken as a stimulant with meat before a lion hunt to give warriors courage. The moran surround a big male lion, then rush in with their spears – "Fantastic!" says Myles, who has seen this twice. "Not one hangs back, they all want to be first. And when the wounded lion knows it must break out of that circle, and charges, and gets one of them down, he just curls up under that buffalo-hide shield. The others are in there so quick that he's up a second later. I saw two lions killed, and not one of those chaps ever got a scratch!"

It is said that many of the best moran died of infection in the years that followed the great rinderpest plagues, when the proliferating lions, having finished the dead cattle, turned to the live ones; even a slight mauling from a lion or leopard can be fatal, since the smears of carrion adhering to the teeth and claws make the wounds septic. Today the Maasai are forbidden to kill lions or steal cattle, much less spear their fellow Africans. In an effort to damp their warlike nature, the buffalo-hide shields, black, white, and red, have been taken away from them, although spears may be carried as a defense against wild animals, and are still used occasionally on people; a white man was killed only a few years ago in the region of Narok. The Maasai have been compared[6] to predators such as wild hunting dogs that seem strangely delicate in their adjustments to their environment, and fade quickly in the face of change. When jailed by the colonial authorities, they died so regularly that a system of fines had to be set up instead.

Turner has a high opinion of the Maasai, of their independence and their physical courage and their ferocity as warriors, and he favors a popular theory that they blocked the northward advance through East Africa of the formidable Ngoni Zulu of the South. "The Zulus were well organized, you see, none of this other Bantu lot could do a thing with them; took the Maasai to stop them. They never got farther north than the Maasai Steppe!" Myles's face is not often alight with such enthusiasm – "Oh, they're *wonderful* people!" He compared them to the Somali of Kenya's Northwest Frontier, and laughed in sympathy with those British officials who, after only a few months out in Africa, became "white Maasai" or "white Somali" – "No, no! Wouldn't hear a word said against them!" Even Lord Delamere had been a champion of the Maasai, who have an unquenchable sense of their own aristocracy, and won the admiration of the whites by looking down on them.

Myles much regrets the passing of the days when stately files of Maasai raiders in black ostrich plumes and lion headdress, spear points gleaming, crossed the plains without a sideways glance. He is proud of his library of Africana, and has read virtually all of the early accounts – the missionary-explorers like Krapf and Rebmann who first saw the snow peaks of Kenya and Kilimanjaro, and Livingstone and Speke and Burton, who explored the lakes, and Joseph Thomson, the first man to traverse Maasai Land, in 1883, and Count Teleki, who discovered Lake Rudolf, and the ivory hunters such as Frederick Selous and Arthur Neumann and Karamoja Bell, who were of necessity explorers, too. But the time of the hunter-explorers was coming to an end in 1909, when the cousins Hill who had settled on the Kapiti Plains southeast of Nairobi let Theodore Roosevelt hunt lions on their ranch and became the first of the "white hunters". Selous, who escorted Roosevelt (he died a few years later in the German wars in Tanganyika) was the last of the great hunters of the nineteenth century, and those who came after, such as John A. Hunter, began their careers as meat hunters for the Mombasa railroad, or in game control. By the 1920s, Hunter and Philip Percival, whose brother Blayney was the first game warden in the Kenya Colony, were the most renowned of the "white hunters", whose small numbers included Percival's partner, Baron Bror von Blixen, as well as his estranged wife's lover, Denys Finch-Hatton, who was to become the hero of *Out of Africa*.

In East Africa, hunters have ever been great liars, and except as fuel for nostalgia, their exploits make repetitious reading, clogged as they are with stupefying lists of the carcasses left behind and encounters with death so constant as to cancel one another out. Nevertheless a great many of the adventurers were extraordinary men, and much of the seeming exaggeration in their accounts comes less from inflamed imaginations than from the compression of the inevitable adventure into a few pages, unleavened by all the quiet days in between.

The rangers had built an enormous fire which lit up the north face of Naisera. We stood at the fire with stiff drinks. Myles was raised in the Kenya Highlands, and for many years had worked with game control, killing animals for the farmers of Mt Kenya; he reckons that he shot seven hundred buffalo. After three years of this, he was offered a job by Ker and Downey as a white hunter, and traveled all over Africa. He recalls a mid-morning encounter outside the Norfolk Hotel with Ernest Hemingway, whose work he much admires. "Hemingway was a friend of my clients, and invited me into the bar for a drink. I told him thanks very much, but I hadn't finished up – we were going off on safari, you see." Hemingway was very offended. "Any man who doesn't drink with me fights with me," the great man told him.

Eventually Myles married a girl who worked at Ker and Downey, and in this period, like many hunters before him, he turned from hunting to protection of the game. "I was sick of killing animals," he told me. "Thought I'd try a bit of the other side." Myles was then thirty-five, which John Owen, the former director of the Tanzania parks, considers to be the age when most men outgrow shooting big animals. As a District Commissioner in the south Sudan, Owen killed a good number of elephant, and he is not sheepish about it in the least; he feels to this day that the present trend toward photographing animals instead of shooting them is like flirting instead of making it – there bloody well ought to be a certain risk involved.

Most professionals agree that a hunter who takes no risk is no hunter at all; since he lives by violence, he ought to be prepared to die that way. Yet they also agree that in the modern hunting safari there is virtually no risk to anyone but the professional, who may have less to fear from the wild animals than from his clients. A story is told of one of the Greek shipping magnates who took with him a bodyguard of three hunters, then damaged his expensive gun by dropping it when an elephant screamed; the gun's discharge sent it skidding across the rocks, and the bullet just missed one of his guards. Latin Americans, especially, think themselves unmanly if they do not pursue their own wounded animals into dangerous situations, and one hunter speaks of a Brazilian who kept firing furiously over his head as he crawled into dark bush after a wounded leopard – the hunter got it with a lucky shot at the white flare of its teeth – then refused the trophy with disdain until told that it had value, whereupon he claimed it. Another who had wounded a lion handed the hunter a movie camera, instructing him to film the inevitable charge and the destruction of the lion. "Don't shoot," he begged, "unless he has me down." The hunter refused, on the grounds that the loss of a client meant the automatic loss of his own license. (In the good old days, when hunters were not penalized in this way, one of their number obeyed such rash instructions to the letter, and the filmed record of his client's demise, together with his personal effects, was duly sent home to his loved ones.)

Myles had no use for his Latin American clients, who were notorious for killing every animal they were legally entitled to, whether they meant to take it home or not. Once he walked out on such a safari, asking the Nairobi office to send out another hunter. Whatever one may think of hunting, there is a great difference between the true hunter and the butcher, and Myles recognized it: the love of the hunter for the hunted, while scarcely of the spiritual quality attained by the Bushman or Dorobo, is no less real for having been sentimentalized and overblown. But killing without hunting, for mere souvenirs, describes most of the motorized or airborne excursions that pass today for the hunting safari. Also, the professional hunters are no longer a small band of colorful adventurers as they were in the early days when Fritz Schindelar, riding a white horse, risked and received a fatal attack from a charging lion. In Turner's time, after World War II, there were already eighteen hunters; today sixty or seventy are licensed, and their numbers increase as the animals decline.

In his days as a hunter, Myles depended heavily on his Dorobo gun bearers and trackers, who moved quietly and missed nothing: "They've incredible hearing. Not only did they know that a big animal was laying up in there, but they'd know just how far away it was, and whether it was a buffalo or rhino. They could hear him breathing." And it was from Myles that I first heard of the primitive Tindiga hunters east of Lake Eyasi, some sixty miles to the south, where he had once gone on safari. "One day we passed a small man with a bow, sitting on a rock by a small pool. Two weeks later, when we came back through, he was still there; he hadn't moved. He'd got one zebra in the interim."

According to Myles, the wild Tindiga were still independent of surrounding tribes, unlike the Pygmies and Llo-molo and Dorobo, and had even retained their ancient tongue, which was a click-speech like that of the Bushman. Avoiding all others, they moved in small bands through the hills surrounding the hot arid Yaida Valley. I asked Myles if one could visit them, and he shrugged: there might be a few at the Yaida game post, but the wild ones would be very hard to find.

A cold night wind off the Gols whipped the steep walls of Ngata Kiti, and this wind, by morning, had shifted into the northeast. "Dry weather wind," Myles muttered, sipping tea at the morning fire. "Blows the dhows south from Arabia." Though it is generally erratic, the northeast monsoon blows from late October or November through February; the southeast monsoon blows the rest of the year. In summer, the land has dried to tinder, and the dry wind keeps everyone in a bad temper: black man and white actually grin, says Myles, at the first sign of the rains.

Leaving camp and the truck behind, we went eastward down the valley, taking along a driver and two rangers. Animals were scarce, and became scarcer. A hyena in the distance had this region to itself, to judge from the number of ungnawed bones along the way. The valley was much rougher than expected, and two hard hours passed before we came onto a rise that descended to the Salei Plain. To the south, in a kingdom of black rains, the Crater Highlands mounted toward the rim of Ngorongoro, thirty miles away; away from the Ngorongoro road, the Crater Highlands, girt by dead volcanoes that rise ten thousand feet and more into their clouds, are little known. Northeast was the rim of the escarpment, and beyond it and far below lay the great lonely Lake Natron, stretching away to the Kenya border. Straight ahead, lost in the clouds, Ol Doinyo Lengai rose nearly ten thousand feet from the Rift Valley floor.

The Salei Plain, which forms a broad step between the Gols and the brink of the escarpment, is a bitter place of tussock and coarse bush that rises from gray cindery ash of the volcanoes, and for a time it seemed that its creatures were all solitary – one hyena, one giraffe, a rhino – as if only here, in this land too poor to support predators, such outcast animals could survive. The big coarse grass, too high to walk through with impunity, hid stones that could gut a car, and progress, which had been slow all morning, became slower still. In eleven hours of lurching and jarring, with one half-hour stop, we were to travel less than eighty miles.

Once our route crossed an old track of the Somali traders who make their way to the Sonjo villages that overlook Lake Natron; their most popular product is Sloan's Liniment, taken internally as a beverage and nostrum. The Sonjo are a xenophobic tribe of Bantu speakers who defend an enclave in this remote corner of Maasai Land. Like many eastern Bantu groups of hill regions, they may have a strong Caucasoid strain in their blood from the Hamitic tillers they displaced, for the average Sonjo is lighter in color than the Maasai. With the digging stick that is their only tool, they practice irrigation farming, eked out by goats and poaching. Maasai still raid their outlying camps, and the Sonjo construct fortified villages and fend off attacks with poisoned arrows. Today, the six villages still existing are built on the escarpment slopes on this west side of Lake Natron, and all overlook Ol Doinyo Lengai, which like the Maasai they consider to be the Mountain of God. It was Ngai who gave the digging stick to the Sonjo and Kikuyu, to whom the Sonjo are linguistically related, although the Sonjo themselves have a tradition of common origin with the Ikoma of Lake Victoria, with whom they still share such obscure customs as scarring infants above the left scapula and under the left breast.[7] The Ikoma and Sonjo are eighty miles and at least two centuries apart, for the tribes were probably separated by the coming of the Maasai.

The Sonjo are bad people, Leite says, teasing the Ikoma driver about Bantu fears of the Maasai and of wild animals; how could it be that people so frightened of animals could be famous poachers, like the Ikoma and the Sonjo? The driver's tribe is held in low regard by Maasai and white alike, though it must be said that the Maasai despise all Bantu tribes, known collectively as *il-meek*. The most charitable view that one hears of the Ikoma is that centuries of exposure to the tsetse fly have leached away their human virtues. "Murder *everything*," Myles says. The Ikoma driver, one of the rare survivors of a black mamba bite, remarked that all Maasai were cattle thieves, which of course is true.

The second ranger was Corporal Nyamahanga, an Ikuria from Mara province at the Kenya border. Last year a poacher fired two poison arrows at Myles and the corporal, and Myles said, "Pot him," which Corporal Nyamahanga did. "Had three great whacking buckshot holes in his forehead. Bandaged him up, but I thought he was a goner. Couldn't get him to hospital that night, we were twenty mile from our vehicles, and next morning I said to Corporal Nyamahanga 'Is he dead?' 'No sir, he's eating a good breakfast!'" Myles turned to gaze at me, disgusted. "Survived a charge of buckshot in the head, he did; took him to hospital at Musoma." He contemplated the corporal, a very strong big serious man whose black laced boots curled up sharply at the toes. "Good people, the Ikuria, and Corporal Nyamahanga is a good man – great runner, too. I'll make him sergeant as soon as there's a place."

The Land Rover groaned on through a thickening heat, but the rim of the escarpment kept retreating; each ridge disclosed new gullies and rough broken ground. Up one gully that deflected us off to the north came a lone Maasai, with a few cattle; he disdained to show surprise at meeting a vehicle in this waste where no vehicle, it seems certain, had ever been before. In his faded red toga, face a mask, the only human figure that was seen on the safari to the Gol Mountains scarcely turned to watch us pass. On a journey, the Maasai say, if a man is met who walks alone, the journey will be unsuccessful. So it proved this day, for we never reached the rim of the escarpment.

Ol Doinyo Lengai, though shrouded, was a heavy presence in the sky. Lost bands of kongoni and gazelle, wandered down out of the highland clouds, waited for everything and nothing on the edges of the cinder plain, and on a rise stood a stone oryx with one horn. The horn was long and straight and whorled; here was the unicorn. The beisa oryx is a strong gray antelope, wary and quick and spirited; oryx have been known to kill attacking lions. This one, given sudden life, went off at a fast trot. Far down the slope its herds were already moving at our approach. Myles said that in this region, where the animal is rare and wild, the hunter who killed an oryx usually earned it.

On the level ground, the game trails radiated out in cracks from the dry water-holes. Near one hole a dead zebra, still intact, had drawn a horde of griffons from the sky. The zebra did not look diseased, and we searched it for sign of Sonjo arrows, but there was nothing; it had merely died. Straightening up again, black men and white stood stunned beneath a leaden firmament, awaiting impulse: there was no sound but our own boots on the cinders. At midday Lengai loomed through the clouds and again vanished. Heat and silence became one. Adding their silence to the silence, the griffons waited.

The Land Rover retreated westward, toward the east face of the Gols. A band of green lined the bases of these cliffs, where the rare rains came down out of the mountains, and plains game stood expectant in the low still woods. Under the cliffs was a Somali track, headed south toward the mouth of Ngata Kiti, where we climbed out of the Salei in late afternoon. Soon the air was cool, and we paused on the slope, gazing back toward Lengai, which had come up out of its clouds to watch us go. The Mountain of God is a magnificent pure cone, a true mythic volcano, shrouded in pale ash so fine that it mists into the canopies of clouds, making the whole mountain an illusion.

Now the sun appeared, and the air dried; the pale tones of Ngata Kiti came to life. Round-haunched zebra stood, tails blowing, on a round curve of a hill, each wild horse in silhouette against the sky. A cheetah appeared, and then two more, moving westward up the valley; the animal survives in such dry country by lapping blood from the body cavity of its kill. The walk of lions is low-slung and easy, and leopards move like snakes, striking and coiling; the cheetah's walk looks stiff and deadly as if it were bent on revenge. The three cats were traveling, not hunting, and did not look back.

Three miles from Naisera, we got down from the Land Rover to walk home. Bouncing away, the Africans stared back at us as if we had gone mad. Then the car stink was gone, and the motor; the twilight valley rang like a great bell.

On the plain lay a tawny pipit, dead, raked by a hawk. Somewhere jackals were keening, and a restless lion roared from across the valley. Then owls emerged, and in the growing dark, the white bellies of gazelles flashed back and forth like flags in a ghostly dance. From the mouth of a burrow peered four faces of bat-eared foxes, and from Naisera came a troop of mongoose, looping out in single file over the plain; it was the time of the night hunters.

Today we were beaten, but another day we would come back. At the evening fire, we planned a foot safari that would take us southeast across the wild Loita Hills of Kenya to the Sonjo villages, and down along the western shore of Natron; we would climb Lengai, then continue south into the Crater Highlands, to Ngorongoro.

At dawn we left the Gol behind, turning north toward Loliondo. A wind from the northeast was high and cold, a wind of hawks and eagles, and beyond Lemuta, the delicate pearl-and-chestnut kestrels dipped and rose, snatching dung beetles from the hard-caked ground. Farther on, four steppe eagles in a half-circle at the mouth of a hole fed with ravenous dexterity on a hatching of termites. Africa is a place of incongruities, as if its species were still evolving – kingfishers that live in the dry woods, owls that seize fish, eagles that eat insects. And doubtless the great variety of raptors here is accounted for by their versatility of habit: nothing is overlooked, and nothing wasted.

Across the plain came a strange hyena that behaved like no hyena we had ever seen. Though unpursued, and pursuing no other creature, it ran hard, and though its head was half-averted in the manner of hyenas, its tail was raised, not tucked in the usual way between the legs, and it came straight for the car instead of fleeing it, only turning off in the final yards, still unafraid, still searching.

Myles stared after it in real surprise: he would demand a scientific explanation of such behavior from his friend Hans Kruuk. (Dr Kruuk, the hyena specialist at Serengeti, has a high opinion of the charm, playfulness, and cleanly habits of these creatures in captivity, and keeps one as a pet.) Hunters and game wardens are the traditional authorities on animal behavior, but today their opinions are regularly challenged by biologists and ecologists, and Myles, who works closely with the people at the Serengeti Research Institute, feels obsolete, "Scientists are in charge of the animals these days," he said shortly. "We just keep things going for them. But now and then we catch them out – there are still a few things they don't know."

The vehicle traversed the lonely rises, rolling a thin dust cloud toward the west. Myles wished to show me an enormous fig that stands by itself far off beyond Barafu Kopjes. These hard plains are bare and bony, with only a whisper of grass, yet the animals keep to the ridges, where the grass is shortest. In a tilted world, the wildebeest went streaming down the sky, black tail tassels hung on the wind behind, all but a solitary bull, thin-ribbed and rag-tailed, old beard blowing. Perhaps he felt his death upon him, for he paid no attention to our intrusion. Soon he had the whole sky to himself.

The giant fig, which looks like a small grove in the distance, is at least as old as man's recorded history on this plain. Its spread is not less than one hundred and fifty feet, the size of six ordinary figs, and it is a tree of life. Cape rooks, kestrels, owls, and the shy brown-chested cuckoo were in residence, and none would willingly leave the tree because there are no other trees for miles around. One owl that moved onto a nearby rock was punished by the kestrels; at each blow from above, it shifted its feet and shuffled its loose feathers.

The tree has a Maasai hearth built into its thick base, and a flat stone near at hand for sharpening spear blades. One day I would like to sit under this tree that has drawn so much fat wood and fleshy leaves out of near-desert, and stare for a week or more into the emptiness. One understands why these monumental figs take on a religious aura for the Africans; they are thought to symbolize the sacred mountains, and the old ways of close kinship with the earth and rain, Nature and God. The Mau-Mau leader Kimathi used such figs for prayer as well as message depots, and his people said of one great tree that it would fall of its own accord when Kimathi was taken. In the police inspector's unsuperstitious account[8] of the hunt for Kimathi, the tree in question fell within that hour.

Even the most pragmatic narratives of life in Africa must touch on what H. M. Stanley was pleased to call "my dark companions and their strange stories" – the pervasive witchcraft and sorcery, which may be legitimate, in one's best interests, or may be used wrongfully, taking the law into one's own hands. The Kikuyu recognize nine categories of magic besides charms (protective magic) and sorcery (destructive magic), and strange powers are by no means limited to the witch doctor, but are freely applied by all. Thus his captor was awed by Kimathi's uncanny sense of impending danger, as Karen Blixen was awed by the instincts of her servants, who would always know of her return and would be at the railroad to meet her. C. P. J. Ionides, the great reptile man of southeast Tanzania, was mystified by the preventive cure administered to him by an African which appeared to have made him immune, or nearly so, to dangerous snake bites.[9] A doctor who has worked with Africans for thirty years has told me in detail of the spells and curses, especially popular among wives of unwanted husbands, that can cause a healthy person to give up and die in a few days of strange wasting diseases: he resigns himself to death because a witch has eaten his "life soul". Or a man whose wife is unfaithful while he is off hunting is subject to death or serious injury from wild animals.[10] Fetishes are in common use: certain Karomojong are cursed with drought if someone experienced in these matters places an ostrich head on a mountain top with its bill pointed at their village.

A witch has mystical resources not possessed by the mere sorcerer, and will often remain at home while his "shadow-soul" is abroad in the form of a night animal. A missionary tells[11] of an old witch doctor in a tribe plagued by lions who for years refused to be converted; then a hunter was sent in by the Game Department, and soon thereafter, the old man became a Christian. When asked why, he shook his head in resignation. "Why not?" he said. "You've shot my lions." Cults of leopard-men[12] and lion-men who kill with claws are both well known, and the lion-men, if they exist, may cloak their work behind that of a real man-eater, as was thought to have been the case in the widespread deaths in 1920 and again in 1946 among the Turu in the region of Singida, in south-central Tanzania, which came to a prompt halt when an investigation was begun: "Too many eyes are watching now," said a Turu chief.[13] Another chief in the same region predicted to a British District Officer that elephants would take care of a local man who was annoying the village by holding up an irrigation scheme, and shortly thereafter a herd of elephant came through the nearby banana groves without touching a tree and utterly destroyed the shamba of the offender.[14]

Most rural Africans have knowledge of animals controlled by gifted individuals – not always witch doctors – whose spirits inhabit them: the man-eaters of Tsavo were especially feared due to their occupancy by human spirits, and many tales are told in many parts of Africa of hyena spirits in human form who are detected by some such sign as a mouth in the back of the head.[15] A werewolf hyena is often an old witch woman, "trotting along the river now, baring her teeth in the night air",[16] and the Bantu of Tanzania know of those who ride hyenas in the night. Peasants are more witch-ridden than hunters and nomads, and among the Mbugwe, tillers of sorghum and millet who settled on the bare mud flats south of Lake Manyara as a protection against Maasai raids, more than half the adult population are considered witches who control all the hyenas or "night cattle" in the region, and sometimes lions into the bargain; fear of black magic is so prevalent that people eat in the darkness of their huts rather than expose their food to the evil eye of others, and when in the bush hide their food with their clothes or go to eat alone behind a tree.[17] That several people in the Manyara region have been taken by lions in recent years will only affirm the beliefs of the Mbugwe.

Belief in lycanthropy involving lions and hyenas, like the summoning of beasts to carry out specific deeds, is not only widespread but in many cases very difficult to put aside as superstition; these events have a reality in the ancestral intuition of mankind that cannot be dismissed simply because it cannot be explained. The story I like best – because it is mythic and rings true, whether or not it actually took place – was told me by a lady whose husband had it from the hunter Bror von Blixen, a practical sort, so it is said, not given to flights of fancy. One day on safari Blixen was begged by natives of the locality to deal with a dangerous hyena that was raiding the village stock at night; no one dared to kill it himself for fear of reprisal from its witch. Blixen agreed, but his staff would not keep watch with him: to kill Fisi, the Hyena, would bring evil luck. Finally Blixen prevailed on his gun bearer to go along, and later this man bore witness to what happened.

The moonlight was crossed by the silhouette of a hyena, and when Blixen fired, wounding it, the creature dragged itself into a thicket. They followed the blood trail to a bush, from the far side of which the hyena soon emerged. Blixen's second shot killed it, and the two men went forward. Where the hyena had fallen, in the moonlight, lay the body of an African.

The great fig west of the Gol Mountains overlooks a dry korongo, and nearby there is a Maasai cattle well. In the well lay a drowned hyena so blue and bloated that the rotting skin shone through the wide-stretched hairs. Though it had been there many days, no scavenger had touched it. Even its eye was still in place, fixed malevolently upon the heavens.

We headed south. Miles from where it had first appeared, the lone hyena rose out of the land, and this time it came even closer, loping along beside the car, tail high and bald eye searching. We wondered then if this haunted beast was hunting for its mate, and if the mate might be the hyena in the well. But we did not know, and never would, and the mystery pleased us.

6 Rites of Passage

We have to share our land with wild and dangerous animals. We have to learn to give way to the elephant, the rhinoceros, the lion, etc., and this has not been our way of life. Many of us have lost children, others have lost relatives and stock to these animals which belong to the Government. The Government has value for these animals but they are of no value to us any more. The only value of these animals which we knew about is that they used to be the source of our traditionally important trophies, such as kudu horns used for war signals, lion manes worn as a sign of gallantry by the morrans (young warriors), buffalo hides for shields, elephant tusks for ornaments worn by the morrans, etc. The use of these things in our daily life is quickly becoming a thing of the past. This value of wildlife being gone, we know of no other value whatever and yet our cattle are being killed and our people either being killed or injured by these animals. We are fined or imprisoned when we kill these animals for food even in times of extreme famine despite the fact that we share our land with them. The presence of these animals in our district means loss of lives and stock every year and nothing else.

D. M. Sindiyo (*a Maasai warden, paraphrasing the arguments of the Samburu*)[1]

At Lemai on the Mara River, eighty miles north of Seronera near the Kenya border, the Ikuria Bantu were displeased because part of their lands north of the Mara had been appropriated for the Serengeti park; they were harassing the Lemai guard post at night with threats and stones. Myles Turner flew an extra ranger to Lemai to strengthen the garrison, and I went along. We circled a concentration of six hundred buffalo near the Bangai River, then flew onward, passing east of the old Ikoma fort, built by the Germans in 1905 as a defense against rebellious Ikoma. Beyond Ikoma was another great herd of buffalo, black igneous lumps in the tsetse-ridden land. Zebra shone in the morning woods, but a rhino was as dull as stone in the early light.

To the north and west, over Lake Victoria, the cloud masses were a deepening gray-black; at times the plane flew through black rain. These lake basin storms are the worst in East Africa, building all day and coming to a boil in late afternoon. But the clouds were pierced by shafts of sun, and the plane cast a hard shadow on thatch roofs, bomas, and patchwork gardens scattered along the boundary of the park. Half-naked people stood outside the huts; they did not wave. "*Wa-Ikoma*," Myles said. "Poachers." Poaching has always been a problem on park borders, all the more so because no park in East Africa is a natural ecological unit that shelters all its game animals all year round. To contain the natural wanderings of its herds, the Serengeti park, five thousand square miles in extent, would have to be doubled in size, expanding east to the Crater Highlands and northward into Kenya, through the Maasai Mara to the Mau Range. Human population increase and the lack of protein in lands which suffer from advanced protein deficiency in the poor have made the poaching of wild game a widespread industry, and an estimated twenty thousand animals are killed each year in the Serengeti area alone. Poisoned arrows, which are silent, are still preferred to rifles, but traps and steel wire snares have replaced the traditional snares woven of the bayonet aloe or bow-string hemp that gave its Maasai name to Olduvai Gorge.

The parks are the last refuge of large animals, which in most of East Africa are all but gone. The game departments are chronically bereft of funds, staff, and the technical training to protect the game, and most of their resources are devoted to destroying animals worth far more in meat and tusks and hides than the shamba being protected in the name of game control. Where animals are not shot out, poached, or harried to extinction, they are eliminated by human settlements at the only water points for miles around, or their habitat vanishes in the fires lit to bring forth new grass. Thus the survival of the animals depends on the survival of the parks, among which the Serengeti has no peer.

For purposes of efficiency when dealing with poachers and to inspire the African judiciary to impose meaningful sentences, all poachers are classed together as brutal hirelings of unscrupulous Asian interests in Nairobi or Dar es Salaam; traps, snares, and poisoned arrows maim and torture many more animals than are actually retrieved, and of late the gangs have become motorized, crossing park boundaries at will. In this official picture of the matter there is considerable truth, but it is also true that the majority of "poachers" are people of the region who are seeking to eke out a subsistence diet as they have always done. The parks for which their lands have been appropriated, and which they themselves have no means to visit even if they were interested, give sanctuary to marauding animals that are a threat to domestic stock and crops, not to speak of human life, and their resentment is natural and just. It is no good telling a shamba dweller that tourist revenues are crucial to the nation when his own meager existence remains unaffected, or affected for the worse. "The nation", the concept of national consciousness, has not penetrated very far into the bush; as in the Sudan, there are many tribesmen who have no idea that they are Kenyan or Tanzanian and would care little if they knew. Even the urban African benefits little from the tourist economy, not to speak of the revenues of the parks, which are resented as the private preserves of white foreigners and the few blacks at the top. Not long ago it was estimated that only one East African in twelve had ever seen a lion, though lions are common in the park at the very outskirts of Nairobi, but one is not allowed into the parks without a car, and very few Africans have access to a car, far less own one. The average citizen has more fear of than interest in wild animals, which most Africans regard as evidence of backwardness, a view in which they were long encouraged by European farmers and administrators. Far from being proud of the "priceless heritage" so dear to conservation literature, they are ashamed of it.

Nor is poaching a simple matter of free meat. Rural Africans in the vicinity of game reserves and parks quite naturally believe that the numbers of wild animals are inexhaustible, and see no reason why they should not be harvested as they have always been. Hunting, with its prestige for the good hunter, is a ceremony and sport as it is for westerners; its place in his economy as well as its risk to the poorly armed native hunter make it considerably less decadent. And no one can explain why killing animals is permitted to foreigners in search of trophies but not to citizens in search of food. Yet to permit random poaching by local hunters would encourage ever bolder operations directed by outsiders and carried out by professionals who do not hesitate to turn their poisoned arrows on African game rangers; arrow poisons are obtained from several plants (two Apocynaceae, an amaryllis, and two lilies), but the one used most commonly in this region comes from the shrubby dogbane (*Acokanthera*) which has no antidote, and can kill in a matter of minutes. Still, bows are no match for rifles, and ordinarily, the poacher dies instead.

Last year four poachers died in the Serengeti. One was shot down by the rangers after firing his fourth poisoned arrow. Two corpses were found under a tree, caught by a fire probably set by themselves, for grasslands near a water course are often burned to give the hunters a better view and to make sure that their poisoned arrows are not lost; also, the use of bangi (the marijuana hemp, *Cannabis*, brought to the east coast in the earliest trade with Asia) and homemade spirits is popular in the poachers' camps, and perhaps the two were taken by surprise. The fourth was mangled and decapitated by a maimed buffalo caught in his wire snare. Myles was anxious to display the poacher's head as cautionary evidence in the small museum at Seronera, but was dissuaded by John Owen, who felt that the public display of an African head might be taken amiss. The head is on view in Turner's office, over the legend (from an Italian graveyard)

> I have been where you are now,
> And you will be where I have gone

Myles Turner is sympathetic with the Ikuria, who are one of the peoples he admires. "The land is all they have," he says. But he is a traditionalist in his dealings with the Africans, and though he joked with the ranger in the plane, the jokes were firm. When his plane appeared over Lemai, a half dozen of his "Field Force" rushed to the airstrip, where they were lined up more or less smartly by their corporal. In green drill shorts, shirts, berets, and black puttees, they made a fine-looking line, and when Turner stepped down from the plane, they sprang backwards to attention, slapping rifles. "Jambo, Corporal," Turner said, by way of greeting and approval, then put the rangers at their ease. Plainly the men enjoyed these formalities as much as Myles did, and at the same time were amused. Myles gave them letters and news of their families, and they gave him messages to send back. Then we marched down to the Mara in a military manner to inspect the hippos.

Hippos can weigh twice as much as buffalo, or a ton and a half each. Like whales, they are born in the water, but ordinarily they feed on land, and their copious manure, supporting rich growths of blue-green algae, is a great boon to fish. Here they had piled up in the river rapids, where the lateritic silt had turned them the same red as the broad-backed boulders. On land, the hippopotamus exudes a red secretion, perhaps to protect its skin against the sun, and Africans say that it is sweating its own blood. With their flayed skin, cavernous raw mouths, and bulging eyes, their tuba voices splitting the wash of the Mara on its banks seemed like the uproar of the damned, as if, in the cold rain and purgatorial din, just at this moment, the great water pigs had been cast into perdition, their downfall heralded by the scream of the fish eagle that circled overhead.

East of Soit Naado Murt, on the Girtasho Plain, a burrow had been taken over and enlarged by wild hunting dogs, which differ from true dogs in having a four-toed foot. In the Girtasho pack were eleven dogs and three bitches, black with patches of dirty white and brindle, and the invariable white tip to the tattered tail. Wild dogs are mangy and bad-smelling, with bat ears and gaunt bodies, yet they are appealing creatures, pirouetting in almost constant play, and rolling and flopping about in piles. Perhaps distemper keeps their numbers low,[2] for they are faithful in the raising of their young, and the most efficient killers on the plain.

Wild dogs are nomadic most of the year, attending the migrations of the herds, but when a bitch whelps, they remain with her and bring her food. Ordinarily one dog – not necessarily the mother – remains with the pups when the pack goes out to hunt, and five dogs have been known to raise nine pups after their mother – the pack's only bitch – had died. At the den one afternoon, four pups were frolicking from dog to dog, and one of the dogs dutifully disgorged some undigested chunks of meat, but the pups were bothered by the bursts of thunder, looking up from their food to whine at the far, silent lightning. A mile to the westward, zebra herds moved steadily along the skyline. When the rain thickened, the pups tumbled down into their den, and the adults gathered in a pile of matted black and brindle hair to shed the huge tropical downpour. Toward twilight, the rain eased and the dog pile broke apart, white tail tips twirling; the animals frisked about the soggy plain, greeting anew by inserting the muzzle into the corner of another's mouth, as the pups do when begging for food. When they are old enough to follow the hunt, the pups will be given first place at the kill.

Four dogs led by a brindle male moved off a little towards the west; they stood stiff-legged, straining forward, round black ears cocked toward the zebra herds which, agitated by the storm, were moving along at a steady gallop. Then the four set off at a steady trot, and the others broke their play to watch them go. Three more moved out, though not so swiftly, and George Schaller followed the seven at a little distance. Soon the remaining animals were coming, all but one that remained to guard the den. Only the first four were intent; the rest stopping repeatedly to romp and crouch or greet the stragglers. Then these nine would run to catch the four, loping along on both sides of the moving vehicle, casting a brief look at us as they passed. Ahead, the leaders trotted steadily, and the nine stragglers, overtaking them, would again break off to romp and play.

The four lead dogs, nearing the herds, broke into an easy run; the zebras spurted. Perhaps the dogs had singled out a victim – an old or diseased horse, a pregnant mare, a foal – for now they were streaming over the wet grass. Rain swept the plain, and gray sheets blurred the swirling stripes, which burst apart to scatter in all directions. The dogs wheeled hard, intent now on a quarry, but lost it as the horses veered, then milled together in a solid phalanx. A stallion charged the dogs, ears back, and they gave way.

The chase of a mile or more had failed; the wild dogs frisked and played. But now all thirteen were intent, and in moments they were loping back past the waiting vehicle, headed west. The leaders were already in their hunting run, bounding along in silence through the growing dark like hounds of hell, and the others, close behind, made sweet puppy-like call notes, strangely audible over the motor of the car, which swerved violently to miss half-hidden burrows. All thirteen stretched cadaverous shapes in long easy leaps over the plain. In their run, the dogs are beautiful and swift, and came up with the herds in not more than a mile. Then the dark shapes were whisking in and out among the zebra, and a foal still brown with a foal's long guard hairs quit the mare's side when a dog bit at it, and was surrounded.

A six-month zebra foal, weighing perhaps three hundred pounds, is too big to be downed easily by thin animals of forty pounds apiece. The dogs chivvied it round and round. One dog had sunk its teeth into the foal's black muzzle, tugging backwards to keep the victim's head low – this is a habit of the dogs, to compensate for their light weight – and the dog was swung free of the ground as the foal reared, lost its balance, and went down. Now the mare charged, scattering the pack, and when the foal jumped up as if unhurt, the two fled for the herd. But the dogs overtook the foal again, snapping at its hams, and braying softly, it stopped short of its own accord. Again a dog seized its muzzle, legs braced, dragging the head forward, as the rest tore into it from behind and below. At the yanking of its nose, the foal's mouth fell open, and it made a last small sound. Once more the mare rushed at the dogs, and once again, but already she seemed resigned to what was happening, and did not follow up her own attacks. The foal sank to its knees, neck still stretched by the backing dog, its entrails a dim gleam in the rain. Then the dog at its nose let go and joined the rest, and the foal raised its head, ears high, gazing in silence at the mare, which stood guard over it, motionless. Between her legs, her foal was being eaten alive, and mercifully, she did nothing. Then the foal sank down, and the dogs surged at the belly, all but one that snapped an eye out as the head flopped on the grass.

Unmarked, the mare turned and walked away. Intent on her foal, the dogs had not once snapped at her. Noticing the car twenty yards off, she gave a snort and a jump sideways, then walked on. Flanks pressed together, ears alert, her band awaited her; nearby, other zebra clans were grazing. Soon the foal's family, carrying the mare with it, moved away, snatching at the grass as they ambled westward.

The foal's spread legs stuck up like sticks from the twisting black and brindle; the dogs drove into the belly, hind legs straining. They snatched a mouthful, gulped it, and tore in again, climbing the carcass, tails erect, as if every lion and hyena on the plain were coming fast to drive them from the kill. All thirteen heads snapped at the meat, so close together that inevitably one yelped, but even when two would worry the same shred, there was never a snarl, only a wet steady sound of meat-eating. When the first dog moved off, licking its chops, the foal's rib cage was already bare; not ten minutes had passed since it had died. Then the hyenas came. First there were two, rising up out of the raining grass like mud lumps given life. They shambled forward without haste, neither numerous nor hungry enough to drive away the dogs. Then there were five in a semicircle, feinting a little. A dog ran out to chase away the boldest, and then two of the five, with the strange speed that makes them deadly hunters on their own, chased off a sixth hyena – not a clan member, apparently – that had come in from the north through the twilight rain.

Six of the dogs, their feeding finished, wagged long tails as they romped and greeted; there was just enough light left to illumine the red on their white patches. The rest fed steadily, eyes turned to the hyenas as they swallowed, and as each dog got its fill and forsook the carcass, the half-circle of hyenas tightened. The last dog gave way to them without a snarl. The forequarters were left, and the head and neck, and all the bones. For the powerful jaws of the hyena, the bones of the plains animals present no problem. Hoofs, bones, and skin of what had been, ten minutes before, the fat hindquarters of a swift skittish young horse lay twisted up in a torn muddy bag; the teeth of its skull and the white eye sockets were luminous. At dark, as the tail tips of the dogs danced away eastward, the hyena shapes drew together at the remains, one great night beast sinking slowly down into the mud.

I once watched a hyena gaining on a gnu that only saved itself by plunging into the heart of a panicked herd; the hyena lost track of its quarry when the herd stampeded. The cringing bear-like lope of these strange cat relatives is deceptive: a hyena can run forty miles an hour, which is considered the top speed of the swift wild dog. Cheetah are said to attain sixty but have small endurance; I have seen one spring at a Thomson's gazelle, its usual prey, and quit within the first one hundred yards. Hyenas, on the other hand, will run their prey into the ground; there is no escape. And in darkness they are bold – a man alone on the night roads of Africa has less to fear from lions than hyena. In the Ngorongoro Crater the roles ordinarily assigned to lions and hyenas are reversed. It is the hyenas, hunting at night, that make most of the kills, and the lions seen on the carcasses in daytime are the scavengers. Hans Kruuk has discovered that the crater's hyenas are divided in great clans, and that sometimes these hyena armies war at night, filling the crater with the din of the inferno.

The natural history of even the best-known African mammals is incomplete, and such hole dwellers as the ant-bear, the aard-wolf, and the pangolin have avoided the scrutiny of man almost entirely. It is not even known which species excavate the holes, which may also be occupied by hyenas, jackals, mongooses, bat-eared foxes, aard-wolves, porcupines, ratels or honey badgers, and, in whelping season, the wild hunting dog. Often the burrows are dug in the bases of old termite hills, which stand on the plain like strange red statues of a vanished civilization, worn to anonymity by time. The termites are ancient relatives of the cockroach, and in the wake of rains they leave the termitaria in nuptial flight; soon their wings break off, and new colonies are founded where they come to earth. Were man to destroy the many creatures that prey on them, the termite mounds would cover entire landscapes. The African past lies in the belly of the termite, which has eaten all trace of past tropical civilizations and will do as much for the greater part of what now stands. At the termitaria, one may look at dawn and evening for such nocturnal creatures as the striped hyena, with its long hair and gaunt body, but in my stays in the Serengeti I never saw this wolf-sized animal that lived in the ground beneath my feet.

One day I surprised a honey badger some distance from its earth, and followed it for a while over the plain. This dark squat animal has long hair and a thick skin to protect it from bee stings, and like most of the weasel tribe, it is volatile and ferocious, with a snarl more hideous than any sound I heard in Africa. The ratel moves quickly, low to the ground, and in its dealings with man is said to direct its attack straight at the crotch.

Another day, observing hyenas with Hans Kruuk, I was lucky enough to see a pangolin, which has overlapping armor on its back and legs and tail. The pangolin has been much reduced by a Maasai notion that its curious reptilian plates will bring the wearer luck in love. At our approach it ceased its rooting in the grass and, with an audible clack, rolled up into a ball to protect its vulnerable furred stomach. We contemplated it a while, then left it where it lay, a strange mute sphere on the bare plain.

*   *   *

In March, renewal of the southeast monsoon brings the long rains. Rains vary from region to region, according to the winds, and since the winds are not dependable, seasons in East Africa have a general pattern but can seldom be closely predicted. The cyclical wet years and years of drought are a faint echo of the pluvials and inter-pluvials of the Pleistocene. In 1961 drought had destroyed thousands of animals; the next year floods killed thousands more. In the winter of 1969 rain fell in the Serengeti almost daily, and no one knew whether the short rains of late autumn had failed to end or the long rains of spring had begun too early. A somber light refracted from the water gleamed in the depressions, and the treeless distances with their animal silhouettes, the glow of bright flowers underfoot, recalled the tundras of the north to which the migrant plovers on the plain would soon return.

The animals had slowed, and some stood still. In this light those without movement looked enormous, the archetypal animal cast in stone. The ostrich, too, is huge on the horizon, and the kori bustard is the heaviest of all flying birds on earth. Everywhere the clouds were crossed by giant birds in their slow circles, like winged reptiles on an antediluvian sky.

One morning the dog pile broke apart before daylight and headed off toward the herds under Naabi Hill. Unlike lions, which often go hungry, the wild dogs rarely fail to make a kill, and this time they were followed from the start by three hyenas that had waited near the den. The three humped along behind the pack, and one of the dogs paused to sniff noses with a hyena by way of greeting. In the distance, zebras yelped like dogs, and the dogs chittered quietly like birds as they loped along. As the sun rose out of the Gol Mountains, they faked an attack on a string of wildebeest and moved on.

A mile and a half east of the den, the pack cut off a herd of zebra and ran it in tight circles. There were foals in this herd, but the dogs had singled out a pregnant mare. When the herd scattered, they closed in, streaming along in the early light, and almost immediately she fell behind and then gave up, standing motionless as one dog seized her nose and others ripped at her pregnant belly and others piled up under her tail to get at her entrails at the anus, surging at her with such force that the flesh of her uplifted quarters quaked in the striped skin. Perhaps in shock, their quarry shares the detachment of the dogs, which attack it peaceably, ears forward, with no slightest sign of snapping or snarling. The mare seemed entirely docile, unafraid, as if she had run as she had been hunted, out of instinct, and without emotion: only rarely will a herd animal attempt to defend itself with the hoofs and teeth used so effectively in battles with its own kind, though such resistance might well spare its life.[3] The zebra still stood a full half-minute after her guts had been snatched out, then sagged down dead. Her unborn colt was dragged into the clear and snapped apart off to one side.

The morning was silent but for the wet sound of eating; a Caspian plover and a band of sand grouse picked at the mute prairie. The three hyenas stood in wait, and two others appeared after the kill. One snatched a scrap and ran with it; the meat, black with blood and mud, dragged on the ground. Chased by the rest, the hyena made a shrill sound like a pig squeal. When their spirit is up, hyenas will take on a lion, and if they chose, could bite a wild dog in half, but in daylight, they seem ill at ease; they were scattered by one tawny eagle, which took over the first piece of meat abandoned by the dogs. The last dog to leave, having finished with the fetus, drove the hyenas off the carcass of the mare on its way past, then frisked on home. In a day and a night, when lions and hyenas, vultures and marabous, jackals, eagles, ants, and beetles have all finished, there will be no sign but the stained pressed grass that a death ever took place.

All winter in the Serengeti damp scrawny calves and afterbirths are everywhere, and old or diseased animals fall in the night. Fat hyenas, having slaked their thirst, squat in the rain puddles, and gaping lions lie belly to the sun. On Naabi Hill the requiem birds, digesting carrion, hunch on the canopies of low acacia. Down to the west, a young zebra wanders listlessly by itself. Unlike topi and kongoni, which are often seen alone, the zebra and wildebeest prefer the herd; an animal by itself may be sick or wounded, and draws predators from all over the plain. This mare had a deep gash down her right flank, and a slash of claws across the stripings of her quarters; red meat gleamed on right foreleg and left fetlock. It seemed strange that an attacking lion close enough to maul so could have botched the job, but the zebra pattern makes it difficult to see at night, when it is most vulnerable to attack by lions, and zebra are strong animals; a thin lioness that I saw once at Ngorongoro had a broken incisor hanging from her jaw that must have been the work of a flying hoof.

Starvation is the greatest threat to lions, which are inefficient hunters and often fail to make a kill. Unlike wild dog packs, which sometimes overlap in their wide hunting range, lions will attack and even eat another lion that has entered their territory, snapping and snarling in the same antagonistic way with which they join their pride mates on a kill, whereas when hunting, they are silent and impassive. In winter when calves of gazelle and gnu litter the plain, the lions are well fed, but at other seasons they may be so hungry that their own cubs are driven from the kills: ordinarily, however, the lion will permit cubs to feed even when the lioness that made the kill is not permitted to approach.[4] Until it is two, the cub is a dependent, and less than half of those born in the Serengeti survive the first year of life. In hard times, cubs may be eaten by hyenas, or by the leopard, which has a taste for other carnivores, including domestic cats and dogs.

A former warden of the Serengeti who feels that plains game should be killed to feed these starving cubs is opposed by George Schaller on the grounds that such artificial feeding would interfere with the balance of lion numbers as well as with the natural selection that maintains the vitality of the species. Dr Schaller is correct, I think, and yet my sympathies are with the predator, not with the hunted, perhaps because a lion is perceived as an individual, whereas one member of a herd of thousands seems but a part of a compound organism, with little more identity than one termite in a swarm. Separated from the herd, it gains identity, like the zebra killed by the wild dogs, but even so I felt more pity for an injured lion that I saw near the Seronera River in the hungry months of summer, a walking husk of mane and bone, so weak that the dry weather wind threatened to knock it over.

The death of any predator is disturbing. I was startled one day to see a hawk in the talons of a Verreaux's eagle-owl; perhaps it had been killed in the act of killing. Another day, by a korongo, I helped Schaller collect a dying lioness. She had emaciated hindquarters and the staggers, and at our approach, she reeled to her feet, then fell. In the interests of science as well as mercy, for he wished an autopsy, George shot her with an overdose of tranquilizer. Although she twitched when the needle struck, and did not rise, she got up after a few minutes and weaved a few feet more and fell again as if defeated by the obstacle of the korongo, where frogs trilled in oblivion of unfrogly things. I had the strong feeling that the lioness, sensing death, had risen to escape it, like the vultures I had heard of somewhere that flew up from the poisoned meat set out for lions, circling higher and higher into the sky, only to fall like stones as life forsook them. A moment later, her head rose up, then flopped for the last time, but she would not die. Sprinkled with hopping lion flies and the fat ticks that in lions are a sign of poor condition, she lay there in a light rain, her gaunt flanks twitching.

The episode taught me something about George Schaller, who is single-minded, not easy to know. George is a stern pragmatist, unable to muster up much grace in the face of unscientific attitudes; he takes a hard-eyed look at almost everything. Yet at this moment his boyish face was openly upset, more upset than I had ever thought to see him. The death of the lioness was painless, far better than being found by the hyenas, but it was going on too long; twice he returned to the Land Rover for additional dosage. We stood there in a kind of vigil, feeling more and more depressed, and the end, when it came at last, was shocking. The poor beast, her life going, began to twitch and tremble. With a little grunt, she turned onto her back and lifted her hind legs into the air. Still grunting, she licked passionately at the grass, and her haunches shuddered in long spasms, and this last abandon shattered the detachment I had felt until that moment. I was swept by a wave of feeling, then a pang so sharp that, for a moment, I felt sick, as if all the waste and loss in life, the harm one brings to oneself and others, had been drawn to a point in this lonely passage between light and darkness.

Mid-March when the long rains were due was a time of wind and dry days in the Serengeti, with black trees in iron silhouette on the hard sunsets and great birds turning forever on a silver sky. A full moon rose in a night rainbow, but the next day the sun was clear again, flat as a disc in the pale universe.

Two rhino and a herd of buffalo had brought up the rear of the eastward migration. Unlike the antelope, which blow with the wind and grasses, the dark animals stood earthbound on the plain. The antelope, all but a few, had drifted east under the Crater Highlands, whereas the zebra, in expectation of the rains, were turning west again towards the woods. Great herds had gathered at the Seronera River, where the local prides of lions were well fed. Twenty lions together, dozing in the golden grass, could sometimes be located by the wave of a black tail tuft or the black ear tips of a lifted head that gazed through the sun shimmer of the seed heads. Others gorged in uproar near the river crossings, tearing the fat striped flanks on fresh green beds – now daytime kills were common. Yet for all their prosperity, there was an air of doom about the lions. The males, especially, seemed too big, and they walked too slowly between feast and famine, as if in some dim intuition that the time of the great predators was running out.

Pairs of male lions, unattached to any pride, may hunt and live together in great harmony, with something like demonstrative affection. But when two strangers meet, there seems to be a waiting period while fear settles. One sinks into the grass at a little distance, and for a long time they watch each other, and their sad eyes, unblinking, never move. The gaze is the warning, and it is the same gaze, wary but unwavering, with which lions confront man. The gold cat eyes shimmer with hidden lights, eyes that see everything and betray nothing. When the lion is satisfied that the threat is past, the head is turned, as if ignoring it might speed the departure of an unwelcome and evil-smelling presence. In its torpor and detachment, the lion sometimes seems the dullest beast in Africa, but one has only to watch a file of lions setting off on the evening hunt to be awed anew by the power of this animal.

One late afternoon of March, beyond Maasai Kopjes, eleven lionesses lay on a kill, and the upraised heads, in a setting sun, were red. With their grim visages and flat glazed eyes, these twilight beasts were ominous. Then the gory heads all turned as one, ear tips alert. No animal was in sight, and their bellies were full, yet they glared steadfastly away into the emptiness of the plain, as if something that no man could sense was imminent.

Not far off there was a leopard; possibly they scented it. The leopard lay on an open rise, in the shadow of a wind-worn bush, and unlike the lions, it lay gracefully. Even stretched on a tree limb, all four feet hanging, as it is seen sometimes in the fever trees, the leopard has the grace of complete awareness, with all its tensions in its pointed eyes. The lion's gaze is merely baleful; that of the leopard is malevolent, a distillation of the trapped fear that is true savagery.

Under a whistling thorn the leopard lay, gold coat on fire in the sinking sun, as if imagining that so long as it lay still it was unseen. Behind it was a solitary thorn tree, black and bony in the sunset, and from a crotch in a high branch, turning gently, torn hide matted with caked blood, the hollow form of a gazelle hung by the neck. At the insistence of the wind, the delicate black shells of the turning hoofs, on tiptoe, made a dry clicking in the silence of the plain.

7 Elephant Kingdoms

To Game Warden
Sir,
I am compelled of notifying your Excellence the ecceptional an critical situation of my people at Tuso. Many times they called on my praing me of addressing to your Excellence a letter for obtain a remedy and so save they meadows from total devestation. I recused for I thought were a passing disease, but on the contrary the invasion took fearfully increasing so that the natives are now disturbed and in danger in their own huts for in the night the elephants ventured themselves amid abitation. All men are desolate and said me sadfully, "What shall we eat this year. We shall compelled to emigrate all . . ."

With my best gratefully and respectful regards,
Yours sincerely, a Mission Boy[1]

We are the fire which burns the country. The Calf of the Elephant is exposed on the plain.
from the Bantu[2]

One morning a great company of elephants came from the woodlands, moving eastward toward the Togoro Plain. "It's like the old Africa, this," Myles Turner said, coming to fetch me. "It's one of the greatest sights a man can see."

We flew northward over the Orangi River. In the wake of the elephant herds, stinkbark acacia were scattered like sticks, the haze of yellow blossoms bright in the killed trees. Through the center of the destruction, west to east, ran a great muddied thoroughfare of the sort described by Selous in the nineteenth century. Here the center of the herd had passed. The plane turned eastward, coming up on the elephant armies from behind. More than four hundred animals were pushed together in one phalanx; a smaller group of one hundred and another of sixty were nearby. The four hundred moved in one slow-stepping swaying mass, with the largest cows along the outer ranks and big bulls scattered on both sides. "Seventy and eighty pounds, some of those bulls," Myles said. (Trophy elephants are described according to the weight of a single tusk; an eighty-pound elephant would carry about twice that weight in ivory. "Saw an eighty today." "*Did* you!")

Myles said that elephants herded up after heavy rains, but that this was an enormous congregation for the Serengeti. In 1913, when the first safari came here,[3] the abounding lions and wild dogs were shot as vermin, but no elephants were seen at all. Even after 1925, when the plains were hunted regularly by such men as Philip Percival and the American, Martin Johnson, few elephants were reported. Not until after 1937, it is said, when the Serengeti was set aside as a game reserve (it was not made a national park until 1951), did harried elephants from the developing agricultural country of west Kenya move south into this region, but it seems more likely that they were always present in small numbers, and merely increased as a result of human pressures in suitable habitats outside the park.

Elephants, with their path-making and tree-splitting propensities, will alter the character of the densest bush in very short order; probably they rank with man and fire as the greatest force for habitat change in Africa.[4] In the Serengeti, the herds are destroying many of the taller trees which are thought to have risen at the beginning of the century, in a long period without grass fires that followed plague, famine, and an absence of the Maasai. Dry season fires, often set purposely by poachers and pastoral peoples, encourage grassland by suppressing new woody growth; when accompanied by drought, and fed by a woodland tinder of elephant-killed trees, they do lasting damage to the soil and the whole environment. Fires waste the dry grass that is used by certain animals, and the regrowth exhausts the energy in the grass roots that is needed for good growth in the rainy season. In the Serengeti in recent years, fire and elephants together have converted miles and miles of acacia wood to grassland, and damaged the stands of yellowbark acacia or fever tree along the water courses. The range of the plains game has increased, but the much less numerous woodland species such as the roan antelope and oribi become ever more difficult to see.

Beneath the plane, the elephant mass moved like gray lava, leaving behind a ruined bog of mud and twisted trees. An elephant can eat as much as six hundred pounds of grass and browse each day, and it is a destructive feeder, breaking down many trees and shrubs along the way. The Serengeti is immense, and can absorb this damage, but one sees quickly how an elephant invasion might affect more vulnerable areas. Ordinarily the elephant herds are scattered and nomadic, but pressure from settlements, game control, and poachers sometimes confines huge herds to restricted habitats which they may destroy. Already three of Tanzania's new national parks – Serengeti, Manyara, and Ruaha – have more elephants than is good for them. The elephant problem, where and when and how to manage them, is a great controversy in East Africa, and its solution must affect the balance of animals and man throughout the continent.

Anxious to see the great herd from the ground, I picked up George Schaller at Seronera and drove northwest to Banagi, then westward on the Ikoma-Musoma track to the old northwest boundary of the park, where I headed across country. I had taken good bearings from the air, but elephants on the move can go a long way in an hour, and even for a vehicle with four-wheel drive, this rough bush of high grass, potholes, rocks, steep brushy streams, and swampy mud is very differ-ent from the hardpan of the plain. The low hot woods lacked rises or landmarks, and for a while it seemed that I had actually misplaced four hundred elephants.

Then six bulls loomed through the trees, lashing the air with their trunks, ears blowing, in a stiff-legged swinging stride; they forded a steep gully as the main herd, ahead of them, appeared on a wooded rise. Ranging up and down the gully, we found a place to lurch across, then took off eastward, hoping to find a point down-wind of the herd where the elephants would pass. But their pace had slowed as the sun rose; we worked back to them, upwind. The elephants were destroying a low wood – this is not an exaggeration – with a terrible cracking of trees, but after a while they moved out onto open savanna. In a swampy stream they sprayed one another and rolled in the water and coated their hides with mud, filling the air with a thick sloughing sound like the wet meat sound made by predators on a kill. Even at rest the herd flowed in perpetual motion, the ears like delicate great petals, the ripple of the mud-caked flanks, the coiling trunks a dream rhythm, a rhythm of wind and trees. "It's a nice life," Schaller said. "Long, and without fear." A young one could be killed by a lion, but only a desperate lion would venture near a herd of elephants, which are among the few creatures that reach old age in the wild.

There has been much testimony to the silence of the elephant, and all of it is true. At one point there came a cracking sound so small that had I not been alert for the stray elephants all around, I might never have seen the mighty bull that bore down on us from behind. A hundred yards away, it came through the scrub and deadwood like a cloud shadow, dwarfing the small trees of the open woodland. I raised binoculars to watch him turn when he got our scent, but the light wind had shifted and instead the bull was coming fast, looming higher and higher, filling the field of the binoculars, forehead, ears and back agleam with wet mud dredged up from the donga. There was no time to reach the car, nothing to do but stand transfixed. A froggish voice said, "What do you think, George?" and got no answer.

Then the bull scented us – the hot wind was shifting every moment – and the dark wings flared, filling the sky, and the air was split wide by that ultimate scream that the elephant gives in alarm or agitation, that primordial warped horn note out of oldest Africa. It altered course without missing a stride, not in flight but wary, wide-eared, passing man by. Where first aware of us, the bull had been less than one hundred feet away – I walked it off – and he was somewhat nearer where he passed. "He was pretty close," I said finally to Schaller. George cleared his throat. "You don't want them any closer than that," he said. "Not when you're on foot." Schaller, who has no taste for exaggeration, had a very respectful look upon his face.

Stalking the elephants, we were soon a half-mile from my Land Rover. What little wind there was continued shifting, and one old cow, getting our scent, flared her ears and lifted her trunk, holding it upraised for a long time like a question mark. There were new calves with the herd, and we went no closer. Then the cow lost the scent, and the sloughing sound resumed, a sound that this same animal has made for four hundred thousand years. Occasionally there came a brief scream of agitation, or the crack of a killed tree back in the wood, and always the *thuck* of mud and water, and a rumbling of elephantine guts, the deepest sound made by any animal on earth except the whale.

Africa. Noon. The hot still waiting air. A hornbill, gnats, the green hills in the distance, wearing away west toward Lake Victoria.

Until recent years, when the elephant herds have become concentrated in game reserves and parks, it has been difficult to study elephants, since one could not stay close enough to the herds to observe daily behavior. Even now, most students of the elephant are content to work with graphs, air surveys, dead animals, and the like, since behavioral studies are best done on foot, a job that few people have the heart for. An exception is Iain Douglas-Hamilton, a young Scots biologist who was doing his thesis on the elephants of Lake Manyara.

Lake Manyara, like Lake Natron, is a soda lake or magadi that lies along the base of the Rift Escarpment. The east side of the lake lies in arid plain, but the west shore, where streams emerge from the porous volcanic rock of the Crater Highlands, supports high, dark groundwater forest. The thick trees have the atmosphere of jungle, but there are no epiphytes or mosses, for the air is dry. On the road south into Lake Manyara Park, this forest gives way to an open wood of that airiest of all acacias, the umbrella thorn, and beyond the Ndala River is a region of dense thicket and wet savanna. The strip of trees between lake and escarpment is so narrow, and the pressure on elephants in the surrounding farm country so great, that Manyara can claim the greatest elephant concentration in East Africa, an estimated twelve to the square mile. For this reason – and also because the Manyara animals are used to vehicles, and with good manners can be approached closely – it is the best place to watch elephants in the world.

In the acacia wood that descends to the lake shore, elephants were everywhere in groves and thickets. Elephants travel in matriarchal groups led by a succession of mothers and daughters – female elephants stay with their mothers all their lives – and this group may include young males which have not yet been driven off. (Elephants not fully grown are difficult to sex – their genitals are well camouflaged in the cascade of slack and wrinkles – and unless their behavior has been studied for some time, the exact composition of a cow-calf group is very difficult to determine.) Ordinarily the leader is the oldest cow, who is related to every other animal; she may be fifty years old and past the breeding age, but her great memory and experience is the herd's defense against drought and flood and man. She knows not only where good browse may be found in different seasons, but when to charge and when to flee, and it is to her that the herd turns in time of stress. When a cow is in season, bulls may join the cow-calf group; at other times, they live alone or in herds of bachelors. When I drove near, the bulls moved off after a perfunctory threat display – flared ears, brandished tusks, a swaying forefoot like a pendulum, the dismantling of the nearest tree, and perhaps a diffident scream; sometimes they ease their nervous strain by chasing a jackal or a bird. With cows, as well, aggressive behavior is usually mere threat display, though it is wiser not to count on it.

The person best acquainted with these elephants is Iain Douglas-Hamilton, who had set up a small camp on the Ndala or Buffalo River, eight miles into Lake Manyara Park. The camp is perched above a gravel bend in the Ndala, a surface stream that courses down over ancient crystalline rock in a series of lovely waterfalls and pools and empties into the lake a mile below. Though the pools are cool, and deep enough to splash in, one swims at the risk of bilharzia, an extremely disagreeable intestinal invasion by trematode larvae passed into sluggish water via hominid feces: the larvae enter a small fresh-water snail that in turn releases the cercaria life stage into the water, and the cercaria enter the pores of baboons and men. Many people have contracted bilharzia in this pool, including Douglas-Hamilton, who is not the sort to be dismayed by such ill provenance, and will almost certainly risk and receive another dose of a disease which, without long and tiresome treatment, may be debilitating and even fatal.

When I drove into camp, its proprietor was standing outside his modest research laboratory with his pretty mother, Prunella Power, who was here on a visit from England. He is a strong good-looking young man with blond hair and glasses, wearing faded green drill shorts and shirt and old black street shoes without laces or socks (he also has an excellent pair of field boots which he wears when they turn up). He took my note of introduction and stuffed it in his pocket, and I doubt if he has read it to this day. "You'll stay with us, won't you?" he said straight off. "Have you had tea? Well, do come along then, we're just off elephant-watching." I got out of my Land Rover and into his, and we set off with a turn of speed toward the lake, where Douglas-Hamilton drove straight up to an elephant herd and began taking notes. His approach was so abrupt, so lacking in finesse, that the whole herd was engaged in threat display, with much shrill screaming. "Silly old things," said Iain, scarcely looking up. "Frightful cowards, really. Silly old elephants," He gazed at them with affection. "Oh, damn!" he said, as a big cow came blaring through the bushes. "That's Big Boadicia – she'll charge us, I expect." But Boadicea, the matriarch, held back as a younger cow charged instead. I expected Iain to drop his notebook and go for the wheel, but he merely said, "This one doesn't mean it." The young cow stopped a few yards short of the hood. Her bluff called, she backed up, forefoot swinging, and began what is known to behaviorists as displacement feeding, by way of expending her chagrin. Forefoot still swinging sideways, she wrenched at a tussock of green grass, and we were close enough to observe a trick I had never heard about – as the elephant tugs on grass, it mows it with the sharp toenails of its heavy foot, which is swinging in the rhythm of a scythe.

Iain and his mother had been asked to dinner by Jane and Hillary Hook, who were presently encamped with their safari clients in the ground-water forest near the entrance to the park; as I also knew the Hooks, I was taken along. Though not late, Iain drove like hell, slowing only to permit a puff adder to cross the road; in the headlights, the venomous thing, too fat to writhe, inched over the ground like a centipede. Rounding the bend a moment later, we found our way barred by a huge stinkbark, much too big to move, that wind had felled across the road at a point where the left side was steep uphill bank and the right a steep bank down. "I'm not missing dinner!" Iain cried, and forthwith gunned his car off the embankment into the jungle dark, in an attempt – I assume – to bypass the offending stinkbark. The undercarriage of the car struck one of several hidden stumps with an impact that drove the driver's mother into the roof, and inevitably, within seconds, the car was hung up, both front wheels spinning in the air. Iain grabbed up a monstrous jack and hoisted the transmission and axle clear of the stump. "Now I'll drive straight off the jack," he called to me. "Do catch it, will you?" I jumped away from the spinning jack as he drove off it, staring in astonishment as this inspired youth, in a series of wild spurts and caroms, bashed his way back to the road.

On the return trip, Mrs Power was guided around the fallen tree on foot by

Hillary's flashlight. Down below, also on foot, I led Iain back over the stumps, then leapt into the open rear as the car made its lunge at the steep bank. At the last moment, it altered course and proceeded into the interior of a thornbush, emerging miraculously onto the road.

"Fantastic!" said Hillary Hook. "I'd never have believed it!"

On the way home, picking thorns out of my face, I was fairly whining in annoyance, and Mrs Power, who is resigned to Iain through love and lack of choice, said, "I rather thought you'd intercede."

"I kept hoping *you* would intercede," I told her crossly. "I have no experience of him, and anyway, you're his mother."

Early next morning, we drove south to the Endobash River. In the shallows of the lake, near a great baobab, lay a dead buffalo, and in the spreading limbs of a nearby umbrella acacia lay a lion. The tree-climbing habit evolved by the lions of Manyara is said to be a defense against the stomoxys fly, which breeds along the water edge; in time of stomoxys infestations, the Ngorongoro lions are arboreal as well, and in the summer of 1970 I saw one climb a tree in tsetse woods of the western Serengeti. But at Manyara, where there is little shelter for lions against attacks by the numerous elephants and buffalo, protection from these animals may also be a factor.

Impala, bright rust red in the early light, scampered prettily in antelope perfection, and buffalo in a herd of hundreds milled back and forth across the track. Near the Endobash were big elephants that Iain did not recognize, and these he approached with circumspection. They had come in from outside the park, where they might have been chivvied and possibly shot at by man; such elephants take offense in very short order. Also, they were browsing in the thick high brush, so that their numbers and whereabouts were still uncertain. And finally, they looked decidedly larger than the home elephants of Manyara, which tend to be small, no doubt because the population is a young one. "These are the baddies," Iain said. He sat slumped behind the wheel of his idling Land Rover, hands in pockets. "Horrible wild uncouth elephants!" he cried suddenly, as if about to shake his fist. "Turn around, you bah-stards, let's have a look at you!" Here in the Endobash last year a band of strange elephants had dismantled his Land Rover around his ears while he and a girl companion cowered on the floor; the vehicle in which we rode, already battered, was its replacement.

The back of Iain's new Land Rover is open, like a short truck bed, and contained, besides spare wheel and jack, a park ranger named Mhoja whom Iain has trained to help him in his elephant surveys. Mhoja, a Nyamwezi from the great Bantu tribe of central Tanzania, was terrified at first, says Iain, but recently, for some unaccountable reason, had become more philosophical about his fate. Nevertheless, Mhoja was tapping urgently on the cab roof, for elephants were moving at us from both sides – we were caught in the middle. "They'll charge us, I expect," said Iain, and they did. He gunned his motor and we crashed between two bushes into the clear.

We went down to the Endobash River, and from there worked west up the Endobash Valley, under the cliffs of the escarpment. Last year in this place, while poking about in the thick bush, Iain and his mother surprised a rhino. Iain, run down, spent three weeks in a hospital at Arusha with a fractured vertebra. Soon after, he was a participant in the crash of a small plane, and decided to take up flying. Iain's father died in an air crash in World War II, and his mother is not happy about his new passion, but she knows better than to try to dissuade him.

One afternoon I volunteered to try Mhoja's position in the rear. As soon as possible, Iain had me surrounded with irate cows, which were menacing the car from all directions, and trying to see all ways at once, I shrank against the cab. Through his rear window, Iain said, "You'll get hardened to it, never fear." Soon a huge bull loomed alongside in threat display, and with his tusks demolished a small tree not fifteen feet from where I cowered, unable to imagine why Douglas-Hamilton was so loath to spare my life. Inching my head around to plead, I looked straight into Iain's camera; he fancied the shot of a frightened face with a big bull elephant filling the entire background. "You're going to want this picture," Iain said.

Annoyed by my annoyance, he said I had no faith: "I know these elephants," he complained later, "I really do." Iain was of two minds about his reputation for recklessness, which he had done nothing to discourage and which had returned to haunt him. "People seem to think I'm some sort of idiot, but I *had* to work close to elephants to do my research." To study not only elephant behavior but the effect of high numbers on the ecology of Manyara required a close record of their movements; therefore he had to know each animal's identity and position in its herd, as well as which herds were Manyara elephants and which were transient in the park. His solution was to photograph each animal with its ears flared, head-on, so that tusks and ear nicks could be used in identification, but the method demanded confrontations with four hundred and twenty agitated elephants. Iain learned the hard way which elephants were bad-tempered, and his confidence that he could distinguish a threat from an honest charge – which professional hunters who have gone out with him are unable to do – encouraged him to give visitors, as he says, "the same excitement, the same fun with elephants that I had when I didn't know anything." But the spreading tales of these adventures have tended to discredit the valuable research Douglas-Hamilton has done in the long days spent closer to wild elephants than anyone had ever gone before.

The elephants at Manyara are presently destroying the umbrella thorn at such a rate that regeneration cannot keep pace with the destruction, and in Iain's view, these lovely trees will be gone from the Manyara park within ten years.

Those not knocked down are stripped so grievously of bark that they cannot recover; either their vascular system is destroyed or they fall prey to the boring beetle that penetrates the exposed wood. On the other hand, elephants have been destroying woodlands for thousands of years, and perhaps destruction is a part of the natural cycle of this acacia, which represses the growth of its own seedlings in its shade. In season, elephants consume great quantities of the seed pods, and as they move continually in search of the varied browse that they require, the seeds are borne elsewhere and deposited – a most auspicious start in life – in an immense warm nutritious pile of dung.

The mature umbrella thorns in the region of Ndala had been noted in transects on a chart, and as it was crucial to his studies to know what had become of them in the course of a year, Iain set out one morning to survey two transects in the forest between his camp and the lake. Since the transects were mostly covered in the kind of thick high bush favored by rhino and old solitary buffalo, he needed a gun to back him up. Mhoja carried a .470 Rigby elephant rifle and I carried a .12 gauge Greeners single shot, said to be useful in "turning" a rhino's charge. "I shouldn't load it until something happens if I were you," said Iain. "It tends to go off by itself." All morning I carried the gun broken with a shotgun shell in my right hand; if *anything* went right in an emergency, I thought, it would be pure dumb luck.

The dawn had something ominous about it, or so it seemed to me, a tinge of gloom that haunted the African morning. The swift sun of the tropics, rising, spun on the white ivory of an elephant high on the slope of the escarpment; ahead, more elephants drifted away through woods that were still in shadow. Where they had forged tunnels through the brush, the brown woodland air spun with glittering webs of emerald spiders, and in a shaft of light between two trees stood a black-and-bamboo leopard tortoise, bright with dew. The sunrise fired a lizard's head, emerged from the cobra shadows of a dead tree, and glinted on a file of driver ants on the way to raid a termite nest. Sun and shadow, light and death. Through an open glade down toward the lake, impala danced.

On foot, the pulse of Africa comes through your boot. You are an animal among others, chary of the shadowed places, of sudden quiet in the air. A fine walk in the early woods turned hour by hour into a wearing trek through head-high caper and toothbrush bush, and as the sun climbed, heat settled in the woods, and colors faded, and dew dried. The thickened bush gave off coarse smells, the gun grew heavy, the step slowed. A humid pall had crossed the sun, and no bird sang. One had to concentrate to be aware, reminding oneself that this midday stillness, when dozing animals may be taken by surprise, is not the hour to walk carelessly in thickets. But a time comes when awareness goes, and one reels sweaty and heavy-legged under the sun, dulled to all signs and signals, like a laggard buffalo behind its herd. This time, for man as well as animals, is a time of danger.

"Like Endobash Plains, this," said Iain, bashing through; even Iain seemed subdued. "Let's have some gun support through here." And when at last we were in the clear again, walking homeward through the woods, he said, "Pushing through bush like that . . . a bit dicey, you know. Doesn't pay to think about it too much; you might not do it. People talk about going too near elephants, but walking these transects each month is a hell of a lot more dangerous." I was happy that the walk was over, and looked with fresh eyes on the rest of the precious day. In the afternoon, in a quiet glade, I watched striped kingfishers sing in a trio. In the urgency of their song, these woodland birds lifted bright wings like butterflies, and trembled.

In mid-February, I made a trip to southern Tanzania to look at the elephant damage in the huge new park along the Ruaha River, and Douglas-Hamilton decided to come along. He was anxious, in fact, to fly us down in his new plane, an ancient Piper with a fuel range barely adequate for the distance even if his navigation were exact. "I've just got my license," Iain said. "It will be an adventure." But the idea was discouraged by John Owen, who had us picked up in Arusha by John Savidge, the warden of Ruaha.

We flew south over the Maasai Steppe, the broad trackless central plateau of Tanzania. On the north–south line, the Maasai Steppe is located at the center of Africa, and at its western edge, Savidge picked up the Great North Road (from the Cape to Cairo; this road was pioneered in the famous five-thousand-mile walk in 1898–1899 by Ewart Grogan). Here and elsewhere north of the Zambezi River, the Great North Road is mostly rude dirt track. The plane crossed a litter of tin roofs in the Kondoa–Irangi hills, where the primitive farming practices of a swelling population have caused the precious topsoil to wash down in great erosion fans onto the naked plain. In Tanzania, intensive agriculture is seen as the solution to malnutrition and unemployment, and a population increase is encouraged. But except in the highlands, the red earths of East Africa are too poor to support permanent agriculture, and where they are fertile, the soils are soon impoverished by the plow, which lays them bare to cycles of fierce sun and leaching rain. In the wet season the ground is muck, and in the dry a hard-caked dusty stone. Wind and rain erode a soil that may have taken centuries to form, and there is desert. In Ethiopia, Madagascar, and throughout East Africa one sees this fatal erosion of thin fragile lateritic soils; the rust red of the laterite comes to the surface of the African landscape like blood welling in scraped skin.

Off to the west lay Dodoma, on the old trading route from Zanzibar and Bagamoyo, on the coast, to Tabora and Lake Tanganyika; through Dodoma came the Arab and Swahili trading caravans that would emerge months later with ivory and long lines of slaves. Speke and Burton passed through here in 1857, and Speke and Grant a few years later, on their way to the discovery of the headwaters of the Nile. Traders, missionaries, and explorers were careful to avoid the country to the north, for Dodoma lies at the south end of the Maasai Steppe, the two-hundred-mile southern extension of Maasai Land. Here the Maasai are alleged, on no good evidence, to have stopped the northward expansion of fierce Ngoni Zulu from southern Africa, or sometimes it is said that the Zulu stopped the southward course of the Maasai, but probably the two tribes never met. By 1840, the Ngoni had already settled in the vicinity of Lake Rukwa, in the Southern Highlands, well south of the northern edge of tsetse-infested forest that would surely have served as a barrier to the Maasai herds.

More likely the Maasai were checked by the fierce Gogo and Hehe in this region. Between 1890 and 1894, the Hehe – now demoralized like the Maasai – were also fighting the appropriation of their land by Germans, who refused to recognize and work with local chiefs and levied on the tribes a repressive system of taxation and forced labor that invited incessant revolt. The Maji-Maji Rebellion, between 1905 and 1907, devastated much of the southern country, and as in the Mau-Mau Rebellion, a half-century later, it was the African who suffered; an estimated one hundred thousand died.

The great Bahi Swamp lay south and west as the plane crossed the northern boundary of the park. This west part of the park is unbroken miombo or dry forest which subsides into acacia scrub and riverain vegetation as the Great Ruaha River slides eastward toward the coast. Miombo, composed mostly of scrubby species of *Brachystegia*, extends east and west for sixteen hundred miles in a vast infertile wilderness. It is hot, dull, and oppressive, and the great emphasis in south Tanzania on bush-clearing and the slaughter of wild animals in futile attempts to eradicate the tsetse fly has made much of it more empty and monotonous than it was before.

We had a pleasant visit at Ruaha, and a good swim in a swirling pool at the edge of the river rapids. Here Iain wished to see who could swim farthest out without being swept away, and I spared one of his nine lives by declining. That evening, a spirited discussion of the elephant problem got us nowhere. Elephants have much increased along the Ruaha since the last native villages in this area were evacuated, and Savidge and his wife were upset by the elephant damage to the lovely winterthorn and baobab near park headquarters; they wanted an elephant control program set up at once. While their feelings were understandable, neither Douglas-Hamilton nor I agreed that slaughter was the solution – not, at least, until all other courses had been tried.

The Ruaha situation was discussed on the first of March at a Kenya–Tanzania elephant meeting convened at Voi, in Tsavo Park. John Owen had been kind enough to invite me to the conference, and on March 1, 1969, I flew with him to Tsavo. We left Arusha in mid-morning, passing south of black Mt Meru and the broad back side of Kilimanjaro and its gaunt eastern peak, Mawensi, that like Mt Kenya is the black hard core of a volcano whose sides have blown away. Straight ahead lay Kenya's Serengeti, a bare steppe with isolated rises. Beyond lay nyika, the wilderness, thousands of square miles of thorn scrub between the highland plateaus and the sea. Soon the plane's shadow was crossing Tsavo. This largest of national parks in Africa, like most, came into being because the area involved, due to tsetse or other pestilence, was considered unfit for anything else, and it is divided into eastern and western sections by the Mombasa Railroad. Surrounding the railroad is an abrupt congregation of small mountains called the Teita Hills, and under the Teita Hills lay Voi.

Our host at Voi was David Sheldrick, warden of Tsavo East and a central figure in the first flare-up in the great elephant dispute that arose in the mid-1960s. His opponent was Dr Richard Laws, at that time head of the Tsavo Research Project and the chief proponent of elephant cropping as a means of stabilizing elephant populations to keep them in balance with contracting habitats. In a paper[5] prepared with the help of Ian Parker, whose Wildlife Services Ltd., Nairobi, did all the shooting, Laws described the elimination of four hundred elephant killed in 1965 on the south bank of the Nile at Murchison Falls, and of three hundred more destroyed at Tsavo. In effect, Laws concluded that the assumption of a general increase in elephant populations was mistaken; that what had increased was the density of elephant populations in certain protected areas, notably the parks; that this increase, at least in part, represented an immigration of elephants into the parks from unprotected areas, and a corresponding lack of places to which to emigrate, due to increasing human pressure at park boundaries; that this interruption of migration patterns, especially in the dry season, often put unnatural pressure on the habitat, which was therefore deteriorating; that one symptom of this deterioration was the rapid conversion of woodland to grassland, a process accelerated by periodic fires; that – quite apart from the progressive elimination of suitable habitat for other woodland species – the invading grassland provided inadequate nourishment for the elephants, which were exhibiting such strong evidence of nutritional deficiency as reduced fertility, increased calf mortality, retarded growth, and even such pathological symptoms of stress as deforming abscesses of the jaw (on the south bank of the Victoria Nile, these abscesses were present in thirty per cent of the killed animals); that, far from increasing, many elephant populations were in the process of a "crash" that, due to elephant longevity, might extend over a half-century; and finally, that this crash, which at

Murchison Falls was well advanced, had already begun at Tsavo, and because of increasing destruction of habitat, might well cause the complete extinction of elephant populations in both places. Laws concluded that these threatened populations would benefit most from an acceleration of the crash brought about by man, in order to save the remaining habitats for the animals that survived.

The Laws–Parker conclusions seemed particularly applicable to Tsavo, where the extended drought of 1960–1961, followed immediately by violent floods, had ravaged the habitat, causing the death of great numbers of elephants and rhino. Tsavo was still in poor condition in 1964, when Laws was invited by the Kenya National Parks to take a preliminary sample of three hundred elephants. Even so, further elephant slaughter on the scale recommended was resisted by Warden Sheldrick, who in the absence of more comprehensive studies felt that natural checks and balances should be permitted to take care of excess elephants. Eventually Sheldrick won the support of the Parks trustees, but meanwhile he had been attacked for the elevation of his own beliefs over trained scientific opinion. Laws spoke bitterly of "preservationists"; since man was responsible for the elephant problem, he was also responsible for its solution, no matter how abhorrent the idea of slaughter. Laws, in turn, was criticized by Sheldrick supporters for turning an honest difference of opinion into a public harangue, and anyway, these people said, Ian Parker's financial interest in cropping operations, present and future, voided the objectivity of the report, which was invalidated in any case by its inadequate attention to vegetation patterns and climatic cycles. (The ad hominem aspects of the dispute were ill-founded on both sides. Sheldrick and Laws both found support among ecologists and biologists then working in East Africa; and while Parker's interest in commercial game cropping may have lent vigor to his beliefs, he had long since demonstrated a sincere and intelligent interest in the welfare of African wildlife. As a member of the Game Department, Parker had worked on anti-poaching campaigns at Tsavo, and subsequently was made manager of the Galana River Game Management Scheme, a pioneering effort to crop wild herds for protein and profit.)

The battle raged in newspapers and journals throughout Africa and beyond, and the smoke of it has not settled to this day. "The Tsavo elephant problem is a classical example of indecision, vacillation, and mismanagement," Laws wrote in a recent paper. Still, his dire forecasts have not yet come to pass, perhaps because a series of favorable seasons have substantially restored the habitats of Tsavo. Most of the conferees at Voi were in sympathy with the anti-cropping views of David Sheldrick, although there were gradations of opinion. Tsavo ecologist Dr Philip Glover, for example, agreed with Dr Hugh Lamprey, head of the Serengeti Research Institute, that elephants would have to be cropped in the Serengeti unless fires there were brought under control. It was concluded that each of the parks presented a separate problem, and that in all cases more study was required before a cropping program was begun. No one agreed with the warden of Ruaha that elephants should be killed there without further ado, and no one sided publicly with the Scientific Officer of the Tanzania National Parks, who said, in effect, that no park elephants should be destroyed under any circumstances. This veteran ecologist, Mr Vesey-FitzGerald, felt strongly that population fluctuations based on natural adjustments to inevitable ecological change within a park were part of long-range patterns not yet understood. He agreed that certain elephant populations were out of balance with their environment but felt that regulatory mechanisms such as loss of fertility would take care of this. There were no known occasions, he declared, when elephants had made their environment uninhabitable to themselves (though Laws's observations at Murchison Falls appear to refute this). While fire should certainly be controlled to lessen the impact of the animals on the habitat, he said, any artificial reduction of populations would interfere with the natural rhythms of the African land. Until a thorough study had been made of all environmental factors, and especially the regeneration of affected vegetation, the slaughter of animals in a national park was a bad mistake and a worse precedent, and probably an impertinence into the bargain.

Of all African animals, the elephant is the most difficult for man to live with, yet its passing – if this must come – seems the most tragic of all. I can watch elephants (and elephants alone) for hours at a time, for sooner or later the elephant will do something very strange such as mow grass with its toenails or draw the tusks from the rotted carcass of another elephant and carry them off into the bush. There is mystery behind that masked gray visage, and ancient life force, delicate and mighty, awesome and enchanted, commanding the silence ordinarily reserved for mountain peaks, great fires, and the sea. I remember a remark made by a girl about her father, a businessman of narrow sensibilities who, casting about for a means of self-gratification, traveled to Africa and slew an elephant. Standing there in his new hunting togs in a vast and hostile silence, staring at the huge dead bleeding thing that moments before had borne such life, he was struck for the first time in his headlong passage through his days by his own irrelevance. "Even *he*," his daughter said, "knew he'd done something stupid."

The elephant problem, still unresolved, will eventually affect conservation policies throughout East Africa, where even very honest governments may not be able to withstand political pressure to provide meat for the people. Already there is talk of systematic game-cropping in the parks on a sustained yield basis, especially since park revenues from meat and hides and tusks could be considerable, and this temptation may prove impossible to resist for the new governments. Or an outbreak of political instability might wreck the tourist industry that justifies the existence of the parks, thus removing the last barrier between the animals and a hungry populace. African schoolchildren are now taught to appreciate their wild animals and the land, but public attitudes may not change in time to spare the wildlife in the next decades, when the world must deal with the worst consequences of overpopulation and pollution. And a stubborn fight for animal preservation in disregard of people and their famine-haunted future would only be the culminating failure of the western civilization that, through its blind administration of vaccines and quinine, has upset the ecologies of a whole continent. Thus wildlife must be treated in terms of resource management in this new Africa which includes, besides gazelles, a growing horde of tattered humans who squat for days and weeks and months and years on end, in a seeming trance, awaiting hope. In the grotesque costumes of African roadsides – rag-wrapped heads and the wool greatcoats and steel helmets of old white man's wars are worn here in hundred-degree heat – the figures look like survivors of a cataclysm. Once, in Nanyuki, I saw a legless man, lacking all means of locomotion, who had been installed in an old auto tire in a ditch at the end of town. Fiercely, eyes bulging, oblivious of the rush of exhaust fumes spinning up the dust around his ears, he glared at an ancient newspaper, as if deciphering the news of doomsday.

The elephant problem is the reverse side of the problem of livestock, which are also out of balance with the environment. In small numbers, cattle were no threat to the African landscape; it is only in the past century, with the coming of the white man, that a conflict has emerged. The Europeans saw livestock as a sign of promise in the heathen: what was good for the white in Europe was good for the black in Africa, and that was that. In addition, the white encouraged a contempt for game, not only as fit food for man but as competitors of cattle and as carriers of the tsetse fly. In Uganda, Zambia, Rhodesia, Tanzania, the solution has been the destruction of the bush and a wholesale slaughter, over vast areas, of the native creatures, in a vain effort to render these regions habitable by men and cattle. Today it is known that the tsetse prefers wart hog, giraffe, and buffalo, paying little attention to the antelopes, so that the vast majority of victims died in vain.

The European and his paraphernalia were all that was needed to upset the balance of man and the African land. It was clear to the simplest African that the wild animals were creatures of the past, destroying his shambas and competing with his livestock for the grass; they stood in the way of a "progress" that was very much to be desired. Game control, tsetse control, fenced water points, poaching –

everywhere the wild animals made way for creatures which even from the point of view of economics seem very much less efficient than themselves. The ancestors of the wild animals have been evolving for seventy million years; the modern species, three quarters of a million years old, form the last great population of wild animals left on earth. Over their long evolutionary course, they have adapted to the heat and rain, to poor soils and coarse vegetation, and because they have had time to specialize, a dozen species can feed in the same area without competing. Rhino, giraffe, and gerenuk are browsers of leaves and shrubs, while zebra, topi, and wildebeest are grazers; buffalo, elephant, eland, impala, and most other antelope do both. Zebras will eat standing hay, and wildebeests and kongonis half-grown grass, leaving the newest growth to the gazelles; the topi has a taste for the rank meadow grass that most other antelopes avoid. Only a few wild herbivores require shade, and all have water-conserving mechanisms that permit them to go without water for days at a time; the Grant's gazelle, gerenuk, and oryx may not drink for months. Cattle, by comparison, must be brought to water every day or two, and waste coarse grasses used by the wild animals.

In addition, the game matures and breeds much earlier than domestic stock, and no fencing, shelter, tsetse control, or veterinary service is required. So far, game ranching experiments in Kenya and Tanzania are still experiments, having failed to anticipate the complex problems, from local politics and prejudices to the mechanics of harvesting in a hot wilderness without roads: the animals soon become so wary that systematic shooting is impossible, at least in areas accessible to service vehicles and refrigerator trucks. For this reason, the emphasis on game-cropping seems less promising than the development of semi-domesticated herds that can be harvested where needed. Whatever the solution, it seems clear that game ranching is a promising approach, all the more so since the tourists on whom East African economies count heavily do not come here to see cattle.

The eland, which mingles readily with cattle and on occasion follows herds into Maasai bomas, has been raised domestically in Southern Rhodesia, South Africa, and Russia, and recent success with buffalo and oryx at Galana River suggests that other animals may also be tamed that will yield more protein with less damage to the land than the scrub cattle. Until this is proven, however, care must be taken not to penalize the pastoral peoples for conditions caused by rain cycles and climate. Amboseli, where wildlife and the Maasai herds share a game reserve that is turning to dust, is often cited as a habitat badly damaged by too many cattle, but recent studies[6] indicate that the deteriorating vegetation is more a consequence of a raised water table with resultant high salinity than of overgrazing. Also, the contention that much of his herd is useless makes no sense to the Maasai, who knows that even the scraggiest of his cows can produce a calf in the next year. But one zebra skin is worth four times the price of such a cow, and eventually the tribe may be compelled to bring their myriad cattle into the economy by raising animals of better quality and permitting more of them to be sold and slaughtered. The population of the pastoral tribes rises between two and three per cent each year, and landscape after landscape, wide open to settlement and the crude agriculture of the first comers, is ravaged by burning, subsistence farming, overgrazing, and erosion. The thin soil is cut to mud and dust by plagues of scrawny kine, following the same track to the rare waterholes, and goats scour the last nourishment from the gullied earth. Certain Turkana, after centuries as herdsmen, are reverting to the status of hunter-gatherers. Having no choice, they have given up their old taboos and will eat virtually anything, from snakes to doum palm roots; in recent years they have been seen picking through thorn trees for the eggs and young of weavers. A similar fate is threatening the Maasai, for once the earth has blown away, plague and famine are inevitable.

Tsavo East is so very vast that to get any sense of it, one must see it from the air. In two planes, we flew north over the waterhole at Mudanda Rock to the confluence of the Tsavo and Athi Rivers that together form the Galana, under the Yatta Plateau; from here, we followed the Yatta northward. This extraordinary formation, which comes south one hundred and eighty miles from the region of Thika to a point east of Mtito Andei, is capped by a great tongue of lava; all the land surrounding has eroded away. The Yatta rises like a rampart from the rivers and dry plains, yet its steep sides present no problem to the elephants, which that day were present on the heights in numbers. The elephants of Tsavo are the most celebrated in East Africa, being very large and magisterial in color, due to their habit of dusting in red desert soil. Yet they were not always common here: the great ivory hunter Arthur Neumann, traveling on foot through the Tsavo region on the way from Mombasa to Lake Rudolf in the last years of the nineteenth century, saw no elephants at all.[7] The two planes cross the high land between rivers. Somewhere here there is a rock heaped up with pebbles tossed onto it for luck by Maasai warriors on the way to raid the Giriama of the coast. Along the far side of the Yatta flows the Tiva, and beyond the Tiva the dry thorn scrub stretches eastward one hundred and fifty miles to the Tana River. Away from the rivers, the only large tree in this nyika is the great, strange baobab, but the baobab, which stores calcium in its bark, has been hammered hard by elephants, and few young trees remain in Tsavo Park. For many tribes, the baobab, being infested with such nocturnal creatures as owls, bats, bushbabies, and ghosts, is a house of spirits; the Kamba say that its weird "upside-down" appearance was its punishment for not growing where God wanted.

Kamba hunters, with a few nomadic Orma Boran and Ariangulo or "Waliangulu" have most of this hostile country to themselves. Like the Kamba, the Ariangulo, a little-known tribe of the nyika that speaks an eastern Hamitic tongue like that of the Galla, are expert trackers and bowmen and have long hunted elephants throughout this region, using arrows tipped with acokanthera poison brewed by the Giriama, and selling ivory to the coastal traders. After 1948, when the Tsavo bush country, considered hopeless for all other purposes, was ordained a national park, a number of Kamba and Ariangulo hunters – or poachers, as they now were called, a matter of some indifference to them – continued in their old ways for several years. In the winter of 1950, in this burning land east of the Tiva, a band of thirty-eight Kamba, tracing a series of waterholes toward Dakadima Hill, found all of them dry. Half of the band set off for the Tiva, on the chance that the seasonal river still held water, and the rest headed south toward the Galana, which was sure to have water but was much farther away. The first group disappeared without a trace; in the second, there was one survivor.[8]

In the years of Mau-Mau, when most wardens were away in the Kenya Regiment, the elephant hunters descended upon Tsavo, but subsequent campaigns led by Sheldrick and Bill Woodley, now warden of the Aberdares National Park, compounded the excess-elephant problem by sending most of the hunters to jail. After serving sentences that were difficult for them to understand, some hunters became safari gun bearers and trackers, or scouts for the Kenya Game Department, and great credit for finding them places must go to Bill Woodley, who would later do the same for ex-Mau-Mau in the Aberdares. A few reverted to poaching, and most have joined the many other Africans whose old way of life has vanished, leaving them without heritage or hope.

I flew back to Tanzania with Douglas-Hamilton, who had brought his new plane to the elephant conference. Iain's plane is twenty years old, and looks it, but it "came with all sorts of spare parts – ailerons and wings and things. I shan't be able to use them, I suppose, unless I crump it." We took off from Voi at a very steep angle – a stalling angle, I was told later by Hugh Lamprey, a veteran flyer who once landed his plane on the stony saddle, fifteen thousand feet up, between the peaks of Kilimanjaro. Despite thunderheads and heavy rain, Iain chose a strange route through the Teita Hills, and I sat filled with gloom as the black rain smacked his windshield. There are bad air currents in the Teita Hills; it was at Voi that Karen Blixen's friend, Denys Finch-Hatton, crashed and died.

Soon I persuaded Iain to give me the wheel, and after that the flight was uneventful. We crossed the Ardai Plain beyond Arusha and the smooth Losiminguri Hills, flying westward toward the dark cliffs of the Rift. But Iain would not suffer the flight to pass without incident, for just as we reached the cliff he said, "I'll take it now." He wigwagged the tourists taking tea on the lawn of the Manyara Lodge, on the rim of the escarpment, and no doubt caused a click of cups by banking in a violent arc over the void and plunging in a power dive at the ground-water forest, a thousand feet below. He then swooped up to cliff level again, and came in to a competent landing.

A year later, when I got back to Ndala, I found Iain in a state of some chagrin. A month after my departure in the spring before, he had walked away from the wreck of his new airplane, which was far beyond the help of his spare parts. And it had scarcely been repaired when he nosed it over in soft sand while attempting to land on the sea beach at Kilifi, on the coast of Kenya. At present he was unable to accompany me on a planned climb of Ol Doinyo Lengai, having been warned by his sponsors and superiors that his reputation was outstripping his accomplishment. Nor could he go on our other planned safari to the Yaida Valley south of the Crater Highlands, where Iain's friend, a young zoologist named Peter Enderlein, was in touch with the small click-speaking Tindiga hunters. Over a whiskey, we agreed that he had done a good deal of difficult and dangerous research that more prudent students of the elephant would never attempt, and that his work or lack of it should be judged on its own merits. It often appeared that the official disapproval had less to do with deficiencies in his research than with his various mishaps, or even perhaps his domestic arrangements at Ndala, which included a friend whom he would marry a year later. Oria Rocco, whose family has a farm at Naivasha in Kenya, is a live marvelous girl with a husky laugh, fierce gentle spirit, and a natural empathy with elephants, being related to the creator of Babar, the splendid elephant of children's books. Worldly as Iain is conservative, she shares his intensity about the present and fatality about the future, and the camp was much more civilized for her presence.

I had not been in Ndala a half-hour before Iain had us in emergency. A cow-calf herd led by an old cow known as Ophelia came up the river bed to drink at a small pool at the base of the falls. The camp lies on the ascending slope of the escarpment, at the level of the falls; just below, the river levels off, flowing gradually toward Lake Manyara, and downriver a short distance, Iain has a makeshift hide or blind. From here, he thought, he could get pictures of the herd with a complex camera device of his own invention which makes double images of the subject on the same negative; using parallax, animal measurements may be made with fair accuracy without destroying the animal itself. (The animal's shoulder height is a clue to its age, and the age structure of the population – the proportion of old animals to young – is an important indication of population health: despite the density of its elephant, Manyara at present has a healthy, "pyramid" population, with many young animals at the base.) Though the device works, it is so unwieldy that another person must be present with a notebook to record the data, and that other person was me.

We descended the steep bank under the camp and made our way downriver to the hide. The herd was busy at the pool, but I disliked our position very much. The animals were cut off; their only escape was straight back down the river past the hide, which was skeletal and decrepit, utterly worthless. And here we were on open ground, a hundred yards downriver from the steep bank leading up to the camp ... "They'll never scent us," Iain decided, setting up his apparatus, an ill-favored thing of long arms, loose parts, and prisms. But scent us they did, before he could get one picture. Ophelia, ears flared, spun around and, in dead silence, hurried her generations down the river bed in the stiff-legged elephant run that is really a walk, keeping her own impressive bulk between man and herd. We didn't move. "I don't think she's going to charge us," Iain whispered. But the moment the herd was safely past, Ophelia swung up onto the bank, and she had dispensed with threat display. There were no flared ears, no blaring, only an oncoming cow elephant, trunk held high, less than twenty yards away.

As I started to run, I recall cursing myself for having been there in the first place; my one chance was that the elephant would seize my friend instead of me. In hopelessness, or perhaps some instinct not to turn my back on a charging animal, I faced around again almost before I had set out, and was rewarded with one of the great sights of a lifetime. Douglas-Hamilton, unwilling to drop his apparatus, and knowing that flight was useless anyway, and doubtless cross that Ophelia had failed to act as he predicted, was making a last stand. As the elephant loomed over us, filling the coarse heat of noon with her dusty bulk, he flared his arms and waved his glittering contraption in her face, at the same time bellowing, "Bugger off." Taken aback, the dazzled Ophelia flared her ears and blared, but she had sidestepped, losing the initiative, and now, thrown off course, she swung away toward the river, trumpeting angrily over her shoulder.

From high on the bank came a great peal of laughter from Oria. Iain and I trudged up to lunch; there was very damned little to say.

Another day we took a picnic to the Endobash River, which descends in a series of waterfalls that churn up a white froth in its pools. To reach it, one must push a short ways through the bush, and Iain, who has had two bad scrapes in this region, was carrying his heavy rifle. At the river, we climbed to a high pool where we stripped and swam in the cool current. Then we sat on a hot rock ledge to dry, and drank wine with Oria's fine lunch. Afterwards, like three Sunday strollers, we walked down the river bed toward the lake. In the sun and windlessness, enclosed by leafy trees, it was intimate and peaceful, with none of that vast anonymity that subdues one in the spaces of East Africa. But we had scarcely started home when the road a quarter-mile ahead was crossed by a herd of elephants. "Endobash baddies!" Iain said, grabbing his notebook. "I'll have to have a look at those! Load up the gun!" Because we would have to approach on foot to get close to these strange elephants, he needed gun support; Oria would take the pictures. We walked quickly and quietly down the river road.

The elephants were upwind of us, and before we knew it we were right among them, so close, in fact, that we dove for cover underneath the high bush beside us when it quaked with the movements of the elephant behind. A moment later, another walked out into the open a few yards ahead. It was a large cow with odd warped tusks. "Oh hell," said Iain, "it's only Jane Eyre after all." Blithely he stepped out onto the road, hailing his old friend, and there was a moment of suspense when the cow turned toward him. Then she went off sideways, ears flapping in half-hearted threat display, and her herd came out through the wall of bush and fell into step behind her.

Iain's disappointment was matched by my own relief, and Oria, who was pregnant, felt as I did: we had gotten off easily. It was a lovely late afternoon, and whirling along the lake track in the open car, exalted by wine and wind, I reveled in the buffaloes and wading birds in the bright water of the lake edge, and the great shining purple baobab that stands on the lake shore between Endobash and Ndala. But just past the Ndala crossing there were two lionesses in an acacia, and one of them lay stretched on a low limb not ten feet above the road. Oria said, "I'll take her picture as we pass underneath," and Iain slowed the Land Rover on the bridge while she set her camera. At Manyara the tree-climbing lions are resigned to cars, and there is no danger in driving beneath one. But this animal was much closer to the road than most, and the car was wide open: Iain had removed the roof to feel closer to his elephants, and even the windshield was folded flat upon the hood. Lions accustomed to cameras and the faces in car windows see human beings in the open as a threat; when the car passed beneath her, the lioness and I scowled nervously, and I felt my shoulders hunch around my head.

Oria said she had missed the shot, and we passed beneath again, and then again, as she shot point-blank into the animal's mouth, which was now wide open. "Once more," she said; both Oria and Iain seemed feverish with excitement. "Christ," I said, scarcely able to speak. "You people – " But already the car had been yanked around, and seeing Iain's stubborn face, I knew that any interference short of a blunt instrument would only goad him to some ultimate stupidity that might get one of us mauled. I considered jumping out, but not for long. The lioness, extremely agitated, had risen to her feet, and a man on the ground might well invite attack. Insane as it seemed, I decided I was safer in the car, which proceeded forward.

The lioness crouched, hindquarters high, pulling her forepaws back beneath her chest, and the black tuft of her heavy tail thumped on the bark. Awaiting us, she flared her teeth, and this time I saw the muscles twitch as she hitched herself to spring: Ears back, eyes flat in an intent head sunk low upon her paws, she was shifting her bony shoulders and hind feet. Apparently Iain noticed this, for when Oria murmured, "She won't jump," he snapped at her, "Don't be so bloody sure." Nevertheless he carried on – I don't think it occurred to him to stop – and a second later we were fatally committed.

The lioness hitched her hindquarters again, snarling so loudly as the threat came close that Iain, who should have shot ahead, passing beneath her, jammed on the brakes and stalled. The front of the car stopped directly under the limb, with the cat's stiff whiskers and my whey face less than a lion's length apart; I was too paralyzed to stir. Land Rover motors spin quietly a while before they start, and while we waited for that trapped lioness to explode around our ears we listened to the scrape of claws on bark and the hiss and spitting and the heavy thump of that hard tail against the wood, and watched the twitch of the black tail tassel and the leg muscles shivering in spasms under the fly-flecked hide. The intensity, the sun, the light were terrifically exciting – I hated it, but it was terrifically exciting. I felt unbearably aware. I think I smelled her but I can't remember; there is only a violent memory of lion-ness in all my senses. Then Iain, gone stiff in the face, was easing the car out of there, and he backed a good long way from the taut beast before turning around and proceeding homeward through the quiet woods.

Nobody spoke. When Oria pointed out more arboreal lions, we ignored her. I felt angry and depressed – angry at having our lives risked so unreasonably, and depressed because I had permitted it to happen, as if I had lacked the courage to admit fear. At camp, I said in sour tones, "Well, you got some fantastic pictures. I'll say that much." And Iain, looking cross himself, said shortly, "I'll never use them – those were for her scrapbook. I can't stand pictures of frightened animals." Two years before a friend of Iain had given him a book of mine on travels in wild parts of South America, and now he commented that I had taken a few risks myself. But calculated risks to reach a goal were quite different from risks taken for their own sake; I was thinking of George Schaller's account of his solitary camp in the grizzly tundra of Alaska, and the care he had taken, the awareness of every step on river stones, of each swing of his ax – the disciplined courage that it took to live alone in wilderness where any mistake might be the last. What we had just done, by comparison, was merely stupid.

For once, Iain failed to argue. He was silent for a while, then said abruptly that he expected to die violently, as his father had, and doubted very much that he would live to see his fortieth year. Should he maintain his present habits, this romantic prediction will doubtless be borne out. "I'd hate to die," he said on another occasion, "but I'd rather risk dying than live nine-to-five." Yet people like Iain who hurl themselves at life with such generous spirit seem to rush untouched through danger after danger, as if the embrace of death as part of life made them immortal.

Months later, when his work at Manyara had ended, Iain came with Oria to America. We discussed elephants and the fine days at Ndala, arriving eventually at the adventure with the lioness. "Those times with the elephants weren't really dangerous," he said; he glared at Oria when she laughed. "Honestly. I knew what I was doing. But that business with the lion was absurd." He shrugged, and after a pause said quietly, "We just did it out of love of life."

At Ndala I lived happily in a thatch-roofed banda, like an African beehive hut with windows and a cement floor. The hut was perched on the high river bank just beside the falls, which washed away all noises but the clear notes of forest birds. Sometimes I climbed the stream above the falls, with its hidden rock pools and small sandy beaches shaded by figs and tamarind, and massive boulders of the ancient rock of Africa laid bare by the torrents of the rainy season. In the winter, a pair of Egyptian geese flew each day into the ravines above the falls; one watched them appear out of the sun over Manyara and vanish into the Rift wall.

In the ground-water forest, a green monitor lizard, four feet long, crosses a brook, and the speckled *Charaxes* butterflies flicker through the shades. In an open glade a fastidious impala lifts its hind leg to shed big drops of rain. At daybreak a dog baboon, taking his ease atop a termitarium, picks his breakfast from a plucked branch of red berries; finding himself observed, he cocks his head, then dismisses his fellow hominoid with a cynical nod. At evening a white-browed coucal, called the water-bottle bird, neck feathers raised, whole body shuddering, delivers that liquid falling song that only intensifies the stillness.

In the winter drought of 1961, Manyara was a pale dead place of scum froth and cracked soda; in 1969 and 1970 the water level was so high that many of the tracks behind the shore were underwater, and much of the umbrella thorn was killed. At twilight one late afternoon near the drowned forest, a herd of elephants fed on mats of dead typha sedge blown over from the far side of the lake. The animals waded to their chests in the greasy waves, trunks coiling in and out, ears blowing. Night was falling in the shadows of the Rift, which rose in a black wall behind the elephants, and from dusky woods came a solitary fluting. As the sun sank to the escarpment, the western sky took on a greenish cast, and the last light of storm caught the whiskers on the pointed lips, the torn flutings of the ears, the ragged switch of a wet tail on ancient hide. The dead forest, the doomed giants, the wild light were of another age, and made me restless, as if awakening ancestral memories of the Deluge.

8 Great Caldron Mountains

There is a void in the life of the African, a spiritual emptiness, divorced as he is from each world, standing in between, torn in both directions. To go forward is to abandon the past in which the roots of his being have their nourishment; to go backward is to cut himself off from the future, for there is no doubt about where the future lies. The African has been taught to abandon his old ways, yet he is not accepted in the new world even when he has mastered its ways. There seems to be no bridge, and this is the source of his terrible loneliness.

Colin Turnbull, *The Lonely African*

... a herd of Buffalo, one hundred and twenty-nine of them, came out of the morning mist under a copper sky, one by one, as if the dark and massive, iron-like animals with the mighty horizontally swung horns were not approaching, but were being created before my eyes and sent out as they were finished.

Isak Dinesen, *Out of Africa*

Between Kilimanjaro and Mt Meru, off the road that winds around the side of Ngurdoto Crater, are soft ponds where hippos push and blow, and here vast beds of floating vegetation, papyrus and pale sky blue petals of nymphea drifting with the wind, may cause a pond to form or vanish before one returns along the road: I noticed this one afternoon while walking homeward to Momela. On my left as I went along, the clouds lifted from the shattered side of black Mt Meru, revealing the jagged walls and the great cinder cone of its exploded crater. Before long, I heard the somber crack of a snapped branch, and rounding a bend, found my path barred by elephants. They were feeding on both sides, and one stood foursquare on the road, legs like stone columns. I was sorry about this, as dark was coming, and there was an elephant in this region that last year, having been approached incautiously, destroyed John Owen's friend, Baron Von Blumenthal. But Desmond Vesey-FitzGerald, who had seen these elephants earlier and antici-pated the confrontation, came to fetch me. I was glad to see his Land Rover, for night came down before we reached his camp.

Vesey, who is the ecologist for Tanzania's national parks, had been kind enough to invite me to Momela, at the foot of Mt Meru, to learn some "bush botany" from himself and his dear friend Mary Richards, a beautiful Welsh lady of eighty-three who, like Vesey himself, had transferred her botanical field work into Tanzania when the political situation in Northern Rhodesia, now Zambia, became a nuisance. ("Can't tell what they'll ask you at the borders anymore – doubt if they know themselves. Used to ask what sex your wife was – probably still do.") But Vesey and Mary were much too busy to bemoan the passing of the grand old days, for he was completing his work on East African grasses, while she was negotiating the purchase of a new Land Rover for a botanical safari into the remote plains behind Kilimanjaro. She had brought along from Zambia her cook Samuel, and as Vesey already had two Samuels in residence, and as these old friends are much given to good-humored shouting, their household is a lively place. Three Samuels or none might appear when one was called, whereas Vesey's cook Chilufia was apt to be there whether wanted or not, agitating in stricken silence for a chance to lay bare a calamity. The gloom of Chilufia is eternal as fire or water, and would no doubt be passed on from father to son.

"That banana pudding, Chilufia! We *don't* wish to see that again!"

And Chilufia rolls a yellow eye in resignation; one suspects Chilufia of laughter in the dark.

Toward Africans, Vesey and Mary have the good will of the earlier generations, recognizing the dignity and loyalty and courage with which Africans repay respectful treatment. Their manner is one of mixed love and exasperation, and just as the African eases his nerves with laughter at the mzungu, the European, so Vesey calms his own, when he can manage it, by laughing at the blacks. Because there is mutual loyalty in this household, blacks and whites may amuse one another in a way that is forgiven on both sides.

". . *fright*fully smart! Stumbling about on the stones, slapping his rifle butt about – practically knocked himself down!" Vesey's cheeks, in mirth, are merry and red and round, under round glasses. "Didn't you see him? Trouble was, he'd lost his gun sling again, had his rifle all tied up with a fearful bit of string . . ."

Vesey and Mary are pioneer African botanists, self-taught, and they are spirited competitors, decrying each other's botanical techniques, deploring the absence of word from "Kew" (the British Botanical Museum at Kew Gardens), fussing over each other's needs, such as proper tags and a decent supply of "polly bags" for collecting specimens. In the evening, over a stiff drink, they compare notes, recalling old times in Abercorn, and old friends like Ionides, called "Iodine", and J. A. Hunter, the hunter and game warden, and Wilfred Thesiger, the desert traveler, and Peter Greenway, the eminent botanist at the Coryndon (for their generation, Nairobi's National Museum, which acquired its new name at the time of Independence, will always be the Coryndon, just as this land will always be Tanganyika). In the back buildings of the Coryndon, I once met Dr Greenway, a dogged bachelor in baggy plus fours and bow tie who was kind enough to sort out a crude collection I had made in the Dahlak Islands in the Red Sea; he is of the same vintage, more or less, as Mary Richards, and was greatly annoyed at young Vesey for failing to stay in touch with him. "I don't know *what* Vesey thinks he's doing down there," Dr Greenway said, "but you may be sure it isn't botany."

I lived in a tent west of the house, which overlooks the Momela Lakes, in a saddle of green hills under Mt Meru. Looking northeast toward Kilimanjaro, there is a broad prospect of the Mgare Merobi region where Joseph Thomson of the Royal Geographic Society first met with the Maasai; Thomson, in 1883, was the first European to cross Maasai Land to Lake Victoria and return. "We soon set our eyes upon the dreaded warriors that had been so long the subject of my waking dreams, and I could not but involuntarily exclaim, 'What splendid fellows!' as I surveyed a band of the most peculiar race of men to be found in Africa." But soon the Maasai were behaving with the aggressive arrogance for which they are well known, and two days later, having gotten word that the Maasai in the country ahead were up in arms, Thomson felt obliged to beat a retreat around the south side of Kilimanjaro. Originally he had planned to go west over the Nguruman region to the lake, but now he was deflected, coming around by way of Loitokitok and Amboseli and heading northwest to Naivasha, Lake Baringo, and Kusumu on a route very close to today's main road from Namanga to these destinations. En route, he named the Aberdare Mountains for the president of the society that had sponsored him and a lovely falls in honor of himself.

It has been said that Thomson's peril was exaggerated by the Chagga people of the foothills of Kilimanjaro, who hoped to relieve him of the trading goods intended for the Maasai. The Chagga were and are today an intelligent, ambitious tribe of Bantu-speaking cultivators who practiced irrigation in the rich highlands; like the Kikuyu, they were driven inland from the coast by northern invaders and they, too, are supposed to have displaced a small race of men with big bows and unintelligible speech, who were driven higher and higher on Mt Kilimanjaro and eventually vanished. Subsequently the Chagga were harassed by the Maasai and displaced by Europeans, yet later became the most powerful tribe in the country. Whether the Chagga and Kikuyu got control of the best land because they are intelligent and ambitious, or whether their intelligence and ambition is a consequence of favorable environment and good nutrition would make an interesting study.

At daybreak, through the tent fly, I could see giraffe heads swaying over the small rises around camp, like giant flowers shot up overnight; the bell note of a boubou shrike distills the windless morning. Giraffes gaze raptly, one ear flicking, before moving off in that elegant slow rhythm that is tuned to the old music of the elephants. Elephants, too, convene here in the night, and sometimes buffalo, chewing their cud as they contemplate man's habitations. Below the camp, the water trails of courting coot melt the surface of Momela, and beyond the lakes, in a realm of shadow, Kilimanjaro's base forms a pedestal for its high cumulus. Birds fly from this dark world into the sunlight of Momela – a quartet of crowned cranes, wild horn note calling from across the water, and ducks that hurry down the clouds – pintail, Cape widgeon, Hottentot teal. In rain, the lakes have the monotone alpine cast of mountain lakes across the high places of the world, but here the monotone is pierced by fierce rays of African color – a rainbow in a purple sky, an emilia blossom, tropic orange, or a carmine feather, drifted down from a diadem of birds crossing the heavens in the last shreds of sunset.

His people tell of a young Bushman who came upon a rock pool in the desert. Kneeling to drink, he saw reflected in the pool a red bird more brilliant than anything he had ever seen on earth. Determined to hold it in his hand, he sprang up with his bow, but there was no sign of the red bird in the sere desert sky. Wandering from place to place, inquiring after the vanished bird, he strayed farther and farther from his homeland. Days gathered into months and years, and in this way, without ever having found what he was seeking, he became old. He had hunted the land over, and talked to the few who might have glimpsed the bird as well as the many who had not, and still his heart could not give up the search. At last, on the point of turning home, he heard that the red bird had been seen from the peak of the north mountain, and he took up his bow and resumed his journey one more time. The mountain was far away across a desert, and when he reached the foothills the old hunter was mortally tired. With the end of his strength, he climbed and climbed into the sky, and on the peak he lay down upon his back, for he was dying. One last time he gazed into the distances, hoping to glimpse the splendid thing in the mountain sky. But the sky was empty, and he sighed and closed his eyes, wondering if his life had been in vain, and died with the sun upon his eyelids and a vision of the bird as he had seen it long ago, reflected in the bright pool of his childhood. And as he died, a feather of a burning red drifted down from the great sky, coming to rest in his still hand.[1]

Dark Meru is gaunt in a pearly sun that illumines the high shards of the blasted crater, and under the peaks the cotton clouds, filling with light, nudge and nestle like balloons in the corners of the dead volcano. Meru is the fifth highest mountain in all Africa, and may once have been highest of all. It is dormant, not extinct; it may have erupted as recently as 1879. An earlier explosion collapsed this eastern wall, and the glacier or crater lake cascaded down the mountain;

the walls, still crumbling, raise clouds of dust on windless days.

On the northeast flank of Meru lies a mountain wilderness still relatively unexplored called the Chaperro. I went there with Vesey and John Beasley, the warden of Ngurdoto, and two askaris of the Meru tribe, Serekieli and Frank. A certain *Podocarpus* species with a finer bark pattern than the more common species occurs on Kilimanjaro, and Vesey was anxious to find out if it was native to Mt Meru as well. *Podocarpus* belongs to a primitive group of conifers related to the yews and, with the East African cedar, forms forests of relict evergreens well over one hundred feet tall. These big trees, in East Africa, are now confined to Meru, Kilimanjaro, and Mt Kenya.

There is a track up into the crater that crosses the fallen crater wall, and one is able to drive a vehicle with four-wheel drive to eighty-four hundred feet, where the forest opens out into a black lava tumulus, with a true montane flora of such Palearctic forms as heath, barberry, crotalaria, bracken fern, and usnea. Under the peak called Little Meru, where elephants mount stolidly to heights of eleven thousand feet, the track works around the rim to the northern face. Here we would descend through the high forest. In the silver sun of the crater mists, a dusky flycatcher, silver gray and dun, on a limb tip silvered with orchid swords and lichen, was utterly in place. This was cloud forest, with violets and buttercups, clover and geranium, and the mossy tree limbs carried ferns and yellow star flowers of stonecrop. Wild coffee and wild orange filled the clouds with scent, and here and there, like giants in the mist, stood arborescent lily and lobelia. Although animals wander high onto the mountain – the eland, klipspringer, and mountain reedbuck occur commonly at twelve thousand feet – the only antelope we saw on the descent was a lone bushbuck, and the birds were scarce: a bar-tailed trogon, red and blue, poised a moment on a limb, and John Beasley picked out an evergreen forest warbler and a broad-ringed white-eye at the edge of a sunny clearing. Meanwhile, we searched in vain for the uncommon conifer.

The forest was opening into glades where the grass, cropped short, was littered with fresh buffalo dung. "They can't be far ahead of us," John Beasley said. Last year Beasley had two ribs broken by a buffalo that caught him as he swung into a tree; he escaped the horn tip but was struck by the heavy boss. The buffalo is said to be the most aggressive animal in Africa, much more dangerous than the rhino, since that beast will often thunder past its target and keep right on going until, at some point in its course, having met with no obstacle and having forgotten what excited it in the first place, it comes to a ponderous halt. The buffalo, on the other hand, turns quickly and is diligent in its pursuit. It is keen of nose and eye and ear, and like the lion, is very difficult to stop once it attacks, often persisting in the work of destruction for some time after the object of its rage or fear is dead.

It will even stalk a man, especially when wounded, coming around on its pursuer from behind, and last year near Momela a man was killed by a lurking buffalo in his own garden.

"*Mbogo!*"

Serekieli, in the lead, was calling back to us, and a buffalo skull as if in sign, lay in the grass, surrounded by fresh spoor. We stood and listened. Before making their move, buffalo may lie in wait until whatever approaches them has gone past. This is customarily ascribed to malevolence or low cunning, but dull wits and slow reaction time may be an alternative explanation. "If they're good-natured, you don't see them," Vesey said crossly. "If they're not, they rush out at you. Terrific nervous tension, I must say." At sixty-two, Vesey is strong and energetic, but feels himself at a disadvantage when it comes to nipping up trees.

Then the suspense got to the buffalo, and the hidden herd rushed away down the mountainside with a heavy cracking, and a long rumbling like a mountain torrent past big boulders. Immediately, another Meru voice called out, "*Kifaru!*" and Vesey mopped his brow. The Meru were pointing at a rhino print as fresh as a black petal, and within seconds a rhino crashed into the brush off to the east. The crash started up a buffalo lying low in the wild nightshade to our left. This lone animal was the one we were afraid of, and as it was much closer than the others, its explosion through the branches caused the wazungu to rush in all directions. Beasley sprinted past, bound for the same tree as myself, as the askari Serekieli, standing fast, fired his gun to turn the charge. The black blur whirled away, and the echo died.

On foot in Africa, one will have this experience sooner or later, and Thomson's encounter with a buffalo in this region could have described our own:

> Men were running on all sides as if the ground had yawned to swallow them up. Some were scrambling up trees, others, paralyzed, hid behind bushes, or any other object. Terror seemed to permeate the air with electric effect, and the short, quick cries of excited, panic-stricken men were heard on all sides. Almost paralyzed myself at this extraordinary but as yet unseen danger, I stood helpless till I was enlightened by one of my men screaming out to me in a warning voice, "Bwana, bwana, mboga!" (Master, a buffalo.) "Good gracious! Where?" I said, as I skipped with agility behind a tree, and peered cautiously past the side in the direction indicated – for be it known that there is not a more dangerous or dreaded animal in all Africa.[2]

The relative menace of what hunters know as "the big five" – elephant, rhino, buffalo, lion, and leopard – is a popular topic of discussion in East Africa. J. A. Hunter, for example, ranked the leopard first, then lion, buffalo, elephant, and rhino, in that order. C. P. J. Ionides also thought the leopard more dangerous than the lion. This prejudice in favor of the carnivores is the prejudice of hunters who have had to finish off wounded animals, and might not be shared, say, by a farmer or field zoologist, who is more likely to be attacked by a large herbivore. In Ionides' opinion, the most dangerous animal to an unarmed person in the bush is a tuskless elephant. Lion attacks are now quite rare, but in the days of widespread game slaughter for tsetse control, a number of lions in these devastated regions turned on man in desperation, and bags of fifty, sixty, and in one case ninety human beings were recorded.[3] For people like myself who lack experience, it is purely a subjective business. I fear all five of the big five with all my heart, but I have least fear of the rhino, perhaps because one may leap aside with a reasonable hope that the rhino will keep on going. Unlike the other beasts of the big five, the rhino, with its poor vision and small powers of deduction, is only anxious to dispel an unsupportable suspense, and is probably as frightened as its foe.

In the next thousand feet of the descent there were rhino wallows and buffalo sign on every side; one kept an eye out for hospitable trees even before an emergency had been declared. In a mahogany, Meru tribesmen had placed a beehive, essentially a hollowed cedar log with a removable bottom, hung from a limb by a wooden hook. (The Dorobo add to the hive's efficiency by hailing the bees in strange high-pitched tones: "Bees, bees, all you who are in this country, come now and make honey here!")[4] In the honey harvest, the bees' wits are thickened with a smoke flare; when the hive is lowered to the ground the addled bees collect where it had hung. Easing his nerves, Vesey hypothesized the converse of the bees:

"Where the bloody hell's the hive?!"

"Right here, you idiot – it's always here."

"Well, it bloody well *isn't*!"

By the time they get through discussing it, the hive is back in place:

"You see? Right there under your nose! Damned bloody fool!"

The great trees, fallen, have opened glades in a wild parkland, and silver deadwood is entwined by a climbing acanth with blossoms of light lavender. In stillness, in wind-shifted sun and shadow, a papilio butterfly, deep blue, is dancing with a Meru swallowtail, black and white, which ascends from the black and white remains of a colobus monkey, knocked from its tree by a leopard or an eagle ...

"*Kifaru!*"

At six thousand feet, in a mahogany grove, a rhino digging is so fresh that it seems to breathe; we hurry past. "I must say," Vesey huffs, "on leave in England, it's nice to walk about a bit and not have some bloody ungrateful beast rush out at you." Once Vesey was chased by an irate hippopotamus that took a colossal bite out of his Land Rover.

A shy lemon dove in a pepper tree . . . more spoor . . .

"*Kifaru!*"

At the crash, we scatter. Horn high, tail high, a rhino lumbers forth out of the undergrowth thirty yards away. The rhino is said to hoist its tail when wishing to depart, but no one appears confident that this is so. From behind my tree, too big to climb, I see Beasley on the limb of a wild coffee, with Vesey crouched below, as the rhino, trotting heavily across the glade, emits three horrible coughing snorts. The askari Frank is somewhere out of sight, but Serekieli stands bravely, legs apart, ready to fire. There is no need – the rhino goes, and keeps on going.

The Africans permit themselves a wild sweet laughter of relief, watching the whites come down out of the trees. Vesey, treed twice in half an hour, is not amused, not yet; he will be later.

"Get on! Get on!" he says, anxious to be off this bloody mountain.

I hoped to see the white-maned Kilimanjaro bush pig, and one afternoon I went down into Ngurdoto Crater with Serekieli, accompanied by a silent boy whom we met along the road; like many people on the paths of Africa, the boy had no appointments and no destination of his own.

Ngurdoto, like the famous Ngorongoro, is extinct, and both have the graduated bowl known as a caldera, which is formed when the molten core of a volcano subsides into the earth and the steep crater sides fall inward. Ngorongoro was unknown to the outside world until 1892, and not until early in this century did the white man find this smaller caldera to the east of Meru. Ngurdoto is larger than it appears – seen from the west rim, the farthest animals on the crater floor are two miles away – but the distance seems more temporal than spatial. Unlike Ngorongoro, there are no tracks or paths inside the crater, and as one peers down from the rim at remote creatures grazing in peace, oblivious of man, there rises from this hidden world that stillness of the early morning before man was born.

An elephant path of pressed humus and round leather-polished stones wound down among the boles of the gallery forest. The sun was high and the birds still, the forest dark and cool. Under the steep rim, out of the reach of axes, rose the great African mahogany and the elegant tropical olive, loliondo. We descended through the forest single file. The steep path leveled out into grassy glades which, being ponds in time of rain, are mostly round. We followed them eastward, under the crater rim, working our way out of the trees. Serekieli, in forest green, carried a shotgun. Like many people come lately to boots, Serekieli tends to clump, but he clumps quietly and is very surefooted; he is a lean handsome man of sad eyes and enchanted smile. Every little while he stopped to listen, giving the animals time to move away. Baboon and wart hog stared, then ran, the hominoids barking and shrieking as they scampered, the wild pigs departing the field in a stiff trot. Moments later we stood exposed in a bowl of sunlight.

Buffalo and a solitary rhino took mute note of us; the world stood still. Flat wet dung raised its reassuring smell in halos of loud flies. We turned west across wild pasture – cropped turf, cabbage butterflies, and cloven prints filled with clear rain – that rings the sedge swamp in the pit of the caldera. A hawk rose on thermals from the crater floor, and white egrets crossed the dark walls; in the marsh, a golden sedge was seeding in the swelling light of afternoon. More buffalo lay along the wood edge at the western wall, and with them rhino and an elephant. The rhinos lay still, but the elephant, a mile away, blared in alarm, and others answered from the galleries of trees, the screams echoing around the crater; the elephant's ears flared wide and closed as it passed with saintly tread into the forest. Bushbuck and waterbuck lifted carved heads to watch man's coming; their tails switched and their hind legs stamped but they did not run. Perhaps the white-maned bush pig saw us, too, raising red eyes from the snuffled dirt and scratching its raspy hide with a sharp hoof. Another time I glimpsed it from the rim at twilight, a ring of white in the dim trees, and one night a year later, descending the mountain, my headlights penned a family band, striped piglets and all, between the high sides of the road, but today it remained hidden.

The buffalo rose and split into two companies, and twelve hundred hoofs thundered at once under the walls. The thunder set off an insane screeching of baboons that spread the length and breadth of Ngurdoto, and a blue monkey dropped from a lone tree in the savanna and scampered to the forest. Some of the milling buffalo plunged off into the wood, but others turned and came straight at us, the sunlight spinning on their horns. Buffalo have good eyesight, and we expected these to veer, but a hundred yards away, they were still coming, rocking heavily across the meadow. We turned and ran. Confused by our flight, they wheeled about and fled after the rest into the thickets. There came a terrific crack and crashing, as if their companions had turned back and the two groups had collided. In the stunned silence, we headed once more for the western wall, but were scarcely in the clear when the rumbling increased again, and the wood edge quaked, swayed, and split wide as the tide of buffalo broke free onto the plain and scattered in all directions.

The hawk, clearing the crater rim, was burnt black by the western sun. From the forest, the hollow laugh of the blue monkey was answered by the froggish racketing of a turaco. Parting leaves with long shy fingers, Serekieli probed for sign of an animal trail that might climb to the western rim. We pushed through heavy growth of sage and psidia, stopping each moment to listen hard, then clap our hands. More than an hour was required to climb out of the heat and thicket to the gallery forest under the crater rim, and all the while the elephants were near, in enormous silence.

The leaves hung still. Bright on the dark humus lay a fiery fruit, white bird droppings, the blood-red feather of a turaco. When, near at hand, an elephant blared, the threat ricocheted around the walls, counterpointed by weird echoes of baboons. Serekieli offered an innocent smile and moved quietly ahead. In another hour we were on the rim, and rested on cool beds of a pink balsam. The wood smell was infused with scents of the wild orange and wild pepper trees, and of *Tabernae montana*, a white-flowered relative of frangipani. Where the western sun illumined the high leaves, a company of colobus and blue monkeys, silhouetted, leapt into the sky, careening down onto the canopy of the crater's outer wall. Somewhere elephants were moving. It was near evening, and in every part the forest creaked with life.

On certain rare mornings at Momela, Mt Kilimanjaro rises high and clear out of clouds that dissolve around it. From the north, in Kenya, it looks celestial, benign; from Momela, it is dark and looming. Such massifs as the Ruwenzoris on the Congo–Uganda border and the High Semien of Ethiopia lack the splendor of Kilimanjaro and Mt Kenya, which stand all alone: at 19,340 feet, Kilimanjaro is the highest solitary mountain in the world. Mt Kenya is a shard of rock thrust upward from the earth, but Kilima Njaro, the White Mountain, has ascended into the sky, a place of religious resonance for tribes all around its horizons.

The glacier glistens. A distant snow peak scours the mind, but a snow peak in the tropics draws the heart to a fine shimmering painful point of joy.

Kilimanjaro is the easternmost of the Great Caldron Mountains, which were born fifteen to twenty million years ago, in the early Pleistocene, when widespread eruptions and tectonic movements buried the ancient rock of Africa beneath volcanoes, volcanic highlands, and the lava plains of what is now Maasai Land. The cones extend east and west from Kilimanjaro to the Crater Highlands, and from Shombole, just north of the Kenya border, south to Mt Hanang. The last active volcano in the Great Caldron Mountains is Ol Doinyo Lengai, which stands by itself between the Crater Highlands and Lake Natron. One travels there by way of Mto Wa Mbu (Mosquito River), a raffish settlement on the dusty road to Lake Manyara and Ngorongoro. From Mto Wa Mbu a dirt track turns off along that part of the Rift wall formed by the Crater Highlands, arriving eventually at the village of Engaruka, thirty-five miles north; from there, it was said, a Maasai cattle path wound around the ramparts of the Highlands to Lengai.

The track to Engaruka, impassable in rain, parts the high grasses of the plain, branching and regathering according to the whims of its rare travelers, and tending always far out to the eastward, to skirt the gullies that snake down from the ravines in the Rift wall. Turning west again toward the mountains, the track arrives at the rim of Ol Kerii, where the land falls a last few hundred feet to the floor of the Rift Valley. In East Africa, one is never far from the Great Rift, which splits the earth's crust from the Dead Sea south to the Zambezi River, and east and west in broken cracks from the Gulf of Aden to the Valley of the Congo. In places, the Rift is forty miles across, a trench of sun and tawny heat walled by plateaus. The floors that contain the Rift's long, narrow north–south lakes were created long ago when the earth sank between parallel fractures, and they are on different levels: Manyara is eleven hundred feet higher than Lake Natron, to the north.

Ol Kerii, the last great step in the descent into the Rift, has a prospect of lost mountains: Kerimasi, at the northeast corner of the Crater Highlands, and Kitumbeine, a shadow in the ancient haze beyond, and Gelai, due north, that guards the lonely sea of Natron. In every distance stand strange shrouded landscapes of the past and future. The present is wild blowing light, the sun, a bird, a baobab in heraldic isolation, like the tree where man was born.

The track descends to the riverain forests and slow swamps of the Engaruka Basin, steeping – no sign of man, no smoke nor habitation, only two giraffes still as killed trees far out in the savanna – and the sense of entering a new world is quickened by new birds. For the first time I behold the bright, marvelous mechanisms known to man as the rosy-patched shrike, white-throated bee-eater, and Fischer's widowbird, named in honor of Thomson's rival, the German naturalist Gustav Fischer, who in 1882 discovered strange ruins at Engaruka in the course of an attempt to cross Maasai Land. But his good name only encumbers the effect of this airy thing that can draw a landscape taut with its plumed tail.

Down the track comes a loud party of Fischer's countrymen, staring bald-eyed from the windows of a white hunter's vehicle – here was one reason why game had been so scarce along the way. And seeing these tourists trundled forth to blaze away at the very last concentration of great animals left on earth, imagining the pollution of their din, the smoke and blood and shocked silence of the plain, and the wake of rotting carcasses, I stared back at them as rudely, filled with rage. Such sport made it all the harder to wean Africans away from contempt for wildlife, which is a matter of education and not culture: the British and South African soldiers stationed at Marsabit during World War II left thousands of animals to rot that had been idly shot down with automatic weapons from the backs of trucks.[5]

The gorges in the west Rift wall are the shadows of dead rivers that in the pluvials came rushing from the highlands, forming a lake in what is now the Engaruka Basin. For centuries, the surviving stream, thought to come from Embagai Crater in the clouds above, has attracted man to Engaruka, which is a settlement of agricultural Maasai (now known as the Arusa) as well as some Sukuma Bantu from the south. Earlier it was inhabited by people skilled in irrigation who left behind an extensive ruin of stone circles, cairns, and walled terracing for cultivation, as well as a dam one hundred feet long; the terracing on the hills above is visible from the track. The remains of another dam lie near the Ngorongoro–Olbalbal road, and some terracing near the north end of Lake Eyasi, but there is no other ruined city.

Engaruka is scarcely touched by archeologists, and its origins are presently unknown. It lies far off the traditional trading routes, an isolated stone-working community of an estimated thirty to forty thousand souls, the largest such ruin in central and south Africa except Zimbabwe in Rhodesia. Zimbabwe was constructed over centuries, beginning no later than the twelfth century and lasting until 1834, when it was overrun by tribes of Zulu, but according to preliminary investigations,[6] Engaruka may be less than three centuries old. If this is true, who were the people who constructed it, and what became of them?

The Maasai say that Engaruka was occupied by an Irakw people when they descended on this region in the eighteenth century. The Irakw tribes, which include the pit-dwelling Mbulu cultivators of the plateaus behind Lake Manyara, are that obscure group with a strange archaic language that has been tentatively[7] related to those Proto-Hamite hunters who were the first to invade East Africa from the north. Or perhaps the Engaruka masons, Irakw or otherwise, derive from the Neolithic Hamites who brought domestic plants and animals into the country and were scattered in the arable highlands of East Africa until a few centuries ago, when they appear to have been surrounded and absorbed by the waves of Negroids, Nilote as well as Bantu, who came after. In Kenya's Kerio Valley, for example, the Maraket people of the Nandi tribes still maintain elaborate irrigation systems, including conduits woven across the steep faces of cliffs, which they say were made by a northern people of strange language, the Sirikwa, who later died in plague: "They built the furrows, but they did not teach us how to build them; we only know how to keep them as they are."[8] (The similar sound of "Sirikwa" and "Irakw" is interesting, considering the obscure history of both groups.)

There is more than a trace of a vanished race in the Bantu-speaking Sonjo, who still practice stone terracing and irrigation only sixty miles away to the northwest, above Lake Natron, and build fortified palisades around their villages that are found nowhere else south of western Ethiopia, where the Neolithic Hamites are thought to have emerged. One recalls that such non-Bantu peoples as the Hima and Tusi herdsmen of Uganda and Ruanda-Urundi have adopted the Bantu tongue, and the name Sonjo brings to mind the "Enjoe", as the Kikuyu called that vanished northern people, known to the Dorobo as the Mokwan, who built stone "hut circles" on the Uasin Gishu Plateau, and were said to have been scattered by the Maasai. These "hut circles", often mere depressions, may have served also as bomas for the long-horned cattle,[9] and are known as "Sirikwa holes": perhaps the Mokwan, Enjoe, and Sirikwa are all one.[10] Present-day Sonjo stone construction cannot compare with the clean unmortared work at Engaruka, but this people have a legend of a lost city known as Belwa, and inevitably one wonders if the light-skinned Sonjo – they are even lighter than the "Nilo-Hamitic" Maasai – retreated to their remote escarpment after the fall of Engaruka.

Tribal traditions being unreliable, one cannot trust the memory of the Maasai, nor count on Belwa, but it is fine, unscientific fun to try to match the pieces of all the traditions in this region of archaic peoples, which are generally supported by the Somali belief that the stonework in the Crater Highlands region is the work of those early engineers who carved the deep wells at Wajir and Marsabit, in the Northern Frontier Province of Kenya – a race of giants, so they say, that came out of Arabia two thousand years ago, and were the ancestors of the tall Tusi. If Engaruka is more than a few centuries old, it may have been an inland settlement that like Zimbabwe traded with the coast. If so, what brought it to an end? Were the Engaruka builders the fierce *il Adoru* of the Maasai tradition of settlement of this region? Or did the end come before the appearance of the Maasai? According to chronicles of the Portuguese, the coastal town of Kilwa was destroyed in 1589, and three thousand of its four thousand inhabitants devoured by marauding hordes of cannibals known as the Zimba. The Zimba, who also sacked Mombasa and were finally routed at Malindi, are another mystery, since the modern Zimba are a Bantu tribe of the savannas of the lower Zambezi among whom cannibalism is not known (though they are related to cannibalistic Bantu of the central forests).[11] No one can say where the historic Zimba came from, nor what caused their locust-like advance, nor where they subsided once their rage was spent, but possibly they brought an end to Engaruka.

Engaruka today is a shady village of irrigation ditches, banana shambas, dogs and chickens, and here the last traces of good track were left behind. The cars wound down along the river, then headed off into dense thicket. The cattle track diminished in the sun and dust, and for miles the cars forced a way through tough acacia scrub with a fierce shriek of thorn on metal. Then footpath became cattle trail again, tending away from the highlands as before, and emerging eventually in a stony plain that extends to the foot of Kitumbeine. Off to the west, the rainy greens of Kerimasi loomed and passed, and then the gray cone of Lengai came into view, drifting out from behind the Crater Highlands like a moon.

In the distance were the hard white spots that in African landscapes signify far herds of cattle, but here the livestock and wild animals were still in balance, as once they were throughout Maasai Land. Everywhere along the track trailed zebra, gazelle, and wildebeest, with a few eland; outside the parks and their environs I had never seen plains game so common since leaving the Sudan nine years before. The plain was inset with fleeting pools, and a hoof-pocked track wandered from water to water. In a land so hard and flat, the pools had no more depth than mirrors, refracting the changing weathers in the sky, and but for the trees and the tramped margins, the water would have seemed a trick of light that would fade as the sun turned. Water lines of teal and dabchick cracked the mirror, and the long-stemmed silhouettes of wading birds stood still. The edges teemed with sandpipers, feeding avidly before night fell; at dark, under the moon, these Palearctic migrants would cross the equator into the Northern Hemisphere, and tomorrow might find them on Lake Rudolf or the Nile. Marabous, sitting back upon their hinges, digested some unspeakable repast, and in the new grass all around, the prosperous insects had drawn down upon their heads great companies of European storks; the tall white birds stood solemnly on every side. Storks are birds of holocaust – they dance in the heat shimmer of fires, peering down among the sparks for fleeing lizards, grass-mice, snakes – and at one time, they attended locust plagues. Now the locusts can be kept under control except in those unstable regions where man has lost control over himself.[12]

At noon two days later, the stork companies rose motionless on the thermals, curling like smoke in tight flocks of many hundreds, higher and higher over Kerimasi and the Crater Highlands, until the flocks were wisps against the clouds. At the crest of a mile-high column of white birds, they set their course, blown down the sky toward the hard blue of the north horizon. The shorebirds were already gone, and of the native water birds, a solitary grebe remained. On the black margins milled thousands of small zebu cattle, mixed with a few giant horned Ankoles and the gaunt twist-horn kine of archaic kingdoms, all of these crowded by low pushing dung-stuck troops of sheep and goat. At the edge of the dust, in earthen robes, the herdsmen leaned upon their spears, faces in shadow. Swallows coursed the dusty herds snatching hot insects, and the noon air danced with the drum of hoofs, wails, whistles, whoops, and tink of bells, bone clicks, bleating, and yelled laughter.

By the water's edge man squatted, worn rags pulled low over his brow against the sun. Manure smell, flies, the stamp and lowing of the herds, the heat. In the shallows a naked dancing boy darted and splashed. Then cloud shadow dimmed the water shine on his round head, and he turned black. In foreboding he paused; the water stilled, and clouds gathered in the water. He picked at his thin body, one-legged in the evanescent pool that will vanish in summer like the haze of green on this burning land.

*   *   *

Grasslands. Eland, swallows, clouds, and wind. A lone Maasai, stalking across the foothills of Kerimasi like a prophet, staff raised, red robe blowing.

The vehicles forsake the track and cut due west across the slopes toward Lengai. These foothills are mostly parasitic cones of the volcanoes; the cones are grassy, with neat craters. Other craters are inset in the level ground, as if the earth had fallen in, and swallows circle around the rim under the blowing grass.

Two tall Maasai rise from the grass, casting wild smiles and their few scraps of Swahili: "*Jambo! Haban gani?*" (What sort of news?) They point toward the volcano, their clubs or rungus like extensions of long bony arms: "*Kilima cha Mungu!*" they cry. Mountain of God! I shake my head and name the mountain in Maasai: "Ol Doinyo Lengai!" And they smile and wave: "Ngai! Ngai!" In Tanzania, in 1968, the wild herdsmen were ordered to give up their airy shukas and wear pants, but the Maasai pay small attention to such laws; far from the roads, they stand exposed, like the wild people of the Sudan. Their cloth is clean and their beads bright, their ornaments of wrought copper and tin are of a quality not found in the curio shops of Arusha and Nairobi, and the holes in their ear lobes, pierced by the hard thorn of the desert date, are stretched by wooden ear plugs that, nearer the roads, are being replaced by aluminum film canisters dropped by the tourists (in a Maasai village between Makindu and Amboseli, I once found some discarded wooden plugs, silken-smooth with years of human grease). At Mto Wa Mbu, Ngorongoro, Namanga, and Narok the Maasai loiterers are much given to begging and jeering outside the Asian dukas, where they squat on their heels in vulture-like congregations and try half-heartedly to hawk to the tourists old beads and spears and milk gourds and rungus and the short double-edged simis in red scabbards. Such tribesmen bear small resemblance to the people so admired by Thomson, and in fact the suppression of their ways led very quickly to the decline of the Maasai, whose fate much resembles that of the Plains Indians of North America. A government report of 1939, hardly a half-century after Thomson saw them first, notes a decline in birth rate and a high incidence of sterility and venereal disease, as well as pervasive alcoholism, license, and general apathy. Efforts to enlist Maasai in the police or King's African Rifles were mostly a failure, and even the few who became educated often returned afterwards to the life of the grasslands, unable to put aside that fierce pride and independence that caused them to reject white settler and missionary alike. Also, in their effort to regain stability after years of plague, famine, and disruption, they clung all the more tenaciously to their old ways. "Mentally impervious to new ideas, and incapable of adapting to new conditions," they were now adjudged inferior in all respects to the peoples they had formerly ruled. But once again, like the Indians of North America, they were measured by western standards – the downfall of the Maasai had been pride, not inferiority, which was the bureaucratic way of accounting for a wild people's disdain for western values. At the same time Maasai aloofness was much romanticized and admired, since unlike the abominable Bantu, and the Kikuyu especially, who dared to resent the usurpation of their lands and were forever underfoot, the tribe kept itself out of the path of progress. "It has often been proved in other parts of the globe that the native, in the advent of the white man, alters his habits or ceases to exist, and it is to be hoped that the Maasai will choose the first of these alternatives," an observer wrote, as early as 1904.[13] The Maasai, having no choice, altered his habits, but in a spiritual sense, he has ceased to exist as well.

The plateau declines toward the pale misty vat of Natron. Around the inland sea, thirty-five miles long, rise lonely mountains: the volcano called Gelai, on the eastern shore, the dark Rift to the west, and at the northern end, in Kenya, Shombole and the Nguruman Escarpment in an horizon of half-mountain and half-cloud, and over all the Mountain of God, presiding.

It is nearly sunset, and Lengai still far away. Seasonal stream beds and ravines that carry the rain off Kerimasi trench the foothills, and time is lost scouring each gully for a place to cross. Already the motors are too hot and finally it is dark; we make camp under the highland walls, hopefully within walking distance of the great black cone that surrounds itself with stars. Two tents are pitched on the grassy slope, and a fire made. Once this is done, we have a glass of rum. Altogether we are six: besides myself, Vesey-FitzGerald and his friend George Reed and a wildlife photographer and mountaineer named Brian Hawkes, and the cook Chilufia, and the Meru ranger Frank who was with us last year on the Chaperro. Vesey is furious with Chilufia and Frank, who have brought along their water bottles as instructed – they hold them up in proof – but have neglected to put water in them. "You're a pair of idiots, do you understand that? I told you so last safari and now I'm telling you again and I expect I'll have to tell you next time, too – you're a pair of idiots!" Vesey manages to laugh before he finishes, and so do the Africans, but all know that this is not a laughing matter, since there is no good water to be found between here and Engaruka, twenty-five hard miles back. Yet two days later, when water is low, Frank fills his bottle from the jerry can in my Rover, then replaces the cap so carelessly that half of our remaining drinking water leaks away.

It is often said that Africans cannot lay straight paths or plow straight furrows, screw bottle caps, use rifle sights – in short, that they have no sense of geometric order, much less time, since there is nothing of this sort in nature to instruct them. "Have to watch these chaps every minute," white East Africans will tell you. "Can't do the first thing for themselves." But perhaps the proper word is "won't". Most Africans are so accustomed to having decisions made for them by whites, and to carrying out instructions to the letter to avoid abuse, that only rarely do they think out what they are doing, much less take initiative. Rather, they move dully through dull menial tasks – working automatically, without thought, may be all that makes such labor bearable – preferring to be thought stupid than to get in trouble, and at the same time gleeful when calamities occur. Stubborn, apathetic, and perverse, they observe the letter of their instructions, not the spirit of them (Bring your water bottles!). They are not responsible for filling the bottles unless told to do so; if the whites will treat them as children, they will act that way.

Chilufia's heart is still in Zambia, and no doubt his mind as well, but I am puzzled by Frank, who is young, ambitious, and alert. Chilufia seems indifferent to being called an idiot; such words are to be shrugged off, like rain. *Shauri ya Mungu*, he might say – this is the affair of God. But Frank dislikes it; he smiles a strange bad smile as if warning me to understand. One difference between Frank and Chilufia is the name Frank – his real name is Kessi.

Frank is anxious to communicate, though he speaks my language poorly, and I scarcely speak his at all. When Vesey isn't listening he uses my first name. The friendliness is genuine, but there is a hair of aggression in it; he scans my eyes for disapproval or rejection. Knowing this and pained by it, I respond enthusiastically, but soon we are overtaken by silence. We cannot communicate after all. Even if we could, we have little to offer but good will and our humanity. Even among white East Africans and black who converse easily in English or Swahili, the problem appears to be mutual boredom, which comes about because both find the interests of the other trivial, and their ideas therefore of small consequence.

The volcano filled the night like a great bell. Over Shombole and the Loita there was lightning, vast silent illuminations that hollowed out the heavy clouds until they glowed like fire seen through smoke. This night and the next, the lightning came every few moments, but the thunder was too distant to be heard. I listened to a solitary nightjar, fixed in the rigidity of its shrill song that under Lengai was a part of the moon silence.

With Hawkes at daybreak I set off toward the mountain. Each carried a small knapsack of tea and water, nuts and raisins, notebook and binoculars; Hawkes had a camera. Lengai was clear of clouds, and the distance to the lava fan seemed perhaps six miles. But in the bad light of the night before, we had made camp on the wrong side of a grid of steep ridges, and between the ridges lay steep bush-choked dongas. For the first two hours of the trek, we slid and clambered up and down and up and down, opposed by hidden rocks and head-high grasses. I did not expect trouble with animals, and we had none, but leopard pug marks in the sand bed of a donga were a reminder that we could not forget about them either; the giant grass that was such hard work could hide a rhino.

At eight, already hot and tired, we stopped on the crest of a ridge and stared bleakly about us. At this rate, two more hours would pass before we reached the mountain, and at least five would be required for the climb. Allowing three hours for the descent and none at all for rest or exploration, we would still face a four-hour return across these badlands after dark. Also, Lengai was gathering its clouds, which would make the climb more difficult. But we had worked too hard to give up now; the going could get easier at any moment, and from the mountainside we might perceive a better route back to the camp. Or so we persuaded each other, trudging on like pilgrims toward the magic mountain. And almost immediately we struck a Maasai cattle track over the ridges to the river of black sand that winds around the base of the volcano. From the black river, the lava plain climbed rapidly to the ridges of Lengai.

Ahead, a dark gorge cleaved the face of the volcano. The ridge that forms the west side of the gorge faces south toward the Highlands, and its lower slope, still visible beneath the clouds on the summit, looked less precipitous than the rest. We walked up the black river bed, then climbed the far bank and traversed the ash plain. Here a zebra had once wandered; into one ghostly print the wind had blown the copper shell of a large beetle. Higher still, the beetle husks were everywhere, glinting in the wind waves of the surface. The fire and ash of its last eruption, in 1967, buried Lengai in a gray lunar snow, all but these withered tips of wind-twitched grass. At the ravine edge stood the husk of a whistling-thorn on which the galls have turned to wood, yet ants inhabited the galls, subsisting, perhaps, on the dead beetles that blow across the wastes; in greener times, these ants protected the new tips of the acacia against browsers such as the giraffe. A stray lizard track excepted, the ants are the one sign of terrestrial life. Footsteps resound, for the Mountain of God is hollow; there is no sense of the present here, only the past.

In the spring of 1969, on a flight from Nairobi to Manyara, and again in the winter of 1970, coming from Seronera to Arusha, I got the pilots to circle the volcano. Buffeted by downdrafts, dodging clouds, the light planes came in over the deep furrows of the flanks and made tight circles over the sickening vat. In its brimstone smokes, dead grays, sulfurous yellows, there was no hint of green, no sign of life.

The slope had steepened. We dropped our packs beside the dead acacia, and standing there, leaning back into the hill, I became aware of butterflies and birds. The first butterfly was as orange as the sun, and the wind hurried it from east to west across the falling desert, its fire so intensified by the flat light that it was still visible where it rounded the mountain and spun away northwest toward Lake Natron. The birds were birds of high rock places – swifts, crag martins, the white

Egyptian vulture – riding the drafts and currents. Then a lark came strangely near before bounding down across the deserts. On the wind this morning I had heard an elusive lark song; perhaps this solitary bird had been the singer.

I put a few nuts and raisins in my pocket and took a sip of water. The desert air of the volcano was so dry that one handled the water with the kind of reverence that the Bushman must feel for the water that he stores in ostrich eggs. Then we were off again. I concentrated on slow steady steps, a steady breath, at pains not to look down. On the narrowing ridge, there were no rocks, no sticks, no handholds of any kind, only the slick surface of the ash; it was dusty but hard, and my light boots could find no grip. Hawkes, who had climbing boots, was doing better, but he was not optimistic. Before the eruption, according to its few veterans, the conquest of Lengai had been arduous but not difficult; now, Hawkes felt, this route, at least, was a job for a four-man team with ropes and ice-axes. On our right hand, the ridge dropped sheer into the black ravine; to the left, one would roll and bounce all the way to the black river for want of something to catch hold of. I stared rigorously upward, where the white vulture, stiff-winged as a kite, was suddenly sucked up into the mists.

We neared the clouds. Far below, small tornadoes or dust devils whipped ash into the air, and the wind blew it in sheets of smoke across the slopes. The mists descended, and a gathering wind nagged at the nerves; Hawkes called down that the going was getting worse. It was late morning, with the steepest rock of the volcano summit still to go, and already I was reduced to hands and knees. Again and again, my shoes lost their grip, making me throw myself belly down to avoid slipping backward and gathering speed for the ultimate descent; so steep was it where I lay flung against the mountainside that I seemed virtually upright. Breathless, heart pounding, I listened to the fate of the small debris cast loose by my desperate scrabbling – a scaling hiss, a silence, and finally from the depths of the ravine a horrid muttering, quite indescribable, the only sound I ever heard upon Lengai. And having heard it a few times, I rolled over on my back to get my breath, and drank a little water, and when I was rested, I quit.

I lay there wind-burned, scaled with sterile dust, my flask clutched in a brown hand that in this light had the fierce sinew of a talon. And my decision was the right one, for no sooner had I made it than the clouds were parted by a brilliant sun. The sun relaxed my body, and in its warmth I felt myself open outward in immense wellbeing, as if a red feather had drifted down into my hand. I lay there languid with relief, enjoying the warm wind and the touch of hair that was straying on my brow, the pure rock water from a cool spring at Manyara, the sun on my hot skin, the feel of breathing, all intensified by the wild beauty of the world. From my seat on the Mountain of God, I ruled Embagai and the green shifting shadows of the

Crater Highlands, climbing away into black clouds like a mythical kingdom. The clouds guarded old volcanoes, Jaeger Summit and Loolmalassin, whose peaks I had never seen. Broad-backed, motionless on the wind, an eagle descended the black river that isolates Lengai from the Highlands. Seen from above, a bird of prey, intent on all beneath, is the very messenger of silence.

A series of small mounds, like stepping stones, emerged from the smooth surface of the ash; half-blind with effort on the climb, I had scarcely noticed them. The mounds formed a distinct line down the crest of the ridge, like rhinoceros prints elevated above the surface, and as it happens this was what they were. Apparently a rhino high up on the mountain had tried to flee the last eruptions – perhaps in vain, since its tracks vanish near the edge of the ravine. There was no sign of a trail leading upward, only down. Its tread had compacted the hot ash, and afterwards the mountain winds had worn away the uncompacted ash all around, until the prints had risen above the surface.

Holding a hoofprint in my hands, I raised my eyes to where that horned lump, as if spat up by the volcano, had taken form in the poisonous clouds and rushed down the fiery ridge. What had drawn it up into the mists? Had it been blind, like the buffalo found in the snow high on Mt Kenya? Imagine the sight of that dark thing in the smoke of the volcano; had an African seen it, the rhino might have become a beast of legend, like the hyena, for it is in such dreamlike events that myths are born.

Anxious to transfix so great a mystery, I chipped two prints clean of packed ash and wedged them into my pack. We descended the volcano, crossed the ash plains, circled dust storms. For four hours on sore feet, I carried the stone prints, but they belonged to the dead mountain, for in the journey they returned to dust.

9 Red God

Epwo m-baa pokin in-gitin'got
Everything has an end.
Maasai saying[1]

One bright day of August I went south from Nairobi on the road that crosses the Ngong Hills and descends through ever drier country, passing the site of hand-ax man at Olorgesaille, and winding down out of the hills to the magadi or soda lakes in the pit of the Rift Valley. Lake Magadi itself is a blinding white, a snow field in the desert, but close at hand, under the stacks and litter of the soda factory, the white is somber, crusted and discolored by strange chemistries. Here a road crosses the soda lake on a narrow dike. Some thirty miles west of Magadi, beyond the Uaso Nyiro River that flows south into Lake Natron, a track turns south through long-grass thorn savanna under the Nguruman Escarpment, curving north again as it climbs onto the plateau.

In Magadi I had been joined by Lewis Hurxthal, a young biologist studying the ostrich, and his beautiful wife Nancy, an artist and designer in charge of educational material put out by the African Wildlife Leadership Foundation in Nairobi. The Hurxthals live on the edge of the Aathi Plain where his favorite birds stalk by, and it was Lew who first instructed me in the esoterica of the cock ostrich, which is unique among birds in the possession of a penis. At this time of year, the cock ostrich flushes red and tumescent in the neck and legs, and both sexes writhe and flounce and run. Careening about, they shuffle their fat wings on their backs like maids tying up apron strings while rushing to answer a bell. Once Lew interrupted a discussion of *querencia*, that territory in the bullring where the bull feels safe, acts defensively, and is therefore dangerous: "*Ostriches*" – and he emphasized the word in a soft reproachful tone, as if his great birds had been slighted – "have charisma, too."

We made camp under big sycamore figs where a clear stream coming down off the Ngurumans flows over shining stones. There are few clear streams in East Africa, and we enjoyed a cool bath in its current, which washed away the danger of bilharzia. Squalls of finches – fire finches, mannikins, cutthroats, rufous-backs, queleas, cordon bleus, grayheaded social weavers, all intermixed like autumn leaves – blew in and out of a bare acacia, descending in gusts to the water's edge and whirring away again, oblivious of the human presence just across the stream. The quelea, or Sudan dioch, is known also as the plague finch, since it sometimes appears in clouds that descend like blowing smoke upon the crops, in a way of locusts. Toward evening some Maasai came down to bathe. These men were descendants of those who fled to Ngurumani, "the farms", after the disastrous civil wars of the nineteenth century; their losses made worse by cattle famine in the wake of a locust plague, they were forced to till the soil or die. Today they are found mostly in the Nguruman region, at Engaruka, and under Mt Meru, where they are called "Warusa". In dress and customs, the agriculturalists still emulate the pastoral clans, and these arranged themselves in the middle of camp activities, so that everything might take place around their legs. "Nowhere have I met such pleasing and manly natives over the whole extent of country I have yet traversed in Africa," wrote Joseph Thomson of this people.

A pleasing and manly native, Legaturi, came along next day on an expedition up the rough track that climbs onto the higher steps of the Ngurumans, from where one has a mighty prospect of the broad green swamps of the lower Uaso Nyiro, the volcano of Shombole, and Lake Natron. Farther on, the track loses itself in tsetse bush, and the going got so rough that Nancy, who was four months pregnant, soon felt sick. While Lew tended to her beneath a tree, I went on with Legaturi up the track, which ended eventually at a safari camp set up by Philip Leakey. Beyond, the Nguruman Escarpment mounted northwestward into the wilderness of the Loita Hills.

Feeling uneasy about the Hurxthals, I turned around immediately and started back. In the hot gray day the tsetses were biting without stint; the mute oval shapes made by their overlapping wings speckled the inside of my windshield, and one smooth brute with bristled eyes lit confidingly upon my arm. Despite the thick heat I put on a shirt – Legaturi was swathed like a mummy in his red toga – though I would have been better off had the shirt been white: tsetses prefer dark animals to light, and apparently abhor the zebra, whose stripes appear to disconcert their dim perceptions.

That dipterid biting flies of the genus *Glossina* were vectors of the trypanosomes that caused nagana in cattle and sleeping sickness in man was discovered in Uganda in 1905, and two years later human beings were evacuated from Murchison Falls and many other regions, including the shores of Lake Victoria, where two hundred thousand people – two-thirds of the regional population – had been wiped out in a great epidemic. To this day, the tsetse fly, which also infests much of Kenya and the greater part of Tanzania, remains unrivaled as an impediment to human progress in East Africa. Yet there is reason to believe[2] that "fly", by eliminating susceptible animals, opened up an ecological niche for ground-dwelling primates and thereby permitted the debut of baboons and man; quite possibly it also discouraged early forms of man that had as much promise as *Homo sapiens* and very likely more. Tsetse has determined man's migration routes and settlements, and defended the interior from invasions from the coast; in regions like western Maasai Land in Kenya, where elimination of tsetse has attracted settlers of the politically powerful Luo and Kikuyu, or in Ruanda-Urundi, where the overthrow of the tall Tusi herdsmen by their Bantu serfs has permitted great areas of grassland to revert to tsetse bush, the fly still nags at the course of Africa.

I returned within the hour to the tree, where Hurxthal rose and came solemnly to meet me. Nancy, eyes wide in a face the color of magadi, was having cramps and feared she might be in labor. We were seven miles beyond our camp, and twenty miles from the Uaso Nyiro game post, which might or might not have a radio that worked; from there it was thirty miles more into Magadi. The first seven miles would be the worst, but all of this track was an ordeal for a girl who might be losing her first child. To calm her and rest her for the journey, it seemed best to make camp where we were. Lew worked unceasingly to soothe his wife and make her comfortable against the heat. Although she kept her head throughout, she was badly frightened, and with damned good reason, or so it seemed to me. Privately, I had lost hope for the child, and there was a period in the first few hours of that endless afternoon when I was very worried about Nancy, who never left the sickbed that we constructed in the back of the Land Rover. I racked my brain to make certain we understood what we would do and in what order in a crisis, at the same time marveling at our heedlessness in taking a pregnant girl so far from help. Most of all, I dreaded that my battered Land Rover would break down beyond repair at a crucial moment. In this gloomy hollow of sere thornbush the gray rainless sky of African summer seemed to weigh upon the earth, I remembered the words of a girl born here in Tanzania "Africa overwhelms me so, especially at twilight, that sometimes I burst into tears."

There is no wealth without children, Africans say, and children are especially precious to the Maasai. "The Kikuyu themselves told me how in the old times the Masai had thought it beneath them to intermarry with Kikuyu. But in our days the strange dying nation, to delay its final disappearance had had to come down in its pride, the Masai women have no children and the prolific young Kikuyu girls are in demand with the tribe."[3] On their fourth day of life, Maasai children are taken outside and presented to the sun, and in the days of the civil wars, so it is said, peace among the tribes was made when mothers from the opposing sides suckled one another's babies.

Legaturi, with an air of lofty detachment, was watching closely from beneath a large commiphora, the bark of which, boiled, is a Maasai medicine. His gestures made plain that Nancy's belly should be rubbed in a certain way, but unfortunately we could not understand him, and as for his commiphora infusion, we had nothing to cook with. Excepting a very light small tent and some canned food, our gear had all been left behind at the camp beside the stream.

By evening Nancy was calmer and more comfortable, despite her dread of the journey the next day. We heated some food tins in a fire, and lacking a lantern, went to bed at dark, the Hurxthals in the Land Rover, and I in their small tent under the tree. Legaturi, disdaining the offer of a place in the two-man tent, had made himself a shelter out of thorn branches, but soon he came tugging at the tent fly, murmuring excuses, and once inside, spat all over its triangular doorway of mosquito netting, to bless this transparent stuff against the passage of night animals. Near Leakey's camp, we had come upon a black-maned lion in the grass, and Legaturi, seated beside me, had hurled defiance at the king of beasts, splitting my ears with the blood curdling whoops and chants used by the lion-killing moran of other days. The lion gazed at him, unmoved. When I drove closer, Legaturi subsided, grabbing up my binoculars and pressing them at me, imploring me to stop right there and take a picture: "*Simba! Simba mkubwa!*" (Big lion!) Closing the car window tight, he had shrunk into his blanket, glazed with fright. If Legaturi is a fair example, the agricultural Maasai have lost that aplomb with wild animals for which the tribe is so well known.

In the middle of the night, a rhino blundered into us. A rude *Chough! Chough! Chough!* at the quaking canvas brought us both upright, and Legaturi seized my knee in a famished grip as if fearful that l'Ojuju, the Hairy One, might rush out to do single combat with the huge night presence whose horn was but a few feet from our faces. He did not let go until the rhino wheeled and crashed away. "*Kifaru!*" Legaturi whispered, finding his voice at last. "*Kifaru mkubma!*"

At daylight, slowly, the Land Rover jolted down off the Ngurumans, Nancy cradled in her husband's arms. Near our first camp we made tea, and for an hour or two she rested. Here Legaturi left us, extending a warm invitation – "*Karibu! Karibu! Karibu!*" – to visit him one day in his en-gang. Then we toiled onward, mile by slow mile, arriving at the Uaso Nyiro in the early afternoon. A professional hunter, Robert Reitnauer, camped there with clients on safari, was able to contact Nairobi by radio-telephone, and Frank Minot of the African Wildlife Leadership Foundation was waiting with an airplane at Magadi, where we arrived just before twilight. Nancy was flown out to Nairobi Hospital, and after a few days' rest was permitted to go home. (The baby was born on December 23, and on Christmas Day Nancy wrote me a letter "propped up in my Nairobi Hospital bed, plied with toast and marmalade, and just having handled and breast fed our daughter for the first time, I'm at a loss to describe my wonder and happiness. . . . She was literally my Christmas present . . . a small pink pumpkin-like creature looking remarkably like Lew.")

I made camp south of Magadi, on a ridge that rose from the white soda. In the sinking sun the flats were red and gray. I washed myself and washed my clothes and hung them from the limbs of a squat commiphora full of young skinks, and in moments the damp clothes crawled with wizened bees that came out of nowhere to suck at the precious moisture. The heat was awesome, as if the bleached grass all round had caught on fire, but the air was so dry that it was comfortable so long as one was naked and moved carefully. I made myself a cup of rum and sat on a rope camp stool under the tree, gazing out across the south end of Magadi toward the Nguruman Escarpment and beyond, to the Loita Hills. Tomorrow I would walk the lunar shores of the great Lake Natron that I had seen so many times off in the distance.

Two winters before, in the Gol Mountains, Myles Turner and I had planned a foot safari over the Loita Hills, which are roadless and little known; George Schaller or Hans Kruuk and the wildlife photographer, Alan Root, might go as well. So far as Myles knew, nobody had ever attempted this trek, which he had dreamed about for many years: "One day I'll do it," he kept saying, as if forgetting that we had already made a plan. Our route would continue southward over the Ngurumans to the Sonjo villages, just across the Tanzania border, then down along the west shore of Lake Natron. A day would be taken to climb Ol Doinyo Lengai, after which we would continue into the Crater Highlands, passing by way of Embagai Crater, and coming out eventually at Nainokanoka or Ngorongoro. But this journey, potentially so much more exciting and rewarding than a shooting safari, had never come about, though Myles and I still talk about it, and hope it will.

The reasons given for the indefinite postponement of the foot safari – length of time involved, conflict of schedules, logistics, leave time, my own failure to maintain touch while away from Africa – were understandable enough, but perhaps there was a part of Myles that did not want the safari he had dreamed of for so long to be over and done with. For then some image of that epic Africa of hope and innocence that lay off there in the blue, the Africa of the ivory hunters, Selous and Neumann, Jim Sutherland and Karamoja Bell, would no longer lie safe in the past and future but in the reality of the present, and with the evaporation of the image, hope would end, and with it a sense of his own life too vital to relinquish. For Myles's tough laconic manner hides the romanticism of a man addicted fatally to the past.

A year ago, before the enterprise came all apart, I sensed that the Loita safari was a dream, and another man's dream at that, and attempted to make the journey in pieces, on my own. I went first to Lengai, for the Mountain of God was the beacon in this strangest and most beautiful of all regions that I have come across in Africa. Later, in the Crater Highlands, with a Maasai friend named Martin Mengoriki, I camped on the rim of Embagai, in the hope of going down into its crater. The rim was an alpine meadow dense with flowers, like a circlet around the cloud in the volcano, and under the cloud a crater lake lay in deep forest. All day we waited for a clearing wind, to locate a way down the steep sides, but instead the cloud overflowed onto the meadow, smothering the senses. Uneasy, Martin said: "It is so quiet," and was startled by the volume of his gentle voice: we could hear a mole rat chewing at the grass roots and the tiny wing flutter of a cisticola across the mist. In a bed of lavenders and yellows, cloud curling past the white bands of its ears, lay a big serval. The cat remained there a long moment, shifting its haunches, before sinking down into the flowers and away.

In the late afternoon, the meadows cleared. Not far off, a band of ravens connived in a dead haegenia, the lone, uncommon tree left at this altitude. Before the mists reclaimed it, I climbed the tree and with a panga chopped down dry limbs for a fire. Already, at twilight, it was very cold, but in this hour of changing weathers, odd solitary light shafts, fitful gusts, the mists were lifting, and treetops of the crater sides loomed through the cloud, then the crater floor, and finally the lake, two thousand feet below, where a herd of buffalo stood like dark outcrops on the shore. Out of the weathers fifteen miles away, the Mountain of God loomed once and withdrew; I glimpsed the ridge that I had climbed, down which that rhino had descended. Then the mists closed, and around the rim of Embagai the fire tones of aloes and red gladioli burned coldly in the cloud.

Two buffalo, tracing their old winding ruts, had ambled up into our campsite from the west. Confronted with the Land Rover, they stopped to study it a while, the last light glinting on their horns. Then they wheeled and rolled away, dropping from view; the mountain horizon, as dark came, was empty.

By morning, clouds had settled heavily into the crater, making the descent impossible. We returned south fifty miles to Ngorongoro across a waste of coarse tussock, wind and bitter cinder where the swirls of ash, puffing through each crack, burned nose and throat. In summer the moors are parched despite dark stagnant clouds that shroud the circle of old volcanoes, ten thousand feet and more, that in many trips across the Crater Highlands, summer and winter, I had never seen. The three villages here are the highest in Maasai Land, and once the car was caught in a tide of milling cattle, a maelstrom of shrouding dust and rolling eyes and a doomed bawling, as if at last the earth had tipped on end. At one time there was forest here, and water was more plentiful, but the Maasai have cut and burned the trees to make more pasture, as they have done also on the west slopes of the Mau Range, and so far they pay no heed at all to those who tell them they are ruining their country.

The three villages between volcanoes have some seventy people each, and because the moors are treeless, the villages are fenced with long split timbers brought up from the ravines; the bony staves, bent black on the barren sky, give a bleak aspect to the human habitations. But inside the stockade, out of the wind, the village called Ol Alilal is a snug place of sun-blown weeds and sheep bleats, warm manure scent, goat kids, new puppies, and grains spread upon a hide – the finger millet, eleusine, domesticated long ago in the highlands of Ethiopia. As in all Maasai villages, the corral is surrounded by low oval huts, ovens of dung stuck on a framework of bent saplings. We crouched to enter. The interiors are intricate, with small wicker-walled compartments, and the innermost chamber has a three-stone hearth and a small air vent for the smoke, with two raised beds inset in the wall, one for the father and mother and the other for children. The woman of the house was hospitable, perhaps because I was there with a Maasai; the next time we came, she said, she would prepare fresh blood-and-milk. Everyone was bold and cheerful, and though white travelers must be rare in this far place, they pretended to take no notice of me. Only the beaded infants stared through the dark circles of flies at their infected eyes. Ordinarily the eyes are never treated, so that many Maasai become blind. One pretty woman wore a necklace of lion claw and a bit of old leather that Martin said was dawa or medicine prescribed by the laibon, and a few trading cowries worn in hope of fertility, since the cowry aperture resembles the vagina.[4] In East Africa the cowry, which was brought here first from the Maldive Islands and had spread all across Africa by the fourteenth century, is used ceremonially in the first three of the great rites of passage, birth, circumcision, and marriage, the fourth rite being death.

Sun, heat, stillness were all one. The dying sun in the Ngurumans gave color to the cooking fire, and after dark came a hot wind that fanned night fires all around the horizon, and drove one tongue of flame onto the ridge above the lifeless lake. Though ready to break camp at a moment's notice, I slept poorly – the moon and wind and fire made me restless. But in a red dawn, the wind died again, and the fire sank into the grass, waiting for night.

South of Magadi the road scatters, and wandering tracks cross the white lake bed. There is water where the wading birds are mirrored, and in the liquid shimmer of the heat, a still wildebeest wavers in its own reflection. An hour later, from the west, the ghostly beast was still in sight; it had not moved.

The track winds southwest toward Shombole. Huge termitaria slouch here and there in the dry scrub, and over toward the Nguruman Escarpment, a whirlwind spins a plume of desert dust up the Rift's dark face into the smoky sky of East African summer. Eventually the track descends again, between the dead volcano and the marsh of Uaso Nyiro. In a water gleam that parts the fierce bright reeds, a woman and a man are bathing. The woman squats, her small shoulders demure, but the man stands straight as a gazelle and gazes, body shining, the archetypal man of Africa that I first saw in the Sudan.

The Shombole track comes to an end at three shacks under the volcano, where a duka serves the outlying Maasai with beads and wire for ornament, red cloth, sweet drinks, and cocoa. I gave a ride to a young morani who guided me with brusque motions through the bush to a stony cattle trail that winds between hill and marsh, around Shombole. Farther on, we picked up two Maasai women, and all four of us were squashed into the front when, in the full heat of the desert afternoon, on hot rocky ground at the mud edge of a rotting swamp in the lowest and hottest pit of the Rift Valley floor, my faithful Land Rover, thirty-five miles from Magadi and ninety-five beyond Nairobi, gave a hellish clang and, dragging its guts over the stones, lurched to a halt.

In a bad silence, the Maasai women thanked me and departed. The boy stood by, less out of expectation of reward or even curiosity, I decided, than some sense of duty toward a stranger in Maasai Land. Squatting on my heels and swatting flies, I peered dizzily at the heavy iron shaft, the sand and stone and thorn stuck to raw grease where the shaft had sheared at the universal coupling, cutting off the transmission of power to the rear wheels. In front-wheel drive, the car would move forward weakly, but my limited tools were not able to detach the revolving shaft from the transmission: dragging and clanging in an awful din of steel and rocks, it threatened to shake the car to pieces.

To cool my nerves, I drank a quart of Tusker beer. The Land Rover had picked a poor place to collapse, but at least it had got me to my destination, and the sun if not the heat would soon be gone. Any time now, the airplane of Douglas-Hamilton, coming to meet me, would be landing on the bare mud flats at the north end of Natron. Tomorrow we were to climb Shombole, and after that, if no repairs seemed possible, Iain could fly out to Magadi and leave word of my straits and whereabouts. But as it happened, Iain and Oria were never to appear: they had sent word to Nairobi that has not reached me to this day. Next morning I rigged a whole series of rope slings, held in place by stay lines from the side, that carried the rotating shaft just off the ground, although they burned through regularly from friction. Setting off at sunrise at three miles an hour, with the frequent stops to repair or replace the sling giving the straining car an opportunity to cool off, I arrived in two hours at the duka. A length of soft iron wire presented me by the proprietor was better than the rope, but not much better, and the last of it wore through as I reached Magadi in mid-afternoon, having made not less than fifteen trips beneath the car, in terrific heat, measuring my length in the fine volcanic ash that a hellish wind impacted in hair, lungs, and fingernails. The kind Asian manager of the Magadi Store and his driver-mechanic replaced the sheared bevel pinion with an ingenious makeshift rig that would see the car safely to Nairobi, but all of this still lay ahead as I stood there looking as stupid as I felt under the gaze of that young herdsman by the shores of Natron.

The time had come for a hard look at my old car's parts and contents. This Land Rover that has seen me so faithfully through East Africa is essentially an enclosed pickup truck with no back seats, preceded everywhere by two racks bolted to its front bumper; each rack holds four gallons of spare gasoline. The broad flat hood or bonnet is designed for a spare wheel, but as a precaution against theft I carry the spare in the back, leaving the bonnet free for pressing plants and preparing food. Inside, the steel shelves that flank the wheel hold books and maps, an adjustable wrench, screwdrivers, pliers, knife, long-beam flashlight, distilled water for the batteries, electrical tape, disinfectant, band-aids, and a roll of tissue for binocular lenses, window-wiping, oil sump dip stick, doubtful forks, and bottoms. There are three seats in the front, and a compartment under the left seat (the steering wheel is on the right) holds a foot pump, tire bars, tube patches, spare fan belt, coil, spark plugs, points, distributor cap and condenser, a siphon tube, a tube of stop-leak for the radiator (raw egg white may be tried in an emergency), yellow elephant soap for fuel line leaks, lacquer thinner (emergency nostrum for failed clutch, when dumped into clutch housing), and four quarts of motor oil. Behind the seats is a large lever jack, a shovel, a long engine crank in case of battery failure, and a panga or machete, useful for meat, firewood, and chopping brush to pile under the wheels when mired.

In the days when this car belonged to the Serengeti Research Institute, the roof was fitted with two hinged viewing hatches that open upward and fall flat on the car roof, one forward and one back, for passengers standing on the truck bed. The hatches permit the entry of fresh air at night, if one is sleeping in the car, and when required a mosquito net can be suspended. Across the narrow benches on each side, which cramp the floor space, I have laid loose boards, from the front seat back to the rear door. The spare wheel is kept beneath the boards, and also rope, insecticide, and kerosene, a two-by-four used as a jack base in sand or mud, an all-purpose tin washbasin, two feet in diameter, bought for sixty cents in the Arusha marketplace, and a spare six gallons of water. On top are two mattresses with bedding and mosquito net, a tin chest of provisions, a carton containing kerosene lamp, stove, pot, pan, teapot, and utensils; a small duffel, a rope-seat stool, a plant press. At night, should space be needed, these things may be stowed beneath the car or in the front, and the two mattresses laid side by side, and when special cargo or many people must be transported, the boards are taken up and stacked, for I have carried at one time or another a whole butchered zebra, drying elephant ears, innumerable townspeople and tribesmen, tortoises, birds, chameleons, and a diseased baboon.

In retrospect, I would recommend this additional equipment: a spare half-shaft, an asbestos filament lantern, a spare fuel pump (or a spare diaphragm, if you are a good mechanic), and a nineteenth-century tract called *Shifts and Expedients of Camp Life*, which includes such critical information as the proper method of mounting a small cannon on the hind end of a camel, to repel boarders and deal crisply with shifta or other unsavory individuals who might be gaining on one from the rear.

*   *   *

Since the disabled car was inland from the lake, it seemed best to walk the last mile to the flats, to greet Iain and Oria and to make certain that I was not overlooked; already I was listening for the droning of the motor that would draw to a point the misty distances down toward Lengai. Accompanied by the morani, I followed a cattle trail between the marsh and a thorny rock strangely swollen by thick pink blossoms of the desert rose. Near the mouth of the Uaso Nyiro, green reeds give way to open flats where the Natron leaves a crust crisscrossed by ostrich tracks. Here the young warrior, mounting the rock, made a grand sweeping gesture of his cape toward the horizons of Maasai Land, and sighed with all his being. The red and blue beads swinging from his ears stood for sun and water, but now the sun was out of balance with the rain, and the grass was thin. The Maasai speak of the benevolent Black God who brings rain, and the malevolent Red God who begrudges it, the Black God living in dark thunderheads and the Red in the merciless dry-season sun; Black God and Red are different tempers of Ngai, for God is embodied in the rain and the fierce heat, besides ruling the great pastures of the sky. Looming thunder is feared: the Red God seeks to pierce the Black God's kingdoms, in hope of bringing harm to man. But in distant thunder the Maasai hear the Black God saying, "Let man be . . ."

From where we stood, awed by the view, white flats extended a half-mile to the water's edge, where the heat waves rose in a pink fire of thousands upon thousands of flamingos. All around the north end of the lake the color shimmered, and for some distance down both shores; on the west shore, under the dark Sonjo escarpments, an upside-down forest was reflected. Southeast, the outline of Gelai was a phantom mountain in an amorphous sky, and in the south, the lake vanished in brown vapors that shrouded Ol Doinyo Lengai.

In this somber kingdom of day shadows and dead smokes, the fresh pinks of flamingos and the desert rose appeared unnatural. What belonged here were those tracks of giant birds, like black crosses in the crystalline white soda, and this petrified white bone dung of hyena, and the hieroglyph of a gazelle in quest of salt that had followed some dim impulse far out onto the flats. I remembered the Grant's gazelles on the Chalbi Desert, and the rhino that had climbed Lengai, and the wildebeest at a dead halt for want of impulse, in the shimmer of the soda lake, at noon. What drives such animals away from life-giving conditions into the wasteland – what happens in those rigid clear-eyed heads? How did the hippopotamus find its way up into the Crater Highlands, to blunder into the waters of Ngorongoro? Today one sees them there with wonder, encircled by steep walls, and the mystery deepens when a fish eagle plummets to the springs east of the lake and rises once more against the sky, in its talons a gleam of unknown life from the volcano.

* * *

We walked out into the silence of the flats. Somewhere on the mud, our foot-prints crossed the border of Tanzania, for Natron lies entirely in that country. I listened for the airplane but there was nothing, only the buzzing of these birds that fed with their queer heads upside down, straining diatoms and algae from the stinking waters even as they squirted it with the guano that kept the algae reproducing – surely one of the shortest and most efficient life chains in all nature, at once exhilarating and oppressive in the mindlessness of such blind triumphal life in a place so poisonous and dead. A string of flamingos rose from the pink gases, restoring sharpness to the sky, then sank again into the oblivion of their millions.

Twilight was coming. The boy pointed to a far en-gang under Shombole. "*Aia*," he said, by way of parting – So be it – and stalked away in fear of the African night, his red cape darkening against the white. "*Aia*," I said, watching him go. Soon he vanished under the volcano. This age-set of moran may be the last, for the Maasai of Kenya, upset at being left behind by tribes they once considered worthless, voted this year to discontinue the moran system and send young Maasai to school. But in Maasai Land all change comes slowly, whether in Kenya or Tanzania. The month before, in the region of Ol Alilal, in the Crater Highlands, there was a new age-set of circumcised boys dressed in the traditional black garments bound with broad bead belts and wearing the spectral white paint around the eyes that signifies death and rebirth as a man, and on their shaved heads, arranged on a wood frame that looked from afar like an informal halo, black ostrich plumes danced in the mountain wind. When their hair grew out again, the boys would be young warriors, perhaps the last age-set of moran.

One of the Ol Alilal moran was very sick, and we took him in to the government dispensary at Nainokanoka. This tall boy of seventeen or eighteen could no longer walk; I carried his light body in my arms to the dark shack where to judge from his face, he thought that he would die. Yet here at least he had a chance that he might not have had at Ol Alilal. Though the Maasai have little faith in witch-craft, they recognize ill provenance and evil spirits, and a person dying is removed outside the fences so that death will not bring the village harm. Eventually the body is taken to the westward toward the setting sun, and laid on its left side with knees drawn up, head to the north and face to the east, right arm crossing the breast and left cushioning the head. There it is left to be dealt with by hyenas. Should someone die inside a hut, then the whole village must be moved, and it is said that the people listen for the howl of the hyena, and establish the new village in that direction. The Maasai are afraid of death, though not afraid to die.

* * *

For a long time I stood motionless on the white desert, numbed by these lowering horizons so oblivious of man, understanding at last the stillness of the lone animals that stand transfixed in the distances of Africa. Perhaps because I was alone, and therefore more conscious of my own insignificance under the sky, and aware, too, that the day was dying, and that the airplane would not appear, I felt overwhelmed by the age and might of this old continent, and drained of strength: all seemed pointless in such emptiness, there was nowhere to go. I wanted to lie flat out on my back on this almighty mud, but instead I returned slowly into Kenya, pursued by the mutter of primordial birds. The flamingo sound, rising and falling with the darkening pinks of the gathering birds, was swelling again like an oncoming rush of motley wings – birds, bats, ancient flying things, thick insects.

The galumphing splosh of a pelican, gathering tilapia from the fresh-water mouth of the Uaso Nyiro, was the first sound to rise above the wind of the flamingos. Next came a shrill whooping of the herdsmen, hurrying the last cattle across delta creeks to the bomas in the foothills of Shombole. A Maasai came running from the hills to meet me, bearing tidings of two dangerous lions – "*Simba! Simba mbili!*" – that haunted this vicinity. He asked nothing of me except caution, and as soon as his warning was delivered, ran back a mile or more in the near-darkness to the shelter of his en-gang. Perhaps the earliest pioneers were greeted this way almost everywhere by the wild peoples – the thought was saddening, but his act had made me happy.

I built a fire and broiled the fresh beef I had brought for three, to keep it from going bad, and baked a potato in the coals, and fried tomatoes, and drank another beer, all the while keeping an eye out for bad lions. I also made tea and boiled two eggs for breakfast, to dispense with fire-making in the dawn. As yet I had no energy to think about tomorrow, much less attempt makeshift repairs; the cool of first light would be time enough for that. Moving slowly so as not to stir the heat, I brushed my teeth and rigged my bed roll and climbed out on the car roof, staring away over Lake Natron. I was careful to be quiet: the night has ears, as the Maasai say.

From the Crater Highlands rose the Southern Cross; the Pleiades which the Maasai associate with rains, had waned in early June. July is the time of wind and quarrels, and now, in August, the grass was dry and dead. In August, September, and October, called the Months of Hunger, the people pin grass to their clothes in hope of rain, for grass is sign of prosperity and peace, but not until the Pleiades returned, and the southeast monsoon, would the white clouds come that bring the precious water. (The Mbugwe of the southern flats of Lake Manyara resort to rainmakers, and formerly, in time of drought, so it is said, would sacrifice an unblemished black bull, then an unblemished black man, and finally the rainmaker himself.) [5]

The light in my small camp under Shombole was the one light left in all the world. Staring up at the black cone that filled the night sky to the east, I knew I would never climb it. There was a long hard day ahead with nothing certain at the end of it, and I had no heart for the climb alone, especially here in this sullen realm that had held me at such a distance. The ascent of Lengai and the descent into Embagai Crater had both been failures, and the great volcanoes of the Crater Highlands had remained lost in the clouds. At Natron, my friends had failed to come and my transport had broken down, and tomorrow I would make a slow retreat. And perhaps this came from the pursuit of some fleeting sense of Africa, seeking to fix in time the timeless, to memorize the immemorial, instead of moving gently, in awareness, letting the sign, like the crimson bird, become manifest where it would.

From where I watched, a sentinel in the still summer, there rose and fell the night highlands of two countries, from the Loita down the length of the Ngurumans to the Sonjo scarps that overlook Lake Natron. In the Loita, so the Maasai say, lives Enenauner, a hairy giant, one side flesh, the other stone, who devours mortal men lost in the forests; Enenauner carries a great club, and is heard tokking on trees as it moves along. [6] A far hyena summoned the night feeders and flamingos in crescents moved north across a crescent moon toward Naivasha and Nakuru. Down out of the heavens came their calls, remote electric sound, as if in this place, in such immensities of silence, one had heard heat lightning.

Toward midnight, in the Sonjo Hills, there leapt up two sudden fires. Perhaps this was sign of the harvest festival, Mbarimbari, for these were not the grass fires that leap along the night horizons in the dry season; the twin flames shone like leopard's eyes from the black hills. At this time of year God comes to the Sonjo from Ol Doinyo Lengai, and a few of their ancient enemies, the Maasai, bring goats to be slaughtered at Mbarimbari, where they howl to Ngai for rain and children.

The Sonjo, isolated from the world, know that it is coming to an end. Quarrels and warfare will increase, and eventually the sky will be obscured by a horde of birds, then insect clouds, and finally a shroud of dust. Two suns will rise from the horizons, one in the east, one in the west, as a signal to man that the end of the world is near. At the ultimate noon, when the two suns meet at the top of the sky, the earth will shrivel like a leaf, and all will die.

10   At Gidabembe

The Abatwa are very much smaller people than all small people; they go
under the grass and sleep in anthills; they go in the mist; they live in the
up country in the rocks ... Their village is where they kill game; they
consume the whole of it, and go away
   an anonymous Zulu[1]

> *Hamana nale kui,*
> *Nale kui.*
> Here we go round,
> Go round.
>   *a Hadza dance*[2]

One winter day in 1969, returning to Seronera from Arusha, Myles Turner flew
around the south side of the Crater Highlands, which lay hidden in its black
tumulus of clouds. The light plane skirted Lake Manyara and the dusty flats of
the witch-ridden Mbugwe, then crossed Mbulu Land, on the Kainam Plateau.
Soon it passed over a great silent valley. "That's the Yaida," Turner told me. "That's
where those Bushman people are, the Watindiga." Down there in that arid and
inhospitable stillness, cut off from a changing Africa by the ramparts of the Rift,
last bands of the Old People turned their heads toward the hard silver bird that
crossed their sky. There was no smoke, no village to be seen, nor any sign of man.
   Later that winter, at Ndala, Douglas-Hamilton had suggested a safari to
Tindiga Land, where his friend Peter Enderlein had lived alone for several years,
and was in touch with wild Tindiga still living in the bush. But Iain was never able
to get away, and a year had passed before I crossed paths with Enderlein in
Arusha, and arranged to visit his Yaida Chini game post in the summer. In July
of 1970 I picked up Aaron Msindai, a young Isanzu from the Mweka College
of Wildlife Management at Moshi, who had been assigned to Yaida Chini. We
loaded Aaron's kit into the back of the Land Rover – a rifle and an iron bed,
clothes, lantern, fuel, food for a month – and headed west, spending that night
at Manyara, and at seven the next morning climbing the Rift wall into the clouds
of the Crater Highlands. In the dense mist, trees shifted evilly, and slow cowled
figures with long staves, dark faces hidden in the gloom, moved past the ghostly
fields of maize and wheat. These are the agricultural Mbulu of the so-called Irakw

cluster, a group still unclassified in the ethnographic surveys, whose archaic language, related to Hamitic, suggests that they have been here in the Highlands a very long time, perhaps well before the Iron Age. Like the Hamitic tribes, the Mbulu practice circumcision and clitoridectomy, but they lack the age-set system and other customs of modern Hamites such as the Galla. Doubtless they have mingled with the waves of Bantu and Nilotic peoples who came later, but many retain a Caucasoid cast of feature: the volatile narrow faces of the men, especially, are the faces that one sees in Ethiopia. The Mbulu live in pits dug into hillsides and covered over with roofs of mud and dung; in former days these pit dwellings or tembes, like low mounds in the tall grass, are said to have hidden the people from the Maasai. Today the tembes give way gradually to tin-roofed huts.

At Karatu, a track turns south onto the fertile Kainam Plateau that forms a southern spur of the Crater Highlands. Off the main road, the Mbulu are not used to cars – in the fifty miles between Karatu and Mbulu I met no other vehicle – and the old run disjointedly along the red sides of the road, while the young jump behind the rocks and bushes. Today was Saba Saba (Seven Seven Day, commemorating the founding of TANU, the Tanganyika African National Union Party, on the seventh day of the seventh month, 1954), and near Mbulu, the track was filled with people streaming along toward the settlement. All were hooded against wind and rain, and from behind, in their blowing shrouds, they evoked the migration of those ancestors of many centuries ago who came down out of the north into a land of Stone Age hunters, the Twa, the Small People, most of whom, like the pit-dwelling Gumba found by the Kikuyu, have vanished into the earth.

From Mbulu a rough track heads west, dropping eventually off the Kainam Plateau into the Yaida Valley. It passes a fresh lake called Tlavi, edged by papyrus and typha, a rare pretty place of swallows and blowing reeds in a landscape of sloping grain fields, meadows, and soft sheltering hills that shut away the emptiness of Africa. The lake turned slowly in the lifting mists, a prism for the first rays of sun to pierce the morning clouds on the Crater Highlands. Beyond Tlavi the road rises into sun and sky and wanders along the westward scarp where highland clouds are parting; below lie the pale plains of a still valley, fifty miles long and ten across, like a world forgotten in the desert mountains. A rough rock track winding downhill is crossed by two klipspringer, yellow and gray; they bound away through low combretum woodland. Under the rim, out of the southeast wind, the air is hot. A horde of flies pours through the air vents, and Aaron strikes at them. He hisses, "Tsetse!"

In the wake of tsetse control programs that ended a few years ago, the Mbulu, already pressed for space due to population increase, overgrazing, and crude farming practices that have badly eroded the Kainam Plateau, began to move down into the Yaida Valley, while the Bantu Isanzu seeped in from the south. From the south also came fierce Barabaig herdsmen, and all of these people compete with the Tindiga and wild animals for the limited water. At the same time, the government, embarrassed that a Stone Age group should exist in the new Africa, has attempted to settle the hunters in two villages, one at Yaida Chini, the other farther west at an American Lutheran mission station called Munguli. Some three hundred now live in the settlements, and a few hundred more are still hiding in the bush.

Today, Tindiga, Mbulu, Isanzu, and Barabaig are all present at Yaida Chini, which may be the one place in East Africa where its four basic language families (Khoisan or click-speech, Hamitic, Bantu, and Nilotic) come together. Yaida Chini is a small dusty settlement strewn along under the line of giant figs by the Yaida River, and a group of Africans celebrating Saba Saba at the pombe bar milled out to greet the Land Rover as it rumbled down out of the hills. These people were mostly Isanzu, barefoot and ragtag in European shirts and pants, but to one side stood a dark thick-set pygmoid girl, and Aaron said, "Tindiga." The girl had a large head with prognathous jaw and large antelope eyes in thick black skin, and by western standards she was very ugly. Unlike the yellow-eyed peasants, who offered shouts as evidence of sophistication, she came up softly and stared seriously, mouth closed, like a shy animal. "Tindiga have a very hard tongue," Aaron told me, ignoring his pombe-drunk people. "My tongue is not the same as theirs, but when I speak, they know." It is Aaron's tribe, the Isanzu, that has assimilated most of the southern Tindiga, and few are left who do not have an Isanzu parent; even "Tindiga" is an Isanzu name for a people whose true name is Hadza or Hadzapi.

Because of tsetse and the scarcity of water, the Hadza once had the Yaida to themselves, and scarcely anything was known of them before 1924, when a district officer of what had become, after World War I, the Tanganyika Territory, reported on a people who hid from Europeans and were even less affected than the Bushmen by the world beyond: ". . . a wild man, a creature of the bush, and as far as I can see he is incapable of becoming anything else. Certainly he does not desire to become anything else, for nothing will tempt him to leave his wilderness or to abandon his mode of living. He asks nothing from the rest of us but to be left alone. He interferes with no one, and does his best to insure that no one shall interfere with him."[3] A few years later, the Hadza were inspected by an authority on the Bushmen, who stated in the peremptory tones of colonial scholarship that "there must have been some connection between this black ape-like tribe and the small delicately built yellow man,"[4] whose habits, thoughts, and language structure seemed so similar.

This second authority, Miss Bleek, agrees with the first one, Mr Bagshawe, that the typical tribesman was very black, short, thick-set, ugly and ill-smelling, with prognathous jaw and large splay feet. The blackness and the cast of jaw were most pronounced in the "purest" specimens, for even in Bleek's day, many Hadza in the south part of their range had an Isanzu parent. She does not comment on Bagshawe's contention that the Hadza is "intensely stupid and naturally deceitful" as well as "lazy", that he "does not understand why he should be investigated . . . it is more than probable that he will lie." Yet Bagshawe feels constrained to note that the Hadza "worries but little about the future and not at all about the past," that he is "happy and envies no man." Bagshawe's perplexed tone is echoed by Bleek, who observed that this unprepossessing people often danced in simple pleasure: "*Hamana nale kui*," they sang. "*Nale kui.*"

> Here we go round,
> Go round.

The early descriptions of the Hadza bring to mind the small men with large bows and strange speech who were driven high onto Mt Kilimanjaro by the Chagga, and also the "people of small stature and hideous features," as L. S. B. Leakey describes[5] the Gumba aborigines found by the Kikuyu in the Kenya Highlands. But in the years since they were first reported, the Hadza have mixed increasingly with the Isanzu, who may eventually absorb them as Bantu tribes have been absorbing hunter-gatherers for two millenniums. A recent student, Dr James Woodburn, does not believe that a characteristic physical type is distinguishable any longer, nor does he accept Miss Bleek's assumption of a linguistic link between these people and the Bushmen (although the link between the click-speaking Sandawe, an acculturated tribe of south Tanzania, and the pastoral Bushman relatives known as the Hottentots is clearly established). On no evidence whatsoever, one is tempted to speculate that the Hadza may represent a relict group of pre-Bantu Negroids of the Stone Age, although there is no proof that the Hadza are a Stone Age remnant, or a remnant at all – very probably, they are as numerous as they ever were. They may even be regressive rather than primitive, a group cast out long ago from a more complex civilization, though their many affinities with the Bushmen make this unlikely. Probably we shall never come much closer to the truth than the people's own account of Hadza origins:

Man, say the Hadza, descended to earth on the neck of a giraffe, but more often they say that he climbed down from a baobab. The Hadza themselves came into being in this way: a giant ancestor named Hohole lived in Dungiko with his wife Tsikaio, in a great hall under the rocks where Haine, who is God, the Sun, was not able to follow. Hohole was a hunter of elephants, which were killed with one blow of his stick and stuck into his belt. Sometimes he walked one hundred miles and returned to the cave by evening with six elephants. One day while hunting, Hohole was bitten by a cobra in his little toe. The mighty

Hohole died. Tsikaio, finding him, stayed there five days feeding on his leg, until she felt strong enough to carry the body to Masako. There she left it to be devoured by birds. Soon Tsikaio left the cave and went to live in a great baobab. After six days in the baobab, she gave birth to Konzere, and the children of Tsikaio and Konzere are the Hadza.[6] "The Hadza," as the people say, "is us."

At the west end of the settlement, downriver, Peter Enderlein has built a house. At the sound of the motor, he came out on his veranda, a tall bare-legged man in shorts, boots wide apart, hands stuck in his hip pockets. We went immediately on an inspection of the ostrich pens, where he is raising an experimental flock for plumes and skins and meat. (In the wild, there is a heavy loss of eggs and chicks to predators of all descriptions, including lions, which are fond of playing with the eggs.) With their omnivorous habits and adaptations to arid country, ostrich could be domesticated in the Yaida, where tsetse and a shortage of surface water – the annual rainfall is less than twenty inches – are serious obstacles to agriculture and livestock. Enderlein, who is employed to investigate the valley's resources, would like to try game ranching here, but he has received little support for this scheme or any other, and for the moment must content himself with shooting the animals instead. Fresh meat is sold cheaply to the local people, or dried for sale elsewhere as biltong; the valuable common animal is the zebra, and the sale of zebra hides to wholesalers is the game post's main source of income.

Pending approval of his projects, Enderlein spends most of his time supplying food for the impounded Hadza, who are not supposed to leave the settlement, much less revert to their old lives in the bush. But hunters have always made the transition to agriculture with the greatest reluctance (the Ik of the north Uganda hills are an exception), and as a rule, the people will consume immediately any livestock or maize seed that is given them, and beat their hoe blades into arrowheads. Neither the dry climate nor their temperament lends itself to tilling, and in consequence they do little but drink pombe. This enforced idleness and dependence will certainly lead to their utter disintegration. Until they can come to agriculture of their own accord, Enderlein is trying to persuade the government to establish the Yaida Valley as a game reserve in which Hadza would be hired as trackers, game scouts, and hunters in a game-cropping scheme like the one that gave work to the Ariangulo elephant hunters in the region of Tsavo. Meanwhile, settlement by outsiders would be concentrated instead of scattered at random over the landscape, destroying thousands of square miles of wildlife habitat for the sake of a few shambas that cut off the water points. The Yaida has the last important population of greater kudu in north Tanzania, in addition to all the usual trophy animals, and as a game reserve, would receive income from game-cropping and hunting fees, which at present, due to lack of roads, are negligible. There are old rock paintings in the hills, many still doubtless undiscovered, and Eyasi Man, the Rhodesioid contemporary of the Neanderthalers, was dug up near Mangola in 1935 by a German named Kohl-Larsen, who also found an Australopithecine here in 1939, two decades before the better-publicized *Australopithecus* was turned up by the Leakeys at Olduvai Gorge. All that is needed to encourage tourists is a good track into the north end of the valley from the main road across the Crater Highlands.

Although he has submitted to the government a careful analysis of game numbers and potential in the valley and an imaginative program of resource management, and although Tanzania's astute president Julius Nyerere is said to agree that the Hadza might come more readily to civilization through game-cropping than agriculture, Enderlein's plans have been regularly aborted by the district politicians, who have replaced European civil servants almost everywhere, and who take care not to approve or disapprove any project of a white man lest they expose themselves to the ambitions of their peers. As in other new African nations, the government endorses the principle of conservation, since conservation seems important to those western countries which are helping it in other ways. But most educated Africans care little about wild animals, which are vectors of the tsetse fly, a threat to crops and human life, and a competitor of livestock, and are also identified emotionally with the white man, white hunters, white tourists, and a primitive past which the new Africans wish to forget. As for the Hadzapi, they are the last tribe in Tanzania that is not administered and taxed, and the sooner they vanish, the better. Like the Twa, Bushman, and Dorobo, the small hunters are looked down upon by their own countrymen, and most of those who come into the settlement soon flee back to their former life of dignity and independence.

Of the Maasai, President Nyerere has remarked quite rightly that the government cannot afford to keep part of its people as a human zoo for tourists, and the same could be said about the Hadza: the time of the hunter is past, and will never return. Yet to judge from wild peoples I have seen in South America and New Guinea, the Hadza would be better left alone until a choice that they can make naturally is provided, for this people is acknowledged by all who have met them to be healthy and happy, with no history of epidemic or famine, and able to satisfy all needs in a few hours of each day. Modern medicine, motor transport, radios, and even shoes may be crucial to the poor man, whose wants are endless, self-perpetuating, whose every acquisition means that he cannot afford something else. The wants of the primitive are few, since he does not envy what he knows nothing of. Poverty and the inferior status that await the acculturated Hadza is no alternative to bush life and the serenity of the old ways, and to take this from him by exposing him to a "progress" he cannot share is to abuse his innocence and do him harm.

But Enderlein is accused of wishing to keep this people in the Stone Age "as the Americans wish for the Maasai", and told not to give game work to idle Hadza, since the government is committed to a national program of agriculture. Tsetse control is to be resumed, and the people sent out to girdle and kill the "useless" tsetse-harboring acacias that keep the valley from turning to a desert, and ever more outsiders are encouraged to settle the Yaida even though two crops out of three are lost to drought, even though the land is blowing away under the sharp hoofs of the cattle.

Enderlein showed me the hard bare flats in the grasslands that spread west to the hills called Giyeda Barakh. "Ten years ago," he said, "the people walked a long way around the grove where my camp is now, there were so many rhino, and they still speak of the great herds of eland and elephant moving through. Ten years from now, this whole valley will be a desert." He spoke sadly of his abandoned projects, of all the potential of the Yaida, of the rock paintings and other mysteries of this region that is still so unexplored – he has never found time to go down into Isanzu Land, where there are caves containing great log drums too enormous to be moved. According to the Isanzu, the drums had been built in an older time, by an older people; one thinks of the oracle drums of the great Bantu kingdoms of the lake country. The Isanzu are superstitious about the drums and keep them hidden.

Enderlein is a handsome Swede with a young officer's moustache and a mouth broken on one side by a fist of long ago. Though tall and strong, his eyes are restless, he looks haunted and tired; the solitude and frustration of his work are wearing him down. Either he commits more time that will probably be wasted, or he abandons three years of hard lonely work and all hope, as he sees it, for the Yaida. "I think it's the loveliest place in Africa. And it's almost an ecological unit, too, much more so than the Serengeti – almost all its animals are non-migratory, or would be if they'd let them get to water. I *hate* to give up, but I'm thirty-one now, and I'm getting nowhere; I just can't waste my life here."

The greatest present threat to the Yaida Valley is the cattle of the Barabaig, a pastoral people from the region of Mt Hanang and the Barabaig Plain, fifty miles to the southeast. On Saba Saba, there were numbers of lean Barabaig in the settlement, drinking pombe with their traditional antagonists, the Isanzu. They are a tall, handsome people whose dress and customs resemble those of the Maasai, and on the basis of language, they are usually linked to the Nandi, who are thought to have displaced them from the region of Mt Elgon, on the Kenya–Uganda border, about two hundred and fifty years ago. But little is known of the Barabaig, who appear to have a strong Hamitic mix; their own tradition is that they are related to the Mbulu, and that both groups came south from the shores of Lake Natron.

Such names as Barabaig, Hanang, and Giyeda Barakh evoke the northern deserts, as do such habits as the cutting of trophies from the bodies of human enemies, a custom of the Danakil of Ethiopia. In any case, they display all the simplehearted ferocity of the desert nomads, and to the Maasai are known as Il-man'ati, "the Enemy", a name reserved for a worthy foe whose warriors, unlike those of the Bantu, are entitled to extend a handful of grass to the Maasai in a plea for mercy. The Mangati, as they are generally known, were once scattered by attacks of the Maasai, but more recently have withstood Maasai encroachment from the west of Lake Eyasi, and have matched them raid for raid; it is their faith that ten Barabaig will overwhelm twenty Maasai. Being farther from the reach of the authorities, their moran have retained the custom of killing a lion in sign of manhood, or a man, for that matter, and what are known as "Barabaig spear-blooding murders" have made them a great source of chagrin to government and neighbors alike. Those murdered are "enemies of the people"[7] – the real or potential thieves of Barabaig cattle, a very broad category which includes all lions and strangers, as well as the mothers of thieves as yet unborn.

One night not long ago in Yaida Chini, a young Hadza girl was pierced through the lungs by a spear hurled from behind. Since the hard-drinking Mangati are the only ones with spears and the wish to use them, it is thought here that the girl was fleeing a Mangati admirer who was unable to resist a running target. The dying girl was discovered by Enderlein's cook who, interpreting her gasps as evidence of helpless drunkenness, took speedy advantage of his opportunity and raped her; it is hard to imagine the poor creature's last conclusions on the nature of her fellow man. The cook, himself drunk, got covered with blood, in which condition he was apprehended, and since no one has spoken up for him, he may stay in jail indefinitely, and perhaps be hung, for a crime of which nobody thinks him guilty.

Last September a Yaida Chini game scout, accompanied by three unarmed companions, caught some Barabaig with a dead giraffe and was unwise enough to attempt an arrest. Outraged, the moran pursued the four for three miles or more, trapping them finally in a cave, where they laid siege all night. In the morning, as the game scout came to the end of his ammunition, the warriors departed. Shortly afterwards they lost one of their number to an elephant that they had actually attacked with spears, but they were never arrested. This age-set of moran has stalked the Yaida for several years, passing through on poaching raids and raids into Maasai Land. "Their habit of killing people and cutting ears, nose, fingers, etc., off the bodies might sound exotic and interesting to somebody faraway from Mangati Land," Enderlein wrote in September, 1969, in a plea for help from the Game Department, "but for my Game Scouts and myself who have to live here and move around where these people are to be found this habit is rather disturbing. Our number is quite small already, and before it is reduced any further we would like to ask for assistance to deal with this dangerous situation."

At sunset the hot wind died, and the dust settled in the stillness; the western hills above Lake Eyasi glowed in a dusty desert sun. In Enderlein's grove the yellow-wing bats hung from the thorns in silhouette, flitted off one by one to meet the dark, while to roosts in the fat figs by the river came companies of storks and vultures, sacred ibis, a solitary pelican, sailing onto the high branches with thick wing thumps, hollow bill clack, and guttural weird protest.

At dark, the yard filled with drunken people, come to invite the white man to a party. In rural villages of East Africa, pombe-drinking consumes half the people's time and money, and the less sophisticated they are, the more hopeless they become. In his concern for the Hadza, Enderlein is trying to get the Mbulu district council to restrict the sale of pombe in this settlement: "We have seven pombe parties at Yaida Chini every week, and the men do their very best to attend all of them." But he knows perfectly well that a restriction is of small value, since anyone can brew the stuff at home.

In an Isanzu hut, we squatted on stools in the dim light and drank from a communal calabash of pombe, which at its best has a woody astringent taste and at its worst beggars description. Y-supports held up the roof beams of the flat-topped hut, and the walls were made of grass and mud caked over with dried dung. The smoke and soft voices, the hunched dark forms catching the ember light on gleaming foreheads, the eyes, the warmth, the slow hands at the hearth protected all there against the emptiness and the cold stars, night sorcery and the hyena riders. Later, the Isanzu danced to four big drums of hide and wood played by swift hands and a tin disc beaten in two-stroke rhythm with a stick, while a chanting old man was answered by fierce chorus. Here, well east of the African lakes, was the echo of the Congo and West Africa. The pounding went on and on and on, and the dry valley quaked with sound like a beaten hide, and faraway on the Giyeda Barakh the night sky glowed in a flame twenty miles long, as if the whole country would go up in fire.

Toward midnight, in a sudden silence of the drums, the yelling Africans cursed the white men, the wazungu, who had gone to bed. One man threw something at the house that banged on the wall and fell to the veranda.

In the morning, Enderlein is exhausted. Lately he has had great trouble sleeping; his eyes twitch, and he does everything with violence. Carving a bird, he seizes the whole carcass in his hand and slings the pieces onto plates. Hunting on the plains, he yanks his car too hard, too fast, and he seems careless with his rifle though he is not. Catching himself, or realizing he has been perceived, he mutters sheepishly, "I haven't taken care of myself; I've let everything go. Perhaps I have bilharzia." He shrugs, indifferent. "When I came out here, I was so keen, but now I am not. The people I try to work with do not care, so I cannot care indefinitely. They let everything go." He nodded his head toward the kitchen. "Last night Mfupi was drunk, and didn't bother to close the gate to the duck pen, and a honey badger got all my birds but two. I ask him to set some rice aside for our safari, and he cooks my entire supply. We need two camp cots, but all twelve cots assigned to Yaida Chini are now missing. A cot that will last fifteen years is ruined in three months – the rest have been lost, or perhaps sold in Mbulu." He shrugged again. "It's the same with everything – the land, the animals. Nobody cares, and all of it is going to go." He went outside and stood on his veranda, boots spread, hands in hip pockets, glaring at an African sky shrouded in fire clouds of smoke and blowing dust. In this valley, the only land that goes unburned is land too overgrazed to carry fire.

We head north under the Yaida Escarpment. Like all mornings in the dry season, this day is born in a dusty sun and restless wind, a desert wind, or so it seems, so vast and empty is the plain from which it comes. There is an old safari track, grown over, but the Land Rover makes its own way through acacia savanna where a slender-tailed mongoose, dark and lustrous, slips like a swift fish through the fading grass. At mid-morning the lower Udahaya is crossed, a slow stream dying in the plain. Slowly we wind toward the south Sipunga Hills.

Somewhere in the Sipunga, perhaps thirty miles north of Yaida Chini, small bands of Hadza hide from the resettlement program, living as they have always lived, by hunting and gathering, a people without pottery or gardens or domestic animals other than the random dog. Probably they will hide from us, as well, unless they see that we are the Hadza whom they trust. Magandula is a game scout and the prestige of his bunduki, or rifle, entitles him to two porters, Gimbe and Giga. Magandula is loud and opinionated; Gimbe and Giga are quiet. Magandula and Gimbe have Isanzu fathers, but Giga, smaller and older, is pure Hadza, black, with heavy jaw and swollen cheekbones and flat nose in a head too big for a small thick body which will never attain five feet in height. Until recently Giga has been living in the bush – he is one of a number of Hadza who drift back and forth between the old life and the new – and as if in sign of his transitional state he is wearing a sandal on his right foot but not on his left. Magandula, on the other hand, is an outspoken convert to the new Africa, and wears bright red socks in black street shoes with broken points.

In early afternoon, under Sipunga, Giga speaks. Off among black wrinkled trunks and silvered thorns he has glimpsed a shift of shadows, and now Magandula is speaking, too: "Tindiga!" he says in tones of triumph, choosing the Isanzu name.

There is more than one, it is a hunting party, crouching low in the golden grass to peer under the limbs; the black of their skin is the old black of acacia bark in shadow. Giga is smiling at them, and they do not run; they have seen Giga, and they have a fresh-killed zebra. Enderlein is grinning freely for the first time since I have known him. "Oh, we are *lucky!*" he says twice; he had not thought we would find the hunters this first day.

A striped hock shines in the fork of a tree; the rest rides on the hunters' shoulders. There are ten Hadza, seven with bows and three young boys, and all are smiling. Each boy has glistening raw meat slung over his shoulders and wrapped around him, and one wears the striped hide outward, in a vest. Except for beads at neck and waist, the boys are naked. The men wear loincloths faded to an olive-earth color that blends with the tawny grass; the rags are bound at the waist by a hide thong, and some have simple necklaces of red-and-yellow berry-colored beads. All wear crude sheath knives in the center of the back, and one has a guinea fowl feather in his hair.

Shy, they await in a half-circle, much less tall than their bows "*Tsifiaqua!*"they murmur, and our people say, "*Tsifiaqua mtana*," and then the hunters say, "M-*taa-na!*" for warm emphasis, smiling wholeheartedly. (*Tsifiaqua* is "afternoon" as in "good afternoon", and *mtana* is "nice" as in "nice day", and *tsifiaqua m-taa-na*, as the hunters say it, may mean, "Oh beautiful day!") I am smiling wholeheartedly too, and so is Enderlein; my smile seems to travel right around my head. The encounter in the sunny wood is much too simple, too beautiful to be real, yet it is more real than anything I have known in a long time. I feel a warm flood of relief, as if I had been away all my life and had come home again – I want to embrace them all. And so both groups stand face to face, admiring each other in the sunlight, and then hands are taken all around, each man being greeted separately by all the rest. They are happy we are to visit them and delighted to pile the zebra meat into the Land Rover, for the day is hot and dry and from here to where these Hadza live, behind the Sipunga Hills, is perhaps six miles of stony walking. The eldest, Mzee Dafi, rides, and others run ahead and alongside, and others stay behind to hunt again. The runners keep pace with the car as it barges across the stones and thorn scrub and on across the south end of Sipunga through the ancestral Hadza land called T'ua. Soon Giga kicks off his remaining sandal and runs barefoot with the rest, and then Magandula, in red socks and shiny shoes, is running, too. Gimbe, a young mission boy from Munguli, sits quietly; he is not yet home.

There is no track, only an intermittent path, and here and there Enderlein heaves rocks out of the way to let us pass. Peter is happy, and he works with exuberance, casting away his pent-up angers. So glad are the hunters of our coming that they hurl rocks, too, but since most of them, Giga included, have no idea what they accomplish, they struggle with rocks that are far off the route, out of pure good will. On the sky rise twin hills walled with soaring monoliths, quite unlike anything I have ever seen; the hills overlook the upper Udahaya Valley, between the Sipunga and the Mbulu Escarpment. Seeing the hills the hunters cry out, leaping rocks, and the swiftest is he with the guinea fowl feather, Salibogo.

Behind the twin portals, on a hillside, rise groves of monumental granites. Approaching this place across a meadow of pink baobabs, Dafi whispers, "Gidabembe." Still there is no sign of habitation. But bright green in the sun are two fresh gourds set out to dry on a rock shelf; the placement of the gourds gives man away. A yellow dog, the first and last such animal we saw in Hadza Land, walks stiff and silent from the bush under a tilted monolith, and from the shadows of the stone a thin smoke rises into the dry sunlight, and a crone the color of dry brush appears among the leaves. In the shadows she stands like a dead stick, observing.

At the next grove of rocks, a stone has toppled in such a way that its flat face, some fifteen feet by fifteen in dimension, is held clear of the ground by the debris of its own fall, forming an open-sided shelter five feet high; similar rock shelters at Magosi, in Uganda, have been inhabited since the Middle Stone Age.[8] Small trees at the cave's twin mouths filter the sunlight, and at the hearth is a cracked gourd, a rag, a dik-dik skin, a bone, all now abandoned, for except in time of heaviest rains, the Hadza live beneath the sky. With hand brooms of grass and twigs, Gimbe and Magandula and the hunters brush loose dust from the cave floor, while squat Giga pushes three hearthstones together and with fingertips and breath draws grass wisps into a fire and places a black pot on the points of stone to boil. Outside, an old woman has appeared, bent under a morning's harvest of orange grewia berries, which are dry and sweet and taste like nuts; offering these, she is given a strip of the zebra meat spread out across a stone. Our people take meat for ourselves, and so do others who come quietly into the glade, for the Hadza have no agonies of ownership. Soon the wild horse is gone. On sharpened sticks Gimbe skewers the red meat, laying two sticks across the fire; the rest he places in the trees to dry for biltong. Our arrival at Gidabembe is celebrated with a feast of tea and zebra, ugali and the fire-colored berries.

Gidabembe, the Hadza say, has been one of their camps for a long time, longer than the oldest of them can remember. It is used mainly in the dry season, when large animals are more easily killed, and people gather into larger groups to be in the vicinity of the good hunters. The main encampment lies uphill from the cave, on a knoll overlooking the river, where four small hearths with thornbush walls are grouped among the stones. Two are backed by upright granite and a third by a fallen tree; no roofs are constructed in this season, for there is no rain. The people are invisible to the outside world, which at Gidabembe is no farther than the glint of a tin duka on the slope of the Kainam Plateau, high on the far side of the valley. Their fires are small and their voices quiet, and they are so circumspect in all their habits that no scent of human habitation is detectable, although they do not bother about the droppings of baboons, which appropriate these rocks when man is absent; the baobab seeds in the baboon droppings are sometimes gleaned for man's own use.[9] Only a rare infant's cry betrays the presence of human beings, for the children play quietly, without squalling. One is among them very suddenly, a community of small people speaking prettily in soft click-speech in the light airs of afternoon. Far below the shelter of the rocks is green forest and the brown wind-sparkled river that in July is already running dry.

Soft voices in leaf-filtered sun, and a child humming, and a warm wind off the highlands that twitches the dry trees and blows color into the embers of the hearth. The earth behind the fire has been softened with a digging stick. Here, at dark, covered only with the thin rags worn in the day, the family lies down together on the small mat of kongoni hide or hay. From the thorn walls hang gourds and arrow packets and bird skins for arrow vanes, and by one hearth is an iron pot, black and thin as a leaf cinder. In these simple arrangements is a ceremonial sense of order in which everything is in place, for the ceremony is life itself, yet these shelters last no longer than the whims of their inhabitants, who may move tomorrow to another place, nearby or far. In the rains, especially, they scatter, for game and water are widespread. Somewhere they draw a few sticks over their heads, with grass matted on top, though they are casual about the rain when food is plentiful. In the dry season, many will return to Gidabembe, by the river, for Gidabembe is permanent, although all but the oldest of its people come and go. The hunter, who must travel light, limits his family to parents and children, and the people move in ever-changing groups, with little sense of tribe. The Hadza have no chiefs, no villages, no political system; their independence is their very breath. Giga speaks of an old man who wandered off last year and was thought lost. Three months later he turned up again, well rested from the stress of human company.

In the day the men and boys remain separate from the women. The men carry a fire drill among their arrows, and wherever Hadza tarry for more than a few minutes, and tarrying occupies much of their life, a small fire will be built. One hearth overlooks the river. Here in the broken sunlight, in the odor of wood smoke, the men and boys squat on their heels, shoulder to shoulder in a warm circle around the fire. With Dafi is his son Kahunda, and Saidi the son of Chandalua, who is still hunting in the land called T'ua; both are beautiful children whose eyes are not yet red from fire smoke, nor their teeth broken and brown. Dafi and Ginawi butcher zebra with deft twists of their crude knives; at Dafi's side is an ancient sharpening stone, glinting with soft iron shavings and concave with many seasons of hard use. Knives and metal arrow points come mostly from other tribes, but sometimes they are hammered cold from soft iron acquired in trade for skins and honey. Sheaths are fashioned from two flat bits of wood bound round with hide and sinew. Until recently, a male Hadza wore the pelt of a genet cat,[10] bound on by the hide thong that holds his knife, but now almost all wear small cloth skirts. Each carries a hide pouch with shoulder strap containing scraps of skin and tendon, tobacco leaves and hemp, a disc of baobab wood, lucocuko, used in gambling, a hunk of vine tuber which, when chewed, serves as a glue for binding arrow vanes, some rag-wrapped hornet larvae medicine or dawa, useful for chest pain, and snakebite dawa, of ingredients known only to a few, which is used in trade with the Mbulu and Mangati, spare arrowheads and scraps of metal, a chisel tool made from a nail, a pipe carved from a soft stone in the river. This pipe, one of the few Hadza objects that is not obtained in barter, is no more than a tube, and the tobacco or bangi will fall from it unless it is held vertical. Both men and women, staring at the sky, smoke the stone pipe with gusty sucks accompanied by harsh ritual coughing which is followed in turn by a soft ecstatic sigh.

Dafi and Ginawi eat zebra skin after burning off the hair, and put aside strips of the thick hide to be used for the soles of sandals, which most though not all of the hunters have adopted. They are joined by a Hadza with oriental eyes, high cheekbones, and a light skin with a yellow cast who brings to mind a legend[11] – not entirely without evidence to support it – that long ago Indonesians penetrated inland from the coast; the Tatoga of this region say that their ancestors came originally from beyond the sea. This man has been to Yaida Chini, and is sorry that Enderlein does not recall his name. "Zali," he says. "It is bad of you to forget. I have told it to you at Yaida Chini."

Certain other sallow Hadza might be Bushmen but for the lack of wrinkles and steatopygous buttocks, and Enderlein says that in their attitudes and ways, the Hadza seem identical to the click-speakers of the Kalahari, whom he has read all about. Bushmanoid peoples once inhabited East Africa, and it is tempting to suppose that the two groups were related long ago. On the other hand, certain Negroid groups such as the Bergdama of southwest Africa had adopted the Bushman culture, and even the Zulu have adopted a click-speech from these Twa or Abatwa, whose old hunting lands they have appropriated. The Bushmen themselves have Negroid attributes that they may not have always possessed – it is not known what their ancestors looked like.

But the yellow-brown Hadza look not at all like Giga, and most of the tribe are of mixed appearance, despite the striking heavy-browed appearance of such individuals as Giga, and Andaranda who killed the zebra, and a man named Kargo who, in size, is a true pygmy, and the large-headed girl at Yaida Chini who was the first Hadza that I ever saw, and one identified on sight, it must be said, by my Isanzu passenger, who had never seen her in his life.

Already the hunters are tending to their arrows, long thin shafts cut from a grewia or dombeya and feathered with vanes of bustard, guinea fowl, or vulture. Bird arrows are tipped with sharpened wood, and each bundle has an arrow with a lance blade of honed iron that is used for small game like guinea fowl and dik-dik. All the rest have single- or double-barbed metal points dipped in black resinous poison, made ordinarily from seeds of the black strocanthus fruit or sap of the desert rose. Both poisons are heart stimulants, consumed safely in meat but fatal when received into the bloodstream. Dafi wraps the poisoned barbs in thin strips of impala hide so that the poison will not dry out; the protection of the hunter is incidental. His long stiff bow of dombeya is also wrapped with circlets of impala, though this is maridadi – decoration. Ordinarily, Hadza bow strings are of zebra tendon, while split tendons of impala are the sinew that binds the arrow vanes onto the shaft.

When not out hunting roots and tubers with their digging sticks, Hadza women remain at their own hearths. Here their children with their big bellies and small prominent behinds dusted gray with hearth ash, play a variety of games with the hard bright yellow fruits of nightshade known as Sodom apples. Gondoshabe sits with Gindu, mother of Andaranda who killed the zebra, and lank-dugged Angate with a tobacco wad behind her ear, and Hanako, young wife of the swift hunter Salibogo, threading beads on long strands of fiber from the baobab, and Giga's daughter Kabaka, who with her baby has run away from the game scout Nangai at Yaida Chini. The women wear the same three garments as the women of the Bushmen: a genital cover, skirt, and carrying bag, formerly of hide, but now of cloth. They sit flat on the ground with legs straight out, toes upright, or squat on their haunches like the men. Though the nomadic Hadza do not burden themselves with metal bracelets, most women wear single headbands of white, red, and blue beads as well as bead armlets, anklets, and knee bands, and like the men, they may have three scars cut on the cheek in decoration. Small boys wear a simple strand of beads around the waist, small girls a rag and small bead apron, while infants may wear fetishes and charms as protection against the touch of menstruating women and the night cries of hurtful birds.[12] Kabaka's baby is immobilized by strings of beads, but for all her wealth Kabaka looks disgruntled, and it is she who raises her voice against the mzungu's presence in the camp. The wild Hadza women pay her little mind; though shyer than the men, they soon disregard the visitors and go on about their business. They grind maize, gather firewood; they dry new gourds bartered from the Mbulu, for they have no pottery, and fetch water from the river in the old. The gourds of cool water stand at angles beside a calabash of bright fresh berries. In this dry place, the sparkle of precious water borne in gourds has a true splendor. Gourds and arrow shafts may be marked with cross-hatching incised between parallel lines, these pairs of lines being set at angles to each other, but otherwise the Hadza have no art besides the decoration of their persons and the simplicity of their lives.

The Gidabembe rocks fall to the river edge, two hundred feet below. On the far side of the river lies low heavy forest, and beyond the forest is acacia savanna with big trees. Mbulu people have come down off the escarpment to clear patches of savanna; their presence has brought the humble duka that glints against the hills. Already a few Mbulu have crossed the river and set up maize shambas in the region of Gidabembe, and meanwhile Mangati filter up into the Sipunga from the south. While as yet there is no sign of overgrazing, this will come. The Mbulu and Mangati have caused the wild animals to scatter, and large game has become scarce during the dry season, when the only water available, in the Udahaya, is cut off by man. Eventually the Mbulu will call upon the Game Department to destroy the last elephant and buffalo, and meanwhile the wild animals are poached relentlessly by tillers and herdsmen alike.

A very few strangers, scattered through this valley, threaten the wildlife on which the Hadza depend, yet the Hadza accept these strangers as openly and cheerfully as they accept us. They cannot know that their time is past, although hunting is much harder now, and soon may be beyond their skills. In the old days, in time of famine, people of other tribes would go into the bush to live with the hospitable Hadza, who have no memory of hunger – despite a passion for honey and meat, they depend on seeds, tubers, roots, wild cowpeas, ivy gourd, borage, and berries of toothbrush bush and grewia, in addition to certain fungi and such seasonal tree fruits as baobab, figs, desert dates (*Balanites*), and tamarind. Excess meat and honey, used formerly in trade for beads and iron and tobacco, is hard to come by, for log hives brought in by the Mbulu are attracting the wild bees, and game is scarce. When the hunting is gone, the Hadza may take to killing stock, as the Bushmen did. Already one Hadza has been speared to death near Mangola for the killing and consumption of a goat.

A few Mbulu and Mangati stroll through Gidabembe, tall and contemptuous; they grin coldly for the benefit of the white man by way of answer to the Hadza greetings. There are two Mbulu shambas within a mile of Gidabembe, and already the Hadza have adopted this Mbulu name for their ancestral place, which in their own tongue is Ugulu. Recently, a family of Mangati has built a typical figure-eight stockade close by; one of the loops of the stockade is used for cattle, and in the other is the rectangular Mangati hut, like an Mbulu tembe but built above the level of the ground. The Mbulu and the men of the Mangati wrap themselves in trade cloth, but Mangati women wear skirts of leather cured in human urine, as Maasai women did in former days. Certain warm-breasted leather-skirted girls of the Mangati, carved northern faces softened by the south, are the loveliest women, black or brown or white, that I have seen in Africa.

At dark, we go with drink onto the rock over the cave and roll a smoke, and stare out over Hadza Land, and listen. Already Peter has relaxed, though he has not slept, and I find him an excellent companion, well informed, inquiring, with an open mind and a capacity for silence, and possessed of an ironic perception that has surely spared his sanity. People who knew him from his sprees on infrequent visits to Arusha had warned me that Enderlein was "bushed", as the saying goes here, from too much time alone out in the bush; they spoke of Peter's beautiful young wife who had found bush life unbearable and had fled two years before, not to return. But a letter sent me in Nairobi gave me confidence that we would get on all right: "I think if you allow yourself two weeks here," he wrote in part, "you would be able to get a fair insight into the valley and its mysteries; if you stay longer, you might well end up at my position, knowing nothing at all. It seems the longer one stays at a place, the less one has to say about it . . ."

For this safari we had settled on two low camp cots, without tent, a few essentials such as rice and tea and rum, and whatever tinned goods might be rattling around in the rear of my old Land Rover. For the rest we would make do as we went along. Even so, our camp was infinitely more complex than the Hadza hearths, and soon seemed littered. Both of us have a passion for traveling light, deploring the ponderous caravansary which Anglo-Saxons in particular tend to conceive of as safaris – the table, camp chairs, ice chests, private toilet tents, truckloads of provender and swarming staff that permit them to lug the colonial amenities of the Hotel Norfolk "into the blue." Like myself, Peter has often been ashamed in front of Africans by the amount of equipment that his white friends required. Yet Africans admire wealth, and anyway, they do not make judgments in such matters, but accept a different culture as it is. The people at Gidabembe, who still trust, are neither subservient nor rude. Here was the gentleness, the loving attention to the moment, that is vanishing in East Africa, as it has vanished in the western world.

Exhilarated, happy, we lie flat out on the high rocks, still warm from the hot sun of afternoon. Peter draws his finger across the sky, starting to laugh. "Fake stars have five points, isn't it true?" he says. "Now I shall try to count how many points the *real* stars have . . ." He laughs quietly for a long time. And later he shouts suddenly, "You see? You see that constellation veering? It's like a kite!

It's like a kite in that one moment just before it falls . . ." And I turn my head to watch him bellow at the universe.

Three months after our stay at Gidabembe, Peter would write as follows from hospital in Arusha:

> It seems my time in Hadza Land has come to an end. I was recently called to a meeting in Mbulu to discuss my project but I found myself the witch in a medieval witchhunt where the bonfire was built and the match already lighted. It seemed I wanted to ruin their efforts of settling the Hadza – of course everybody knows that white men like to see Africans primitive and naked only – and turn them back to the bush. I also payed them money to strip nude so that my friends could photograph them in this state – all of course to discredit the development of the country. Somebody suggested that I shoot more zebras than I account for and keep the money myself. Somebody else knew that the Hadza despised me, etc., etc., etc. So here I am, having chosen to be hospitalized for a while – how can one choose jaundice? – looking for new horizons . . .

In a day the zebra is already gone, and Dafi and Salibogo will rejoin the hunters beyond the Sipunga Hills. We go along to watch them hunt.

A solitary elephant crosses a rise among great baobabs, and they cry out, but except at close range, it is hard to drive an arrow through the thick hide of an elephant. Their bows require a hundred-pound pull[13] from a hunter who weighs little more than that himself, and the poison used here is not strong enough.

On the far side of Sipunga, down toward the Yaida Plain, there are impala, and Dafi and Salibogo run through the scattered trees, moving downwind before cutting back toward the animals. Both are very small and quick, as if in hunters, this small size, like the long legs of the nomadic herdsmen, was a phenomenon of natural selection. In the case of the well-fed Hadza, it would be hard to argue that small size is the consequence of life in a hostile and stunted environment; like hunter-gatherers the world over, they tend to be better nourished than more settled peoples, who must struggle to subsist. Until recently there was no need to hunt hard to get all the meat they wanted, and probably the game will be all gone before they refine their skills. Enderlein once watched Ariangulo trackers brought here from the Tsavo country by white hunters. He says that the Hadza, who hunt alone except when encircling baboons, compare in neither tactics nor persistence with the Ariangulo, who have huge bows with arrows tipped in acokanthera and specialize in hunting elephants.

Magandula, grabbing a bow, trots after the hunters in his black shoes; the self-conscious leer upon his face fails to conceal an innocent excitement. Eventually Salibogo goes on by himself, running bent double over long stretches of open ground, rising and falling, crouching, peering, and snaking at last on his belly to the caper bush where he will lie. The animals drift away from Dafi, who, in the way of lions, drives them gently into ambush, but the wind shifts and the lead animal crosses Salibogo's scent. In the stillness comes the impala's blowing snort, and the bright-eyed ones are gone.

With the impala goes the last good opportunity of the day. Even when Enderlein decides to use his rifle, we come up with nothing. Zebra, impala, and wildebeest are all shy and scarce, and a wildebeest bull struck at long range fails to come down. The day is dry and very hot, and much of this landscape south and west of the Sipunga has been burned by the Mangati; on a black ground, Senegal bustards pick the burnt eggs of guinea fowl. Farther north, in a grassland with low suffocated thorn, there are no animals at all. Overhead passes a pelican, flapping and sailing on its way to distant water, but here the thorn wood and dense dusty grass is empty, and as the morning turns to afternoon, black man and white fall silent. An African landscape full of animals, even dangerous ones, does not seem hostile; life is sustained here, and somewhere there is water. But without animals, the parched grass and bitter thorn, the hard-caked earth, the old sky shrouded by smoke through which a dull sun looms like a blind eye – all seems implacable. The sun god Haine, though worshipped by the Hadza, is remote and ill disposed toward man, and is not invoked. In the dark of the moon the hunters dance all night to insure good hunting and good health, for sometimes a hunter, crouched in night ambush at a waterhole, is taken by the lion, Sesemaya.

At home, hot, tired, and oppressed, we tramp down to the Udahaya. Careless of bilharzia, we lie in the cool flow, six inches deep, that streams over fine copper-colored sand. We wash, dry off on the green bank in a cool north wind, and climb back up to Gidabembe, feeling better. There Gondoshabe and Angate are singing on their knees, breasts swinging across big flat-topped tilted stones on which maize meal is refined by being scraped by a flat rock. The meal pours onto clean impala hide below the stone.

The boy Saidi, preparing his small arrows, sits alone at a fire above the river. All Hadza boys, developing their bow strength from an early age, have weapons suitable to their size that are in constant play and practice, and the glint of a bird arrow risen through the trees of a still landscape is a sign of Hadza presence. Though some men never hunt at all, content to accept charity in return for the loss of prestige, Saidi's intensity and bearing say that he will be a hunter. Squatting on his heels, he trims his vulture plumes and binds them to a shaft with neck ligament of the impala. Four vanes are trimmed and bound on tight in as many minutes, and the binding sealed over with the glue from a chewed tuber. He sights down his new arrow shafts then gnaws at one to soften it for straightening before fitting his arrow tips into shaft sockets dug out with a bent nail. Then he rises and goes off after dik-dik and rock hyrax, which both abound here. The hyrax looks like a sharp-nosed marmot, but on the basis of certain anatomical similarities, notably the feet, it has been determined that its nearest living kin are elephants. Perhaps as a defense against the attack of eagles, the hyrax has the astonishing ability to stare straight upward into the equatorial sun.

Watching Saidi go, Enderlein says, "Do you know what will become of him?" He scowls. "First, when all the game is gone, and the trees, too, he will be forced to go to Yaida Chini. Untrained, he can do nothing, and because he is Hadza he will be treated as inferior everywhere he goes. If he is very lucky, he might become a thief in Dar es Salaam; otherwise he will be just another one of all those faces in the streets, hopeless and lost, with all the dignity that this life gives him gone." He got to his feet, disgusted, and we walked in silence toward the cave, through the beautiful rock monuments and wild still twilight orchards of commiphora like old apple trees, and terminalia with red pods like fruit, and figs, and fruiting grewia bushes, and a small sweet-scented acacia with recurved spines that catch hold of the unwary – the wait-a-bit thorn, from the Swahili *ngoja kidogo*, which means wait-a-little.

At the cave is the game scout Nangai, come on foot from Yaida Chini to fetch back his young wife Kabaka, daughter of Giga. "Who knows why she ran away?" Nangai shrugs, smiling shyly at his sullen wife. Giga, holding his ornamented grandchild to his cheek, rolls his eyes and croons, a love all the more affecting for the great ugliness that, as one comes to perceive this man, turns to great beauty.

Tea is served by sad-faced discreet Gimbe, who says, "*Karibu chai,*" welcome to tea, with the same sweet simplicity with which another African once said to me, "You are nicely welcomed to Samburu." With his wood ladle he stirs maize meal into boiling water to make the thick white paste called ugali that is subsistence in East Africa; ugali, eaten with the fingers, is rolled into a kind of concave ball used to mop up whatever is at hand in the way of meat, vegetables, and gravy. Soon he presents a bowl of water in which the right hand is to be dipped and rinsed prior to eating, because here in the cave our posho, or ration, is eaten from a common bowl. The Moslem washing of one hand comes up from the coast by way of the part-Arab Swahili, once the agents of the trade in slaves and ivory; so does the mbira or "marimba", called irimbako by the Hadza, who have no musical instrument of their own. The mbira, or flat-bar zither, came to East Africa centuries ago from Indonesia. It is a hollow box faced with tuned strips of stiff metal that produces soft swift wistful rhythms of time passing, and the old one here at Gidabembe is passed from hand to hand. It is Giga who plays it by the fire as we dine on ugali and delicate doves shot in the hills.

At Gidabembe Hill, among the monoliths, baboons are raving, and there comes a sudden brief strange sound that brings Giga from his cave. "*Chui*," he whispers. Leopard. But the others shrug – how can one know? The Hadza never like to give opinions. A few days later, in this place, we find the vulture-gutted body of a young leopard on an open slope where no sick leopard would ever lie, and the grass all about has been bent and stamped by a convocation of baboons, as if the creature had been caught in the open by the huge baboon troupe, which had killed it. Yet there was no baboon fur in its mouth, nor any blood or sign of struggle in the grass.

The dark falls quiet once again. From Sipunga comes the night song of unknown birds, and the shrill ringing yip of a distant jackal, and inevitably the ululations of hyenas. The Hadza are comparatively unsuperstitious, and unfrightened of the dark: "We are ready for him," they say of Fisi, reaching out to touch their bows. "Hyena can be a bloody nuisance," Enderlein says, recalling an account, no doubt apocryphal, of a sleeping man who had his foot bitten clean off by a night hyena. He places a dim kerosene lantern near our bed rolls, for we are sleeping outside the cave. At my head is a white hyrax stain on the dark rock, and beside the stain are stacked the rifles. Mosquitoes are few and we sleep without a net, staring up through the black leaves at cruel bright stars. Gimbe is sleeping in the Land Rover, and others sleep on hides inside the cave. Magandula curls up with his bunduki, and Giga is hooked close to the embers. They murmur in their soft deep voices, which drop away one by one. Soon Giga is asleep, and all night he breathes rapidly, like a wild creature stunned and felled while running.

The Hadza see no sense in hunting hard with bow and arrow when there is a rifle in the camp. In hope of meat, people are coming in out of the hills, and there are seven hearths where there were four. The Hadza here are now no less than thirty and a buffalo would feed everyone for days.

Many buffalo, as well as rhino and elephant, live in the forest below Gidabembe. When Peter asks me if I wish to hunt, I tell him I will think about it. Enderlein is a good shot who is shooting badly, who is sleeping badly, whose every action has a trace of rage in it; he is not the companion I would choose for the pursuit of dangerous animals, and especially buffalo, toward which he seems more disrespectful than any hunter I have ever met. "He's too damned careless about buffalo; he's going to catch it one of these days," says Douglas-Hamilton, who is not known for prudence. On the other hand, though I had no wish to shoot a big animal myself, hunting dangerous game is a part of the African mystique that I did not know. And this morning is a soft green morning when death, which never seems remote in Africa, but hangs about like something half-remembered, might come almost companionably . . . be that as it may, I leave my doubts behind.

We descend to the river at daybreak, accompanied by the game scouts Magandula and Nangai, and Mugunga, who is Nangai's young porter, and two wild Hadza, Yaida and Salibogo. Magandula carries Peter's .375, which few hunters consider powerful enough to stop a buffalo, and Nangai brings a .22 for small game. Yaida and Salibogo carry bow and arrows. We ford the river where it winds around the base of Gidabembe, and enter the dense forest single file. Salibogo is in the lead, then Enderlein, Nangai, Mugunga, who carries Peter's pouch of bullets, then Magandula, then myself, and finally Yaida, who looks like a young Bushman. For the first time Magandula is shirtless, and he has a porcupine quill stuck in his hair, but he clings to his red socks and pointed shoes.

Trees in this virgin place are huge – umbrella thorn and soaring fever trees, and here and there a mighty winterthorn (*A. albida*), the noblest of all acacias, these interspersed with fat sycamore figs and sausage trees. But along the animal trails and walling the small glades is head-high thicket, hollowed out, where rhino and buffalo may stand entirely hidden. Their spoor is everywhere, and Salibogo drops behind; there is no need for a tracker. We move carefully and quietly, bending each moment to peer into the grottoes. The trick is to sight any hidden beast before it feels crowded and decides to charge, but the cover is dense, and Enderlein offers a tense grin. "Bloody dangerous bush," he murmurs. "They can see you but you can't see them." In Peter's opinion, rhino are more dangerous than buffalo, being stupid and unpredictable, a "warm-blooded dinosaur," as he says, that has outlived its time; rhinos are apt to rush out blindly where a buffalo would slip away. But I share the more common dread of the low-browed buffalo, shifting its jaws sideways as it chews its cud, light glancing from its horn.

Oblivious birdsong in the early morning wind; warm butterflies spin sunlight through the glades. The Hadza pause every little while to wring dry berries from the grewia bushes, but my own mouth is too dry, I am not hungry. There is exhilaration in the hunt, and also the quick heart of the hunted. I feel strong and light and quick, and more than a match for the nearest tree that can be climbed in haste. These are damnably few: the big trees lack low branches and the small are shrouded with thorn vine and liana. Yaida and Salibogo, like myself, keep a close watch on the trees, and we grin nervously at one another.

In a circular glade, Enderlein crouches, stiffens, and steps back, holding out his hand. Magandula gives him his rifle. In the shadows ten yards to the left, the cave of leaves is filled with a massive shape, as still as stone. A little way back there was fresh rhino track, and Peter thinks this is the rhino. He circles out a little ways, just to make sure. A slight movement may bring on a rhino charge – its poor vision cannot make out what's moving, and its nerves cannot tolerate suspense whereas a sudden movement may put it to flight. I am considering a sudden movement, such as flight of my own, when I see a tail in a thin shaft of light, and the tail tuft in fleeting silhouette, and grunt at Peter, "Buffalo."

A sun glint on the moisture at the nostril; the animal is facing us. The tail does not move again. We stand there for long seconds, at a loss. Enderlein cannot get a fair shot in the poor light, and at such close quarters, he does not want a wounded buffalo. He starts a wide circling stalk of the entire copse, signaling his game scouts to follow. But it is the boy Mugunga who jumps forward, and the game scouts shrug, content to let him go. We follow carefully, but soon the hunters vanish in the bushes. Heat and silence. Soon the silence is intensified by a shy birdsong, incomplete, like a child's question gone unanswered.

The bird sings again, waits, sings again. Bees come and go. Soon Mugunga reappears. The beast will not be chivvied out of hiding, and there is no hope of a clear shot with the rifle. But a poisoned arrow need not be precise. The hunter had only to wait a few hours before tracking, so as not to drive the dying animal too far away, and in this time he would return to camp to find help in cutting up the meat, or if the animal was big, to move the whole camp to the carcass.

Mugunga draws on Yaida's bow, then picks the stronger bow of Salibogo. The Hadza faces fill with joy; they respect the rifle but they trust the bow. Then Mugunga vanishes once more, and the silence deepens. Leaves stir and are still.

The birdsong ceases as the buffalo crashes free, but there is no shout, no rifle shot, only more silence. When the hunters reappear, Enderlein says, "I thought the arrow might bring him out where I could get a shot at him, but Mugunga waited a split second too long, and the bloody brute pushed off, out the far side." Even so we will track this buffalo; Peter keeps the gun. The Hadza move on, bush by bush, glade by glade, checking bent grass, earth, and twigs, darting through copses where one would have thought so large an animal could not have gone. To watch such tracking is a pleasure, but this is taut work, for the buffalo is listening, it has not taken flight. Somewhere in the silent trees, the dark animal is standing still, or circling to come up behind. Wherever it is, it is too close.

In the growing heat, our nerves go dead, and we are pushing stupidly ahead, inattentive, not alert, when the spoor dies, too, and we cut away from the river in search of another animal. But the sun is climbing, and the big animals will have taken to the shade. The chance of catching one still grazing in the open is now small.

In a swampy place the Hadza fall on a tomato bush. The small fruits are warm red, intensely flavored, and we eat what we can and tie the rest into a rag to bring back to Gidabembe. Not that the hunters feel obliged to do this: men and women seek and eat food separately and quickly, to avoid the bad manners of refusing it to others, and occasional sharing between the sexes is a matter of whim. Farther on, Yaida and Salibogo locate honey in a tree, and again the hunt for buffalo is abandoned. Usually a grass torch is stuck into the hole to smoke out the bees, but the Hadza are more casual than most Africans about bee stings, and Yaida is wringing one stung hand while feeding himself with the other. The honeycomb is eaten quickly, wax, larvae, and all. The Hadza also eat hyena, cats, and jackals, though they draw the line at frogs and reptiles, and not every man will eat a vulture.

Hyena prints, and spoor of waterbuck. Nangai kicks at buffalo manure to see its freshness, and it is plain that we have passed the dark silent animals close by. Mugunga, frustrated, shoots a lance at a dik-dik half-hidden by low, intervening branches – he leans into the shot on his left foot as he shoots – and the arrow drives hard into a sapling by the dik-dik's neck. He turns to look at us, shaking his head. We circle slowly toward the Udahaya, striking it at midday far downriver. The hunt is over, and we walk barefoot in the water, shooting doves and hyrax with the .22 as we return upstream. Peter is brooding, but I am still excited by the hunt, and glad to be free of the dense bush, and so I celebrate this moment of my life, the sparkle of gold mica on my brown feet, a pair of pied kingfishers that racket from dead limb to limb, the sweet scent of the white-flowered vernonia, swarming with bees that make honey for the Hadza. And the Hadza seem happy, too: their time is now. Though there will not be nearly enough to go around, it awes them to see the doves fall to our gun. They are used to failure in the hunt, which these days occurs often, and in the future must occur more often still.

A visitor to Gidabembe comes from a small camp in the Sipunga Hills, where he helps take care of a young invalid, apparently an epileptic. Last year this boy was badly burned when he fell into a fire, and was led across the hills to the clinic in Mbulu, but after two days he ran away, back to Sipunga. This spring, left alone in camp, he fell again into the fire and was burned so drastically that he can no longer move.

Magandula has borrowed a wood comb from Giga; perched on a rock, he combs his head for a long time without discernible results. According to Magandula, it is only the influence of civilization that prevents the *Sipunganebe* from deserting the man burned, and the Hadza cheerfully agree: among nomadic hunter-gatherers, who cannot afford responsibility for others, such desertion is quite common. Only last year, Yaida says, a man in fever was abandoned in the mountains: "We left him his bow, but he could not live; surely he was eaten by lions." Magandula, scrubbing his shoes, becomes excited and speaks shrilly: "To live in the bush is bad!

Hasn't the government taught us to live in houses? I want nothing to do with the bush!" In recent years the government has made of the Hadza a symbol of primitive apathy to their countrymen, who are exhorted to increase their numbers and work hard on their shambas – "Don't rot in the bush like the Watindiga!" And tillers from Mbulu come sometimes to Yaida Chini and jeer at them: "How can people be so primitive!" – just as the people of Arusha might speak of the poor peasants of Mbulu, or the people of Dar es Salaam of the provincial folk met in Arusha.

Four naked children have clambered up into a grewia bush and hunch there in the branches, knees under their chins, munching sweet berries while they watch us. Despite big bellies and thin legs, which are lost early, Hadza children are clear-eyed and energetic, and like their parents, they are cheerful. Somewhere it has been suggested that hunter-gatherers seem happier than farmers, and of necessity more versatile and alert than people who live mostly in a rut. But their good spirits may come also from their varied diet, which is far healthier than the ugali and pombe fare of the shamba dwellers they are told to emulate.

Magandula watches the white man watching the small dark naked bodies in the branches. "*Kama nyani*," he jeers, with terrific ambivalence, for Magandula is in pain – "Just like baboons!" He searches our faces for the affirmation that he feared was there before he spoke. "Look at old Mutu, and that old woman!" he bursts out again, pointing, "Life is too hard here!" And the old woman herself, coming home one day with her rag sack, speaks of berries with disdain. "Ugali is better," she declares, to show her acquaintance with maize meal paste, although ugali is woefully poor in both taste and nutrition.

Magandula's emotion is disturbing because he is angry without provocation, therefore afraid, therefore fanatic. And what can Magandula be afraid of? Unless he fears that he has lost touch with his origins, his clans, the earth and the old ways, with no real hope or promise from the new.

As if to bear witness for Magandula, old Mutu comes tottering to his hearth and sinks down in a heap against a stone. He no longer bothers with his bow and arrows, which rot in the bush behind his head; the sad old broken arrows with their tattered vanes are the home of spiders. Mutu is back from begging maize at an Mbulu shamba, and complains as ever of his feet, which are leprously cracked and horned up to the ankle bone. To my touch, his afflicted flesh feels rubbery and dead. Once Mutu walked as far east as Mbulu, where he came by his disease. "Things like *this*" – and he flicks his ruined flesh, contemptuous, lip curling around a villainous old mouthful of snag teeth – "you don't find in the bush." In proof of his corruption by the world, Mutu begs cynically for two *shillingi* – the only Hadza that ever begged at all – and is happy to accept a dove instead. Despite his misery and decrepitude, he has no wish to visit the dispensary at Yaida Chini, and waves away the offer of a ride. Already he has his stone pipe lit, tucking a red cinder into it with his bare fingers, and now he lies back laughing at some ancient joke, coughing ecstatically after the custom of his people.

Twig-legged Mutu is big-bellied as a baby, lying there in the sunlight in his swaddling. He rails at life with unholy satisfaction, and so do the two old women whose hearths adjoin his own at the base of the great tilted rock with the rounded top that might be the gravestone of God. All three worn-out souls are of separate families, and fiercely maintain their family hearths as symbols of the independence which is so vital to the Hadza, although not one has relatives at Gidabembe who might look after him. Yet Mutu has maize and berries for his supper, and so do his two neighbors. And it was Mutu who explained the greatest mystery of life at Gidabembe: how it was, when times were hard, that a scorned people were able to beg maize and tobacco from the Mbulu, who were few and poor here, and living themselves at a subsistence level.

The Hadza claim to perform certain services for the Mbulu, helping them to dig their shambas, tend their stock, and cultivate during the wet season; also, the Mbulu come to them for honey and dawa. But these infrequent services cannot account for the munificence of the Mbulu, and it seems clear from the quantity of maize obtained that the Hadza are not begging, but go to the shambas with every expectation of reward.

For the Mbulu, death is a great disaster, and the evil effects of pollutions that they fear the most are those associated with dead bodies. In former days, bodies were left to the hyenas, as with the Maasai, but nowadays, according to Mutu, who is borne out in every particular by Giga and Nangai, the dead person is buried quickly, after which a Hadza is summoned who is of the same sex as the dead. The Hadza shaves the head of the bereaved, who then strips himself naked and presents to the Hadza his clothes and all belongings of the dead person except money, which is not thought of as polluted, and also four debes (the debe or four-gallon kerosene can is the standard container in the bush) of maize. He or she then copulates with the Hadza, who thereby inherits the disaster, and will die eventually of this act. "He may count his years," cries Magandula, who writhes at Mutu's words but does not deny them, "but it will catch him before long." Mutu is emphatic about his facts, pounding his old hand on the earth to simulate copulation. When he is finished he averts his gaze, shrugging his shoulders. Such was the penalty that his people paid for being poor; there was nothing to be done about it. But Nangai and Magandula say they would not perform such a service; it is only for these wild Hadza, who are so poor that they have no choice. (Perhaps the game scouts spread the word that there were wild Hadza at Gidabembe, for not long after our departure Enderlein sent evil news: "The people there were rounded up and taken to Yaida

Chini, arriving in time for a measles epidemic in which nine Hadza children died.")

Listening politely to the shouts of Magandula, the hunters do not protest. They accept the scorn of their fellow man as a part of Hadza life. On the other hand, they prefer to remain in the bush. "I have got used to it," says Chandalua, who is Yaida's older brother and the father of the boy Saidi. With Dafi, he lives ordinarily in the Giyeda Barakh, on the far side of the Yaida, overlooking Lake Eyasi: Giyeda Barakh, known in their click-speech as *Hani'abi*, "the rocks", will be a last strong-hold of the Hadza. Chandalua's gentle face has the transparence of infinity. Sitting on his warm stone notching an arrow shaft, he smiles approvingly on Magandula, who still scrubs fiercely at his shoes.

A stony path of rhino, man, and elephant leads up into Sipunga, and ascending it one morning, we met four lean Mangati entering the valley armed with spears and poisoned arrows. The arrows are illegal, since only the Hadza are permitted to hunt here without restraint, but rather than kill their scraggy beasts, the meat-eating Mangati poach wherever possible.

Both groups stop at a little distance, regarding each other without pleasure. The tall sandaled Mangati, cowled and scarified with half-circles of raised welts about the eyes, are handsome remote men, with a hard cast to their gaze. They look like legendary desert bandits, and their spears have a honed shine. But our party is the stronger, with two white men and the armed game scout Nangai, as well as Salibogo, Andaranda, and Maduru; we have two rifles and three bows. When Nangai steps forward and takes hold of the poisoned arrows, the Mangati leader abandons his bad smile. He refuses to let go, and his companions, scowling, shift their feet. The youngest, a very beautiful cold-faced morani, not yet twenty, makes contemptuous remarks to Andaranda, who steps past him on his pigeon-toed bare feet and continues up the trail. To save face for both sides, it is decided that the shafts will not be taken, only the arrowheads, and the two groups part in silence, looking back over their shoulders until the others are out of sight.

The few Mangati in the region of Gidabembe are at peace with the Hadza, who have nothing worth taking away. "They do not kill us now," the Hadza say. But the hunters, who are small and peaceable and claim no territory, are neither defenseless nor lacking in courage, and their forbearance has its limits. Not long ago, near Tandusi, to the south, some Hadza caught two Mangati moran in a prized bee tree, and when the Mangati defied a request that they come down, shot them out of it with lance arrows, killing both.

The Mangati, too, pay careful attention to death. An elder's funeral may last nine months, while a monument of mud, dung, and poles some twelve feet high is erected in stages on the grave; at the end of the final ceremonies, as darkness falls, two ancient men crawl naked to the deserted mound and fasten a magic vine about its base, whispering. "Don't hurry, wait for us, we will join you soon." Most women and all children are left to the hyenas, but a female elder of good repute may also be given a small mound on which her wood spoon and clay cooking pot are placed. Toward the end of a brief mourning period, a hole is poked through the clay pot, to signify that her work on earth is done.[14]

We climb steadily through the early morning, across dry open hillsides without flowers. In a broad pile of dik-dik droppings on the trail is a small hole six inches deep and six across. Though it moves in daylight with the shadows of rock and bush, the tiny antelope returns at night to these rabbity heaps out in the open; here it feels safe from stealing enemies, and waits out the long African dark. Dik-dik (so the Dorobo say) once tripped over the mighty dung pile of an elephant, and has tried ever since to reply in kind by collecting its tiny droppings in one place.[15] Man takes advantage of the habit by concealing in a hole a ring of thorns with the points facing inward and down. The dik-dik – meaning "quick-quick" in Swahili – cannot extract its delicate leg, and is killed by the first predator to come along. Whoever is hunting here is not a Hadza, for the Hadza know nothing of traps or snares of any kind.

Rhinoceros, also sedentary in their habits, follow the same trails to water, dust wallow, and browse, and on a grand scale share this custom of adding to old piles of their own droppings, which are then booted all about, perhaps as a means of marking territory but more likely as an aid to orientation in a beast whose prodigious sniff must compensate for its poor eyesight. Rhino piles are common on this path, together with wallows and the primitive three-toed print. Not far away, one or more of these beasts is listening, flicking its ears separately in the adaptation that accounts in part for its uncanny hearing, and making up its rudimentary mind whether or not to clear the air with a healthy charge.

The ridge is open, with thick trees and granite islands; a squirrel sways among strange star-shaped fruits of a sterculia. Andaranda on his short bent legs, a hyrax swinging from his waist, views all about him with a smile. His bare feet, impervious to burrs and stones, thump steadily against the earth, and his hands, too, are tough as stumps, as they must be in a life so close to bees and thorns and fire. The trail arrives at a water point, Halanogamai, which Mbulu or Mangati have fenced off with thorn brush to keep out wild animals. Enderlein attacks the fence without a word, hurling it into high piles for a bonfire, and the Hadza drag wood to the fire that has nothing to do with the thorn fence, the threat of which to their way of life they have not grasped. Maduru gets a thorn branch stuck to his back, and I pick him free. One day, emerging from beneath the Land Rover,

I was picked free by Salibogo, and another day by Gimbe; no African would expect thanks for this basic courtesy, and Maduru did not pause to thank me now.

On the far side of the Sipunga, the track turns north, skirting the heads of narrow gorges; the gorges open out on a broad prospect of the Yaida Plain, pale in the desert sun of summer. All along the rim rise granite monoliths, and at one of these vast rocks known as Maseiba there lived until a few years ago an old Hadza named Seira and his wife Nyaiga. One day, says Maduru, Seira was out hunting hyrax, and had killed five with his bow, but the sixth fell into a dark crevice which hid a snake. Seira, three times bitten – Maduru slaps his arm, then chest, then side – ran home and applied strong snakebite dawa. Feeling better, he lay down to rest. But unlike most hunters, who avoid encumbrance, Seira had two wives, and Nyaiga was very jealous of the second wife, even though she lived at Gidabembe. Nyaiga rubbed arrow poison into Seira's bites and he shortly died.

The Hadza leave the elephant trail, circling west through windy glades toward high rocks bright with orange, blue-gray, and crusting gray-green lichens. Below, a cleft between two portals forms a window on the Yaida plain, and nestled in the cleft, entirely hidden from the world except from the spot on which we stand, is a small ledge shaded by a grove of three commiphora. The myrrh trees stand in heraldic triangles, and set against their scaly trunks are three shelters so well camouflaged by cut branches that the trees appear to grow out of a thicket. In seasons when the commiphora is in leaf, the shelters would not be visible at all.

We descend quietly, watched from hiding by the inhabitants. This place is Sangwe, Maduru whispers, and eight Hadza live here. They are very shy and hide behind the huts, though they have recognized Maduru, and been greeted. All three huts are roofed and lined with grass. The wall of one sustains the next, and the tight interiors are spare and orderly as new bird nests. As at Gidabembe, there is no scent of human waste and no notice taken of the seedy feces of baboons. Between the huts and the ledge rim where the cleft falls away into the canyon is a place scarcely large enough for the cooking fire, and beside the fire, on a kongoni hide, lies a strongly built young Hadza with a twisted eye and a stiff right hand bent back toward his wrist by the burnt hide. Healed flesh on his deformed left foot is a bare pink, but the crust on a hand-sized wound over his heel is oozing. This is Magawa, in whose wild eyes I see the choking struggle in the fire, and the thrashing on his rock of pain in the weeks afterward, under the far, unforgiving eye of the sun god, Haine.

Magawa says that he fled the clinic at Mbulu because he could not live so far from Sangwe, and like Mutu, he has no wish to go to Yaida Chini even though here he must remain a helpless cripple. Maduru decides to go to Yaida Chini in Magawa's place, and instead of remaining behind at Sangwe, he comes with us. The others watch Maduru go, and Magandula would say that in time they, too, will depart, leaving Magawa to the lions.

Nangai and Maduru know of a great rock with red paintings, which in this land may be thousands of years old; more recent drawings, usually abstract, are done in white and gray. Earlier this morning, off the trail, we found a large cave almost hidden in the thicket that had overgrown its mouth; Maduru had not known about this cave, which is occupied at present by bats and hornets but also contains an ancient hearth and vertical red stripes. The Hadza have no special curiosity about red markings, since every tree and boulder in this land which gives them life has its own portent and significations.

We descend the ridge, moving southeast along Sipunga. Maduru points out the holes of bees into which he has wedged stones. If the entrance to a hive must be enlarged to reach the honey, and if stones are handy, one or more may be stuck into the hole until the entrance is reduced again to the size approved by bees. "We put stones here," Salibogo says, "so that the honey will come back." Stones stuck in trees are one of the few signs of the presence of Hadza, who unlike the Mbulu and Mangati are invisible in their environment; they have no idea of wilderness, for they are part of it. At the foot of a ravine a bird comes to the trees with urgent trilling, then flies off again, pursued by Salibogo and Andaranda, who are trilling urgently themselves. This bird is the black-throated honey guide, which has evolved the astonishing habit of leading honey badger and man to the hives of bees and feasting upon the leavings of the raid; if no honey is left for the honey guide, Africans say, it will lead the next man to a snake or lion. But this bird is soon back again, still trilling, having left the Hadza far away under the hill.

Southeastward, under the soaring rock, we follow in the noble paths of elephant. Maduru points at an overhanging wall, like a wave of granite on the yellow sky: Darashagan. A hot climb brings us out at last onto a ledge under the overhang, well hidden by the tops of trees that rise from the slopes below; the ledge looks south down the whole length of the Yaida Valley. There is a hearth here, still in use, and on the wall behind the hearth, sheltered by the overhang, are strong paintings in a faded red of a buffalo and a giraffe. We stand before them in a line, in respectful silence. One day another man, all nerves and blood and hope just like ourselves, drew these emblems of existence with a sharpened bird bone spatula, a twist of fur, a feather, and others squatted here to watch, much as the Hadza are squatting now. The Mbulu and Barabaig have no tradition of rock painting, whereas the Bushmen, before they became fugitives, made paintings very similar to these. The only other red paintings in this country are found in the region of Kondoa-Irangi, in the land of the click-speaking Sandawe.

Andaranda makes a fire and broils hyrax and a guinea fowl. When we have eaten, he picks grewia leaves, and the Hadza trim the leaves and roll tobacco from their pouches. I try Nangai's uncultivated weed, and the Hadza giggle at my coughs. Of the drawings they say shyly, "How can we know?" Pressed, they ascribe them to the Old People or to Mungu (God), searching our faces in the hope of learning which one we prefer: our need to *understand* makes them uncomfortable. For people who must live from day to day, past and future have small relevance, and their grasp of it is fleeting; they live in the moment, a very precious gift that we have lost.

Lying back against these ancient rocks of Africa, I am content. The great stillness in these landscapes that once made me restless seeps into me day by day, and with it the unreasonable feeling that I have found what I was searching for without ever having discovered what it was. In the ash of the old hearth, ant lions have counter-sunk their traps and wait in the loose dust for their prey; far overhead a falcon – and today I do not really care whether it is a peregrine or lanner – sails out over the rim of rock and on across the valley. The day is beautiful, my belly full, and returning to the cave this afternoon will be returning home. For the first time, I am in Africa among Africans. We understand almost nothing of one another, yet we are sharing the same water flask, our fingers touching in the common bowl. At Halanogamai there is a spring, and at Darashagan are red rock paintings – that is all.

In a few swift days of a dry summer this ancient cave in central Africa, blackened by centuries of smoke, has become for me my own ancestral place where fifty millenniums ago, a creature not so different from myself hunched close to the first fire. The striped swallow that nests under the arch was here before man's upright troupes came through the silent baobabs, and so were the geckos, hornets, and small mice that go about their bright-eyed business undisturbed.

Giga and Gimbe mind the cave, which stays cool in the dry heat of the day, and one or the other is always by the fire, playing delicately on an mbira. Meals are at random in the African way, and we have no wish to give them order. We eat before going on a hunt and after we return, and on some days there are two meals and on others four or five. When least expected and most wanted, Gimbe will come with a basin of fresh water – karibu – and then he will stir our posho into his charred pot with his wood spoon and present this warming stuff with a fine stew of whatever wild meat is at hand. In the afternoons, we bathe in the river and stand on the cool banks to dry, and toward twilight almost every night we climb onto the toppled monolith that forms the roof over the cave, and smoke, and watch the sun go down over Sipunga.

To the rock cast like a gravestone, the oldest woman, muttering, comes home each twilight with a bundle of sticks for her night fire. When, out of happiness, I greet her, she gives me the cold cheerless stare of ancient women – Why do you greet me, idiot? Can't you see the way that the world goes? – and totters past me to her hearth without a word. At darkness, in wind, three fires light the rock face, with leaping shadows of the three small human forms, clattering and cawing under the skeleton of their lone tree. But the dance of shadows dies as the fires dim and the three panakwetepi, the "old children", fall silent. The eldest draws bat-colored rags about her, hunched and nodding, and subsides into a little heap of dim mortality. I wonder if she hears hyenas howling.

An Mbulu donkey gives its maniacal cry, and far away on the escarpment, probing slowly across the mountain darkness, shine the hard eyes of a truck, bringing in cheap trade goods for the duka. From the Seven Hearths, the Hadza see the outside world, but the world cannot see them. "This valley, this people – it is a tragedy we are watching!" Enderlein cries. "And it is a sign of what is happening everywhere in this country, in the whole world! Sometimes I really don't think it is bearable to watch it, I have not the heart for it, I will have to leave. And other times, especially when I am drunk, I can see myself as a spectator at the greatest comedy there ever was, the obliteration of mankind by our own hand."

When the air grows cold we come down off the rock. In the cave, Hadza are gathered at the fire, shoulder to shoulder like the swallows, clicking endlessly in their warm tongue, with big sighs and little groans of emphasis and soft *n* and *anh* and *m* sounds, hands moving in and out among the embers, the scraping of a knife blade on a stone, cough, a whiff of bangi, until finally the people of the Seven Hearths depart. The last man squatting, Magandula, crawls off to his sleep with a loud self-conscious sigh that tells the white men, stretched silent as two dead beneath the stars, that the worldly Magandula, although patient to a fault, has no place among such simple folk. Already Giga the fire tender is breathing his night breath that sounds like a man pulled down in flight; I watch his face, asleep, and feel a tingling at the temples. Giga has been in Africa forever, he is the prototypic model of a man, the clay, and one loves not Giga but this being who is mortal, a kind humorous fellow of great presence and no small intelligence who will die. And Gimbe, too, singing his songs and playing his sweet irimbako, and even the brash Magandula, donning his magic street shoes for his flight from the old ways: to perceive them in their sleep – Enderlein, too – is to perceive and to make peace with one's own self.

Toward dawn, Giga hurls faggots on the fire and rolls himself a fat and lumpy smoke and coughs and coughs and coughs to his heart's content, and one forgives him even this. Soon the cricket stops its singing, and after a silence there is birdsong, the bell note of the slate-colored boubou, the doves and turacos, a hornbill. At sun-up comes an electric screeching that signals the passage of swift petal-colored lovebirds.

The Hadza hunch close to their fires, getting warm; when the sun has heat in it, the day begins. Soon the akwetepi, the "little people", come past the cave, first boys with bows, then younger children seeking berries – "*Shai-yaamo!*" they call. And the answer is *Shai-yamo mtana*, to which they echo a soft *m-taa-na*. They pull berry branches down and strip them, laughing. At the fire, long-legged in shorts and boots, the restless white men sip their tea and listen, warming cold hands on their tin cups. In the next days we will go away without the game scout Magandula, who is muttering about poachers in the region, and asks if he might linger in the bush.

The last day at the cave is slow and peaceful. The hunters come down from the Seven Hearths to a discreet fire from where they can spy politely on the visitors; they carve and chew and soften and sight new arrow shafts, bracing them by inserting them between the toes, or cut pipe holes into new pieces of stone found in the river.

"*Dong-go-ko.*" One man sings softly of zebras and lions. "*Dong-go-ko gogosala . . .*" Zebra, zebra, running fast . . .

The women are out gathering roots and tubers, and also the silken green nut of the baobab which, pounded on a stone and cooked a little, provides food for five months of the year. The still air of the hillside quakes with the pound of rock on rock, and in this place so distant from the world, the steady sound is an echo of the Stone Age. Sometimes the seeds are left inside the hull to make a baby's rattle, or a half shell may be kept to make a drinking cup. In the rains, the baobab gives shelter, and in drought, the water that it stores in its soft hollows, and always fiber thread and sometimes honey. Perhaps the greatest baobab were already full grown when man made red rock paintings at Darashagan. Today young baobab are killed by fires, set by the strangers who clear the country for their herds and gardens, and the tree where man was born is dying out in Hadza Land.

From a grove off in the western light, an arrow rises, piercing the sun poised on the dark massif of the Sipunga; the shaft glints, balances, and drops to earth. Soon the young hunters, returning homeward, come in single file between the trees, skins black against black silhouetted thorn. One has an mbira, and in wistful monotony, in hesitation step, the naked forms with their small bows pass one by one in a slow dance of childhood. The figures wind in and out among black thorn and tawny twilight grass and vanish once more as in a dream, like a band of the Old People, the small Gumba, who long ago went into hiding in the earth.

Acknowledgments

For encouraging the making of this book I am particularly grateful to John Owen, whose vision and dedication in a crucial time helped to save African wildlife for the future.

I thank Martha Gellhorn and Truman Capote for recommending me so generously to Dr Owen, and also William Shawn of *The New Yorker* magazine for the unfailing support that has made my travels possible for years.

Frank Minot and his staff at the African Wildlife Leadership Foundation in Nairobi (a branch of the Conservation Foundation in Washington, dedicated to the vital task of turning young Africans toward conservation), and also his wife, Mary, were helpful in innumerable ways that made an important contribution, not least of which was the warmth and hospitality of their lovely house in Langata. Other good friends who took me in with unfailing hospitality were Iain Douglas-Hamilton (Manyara), Peter Enderlein (Yaida Chini), Nancy and Lewis Hurxthal (Embakasi), Patricia and John Owen (Arusha), Ruth and Hugh Russell (Arusha), and Desmond Vesey-FitzGerald (Momela). At Seronera, where I had my own quarters, the parks staff and the scientists of the Serengeti Research Institute were most hospitable, in particular Kay and George Schaller and Kay and Myles Turner. Prince Sadruddin Aga Khan kindly invited me to join his safari in the Ngorongoro Crater in 1970, and another safari there later that year was greatly assisted by the generosity of Mr Solomon Ole Saibull, then conservator of the Crater, who made available his private tent.

In gratitude for kindnesses, information, and assistance, I mention the following in the knowledge that the names of others no less helpful will occur to me when it is too late; those I thank, too, with my apologies:

Terence Adamson (Samburu)
Jock Anderson (NFD)*
Ir. Hubert Braun (SRI)**
M. K. Chauhar (Magadi)
Menryn Cowie (Nairobi) (1961)
Dr Harvey Croze (SRI)**
Mme. Leo d'Erlanger (Seronera)
Reggie Destro (Ngorongoro)
Iain Douglas-Hamilton (Ndala)
Badru Eboo (Nairobi)

* Northern Frontier District
** Serengeti Research Institute

Dr G. Eckhart (Njombe)
Ulla Ekblad (Nairobi) (1961)
Peter Enderlein (Yaida Chini)
Luis Fernandes (Nairobi)
P. A. G. "Sandy" Field (Seronera)
Martha Gellhorn (Naivasha)
Giga (Gidabembe)
J. B. Gillett (East African Herbarium)
Gimbe (Gidabembe)
Aleicester Graham (Langata)
Dr Peter Greenway, OBE (East African Herbarium)
Dr Bernhard Grzimek (Seronera)
Patrick Hemingway (Arusha) (1961)
Jane and Hillary Hook (Kiganjo)
Nancy and Lewis Hurxthal (Embakasi–Ngurumans)
Dr Alan Jacobs (Inst. African Studies–Nairobi)
E. P. K. Kayu (East African Herbarium)
Kessi (Frank) (Mt Meru–Ol Doinyo Lengai)
Prince Sadruddin Aga Khan (Ngorongoro)
Kimunginye (Derati)
Dr Hans Kruuk (SRI)**
John Kufunguo (Ngorongoro)
Dr Hugh Lamprey (SRI)**
Richard Leakey (National Museum)
Leite (Gol Mountains)
Adrian Luckhurst (NFD)*
Sir Malcolm MacDonald (Seronera)
Magandula (Gidabembe)
Martin ole Mengoriki (Embagai)
Mary and Frank Minot (Langata)
Jonathan Muhanga (Manyara)
M. Nawaz (Seronera)
Perez Olindo (Nairobi)
David Ommaney (Nairobi)
Patricia and John Owen (Arusha)
Ian S. C. Parker (Nairobi)
Eliot Porter (NFD)*
Sandy Price (National Museum)
Robert Reitnauer (Ngurumans)
Mary Richards (Momela)
Oria Rocco (Ndala)

Alan Root (Nairobi)
Hilary and Monty Ruben (Nairobi)
Ruth and Hugh Russell (Arusha)
Solomon ole Saibull (Ngorongoro)
Yvonne and John Savidge (Ruaha)
Kay and George Schaller (Seronera)
Serekieli (Mt Meru–Ngurdoto)
David Stevens (Manyara)
Simon Trevor (Nairobi)
Kay and Myles Turner (Seronera)
Desmond Vesey-FitzGerald (Momela)
David Western (Nairobi)
Dr James Woodburn (London)

Finally, I am much indebted to the people who checked the manuscript for mistakes; they are, of course, in no way responsible for errors that may remain.

Most or all of the book was read by Dr John S. Owen and Myles Turner, by ecologists Desmond Vesey-FitzGerald and David Western, and by Hugh Russell, who paid particular attention to the use and spelling of Swahili. In addition, particular chapters benefited greatly from the attentions of the following:

Chapter 1	John S. Owen
Chapter 2	Mary and Frank Minot, Hugh Russell
Chapter 3	Jock Anderson, Richard Leakey
Chapter 4	Dr George Schaller, Myles Turner
Chapter 5	Myles Turner
Chapter 6	Dr George Schaller, Myles Turner
Chapter 8	Desmond Vesey-FitzGerald
Chapter 9	Nancy and Lewis Hurxthal
Chapter 10	Peter Enderlein, Dr James Woodburn (conversation in London)
Glossary	Hugh Russell

Peter Matthiessen

Glossary

(All words are Swahili where not otherwise indicated)

askari	soldier, warden, guard
banda	shed, thatched hut, rondavel
bangi	from Indian *bhang*: (*Cannabis*) hemp, narcotic
bao	ancient pebble game
biltong	dried strips of wild meat
boma	stock corral, thorn-walled shelter
dawa	medicine, charm, talisman
debe	4-gallon kerosene can
donga	gully, ravine, dry except in rains
duka	trading post or general store
en-gang	Maasai: home village
kanga	shawl (of East Indian print batik)
karibu	welcome to . . .
kikoi	(*see* shuka)
korongo	small stream, drainage line
laibon	Maasai: medicine man
magadi	soda, soda lake
mbira	marimba
miombo	dry forest, mostly *Brachystegia*
morani	Maasai; pl. moran: warrior
mswaki	toothbrush bush (*Salvadora*)
mzungu	pl. wazungu: white person, European.
nyika	wilderness (especially dry thorn scrub waste between highlands and the sea)
ol duvai	Maasai: bayonet aloe (*Sansevieria*)
panga	cane- or brush-cutting machete
pombe	local beer (usually from maize)
posho	ration (especially ugali)
shamba	farm plot
shifta	Somali: bandit (literally "wanderer")
shuka	rectangular piece of cloth, printed or dyed, worn as herdsman's cape or toga; also, as kikoi, or man's "skirt" (on the East African Coast)
ugali	maize meal, porridge

Notes

Chapter 1

1. Willard Trask, ed., *The Unwritten Song*, Macmillan, 1966.
2. A. J. Arkell, *A History of the Sudan*, Oxford, 1961.
3. Godfrey Lienhardt, "The Shilluk of the Upper Nile", in *African Worlds*, ed. by Daryll Forde, Oxford, 1954.
4. Trask, *op. cit.*
5. Mary Douglas, *Purity and Danger*, Routledge, 1966.
6. E. E. Evans-Pritchard, *The Nuer*, Oxford, 1940.
7. Geoffrey Parrinder, *African Mythology*, Hamlyn, 1967.

Chapter 2

1. Marjorie Perham, in Preface to *Mau Mau Detainee* by J. M. Kariuki, Penguin, 1964.
2. J. M. Kariuki, *Mau Mau Detainee*, Penguin, 1964.
3. Patrice Lumumba, quoted in *The Horizon History of Africa* by Horizon Editors, McGraw-Hill, 1971.
4. G. P. Murdock, *Africa: Its Peoples and Their Culture History*, McGraw-Hill, 1959.
5. K. R. Dundas, "Notes on the Origin and History of the Kikuyu and Dorobo Tribes", *Man*, no. 78, 1908.
6. Joseph Thomson, *Through Masai Land*, Cass, 1968.
7. Ludwig R. von Hohnel, *Discovery by Count Teleki of Lakes Rudolf and Stephanie*, Cass, 1968.
8. J. H. Patterson, *The Man-Eaters of Tsavo*, Macmillan, 1963.
9. R. Oliver and G. Matthew, *History of East Africa*, vol. I, Oxford, 1963, p. 417.
10. Jomo Kenyatta, *Facing Mt Kenya*, Secker, 1938.
11. Peter Beard, *The End of the Game*, Viking, 1965.
12. Placide Tempels in Basil Davidson, *The African Past*, Grosset & Dunlap, 1964.
13. Peter Beard, *op. cit.*
14. Karen Blixen, *Out of Africa*, Putnam, 1937.
15. Peter Beard, *op. cit.*

Chapter 3

1. Gerhard Lindblom, *The Akamba in British East Africa*, Uppsala, 1920.
2. Elspeth Huxley, *The Flame Trees of Thika*, Penguin, 1962.
3. Dundas, *op. cit.*
4. G. W. B. Huntingford, *The Southern Nilo-Hamites*, Internat. African Inst., 1953.
5. Paul Spencer, *The Samburu*, University of California Press, 1965.
6. J. A. Hunter, *Hunter*, Hamish Hamilton, 1952.
7. Dr Alan Jacobs, correspondence.
8. Spencer, *op. cit.*
9. John G. Williams, *Field Guide to Birds of Central and East Africa*, Houghton, 1964; idem., *Field Guide to the National Parks of East Africa*, Collins, 1968.
10. M. Posnansky, ed., *Prelude to East African History*, Oxford, 1966.
11. Sonia Cole, *The Prehistory of East Africa*, Macmillan, 1965.
12. R. Oliver and G. Matthew, *History of East Africa*, vol. I. Oxford, 1963.
13. *Ibid*
14. G. P. Murdock, *op. cit.*
15. *Ibid*
16. Lindblom, *op. cit.*
17. Jacobs, correspondence.
18. von Hohnel, *op. cit.*
19. Joy Adamson, *The Peoples of Kenya*, Collins, 1967.
20. Kariuki, *op. cit.*
21. Spencer, *op. cit.*
22. Thomson, *op. cit.*

Chapter 4

1. Huntingford, *op. cit.*
2. Murdock, *op. cit.*
3. George B. Schaller, *The Serengeti Lion*, Univ. Chicago Press, 1972 (uncorrected proofs).
4. Frederick C. Selous, *A Hunter's Wanderings in Africa*, London, 1881.
5. Parrinder, *op. cit.*
6. George B. Schaller and Gordon R. Lowther, "The Relevance of Carnivore Behavior to the Study of Early Hominids", *Southwestern Jour. Anthrop.*, vol. 25, no. 4, 1969.
7. Hugh Russell, conversations and correspondence.

Chapter 5

1. C. W. Hobley, "Notes on the Dorobo", *Man*, no. 76, 1906.
2. H. A. Fosbrooke, "An Administrative Record of the Masai Social System", *Tanganyika Notes and Records*, no. 26, 1948 (hereafter cited as *TNR*)
3. *Ibid*
4. Joseph H. Greenberg, *The Languages of Africa*, University of Indiana Press, 1963.
5. Karl Peters, quoted in Fosbrooke, *op. cit.*
6. G. W. B. Huntingford, "The Peopling of East Africa by Its Modern Inhabitants", from *History of East Africa* by R. Oliver and G. Matthew, Oxford, 1963.
7. Robert F. Gray, *The Sonjo of Tanganyika*, Oxford, 1963.
8. Ian Henderson (with Philip Goodhart), *The Hunt for Kimathi*, Hamish Hamilton, 1958.
9. A. Wykes, *Snake Man*, Simon and Schuster, 1961.
10. C. P. J. Ionides, "Southern Province Native Superstitions", *TNR*, no. 29, 1950.
11. Russell, *op. cit.*
12. Colin Turnbull, *The Lonely African*, Chatto, 1963.
13. H. K. Schneider, "The Lion-Men of Singida: A Reappraisal", *TNR*, no. 58, 1962.
14. Elspeth Huxley, *With Forks and Hope*, Chatto, 1964.
15. Parrinder, *op. cit.*
16. Blixen, *op. cit.*
17. Robert F. Gray, "Structural Aspects of Mbugwe Witchcraft", from *Witchcraft and Sorcery in East Africa*, ed. by John Middleton and E. H. Winter, Routledge, 1963.

Chapter 6

1. D. M. Sindiyo, "Game Department Field Experience in Public Education", *E. African Agric. & Forestry Journal*, Vol. XXXIII, 1968.
2. George B. Schaller, conversations.
3. George B. Schaller, *The Serengeti Lion*.
4. *Ibid*

Chapter 7

1. J. A. Hunter, *op. cit.*
2. Henri Junod, from *Life in a South African Tribe*, Macmillan, 1912, quoted in *Technicians of the Sacred* by T. Rothenburg, Doubleday, 1968.

3. Stewart Edward White, *The Rediscovered Country*, Doubleday, 1915.
4. R. M. Laws and I. S. C. Parker, "Recent Studies on Elephant Populations in East Africa", *Symp. Zool. Soc.*, 1968.
5. *Ibid*
6. David Western, conversations.
7. Arthur Neumann, *Elephant Hunting in East Equatorial Africa*, London, 1898.
8. Dennis Holman, *The Elephant People*, Murray, 1967.

Chapter 8

1. Adapted from Colin Turnbull, *Tradition and Change in African Life*, Barmerlea, 1967.
2. Thomson, *op. cit.*
3. Ionides, in Wykes, *op. cit.*
4. G. W. B. Huntingford, "The Social Organisation of the Dorobo", *African Studies*, no. 1, 1942.
5. Huxley, *op. cit.*
6. L. S. B. Leakey, "Preliminary Report on . . . Engaruka Ruins", *TNR*, no. 1, 1936.
7. Murdock, *op. cit.*
8. Elspeth Huxley, *A New Earth*, Chatto, 1960.
9. Posnansky, *op. cit.*
10. Gray, *op. cit.*
11. Murdock, *op. cit.*
12. Leslie Brown, *Africa: A Natural History*, Hamish Hamilton, 1965.
13. Sir A. Claud Hollis, *The Masai*, Oxford, 1935.

Chapter 9

1. Hollis, *op. cit.*
2. Frank Lambrecht, "Aspects of the Evolution and Ecology of Tsetse Flies . . .", from *Papers in African Prehistory* by J. D. Fage and R. A. Oliver, Cambridge, 1970.
3. Blixen, *op. cit.*
4. Adamson, *op. cit.*
5. Gray, *op. cit.*
6. Myles Turner, conversations and correspondence.

Chapter 10

1. From Olivia Vlahos, *African Beginnings*, Viking, 1967.
2. Dorothea Bleek, "The Hadzapi or Watindega of Tanganyika Territory", *Africa*, no. 3, 1931.
3. F. J. Bagshawe, "The Peoples of the Happy Valley", *Jour. of the African Society*, Part II, no. 24, 1925.
4. Dorothea Bleek, "Traces of Former Bushman Occupation in Tanganyika Territory", *South African Jour. Sci.*, no. 28, 1931.
5. L. S. B. Leakey, *Stone Age Cultures of Kenya Colony*, Cambridge, 1931.
6. Peter Enderlein, conversations and correspondence.
7. George J. Klima, *The Barabaig*, Holt, Rinehart and Winston, 1970.
8. Posnansky, *op. cit.*
9. James C. Woodburn, "Hunters and Gatherers", Brit. Mus. brochure, 1970. See also Selected Bibliography.
10. *Ibid*
11. G. M. Wilson, "The Tatoga of Tanganyika", *TNR*, no. 33, 1952.
12. Woodburn, *op. cit.*
13. B. Cooper, "The Kindiga", *TNR*, no. 27, 1949.
14. Klima, *op. cit.*
15. R. A. J. Maguire, "Il-Torobo", *TNR*, no. 25, 1948.

Selected Bibliography

Abrahamson, H. *The Origin of Death*. Kegan Paul, 1952.

Adamson, Joy. *The Peoples of Kenya*. Collins, 1967.

Arkell, A. J. *A History of the Sudan*. Oxford, 1961.

Bagshawe, F. J. "The Peoples of the Happy Valley", *Jour. of the African Society*, Part II, no. 24, 1925.

Beard, Peter. *The End of the Game*. Viking, 1965.

Bleek, Dorothea. "The Hadzapi or Watindega of Tanganyika Territory", *Africa*, no. 3, 1931; *idem*, "Traces of Former Bushman Occupation in Tanganyika Territory", *South African Jour. Sci.*, no. 28, 1931.

Blixen, Karen. *Out of Africa*. Putnam, 1937

Brown, Leslie. *Africa: A Natural History*. Hamish Hamilton, 1965.

Carrington, Richard. *Elephants*. Chatto, 1958.

Cave, F. O., and James D. MacDonald. *Birds of the Sudan*. Oliver & Boyd, 1955.

Clark, J. Desmond. *The Prehistory of Africa*. Praeger, 1970.

Cole, Sonia. *The Prehistory of East Africa*. Weidenfeld & Nicolson, 1964.

Cooper, B. "The Kindiga", *Tanganyika Notes and Records* (hereafter *TNR*), no. 27, 1949.

Davidson, Basil. *The African Past*. Longmans, 1964.

Douglas, Mary. *Purity and Danger*. Routledge, 1966.

Douglas-Hamilton, Iain. "The Lake Manyara Elephant Problem", unpub. ms., 1969.

Dundas, K. R. "Notes on the Origin and History of the Kikuyu and Dorobo Tribes", *Man*, no. 78, 1908.

Dyson, W. S., and V. E. Fuchs. "The Elmolo", *Jour. Royal African Inst.*, no. 67, 1937.

Enderlein, Peter. "The Yaida Valley", unpub. ms.

Evans-Pritchard, E. E. *The Nuer*. Oxford, 1940.

Fage, J. D., and R. A. Oliver. *Papers in African Prehistory*. Cambridge, 1970.

Fordham, Paul. *The Geography of African Affairs*. Penguin, 1965.

Fosbrooke, H. A. "An Administrative Record of the Masai Social System", *TNR*, no. 26, 1948; *idem*. "A Stone Age Tribe in Tanganyika", *South African Arch. Bull.*, no. II, 1956.

Graham, Aleicester. "The Lake Rudolf Crocodile", unpub. ms.

Gray, Robert F. *The Sonjo of Tanganyika*. Oxford, 1963; *idem*, "Structural Aspects of Mbugwe Witchcraft, " in Middleton and Winter *Witchcraft and Sorcery in East Africa*. Routledge, 1963.

Greenberg, Joseph H. *The Languages of Africa*. University of Indiana, 1963.

Gregory, J. W. *The Rift Valley and the Geology of East Africa*. Seeley, Service, 1910.

Gulliver, P., and P. H. Gulliver. *The Central Nilo-Hamites*. Internat. African Inst., 1953.

Henderson, Ian (with Philip Goodhart). *The Hunt for Kimathi*. Hamish Hamilton, 1958.

Hobley, C. W. "Notes on the Dorobo", *Man*, no. 76, 1906.

Hollis, Sir A. Claud. *The Masai*. Oxford, 1935.

Holmon, Dennis. *The Elephant People*. Murray, 1967.

Horizon Editors. *The Horizon History of Africa*. McGraw-Hill, 1971.

Hunter, J. A. *Hunter*. Hamish Hamilton, 1952.

Huntingford, G. W. B. "The Peopling of East Africa by Its Modern Inhabitants", in Oliver and Matthew, *History of East Africa*, vol. I, Oxford, 1963; *idem*, "The Social Organisation of the Dorobo," *African Studies*, no. 1, 1942; *idem*, *The Southern Nilo-Hamites*. Internat. African Inst., 1953.

Huxley, Elspeth. *The Flame Trees of Thika*. Penguin, 1962; *idem*, *A New Earth*. Chatto, 1960; *idem*, *With Forks and Hope*, Chatto, 1964.

Ionides, C. P. J. "Southern Province Native Superstitions", *TNR*, no. 29, 1950.

Junod, Henri. *Life in a South African Tribe*. Macmillan, 1912, quoted in *Technicians of the Sacred* by J. Rothenburg, Doubleday, 1968.

Kariuki, J. M. *Mau Mau Detainee*. Penguin, 1964.

Kenyatta, Jomo. *Facing Mt Kenya*. Secker, 1938.

Klima, George J. *The Barabaig*. Holt, Rinehart and Winston, 1970.

Laws, R. M., and I. S. C. Parker. "Recent Studies on Elephant Populations in East Africa", *Symp. Zool Soc.*, 1968.

Leakey, L. S. B. *Adam's Ancestors*. Harper (Torch-books), 1960; *idem*, "Preliminary Report on an Examination of the Engaruka Ruins," *TNR*, no. 1, 1936; *idem*, *Stone Age Cultures of Kenya Colony*, Cambridge, 1931.

Leakey, Richard. "In Search of Man's Past at Lake Rudolf", *Nat. Geog.*, 1969.

Lee, Richard, and I. Devore, eds. *Man the Hunter*. Aldine, 1968.

Lienhardt, Godfrey. "The Shilluk of the Upper Nile", in *African Worlds*, ed. Daryll Forde, Oxford, 1954.

Lindblom, Gerhard. *The Akamba in British East Africa*. Uppsala, 1920.

Maguire, R. A. J. "Il-Torobo", *TNR*, no. 25, 1948.

el Mahdi, Mandour. *A Short History of the Sudan*. Oxford, 1965.

Meinertzhagen, Col. Richard. *Kenya Diary: 1902–1906*. Oliver & Boyd, 1957.

Middleton, John, and E. H. Winter, eds. *Witchcraft and Sorcery in East Africa*. Routledge, 1963.

Murdock, G. P. *Africa: Its Peoples and Their Culture History*. McGraw-Hill, 1959.

Neumann, Arthur. *Elephant Hunting in East Equatorial Africa*. London, 1898.

Oliver, R., and J. D. Fage. *A Short History of Africa*. Penguin, 1962.

Oliver, R., and G. Matthew. *History of East Africa*, vol. 1, Oxford, 1963.

Parrinder, Geoffrey. *African Mythology*. Hamlyn, 1967.

Patterson, J. H. *The Man-Eaters of Tsavo*. Macmillan, 1963.

Posnansky, M., ed. *Prelude to East African History*. Oxford, 1966.

Praed, C. W. Mackworth, and Capt. C. H. B. Grant, *Birds of East and North East Africa.* Longmans, 1952.

Radin, Paul. *African Folktales.* Bollingen, 1952.

Ricciardi, Mireilla. *Vanishing Africa.* Reynal, 1971.

Schaller, George B. *The Serengeti Lion.* Univ. Chicago Press, 1972 (uncorrected proofs).

Schaller, George B., and Gordon R. Lowther. "The Relevance of Carnivore Behavior to the Study of Early Hominids", *Southwestern Jour. Anthrop.*, vol. 25, no. 4, 1969.

Schneider, H. K. "The Lion-Men of Singida: A Reappraisal", *TNR*, no. 58, 1962.

Selous, Frederick C. *A Hunter's Wanderings in Africa.* London, 1881.

Sindiyo, D. M. "Game Department Field Experience in Public Education", *E. African Agric. and Forestry Journal*, vol. XXXIII, 1968.

Spencer, Paul. *The Samburu.* University of California Press, 1965.

Thomas, Elizabeth Marshall. *The Harmless People.* Secker, 1959.

Thomson, Joseph. *Through Masai Land.* Cass, 1968.

Trask, Willard, ed. *The Unwritten Song.* Macmillan, 1966.

Turnbull, Colin. *The Forest People.* Chatto, 1961; *idem, The Lonely African.* Chatto, 1963; *idem, Tradition and Change in African Tribal Life.* Barmerlea, 1967.

Van der Post, Laurens. *The Lost World of the Kalahari.* Hogarth Press, 1958.

Vesey-FitzGerald, Desmond. "Elephants in National Parks: A Problem of the Environment", unpub. ms., 1969.

Vlahos, Olivia. *African Beginnings.* Viking, 1967.

von Hohnel, Ludwig R. *Discovery by Count Teleki of Lakes Rudolf and Stephanie.* Cass, 1968.

White, Stewart Edward. *The Rediscovered Country.* Doubleday, 1915.

Williams, John. *Field Guide to the Birds of Central and East Africa.* Houghton, 1964; *idem, Field Guide to the National Parks of East Africa.* Collins, 1968.

Wilson, G. M. "The Tatoga of Tanganyika", *TNR*, no. 33, 1952.

Woodburn, James C. "The Future of the Tindiga", *TNR*, no. 58, 1962; *idem,* "Hunters and Gatherers", British Museum brochure, 1970.

Wykes, A. *Snake Man.* Simon and Schuster, 1961.

PART 2

African Silences

For George Schaller, Jonah Western,
Iain Douglas-Hamilton, Alec Forbes-Watson,
Peter Enderlein, Brian Nicholson, and
other mentors and companions of immemorial
long days on foot in Africa.

Of Peacocks and Gorillas: Zaire (1978)

In 1913 the young ornithologist James Chapin of the American Museum of Natural History, doing field work in what was then the Belgian Congo, discovered the rufous wing quill of an unknown bird in an African's headdress. He kept that feather for many years without finding anyone, white or black, who could identify the bird. In 1934, in the African museum at Tervueren, near Brussels, he matched the feather to the hen of an old pair of stuffed fowls that were thought to be juvenile domestic peacocks. The cockbird was dark blue and green, with a russet neck patch, while the hen was green above, russet beneath. The hen had peafowl-like eyes on the green feathers, and both sexes had peafowl-like crests; and while not true peafowls (*Pavo*), they turned out to be the only known African representatives of the great pheasant tribe, Phasianidae, separated by thousands of miles of desert and mountain from their nearest relatives in Asia. Subsequently, in 1949, the animal collector Charles Cordier obtained a small number of these birds trapped by local people near the lowland village of Utu, in the Congo Basin, though he himself never saw the species in the wild. These seven "Congo peacocks" (*Afropavo congensis*) were exhibited at the Bronx Zoo in the 1950s, and subsequently a small captive flock was established at the Antwerp Zoo.

In the spring of 1978 *Audubon* magazine sent a small expedition in search of *Afropavo congensis*. Its leader was the British ornithologist Alec Forbes-Watson, who had known James Chapin and still regards him as "the best ornithologist who ever worked in Africa"; according to Forbes-Watson, Chapin was the only known non-African who had ever seen the Congo peacock in the wild. Alec was to be assisted by his friends George Plimpton and George's sister Sarah, who had been keen birdwatchers as children and have taken it up again in recent years; while in Africa they would also search for the three other "most desirable" birds on this huge continent – not "little brown birds", as Forbes-Watson describes them, but species that are spectacular as well as rare. "The peacock is first, indubitably," Alec had told me in Nairobi in 1977. "Then comes the shoebill stork, the lyre-tailed honey guide, and the bareheaded rock fowl. On the fifth bird, no two ornithologists would agree; you'd get an argument whichever one you chose. The Pel's fishing owl, perhaps, or the yellow-crested helmet shrike, or the wattled crane." He discounted as unrealistic any search for the Prigogine's owl, or Congo bay owl, a nocturnal forest relative of the barn owls with a mask-like face; *Phodilus prigoginei*, known from a single specimen found dead in 1951 at Muusi in the Bukavu highlands, has never been observed alive. Unlike *Afropavo*, it belongs to the same genus and resembles the Asian form, *P badius*, and therefore its voice might be similar as well (for those who might wish to listen for it, the call of the Asian owl has been described as a high, whistling *ülee-uu üwee üwee üwee üwee*). Alec himself had already seen the lyre-tailed honey guide and the rock fowl, both of which occur on Mount Nimba in Liberia; as far as was known, the Congo peacock (if it still existed) was confined to the lowland forests of Zaire. For the shoebill, the most accessible location seemed to be the Bangweulu swamp in Zambia.

My hope was to join Forbes-Watson and the Plimptons at Mount Nimba in late March 1978 in time to see the rock fowl and the honey guide, then accompany them on the search for *Afropavo* in Zaire. On Friday, March 24, I was at Man in western Ivory Coast, where I was assisting in a wildlife survey; Mount Nimba was less than a hundred miles away. But local informants assured me the journey was not possible, and by the time I'd made my way back to the coast and got a flight to Roberts Field, Monrovia, it was already Monday afternoon, when my friends would be preparing to depart Mount Nimba. Frustrated, I remained at the airport hotel.

Plimpton turned up early on Tuesday, between plumages. He was heeled over in the hot and humid sun by random baggage that included a stray tripod without telescope, and he wore a trim street hat, hot woolen blazer, soiled bush shirt, and checked Bermuda shorts. His face was flushed with sunburn and the heat, and his very long pale legs were livid from attacks by jungle insects – here was a birdman, tried and true! We spent an agreeable morning at the bar celebrating his tenth wedding anniversary and making plans for a rendezvous a fortnight later in Zaire. At Mount Nimba, he said, all three of them had seen the rock fowl (which, like *Afropavo* and Prigogine's owl, may derive from an invasion of Asian fauna in the far past, and is separated from its closest relatives by thousands of years as well as miles), and Alec and Sarah had every hope of catching up with the lyre-tailed honey guide this very day. He had heard there was a track across the Liberian frontier that joined the road to Man, and he regretted that I had not found it.

Having wasted three days in airports and hotels, I hoped Plimpton was mistaken, but Forbes-Watson, arriving the next morning, assured me he was not; a new road across the border to Mount Nimba had been put through about three months before, he said, ordering a beer and sitting back to enjoy my expression. Had I used it, he continued, I would certainly have seen both the rock fowl and the honey guide, which he and Sarah had observed in its extraordinary courtship flights the day before. (It was James Chapin who had first linked the lyre-tailed honey guide to the weird "song" it makes at courtship time with the odd curving feathers of its tail.) Alec happened to know that I had already seen the shoebill stork in the great marsh called the Sudd, in the south Sudan, and he regretted my bad luck even as he took delight in my chagrin: "You know, of course, that had you been with us yesterday, you would now be the only living ornithologist to have seen three of our four birds." Because our plane had broken down in Dakar and would not arrive here until next daybreak, eighteen hours late, I spent yet another day of airport life digesting this exasperating news and taking such comfort as I could in the lovely pratincoles that coursed at dusk along the jungle walls of the St. Paul River. To console me Alec pointed out my first white-throated blue swallow, which sat dejectedly on the pilings of the hotel dock.

While still in London Forbes-Watson had tried to make connecting reservations that would take us on from Kinshasa, east of Zaire's Atlantic coast, to Bukavu, in the center of the continent, but Air Zaire had not once answered its phone. Arriving in Kinshasa on Thursday morning, March 30, we were informed that there was not room on any flight to Bukavu until the following Tuesday. After a number of dispiriting encounters with lesser officials, we boldly sought out the *chef de base*, in charge of the whole airport, who promptly called in the Air Zaire man and ordered him to put us on the next day's flight to Goma, whether there was room or not. In Goma we would surely find a means of reaching Bukavu, eighty miles off to the south. Anything was better that staying in Kinshasa, where the rains had arrived in flood just two days before and where we would certainly go broke in very short order. Zaire has been staggered by inflation since the drastic fall in the world price of copper ore in 1974, and its transportation difficulties, always serious in a land so vast ("Without a railroad, the Congo isn't worth one red cent!" declared Henry Morton Stanley), have been severely compounded by the escalating price of fuel; advertisements in the Kinshasa paper offer new cars ordered from Europe for which the owners have not bothered to turn up.

The city on the Zaire River (formerly the Congo) seems haunted by the corruption and brutality of its days as Léopoldville, seat of power of the cruel and terrible King of the Belgians, whose "Congo Free State", with its murderous abuse of conscripted labor (the Zairois estimate that ten million people died in the period between 1880 and 1910) continued the depopulation of this shadowed country that the terrible days of slaving had begun. The Belgian Congo colonial administration, though less brutal, continued the exploitation of the country while doing nothing to educate the people for the transition that was already inevitable, and when independence came at last, in 1960, there was no bureaucratic structure to maintain order. The consequence was anarchy and chaos, including the murder of the legitimate prime minister, Patrice Lumumba, the only leader with a national following, followed by installation of a puppet colonel who would dutifully endorse the further exploitation of the country's resources.

The saying *"Plus ça change, plus c'est la même chose"* is bitterly true in the former Belgian Congo. Some privileged blacks now share the booty with the whites (in 1972, Zaire imported more Mercedes automobiles that any country in the world), but as in the colonial days the land is being ransacked by foreign investors, and whole forests will fall for the enrichment of a few, with no thought whatever for the people or the future. To a degree unusual even in modern Africa, graft and corruption are a way of life, and their chief proponent is President-for-Life Mobutu Sese Seko, who was imposed on a war-weary land by American and European interests. (In September of 1960 this Colonel Mobutu, thrust forward by the United States, seized control of the central government from the legitimate prime minister Lumumba. In 1965, he consolidated his military dictatorship, and he has ruled the country ever since. As in the case of Houphouët-Boigny, Idi Amin, Jean-Bédel Bokassa of the Central African Republic, and many other African despots, Mobutu is assumed to have acquired an immense personal fortune at the expense of his precarious new nation.) Even as this sick old capital of King Léopold sags and collapses, Mobutu spends millions on his play city at his home village Gbadolite, south of the Ubangi, complete with unused international airport, two presidential palaces, a Swiss dairy farm, and elaborate plans for a private Disneyland. With a personal fortune of four billion dollars, skimmed from his patrons' exploitation of Zaire's immense natural resources in copper, industrial diamonds, gold, cobalt, timber, and water, Mobutu can afford it. In this huge, famine-haunted country where next to nothing is undertaken for the public welfare, our man in Zaire is the richest ruler in all Africa and perhaps the world.

The scattered vehicles that pass in the night streets are mostly old taxis or expensive cars belonging to the prospering Europeans or to favored Zairois in the good graces of the president. As if oblivious of human life, the automobiles speed through the hordes of Africans who wander the dark and dingy streets in quest of some means of survival, and the hordes close again behind them. The rotting old colonial mansions use spiked fences and watchdogs and armed guards to ward off refugees from the starving countryside, whose tin huts and shantytowns and half-finished or burned-out cement-block shelters crowd right up to their barbed-wire walls and spread like a crusting mold along each potholed boulevard and muddy byway. To forestall starvation, the refugees grow vegetables in the gaps in the cracked concrete of the broken city. In the utter breakdown of municipal systems, there is no way to control Kinshasa's population, which is thought to be close to four million, and this in a city that entirely lacks the most rudimentary sanitation system. Litter and sewage have become a part of the human habitat. At N'dola airport, where the refugees overflow the ramshackle hangars and abandoned service buildings, human excrement is all over the runways.

The Zairois seem proud of their one city, which they refer to affectionately as "Kin". To the Europeans, mostly Belgian, who put up with life in this depressing place because it is so profitable, Kin is known as Poubelleville, or Garbage Can Town.

Zaire is eighty times the size of Belgium – larger, in fact, than all of Europe – and the next day we flew a thousand miles in order to reach Goma, which lies on the frontier with Rwanda. At Goma airport, awaiting our baggage, we discovered that another Air Zaire plane out on the airstrip was the connecting flight to Bukavu, the only one that would leave before next week. Air Zaire at Kinshasa had not told us of this plane, far less booked us on it, though they knew we wished to go to Bukavu; perhaps they resented the intercession on our behalf by the *chef de base*, but more likely they knew nothing about it. The Goma agents would not discuss the matter until we had reclaimed our baggage, by which time the plane was filled, or so they said; we later learned from passengers who made this flight that a number of seats had been empty after all. The Zairois themselves refer to their national airline as "Air Peut-être" ("Air Perhaps") and estimate that the chances of any scheduled flight being completed are less than fifty-fifty, often for no better reason than a decision by the pilot, almost anywhere en route, that he has had enough flying for that day. "Sometimes they change schedules in midflight," one Belgian told me. "One never knows *where* they are. Perhaps this is why they are never hijacked." For the next five days, in any case, there would be no plane to Bukavu, nor (for want of fuel) was there a bus, nor a hired car for less than $350, nor any space on the Sunday boat south on Lake Kivu.

George Schaller's *The Year of the Gorilla* remains the best book I know of on this area. When Schaller came here in 1959, the year before Zaire gained its independence, Goma was still a neat and charming Lake Kivu resort, a "European center" for Belgian *colons* and tourists alike; by the time he left, in late 1960, the civil strife that would devastate the country had begun. Today the weeds have taken over the walks and formal gardens. The open-air cafés are gone, the pleasant pastels of the storefronts are sadly faded, there is nothing in the stores, and nothing works; the telephone is chronically out of order, the water system is breaking down, and nobody is left who can fix either. To escape the place, we decided to visit the Virunga National Park.

As early as 1889 Léopold II had set up reserves to save the elephants from black people in order that they might be killed by whites. Additional reserves were created by Prince Albert in 1890, but the Virunga Park – the former Albert National Park, in what was then the Belgian Congo – was the first true national park in all of Africa; it was established in 1938 on the recommendation of Carl Akeley, who had collected five gorillas here a few years earlier for the American Museum of Natural History. Since then the park has been considerably enlarged, before and after the independence of Zaire in 1960.

When I first came to Africa, in the early winter of 1961, it was assumed that the Albert Park and all its animals were being ravaged and destroyed by the hordes of insensate Africans who were making life so miserable for the colonials; but this report turned out to be as exaggerated as many others, and much credit should be given to the park's African guards, who went unpaid for several years and defended what is now Virunga against the worst of the depredations. At the park entrance there is a plaque commemorating the brave twenty-three who "died for the elephants" in those dark years. Jacques Verschuren, who wrote a moving book about these men, is the former director of the Institut National pour la Conservation de la Nature (INCN), which administers Zaire's seven national parks; these include vast forest tracts in the interior as well as the group of beautiful reserves among lakes and mountains of the Rift. Because of a strong park tradition as well as a small human population, all seven parks continue to do well.

On Saturday morning we arranged a ride to Nyiragongo, the southernmost of the Virunga volcanoes, which rise to the south of Ruwenzori or "Mountains of the Moon", just below the equator between East Africa and northern Zaire. Several of the "fire mountains" are still active, and only a year before, on January 10, 1977, Nyiragongo quite suddenly erupted. As five coulees, or lava rivers, poured down its steep sides, the entire Bahutu village of Bukuma utterly vanished and more than two hundred people died. Destroying the prison and many other buildings, the flow reached the northern outskirts of the town of Goma in just twenty-seven minutes, rolling within a half-mile of the airport, with its large depot of fuel; had the lava touched that depot, it is said, half of Goma would have been destroyed. The northward road into the Virungas vanished, and not for a month did the lava cool sufficiently to carve out the new road; a pretty graveyard in a grove of tall mimosas not far east of the road was one of the few locations that was spared. A few scorched skeletons of trees still stand in the shining fields, and these are being chopped for fuel by survivors of the cataclysm, who straighten here and there, in silhouette, to watch us pass.

Climbing the hill, we look across to dense plantations in Rwanda. This region of volcanic ash forms a rich and well-drained soil – one of the few good soils in all of Africa – and Kivu Province, despite civil wars and economic setbacks, continues to produce good crops of tea and coffee, bananas, cinchona, and pyrethrum. There is no smoke from the volcanoes, and on islets of high ground new gardens and banana groves have been established, but one day in the not far distant future, Nyiragongo – the mother of the spirit Gongo – will erupt again.

Augustus Gabula, the young Bahutu warden who guided us uphill on Nyiragongo, was near the summit when the 1977 eruption took place; his family in their village on these lower slopes had four minutes to flee before their hut was destroyed. Augustus himself ran down through a tongue of forest between lava rivers, his path broken by an elephant herd that was stampeding off the mountain. Perhaps because, as mammalogist Jean Dorst informs us, "Having the legs straight with the bones placed vertically one above another, they are quite incapable of leaping" not all of Nyiragongo's elephants survived. Augustus led us two or three miles up the main flow to a place where a group of six beasts had been overwhelmed; probably they were asphyxiated as this outpouring of lava burned up the oxygen across the mountainside. Among the hollows in the lava field are scattered a group of amorphous molds left by burnt hardwood trees and large white bones. A few liverworts and *Osmunda* ferns now prosper in these crannies. In one of the graves the whole form of the elephant is still discernible, even the holes made by its tusks (long since removed) and a sad, curved tube of stone where the trunk lay. These were forest elephants (once considered a distinct species), and some of them were young. Although there is no forage near the graves, only marigold, coarse bracken, and shrubby acanthus with pale lavender thorned flowers, a number of elephants have made their way out onto the cooled lava and communed for a time with the six encased in stone, to judge from the copious amount of dung around the gravesites.

Toward noon, clouds shift and rain comes blowing through the forest, leaving behind a hot and humid sun. The Kivu–Ruwenzori chain is the heart of the African highland-forest habitat, which has outposts in Ethiopia, in the Kenya highlands, and on Mt Meru and Mt Kilimanjaro in northern Tanzania, as well as far westward on Mt Cameroon. All of these places share many species of flora and fauna. At the lava's edge broad carpets of large pale yellow composites mark the transition zone, and within the forest the tree limbs are thickened by moist gardens, mostly fern and orchid. The flowers I recognize are pink *Impatiens*, peas, the gloriosa lily, and a large hibiscus with blossoms of a dark, sinister lavender. Strangely, butterflies are few, and other than elephant trails, with their fresh dung, there is little sign of animals. But a small troop of the beautiful L'Hoest's monkey barks at our appearance, then retreats with dignity across a tongue of lava; these semiterrestrial cercopithecines are shining black with a bright chestnut oval patch from the shoulders to the base of the long tail and with a striking mass of fluffy white whiskers, and one has an infant clasped to her belly. Compared with its relatives, the mona and blue monkeys, which are widespread in West and East Africa, respectively, the L'Hoest's monkey has an odd, small, scattered range, being confined to the mountains of eastern Zaire, Mt Cameroon, and the island of Fernando Poo, in the Gulf of Guinea.

Since most of my African travels have been made in the thorn scrub and savanna of the plains, I am not familiar with the highland avifauna and am happy to have Forbes-Watson as a guide. Alec has seen more species of African birds than anyone alive (not his own claim – I have heard it made for him by others), and on Nyiragongo, we identify some forty species, more than half of which are new to me. Sarah Plimpton is delighted by the courtship displays of puffbacks and sunbirds, the wistful notes of flycatcher and cuckoo, the flocks of olive pigeons, high and dark, passing overhead. A strange, sad, single note is made by Lagden's bush shrike, which has the striking golden-yellow breast and belly of its East African relatives; we also take note of a regal sunbird – a sunlit male on a bare limb – a red-faced woodland warbler (not red-faced at all; it looks as if it had dipped its face into a peach), and a white-tailed blue flycatcher, flaring the white outer feathers of its tail to catch up sun. For Forbes-Watson these four species are "life birds", as they are known to the bird fraternity, the first of their species he has ever seen, and Sarah and I feel privileged to see them with him; the last time Alec had as many as three life birds in a single day was years ago, on his first visit to Mt Cameroon.

Forbes-Watson is an East African colonial raised up in the "White Highlands", a veteran of the Kenya Regiment in the Mau-Mau days, and a former game warden who likes other wardens and white hunters and is liked by them, yet is amused by the "old boy" element that takes its own romantic mystique so very seriously. I first met him in Nairobi eight or nine years ago, and though we haven't known each other well, we have many friends in common and find that we agree about almost all of them. "I grew up with these chaps, you see," Alec says gently, "and some of them are still trying to pretend that East Africa is like it was, and it just isn't." (Unlike many white East Africans, Alec speaks fluent ki-Swahili, not just the up-country kind used on safari; since he does not cling to the colonial mentality, he truly enjoys talking to Africans and feels quite at home in eastern Zaire, where Swahili is in common use.)

On Sunday, when we rise at 5.30 a.m. to take the steamer from Goma to Bukavu, people are descending toward the lake with all sorts of buckets and containers; apparently the waterworks is out completely. A little boy toting water back uphill has been toppled by a jerry can that is much too big for him, and two small friends try to lift it back upon his head as he totters in a circle on the road edge. Beyond the cove where the water is being taken, more crowds are streaming alongshore toward the ferry. Many are passengers – one woman bears a very large, bright yellow suitcase balanced on her head – but most of these must be mere well-wishers. Or so we hope, since the old boat has no seats at all and in any case will be loaded up like an aquatic bush taxi with as many *citoyens* as can be crammed aboard.

Lake Kivu, at nearly five thousand feet, is the highest of the central lakes that fill the depressions in the mighty rift that splits the continent, and its ice-clear, dark blue waters, set about by high mountains of Zaire and Rwanda, make it one of the loveliest places in all Africa. The Zairois claim that it is Africa's highest lake (Kenya's Lake Naivasha and Lake Nakuru are both higher) and that, due to the great amount of methane gas derived from rotting vegetation on the lake bottom, its waters are poisonous and without life. But this morning we saw that these waters may be used by humans if need be, and some small tilapia at the dock pilings explain the activities of an African cormorant, seen diving yesterday some distance off the shore. However, these fish are not large enough to sustain any real fishery; the few pirogues seen on the lake are mostly transporting bananas and other produce from outlying islands and villages to Goma.

Soon the *Etoile* is passing close to the west shore of Idjwi Island, a forested ridge, sparsely inhabited, that dominates the center of the lake, and toward mid-morning a brief stop is made to drop off something at a mission village. In a cove, under banana fronds, boys are fishing for the small tilapia with wispy poles, and other boys dart forward in pirogues to offer golden pineapples to the passengers. Jokes, coins, and pineapples fly back and forth across the rails, and in less than a minute the *Etoile* is under way again along Idjwi's western shore, it high wake threatening the numerous pirogues that harvest the island plantations; the boatmen wave at us in fear and grandly we wave back.

On Lake Kivu the pirogue looks crude, and its paddle is carved like a deep scoop that cups the water; the paddling motion is a wild overhand that throws arcs of water forward across the shoulders – an inefficient paddle and a poor technique, or so it appears, suggesting the absence of a real fishery tradition. (Most African paddles have the graceful shapes of hearts or blades, as in the great basin of the Amazon, and across the centuries the long pirogues of both Congo and Amazon, sharp-pointed at both ends, have arrived at a near-identical, clean, pure design.) Yet the Kivu pirogues carry immense loads of bananas across wide stretches of open water that are often rolled by squall and wind; sometimes one can scarcely see the paddlers, three of whom may be squashed into the stern.

Beyond Idjwi the *Etoile* returns to the mainland shore, among myriad small, pretty channel islands. Two gray-headed gulls, a distant stork, a white egret point up the surrounding emptiness of sky and mountain; to the southwest rise Mt Kahuzi and Mt Biega. Then the *Etoile* rounds the southernmost of five peninsulas ("a hand of verdure dipped in the lake," the guidebook says) and docks in the tranquil harbor of Bukavu.

Across the cove lies a collection of odd boats, retired for reasons of old age or want of fuel. The largest and most ancient craft, a wonderful old steamboat of the early century, is the retired lake ferry of colonial days, *Le General Tombeur*, now renamed *Lt. Col. Potopoto*. Lieutenant Colonel Potopoto – whose name, in the local Lingala tongue, means "mud" – was one of the many heroes of the recent revolution, and his lettered name is the only new paint on this faded ship. Under the name *Lt. Col. Potopoto* the ferry has never left the dock.

The red roofs of Bukavu on its five peninsulas are strikingly inset in green plantations of tea and coffee, cinchona and pyrethrum, broken by forest stands of gum and pine on hills that rise perhaps fifteen hundred feet above the lake. Like Goma, the town lies on the border with Rwanda, which furnishes eastern Zaire with goods no longer available in this country. In Zaire fuel at the official price is not available, and even the government bureaus here must sometimes depend on black-market gasoline, which during one week in early April of 1978 rose from twenty-five to thirty dollars per gallon. At that price one might well wonder if gasoline or smuggled ivory or other contraband lies beneath those cargoes of bananas that are plied back and forth across the lake.

For want of gas no taxis have come down to meet the boat. Consigning our gear to three young boys, we walk slowly up into the town. The colorful broad boulevards of flowering cassia and coral trees are strangely empty, and so are the shops that, at the time of Schaller's visit in 1959, carried "the latest imports from Brussels, Paris, and Copenhagen". The paint has faded, all the street cobbling is coming up; there are no tourists and few cars. The shortage of gas has saved the life of a driver of a truck that lost its brakes on the incline of this street and rolled downhill backward, overrunning the gas pumps in the station. The garage roof now pins the truck in place; had those pumps been full, not only the truck but the Hotel Residence itself would be no more.

In other days this hotel was known as the Residence Royale, and though the statuary has been removed from niches in the marble stairwells, one may still contemplate the grandeur of days past in some old stuffed heads, huge portraits of the great buildings of Belgium, an antique elevator that can only be stopped by hurling the door open at the right floor, a dining salon in rococo plush, and other appointments of more spacious times. In our efforts to economize we take rooms in the *quatrième catégorie*, but even these have their own vast bathrooms and a lake vista or at least a prospect of the boulevard, as well as a view of the Pêle-Mêle Garage across the street.

Having got to Bukavu, we must now work out a way to cross the mountains of the rift and descend into the jungle haunts of the Congo peacock. According to Forbes-Watson the nearest village to the place where Chapin saw the peafowl is called Utu, which lies not far from Walikale, about a hundred miles to the northwest, along the jungle road to Kisangani (the former Stanleyville). This road descends from the Kahuzi-Biega Mountains, where we hope to make camp long enough to get a good look at gorillas. But since it costs twenty-five dollars simply to go out to the airstrip, we could scarcely consider hiring a car even if someone could be found to take us. Planes or supply trucks that serviced Christian missions at Walikale or the tin-mine station in the region, at Obaye, seemed our best hope, for only a large corporation or a mission could put together enough fuel for such a journey.

A Catholic mission has a station out at Walikale, and we sought to befriend the *monseigneur* at the cathedral, which is located high on the hill above Bukavu, surrounded by candelabra cypress and the remains of flower gardens, turned over now to manioc and maize. The *monseigneur* (an African) assured us that the Walikale mission was not under his jurisdiction and that anyway, only the Protestants had planes. We sought out a Mr and Mrs Fred Bahler of the Grace Mission, who proved hospitable, serving us coffee and cookies in their house above the lake and contacting the mission pilot on our behalf, but the pilot was already overbooked and could not help us. The Bahlers thought that we should see Adrien Deschryver, a former professional hunter who flew a plane for the national parks that might be chartered; and they repeated a story we had heard in Goma. A few years ago an American woman, Lee Lyon, had seen the Congo peacock in the wild and taken pictures of it, not at Utu but at Uku, which means "over there". Ms Lyon had been killed a few years earlier by a young elephant while photographing an elephant-capture program in Rwanda, but Deschryver had been with her at Uku and could give us all the details of the story. Apparently Deschryver was away, but since he lived on the same road as the Bahlers, they would be happy to leave our message at his house.

Subsequently we talked to Citoyen Muzu head of the local government bureau of mines, who sat with a number of unemployed friends in a huge office of the colonial period, under a high ceiling with big holes in it; like so many bureaucratic offices in the new Africa, this one makes plain that the real business is transacted elsewhere. Earlier Muzu had told us that he not only knew the Walikale area but had seen the famous *paon de Congo*; now he seemed less sure that this was true. By not repeating it, Muzu withdrew an earlier suggestion that he escort us in person to the peacock. No, he said, we must go to the Société Minérale de Kivu (Sominki), which actually ran the mines down in the jungle.

Partly because of Sarah's wide-eyed charm, the Belgian mine agents were very helpful; there was a truck that went down to the jungle every week, and we were welcome to ride upon it, on the condition that we would provide for ourselves and be ready to depart at the driver's convenience. But today was Monday, and the truck would not leave until later in the week, and time was running out; my visit to the jungle now depended, in effect, upon Adrien Deschryver, and no one knew when Deschryver would return.

That afternoon, for want of a better plan, we went down to the national parks office to talk to Citoyen Mushenzi, whose name means "mongrel" or "bastard" in Swahili. Mushenzi, an amiable and helpful man who gave us permission to camp at Kahuzi-Biega National Park as well as a note of introduction to its chief warden, is said to be amused by his own name, though we did not feel it was a joke that we should share. At the parks office there was an infant gorilla, apparently abandoned by its parents at Kahuzi-Biega; the young gorilla was completely trusting of human beings, and when it reached out to me, I took it up as one would a young human, cupping its small seat in my hand. It was entirely relaxed, astonishingly so, a solid little coarse-haired thing of no more than twenty pounds that leaned its head quietly against my chest as it gazed about, eliciting an unfamiliar surge of maternal feeling.

Jacques Goossens of the local travel office was kind enough to invite us out to his pleasant house for an aperitif in the late afternoon. On the way he pointed out a sort of monument, the tail of a white fighter plane sticking up out of a field. The downed plane had belonged to Jacques Schramm, the notorious mercenary for the international cartel that had attempted to separate the rich province of Katanga (now Shaba) from the new Zaire and thereby keep the copper wealth all to itself. As luck would have it, Schramm had not been aboard the doomed plane; somewhere in some warring African country, it was said, the man was still in his old line of work.

Goossen's house sits on the easternmost of the five Bukavu peninsulas, and the Rwanda border lies but a short distance away, across the swift Ruzizi stream that flows south into Lake Tanganyika. Except for a period in the late 1960s, when the Belgians were made to feel unwelcome, Jacques Goossens has worked in this country for forty years, and he speaks the equatorial Lingala tongue that is understood in most parts of Zaire. Unlike many former *colons*, Goossens would like to see the new Africa succeed, and although he met Patrice Lumumba once and didn't like him – "He was a big mouth," says gentlemanly Goossens – he thinks that Lumumba had no choice but to fight the secession of Katanga and try to hold this country in one piece. Like most people in Zaire, both white and black, Goossens supposes that the CIA had its long finger in Lumumba's murder and that United Nations Secretary-General Dag Hammarskjöld was murdered, too, in the same year, for the same reason: international big money was at stake, and both men were in the way. Hammarskjöld directed the UN attempt to conquer Katanga and reunite Zaire, and people forget, our host observes, that Hammarskjöld's brother was director of the cartel's competition, Anaconda Copper. Goossens shrugs. It has been a long time since anything surprised this charming, wise, and weary European.

In February of 1961, hitching rides south from Khartoum, I was stranded for some days in Equatoria. These were the bloody days that followed the Katanga secession, and Belgian refugees were streaming across the border into south Sudan; the small hotel at Juba was overflowing, and its grounds were littered with abandoned cars, broken down or out of gas. In mid-February I was at Nimule, across the border from Uganda, and, with two other whites met on the journey, came rather too close to being killed in the burst of anger that swept like a flash fire across Africa.

Those days at Nimule I recall as the longest in my life. There was no point in trying to cross the border, as the nearest town was far away across an arid plain. For fear of missing the stray vehicle that might pass through, we waited forever at the guard post, and during this period – though we never knew the reason for the crisis until days later, when finally we got away into Uganda – Patrice Lumumba, the firebrand of the new Africa, was murdered at Katanga in the Congo.

Overnight the friendly Sudanese became bitterly hostile. Guards and villagers gathered in swarms, their pointing and muttering interspersed with shouts and gestures. We could not understand what was being said, but it seemed clear that our crime was being white – so far as we knew, there were no members of our race closer than Juba, a hundred miles away – and that our fate was being decided. (Numbers of whites were killed that year in Africa; a thousand died in Angola alone.) Until then, the people of Nimule had been gentle and hospitable. The schoolmaster had offered us his hut, and even his own cot, and when our food ran out, the border guards shared their calabash of green murk and tripes into which three dirty white hands and seven or eight black ones dipped gray, mucilaginous hunks of manioc . . .

After a day and night of dread, peremptorily, we were summoned once more to eat from the communal bowl. Doubtless the schoolteacher had interceded for us, though he had been at pains to seem as hostile as the rest. I knew we must accept the food to avoid discourtesy, and the South African agreed; bravely he gagged down his tripe, retiring immediately behind a hut to puke it up again . . . *

The Tree where Man Was Born.

A fortnight later, on a plane from Nairobi to Bombay (I was off on an expedition to New Guinea), I found myself next to a mercenary pilot who was drinking hard, unable to get drunk; he felt threatened because he "knew too much" and was getting out of Africa as fast as possible. As I recall, this man was an Australian. He'd just come from the Congo, where he'd seen enough dirty work, he said, to last a lifetime; he described a recent episode in which some Africans had ordered him to fly a political prisoner to an airstrip in Katanga, where the prisoner was first beaten and then murdered; the killing bothered this man less than the sadistic beating that preceded it. It was not until long afterward, when the circumstances of Lumumba's death became known, that I took this tale as seriously as it deserved.

Considering the violence and rapine that have torn this land from the bloody slaving days of the early nineteenth century to that shameful period of recent years when Belgian interests, backed by international cartels, encouraged the copper-rich Katanga province to secede and thereby set one group of Zairois against another in a horrifying civil war that made a travesty of the country's independence – considering that, it amazes me not that so many Belgians have been permitted to return here – for the Zairois know all too well that they need help from Europeans until a new education system can replace them – but that Belgians, French, and white people in general are treated with such politeness and forbearance. Perhaps, out of all their years of horror, the Zairois have acquired a sense of identity, a national purpose that transcends the tribalism of the past; perhaps their acceptance of the white man's poor opinion of them has been displaced by a more cynical opinion of the white man. Since 1972, the Zairois call each other *citoyen* and are encouraged to discard Christian or European names in favor of "authentic" ones; thus, Alexandre Prigogine, a mixed-blood Tusi nephew of the celebrated ornithologist and the operator of a tour service in Goma, has dubbed himself Negzayo Safari. The women in their elegant long caftans braid their hair in marvelous patterns, while the men have abandoned European shirts and ties in favor of the *abas-cost* (*à bas le costume*, or "down with suits"), a light bush jacket. T-shirts are popular with the nation's youth, particularly shirts that advertise professional teams in the United States, including a mysterious baseball club called the Boston Giants. Despite hard times and a harsh regime, the people appear happy, and perhaps they hope that the immense resources of Zaire will one day be well organized to the profit and benefit of the Zairois themselves.

Most Zairians are wry about their president, Mobutu Sese Seko, whose some-what foolish photographic likeness in big glasses, leopard cap, and leopard foulard presides over every public room and office in the country. At present his discredited regime is exceeded only by the governments of Equatorial Guinea and South Africa in the brutality of its political repression. The Zairois are beginning to resent this "leader" who is so fond of demanding sacrifices for the Popular Revolutionary Movement. The Belgians also bled Zaire, but at least they knew how to run the country.

Drink in hand, I listen contentedly to the evensongs of a tropical boubou and a robin chat, as Goossens speaks about the great days of the early 1970s, when the prospects for Zaire and for the Zairois seemed almost limitless. At that time, he was stationed at Banana, the seaport for Kinshasa and the only port on the short coast of this huge country. One day early in 1974 he received a wire from the ministry of tourism, instructing him to prepare accommodations for the forty-five hundred tourists arriving by sea for the world-championship prizefight between Muhammad Ali and George Foreman. Since Banana could scarcely accommodate five hundred, the news of the huge ship threw the town into panic; huts for the tourist hordes were thrown up on every side without regard for sewage disposal or the threat of plague. But the Great Boat for Banana was as illusory as prosperity for Zaire; it never appeared, and Goossens wonders whether it ever existed at all.

Returning from Goossens's house that evening, we passed the car of Adrien Deschryver, who turned up next day to meet with us in La Fiesta Bar. At thirty-eight, Deschryver is a husky, blunt, laconic man with short-cropped dark hair gone a little gray and the restlessness of somebody in pain; though courteous enough, he offers little, averting his flat, pale blue eyes and smiling a private knowing smile that he means you to see. As a young man Deschryver was trained in taxidermy by James Chapin and had assembled a collection of some seven hundred skins of local birds. All of these, together with his library, were lost during the period of the revolution; he has never had the heart to start again. "*C'est un homme bizarre*," Goossens had told us, accounting for Deschryver's reputation for being difficult. "He has had a lot of trouble in his life. I don't know if that is a good reason, but it is a reason."

Lee Lyon was with him several years ago, Deschryver says, when he saw two Congo peacocks, still alive, that were snared at Hombo; it was not true that she had seen the peacock in the wild. "She was never away from me," he adds enigmatically, "so I would know." He seems to doubt that Chapin saw the peacock, although Forbes-Watson loyally assures us that he did. (In *Birds of the Belgian Congo*, Chapin says that he hunted for the bird in 1937; he does not say that he found it. William G. Conway, the director of the New York Zoological Society, tells me that he once asked Chapin whether he had actually seen the bird and that Chapin said he had not. However, Chapin's notes record that on July 16, 1937, near Ayena, "I noticed something dark running under the bushes of the forest floor, and called to Anyasi. He pursued it, fired, and then I saw a fine male 'peacock' rise with noisy wingbeats and escape.") With Lee Lyon, Deschryver had hoped to film the peacock, but since her death he has lost heart for this project. However, our keen interest seems to reawaken his own; he agrees to join our party in the search. In Deschryver's opinion the best place to start is the region of the mine camp at Obaye. He will fly us there early on Friday and stay over until Sunday or Monday, when I must return with him to Bukavu and go to Rome. Meanwhile, we shall visit Kahuzi-Biega and spend two days – we hope – with the gorillas.

Kahuzi-Biega is in the mountains twenty miles above Bukavu, and at seven in the morning a taxi was found with enough fuel to take us up there, though not back; the driver planned to coast down all the way. Before departing, he stopped to borrow the spare tire that is shared by Bukavu's old taxi fleet, and a good thing, too, as he had a flat not fifteen minutes out of town. Since his car had no jack, we found some villagers to help us hoist the taxi into the air while the tire was changed. Afterward we proceeded without incident uphill through the plantations, until the *Hagenia* trees appeared that marked the beginning of the montane forest.

Since arriving in Bukavu three days ago, we have not seen a single tourist and had hoped to have the gorillas to ourselves. But as luck would have it, two car-loads of Belgian visitors turn up right behind us at the village of Bashi Bantu people by the park entrance. We have permission to camp here overnight, and the head warden, or *conservateur assistant*, has promised us our own guide for tomor-row, but today only one guide is available, and so all visitors must stay together. These six people who are to be *nos copains de safari* intend to take with them a very large brown-and-yellow plastic ice chest full of lunch. Rather than lug it up the mountain by its handles, the unfortunate African assigned to it steps into the bushes and with his panga cuts some strips of flexible green bark for "bush rope"; with this he rigs himself a tumpline in order to carry the big chest on his back.

Disgruntled, we walk through the Bashi village and follow a path cross-country on the mountain. Though still early, the day is hot and humid. Our little band, following the three small Batwa trackers – *les pisteurs* – pushes through tangles of coarse bracken, elephant grass, cane, and lianas between the tall trees and the overgrown plantations. Since there is little forage in unbroken forest, the gorillas are drawn to the abandoned fields of the Bantu peoples' shifting cultivation, where the sun encourages a variety of leafy growth, and are often found too close to the villages for their own good. The trackers descend into swampy streams and up again into the forest, investigating the paths made by the apes and the freshness of their droppings; since gorillas are entirely vegetarian and must eat vast amounts by way of fuel, the droppings are abundant, large, and rather greenish, with a mild sweet smell.

In mid-morning there comes a sound of cracking limbs from a tree copse on the far side of a gully; the small *pisteurs* are pointing with their pangas. But one of our *gaie bande*, a silver-haired man who looked flushed even before he started, has not kept up; he is back there doubled up over a log, suffering heart flutters, attended not by his own party but by Forbes-Watson. "I thought I had a corpse on my hands," said Alec later; he was unable to persuade the man to remove the cameras that were dragging down his neck. Meanwhile, I am warning his compatriots about nettles, about the sharp spear points made by panga cuts on saplings, about false steps, mud slides, safari ants –

"*Ngaji!*"

The first gorilla is a large dark shape high in a tree, a mass of stillness that imagines itself unseen. Then, near the ground, a wild black face leans back into the sunlight to peer at us from behind a heavy trunk, and the sun lights the brown gloss of its nape. Soon a female with a young juvenile is seen, then – *le gros mâle! Voila!* There is high excitement as a huge silver-backed gorilla, rolling his shoulders, moves off on his knuckles into the tangle. The shadows close again, the trees are still. In the silence we hear stomach rumbles, a baboon-like bark, a branch breaking, and now and then a soft, strange "tappeting" as a gorilla slaps its chest; this chest slapping is habitual and not usually intended as a threat.

Midday has come. The gorillas have retired into deep, hot thicket, and no one thinks it a good idea to push them out. The dapper *conservateur assistant*, who likes to be called M. le Conservateur, has come up with more guides, and trackers, leading a highly colored troop of tourists that also includes a group of adolescents. Vivid as a parakeet in a suit of green, M. le Conservateur strides up and down before the silent thicket, warning the whites of the dangers from great apes while declaring himself ready to assume responsibility. Clearly he senses a threat to his authority from a dashing Belgian in his group, whose playsuit, as bright blue as his own is green, has assertive brass studs up and down the fly; this fellow's fingers are hooked into his belt whenever his arms are not akimbo. Frowning deeply to indicate the seriousness of the situation, the Belgian joins the *conservateur assistant* in peering meaningfully in all directions; their stance declares their intention to defend the women and children from attack by incensed gorillas that might come at us suddenly from any quarter.

And so the apes doze in their bush, while the human beings wait dutifully in the damp sun. Pale children fret – and doubtless a few black hairy ones, back in the bush, are fretting, too – and a mother distracts her youngest child by swathing it like a mummy in pink toilet paper, thereby enhancing the festive colors of this jungle scene.

A Klaas' cuckoo sings, long-crested hawk eagles in courtship sail overhead, and from the thicket comes the sweetish chicken-dung aroma of gorillas, accompanied by low coughs and a little barking. It is a stand-off. On one side of this big thicket perhaps thirty large and hairy primates are warning the restless young among them to be quiet, and on the other, a like number of large, hairless ones are doing the same thing. But all at once the suspense is broken by the ceremonial opening of the plastic ice chest, which incites a rush upon the lunch; the meat sandwiches and hardboiled eggs that appease the hairless carnivores assail the platyrrhine nostrils of the hairy herbivores back in the bush, for there comes a wave of agitation from the pongid ranks. The thickets twitch, shifting shadows and a black hand are seen; the humans stop chewing and cock their heads, but there is no sound. The gorilla, like the elephant, is only noisy when it chooses, as in the definition of the true gentleman, "who is never rude except on purpose"; and the sad face of a juvenile, too curious to keep its head low as it sneaks along a grassy brake, is the first sign that the apes are moving out.

Gorilla gorilla goes away under cover of the bushes, easing uphill and out across the old plantation and down again into dark forest of blue gum, leaving behind a spoor of fine, fresh droppings. Up hill and over dale comes *Homo* in pursuit, but *Gorilla* is feeling harassed now, and *Homo* is driven back from the forest edge by the sudden demonstration charge of a big-browed male who has been hiding in a bush. An oncoming male gorilla of several hundred pounds, with his huge face and shoulders and his lengthy reach, commands attention, and when the black mask roars and barks, showing black-rimmed teeth, we retreat speedily. The gorilla sinks away again into the green. To a branch just above comes a big sunbird with long central tail feathers – "Purple-breasted!" cries our dauntless birdman. "*That's* a new one!"

Finding their voices, the frightened guides yell at the gorilla, "*Wacha maneno yako!*" a Swahili expression often used to silence impertinent inferiors; loosely it means, "Don't give me any of your guff!" One of the Bashi, Seaundori, is scared and delighted simultaneously; grinning, he first asks eagerly if all had seen the charge of the gorilla, and then, imagining he has lost face by betraying excitement, he frowns as deeply as M. le Conservateur himself and fires nervous and unnecessary orders. The visitors, too, are babbling in excitement; only the small Batwa trackers, grinning a little, remain silent. They follow the gorillas, never rushing them, just flicking steadily away with their old pangas in the obscuring tangle of lianas. Even when the creatures are in view and no clearing is needed, the trackers tick lightly at the leaves as if to signal their own location to the gorillas and avoid startling them and provoking a panicked charge. This is the only danger from gorillas, which are as peaceable as man allows. Though a leopard has been known to kill an adult male, *Gorilla* has no real enemies except for *Homo,* and after years of protection at Kahuzi-Biega two of the three gorilla troops that are more or less accessible have placed an uneasy trust in man's good intentions. For the second time they permit us to come within twenty feet before the bushes start to twitch and tremble, a sign that the ones still feeding in plain view might be covering for those that are withdrawing. And though our views are mostly brief, there comes a time when *Homo* and *Gorilla* are in full view of each other for minute after minute, not thirty yards apart. The apes are more relaxed than we are and also more discreet, since they do not stare rudely at our strange appearance; on the contrary, they avert their gaze from the disorderly spectacle that we present, lolling back into the meshwork of low branches of big leaves and staring away into the forest as they strip branches of big green leaves and push the wads of green into their mouths. At one point a dozen heads or torsos may be seen at once in a low tier of green foliage just below us; the black woolly hair is clean, unmatted.

I count twenty-six white human beings and ten black ones in a loose line on the steep slope, slipping clumsily on the slick green stalks cut down by the *pisteurs*; at the fore, amateur *cinéastes* are jockeying for position, while from the rear come muffled cries of pain. Once again our path has crossed that of the safari ant, *siafu,* which is biting the hell out of women and children alike. Forbes-Watson and I try to move the tourists from harm's way, but supposing us to be competing for a better snapshot angle, they keep on milling until it is too late. By now Alex is reduced to desperate oaths, apologizing to Sarah for each obscenity and vowing that never, never again will he observe wildlife under such conditions: I wonder what my friend George Schaller, who pioneered gorilla observations when gorillas were still considered very dangerous, would have made of this peculiar woodland scene. To cries of "Silence!" from the adults, much louder than the original disturbance, unhappy children fret in the dark forest, and the *conservateur assistant,* gazing at the sky, makes an erroneous forecast of hard rain by way of an inducement to depart.

In the confusion the gorillas sink again into dense thicket. Departing, they must cross the path made by the trackers in trying to head them off, and at least fifteen pass in view, including *le gros mâle.* With a sudden roar he rears up, huge-headed, from the green wall, as the nervous Bashi guides yell, *"Rongo!"* – "Bluffer!" – and the whites fall over one another in the backward surge: the head of the adult gorilla is so enormous that it seems to occupy more than half the width between the shoulder points. But the threat display seems perfunctory and rather bored; *le gros mâle* regards us briefly before turning to give us a good look at his massive side view and the great slope of his crown. Then he drops onto his knuckles once again and shoulders his way into the forest. From neckless neck to waist he is silver white.

The apes are gone, and man troops down the mountain. Despite the frustrating indignities of this hot day, Alec, Sarah and I are exhilarated and excited, but for our companions their first sight of the wild gorilla was "*très fatiguant*" and even "*un peu déçevant*," or so they write in the park register; one took advantage of this opportunity to register a public complaint about the high price of film here in Zaire. Part of the group identifies itself as "*la famille Poisson*," and it may be that the others were "*la famille Boeuf*".

Before leaving Zaire I crossed paths again with these inheritors of King Léopold's bloody legacy. At Goma airport, their voluminous luggage had been increased by enormous crates of vegetables, one to each person, and they were abusing Air Zaire's black agent for charging them overweight; had they traveled this primitive airline for two weeks only to be repaid with his stupidity? ("*Merci, messieurs*," the agent said.) Tourists would *never* come back to the Belgian Congo as long as they received such ungrateful treatment! The Belgians slap their money down, they wheel, they rant: "*Ça non, monsieur!*"

Next morning we return again to the realm of the gorillas, taking a direction south and west and moving higher on the mountain. Still unsettled by the throngs of yesterday, we had suggested to the *conservateur assistant* that we would be happy to make do with a single tracker and no guide, but this anti-hierarchical idea upset his sense of order very much. (*Les guides ne sont pas les pisteurs! Il y a le Conservateur – c'est moi!* Puis, *les guides!* Puis, *les pisteurs!*) As special visitors with a letter from le Conservateur Mushenzi, we were entitled to two *guides* and three *pisteurs*, and that was that.

I had assumed that the small trackers were Batwa or Twa, the name used by Bantu speakers for all of Africa's small relict peoples, including the Bushman and the Pygmy. But these *pisteurs* are called Mbuti by the guides, and Adrien Deschryver later told me that they are apparently Bambuti or Mbuti hunters from the Ituri Forest to the north who were hunting gorillas in these mountains even before colonial times and maintain a small, separate village about five miles away from the nearest Bashi. Perhaps a certain mixing has occurred, for these little people are not "yellow", as the Mbuti Pygmies of the north are said to be, and may even be a little larger, though none of the three *pisteurs* has attained five feet. They have large-featured faces – big eyes, big jaws, wide mouths, and wide flat noses – in heads that seem too big for their small bodies. But it is the way they act and walk that separates them most distinctly from the guides, for their bearing is so cheerful and self-assured that one is soon oblivious of their small size; they move through the undergrowth and with it, instead of fighting the jungle in the manner of white people and Bantu. In the presence of the guides the leader of the three identifies himself as Shiberi Waziwazi; *waziwazi*, in Swahili, signifies one who comes and goes and is rather derogatory. But later he murmurs that Shiberi Waziwazi is the "African" name given to him by the Bantu, and that his true name, his "forest" name, is Kagwere. At this, the one called Kahuguzi says eagerly that he, too, has a forest name: it is Mukesso! And the forest name of the third Mbuti is Matene. Kagwere's left hand has been shrunken to a claw by fire, and he and Matene have the incised scars between the eyes and down upon the nose that are a mark of the Mbuti. All three have lightly filed brown broken teeth and small, neat, well-made legs, which stick out from beneath diminutive olive-colored raincoats and disappear into olive-colored rubber boots so old and torn that one wonders what might serve to keep them on. This *pisteur* uniform, with rain hats to match, is a sign of high prestige, to judge from the fact that they wear it over rough sweaters in this humid heat even while hacking at the torpid thickets with their pangas. The color hides the Mbuti in these forest shadows, through which, like the gorillas, they know how to move in utter silence, even in these ragged rubber boots.

Before entering the forest the Mbuti set up a kind of altar of sharp sticks stuck upright into the earth; they kneel before it, chipping at the soil in a strange manner with their pangas and crying out some sort of invocation, then pluck fresh leaves and press them down in seeming offering. Yesterday Alec dismissed this ritual as some sort of nonsense *folklorique* for tourists, comparing it to the "Chika dances" in Kenya's Embu region, but later our kind friend Semesaka, headman at the Bashi village and a former soldier in the rebellion (known locally as the *Vita ya Schramm*, or "War of Schramm", after that last and most notorious mercenary in Kivu Province), assured him that it was sincere, and so, today, we pay the ceremony more attention. Afterward Forbes-Watson asks some questions, but because he does so in front of the two Bashi, Kagwere is apparently embarrassed. He says what we had already supposed, that the ceremony is to help in locating the gorillas and to keep the trackers safe; pressed, he says in a false, wheedling tone that the *mungu* they are praying to is Jesus Christ. I watch Mukesso and Matene; they stare at Kagwere, look shy, then begin to laugh, and Kagwere is trying very hard not to laugh himself. We laugh, too, as Alec answers in Swahili, "Oh, come on, now, I'm no missionary!" At this all three Mbuti laugh much harder, but they cannot change the story now, not in front of the Bashi, who look from the whites to the Mbuti and then back again, sullen and mystified. So Forbes-Watson asks what the ceremony meant before the missionaries came into the forest, and the quick-witted Kagwere says, "How could I know? I wasn't here!" At this all three of the little men roll on the ground, and even the two Bashi laugh, and the whites, too.

The trackers point their pangas at high forest to the south, consulting in a rapid murmur as they roll thin cigarettes with makeshift papers. Then they set off up the mountain in a small-stepped amble that reminds me of the Hadza hunters of Tanzania, checking gorilla droppings, following the gorilla paths in search of some fresh sign of feeding; a place is marked where the gorillas have exposed a whole large bed of small white woodland mushrooms, and these will be gathered on the return journey. Tambourine doves hurtle down the path, and from the forest all around come their long, sad, falling notes; we climb onward as a green-blue stretch of Lake Kivu comes in view, down to the east.

Mukesso stops short, he has heard limbs cracking. We hear nothing. But Mukesso is sure, and Kagwere and Matene do not doubt him; the Mbuti strike off into dense jungle, making no effort to keep down the noise, and have not gone a hundred yards when they cross the gorillas' path. The guides are nervous in this tangle, and even the trackers seem uneasy. They stop to listen every little while, ticking the vines and branch tips with their pangas to let the hidden shapes know where they are. One whistles to the others, backs away a little. There is a big dark movement in the nearest bush, only feet away. We see the branches move, glimpse shifting blackness. Then the apes are gone, and the Mbuti do not follow. This place is dangerous, we must wait a little to see which way the apes will go.

Not so long ago, we had been told, a gorilla had killed one of the Mbuti and carried the body about with it for several days, but like the story of the exotic past of the old steamboat *Lt. Col. Potopoto*, this exciting story is not true. It was a Bashi who was seriously bitten, not so long ago, when a panicked gorilla charged past him in making its escape, and this may account for the nervousness of the two guides. Most of the time Seaundori and the other guide, Rukira, are sullen and officious; no doubt they know that we don't feel we need them in the forest, for the *conservateur assistant* is not tactful with his staff, to put it mildly. To track gorillas, to hack paths through the forest is Pygmy work; since the guides carry no rifles, like true askaris, they must know that they serve no purpose here whatever. Like people all over Africa who have lost touch with the old ways, they live in mixed fear and contempt of the wild animals. Seaundori yesterday, Rukira today, were unnerved by the threat display of the great apes, although both must have observed it many times, and so, to save face, they shout a lot of senseless orders and answer questions in querulous, aggressive ways.

Eventually, though we hear nothing, Kagwere jumps quickly to his feet and heads away into the forest, hacking and clipping, with Mukesso and Matene close behind. They trace an old path for perhaps a half-mile, following it around the east face of the mountain, pausing to listen, moving on again. The creatures are now well below us, working their way slowly up the hill; the Mbuti have anticipated their route of forage, we have only to ease along the mountainside, they will come to us. And soon the Bashi, growing bored, stop ordering us about, even let us walk ahead so that we may observe the Mbutis' deadly tracking. "Real bushmen," Forbes-Watson mutters. "I love being with people like this." I do, too, there is nothing I like better.

Soon a young gorilla comes in view, climbing high into a tree. From a point a little farther on, a vast female is visible, sprawled in a comfortable crotch, in sun and shade, perhaps fifteen feet above the ground. Avoiding our stares, she stuffs big, broad leaves into her mouth and pulls a thin branch through her teeth to eat the fresh light bark.

Slowly we sink down into the foliage. Through the wind light of the canopy the sky is blue, and to the nostrils comes the pungence of crushed leaves, the fresh green damp from this morning's rain, the humus smell of the high forest. Overhead a honey guide, a tinker bird sing fitfully; in the thrall of apes we pay them no attention. Observing the big female as she eats, a big male leans back into the vines on the ground behind her; probably he is too heavy now to climb. And seeing his vast aura of wellbeing, one understands the Africans' theory that the gorilla was formerly a villager who retired into the forest in fear of work.

Young gorillas come, still curious about the forest; they play with each other and with the trees, using their opposed toes to brace their climbing. One juvenile lies belly down over a branch, all four limbs dangling; he rolls over and down, to hang by one hand in the classic pose and scratch his armpit. He has wrinkled gray bare fingers and gray fingernails. Briefly he rough-houses with an infant, who flashes a little pale triangle of bare rump that I had not seen before, and the Mbuti laugh, mopping the sweat from their wet faces with handfuls of fresh leaves. For a time the young ape hangs suspended by both arms like a toy gorilla; lacking the discretion of his elders, he leers at man in a thin-lipped, brown-toothed grimace that matches his brown eyes, those eyes with the small pupils in a flat and shining gaze that does not really seem to see us. The gorilla face looks cross and wild and very sad by turns, though scientists assure us that no primate but man is capable of emotive expression.

To sweet-scented dung, like rotted flowers, comes a yellow butterfly; somewhere unseen the flies are buzzing, and a tambourine dove calls. From the undergrowth come deep contented grunts, then stomach rumblings and the sharp crack of a branch that does not break the rhythmic sound of the females' chewing.

Soon the last of the gorillas has swung, climbed, lolled, chewed, cleaned its bottom, beaten its chest in those soft tappeting thumps in different series, lowered to the ground the bellyful of vegetation that makes gorilla legs look small and thin, and vanished once more into the forest. We have watched them for an hour, and we are delighted; we talk little, for there is little to be said. On the way home the Mbuti cut themselves packets of bark strips for making bush rope and gather up the small white mushrooms to take home.

Deschryver had said he would come around on Thursday evening to confirm departure plans for Friday, and when he fails to appear, we find ourselves fretting once again, in this continual frustration about transportation; even Alec, who has stayed calm throughout all the delays and difficulties, grows a bit morose. Neither of us is used to traveling in this helpless way, entirely dependent on expensive, uncertain transport, and we vow that it will not happen again. I keep on saying hopefully that Deschryver must have got in late and is sure to turn up in the morning; now it is 9 a.m., and still he has not come. We are just looking for a car to go in search of him when he turns up at the door of the hotel. He is ready to take us to Obaye, he says, but he cannot stay, since later today he must fly government dignitaries from Goma north into the Ruwenzori. Since otherwise I shall be stranded, I have no choice but to return with him to Goma, on the first leg of my departure.

At the airport entrance, under a big sign reading TOUS POUR MOBUTU, MOBUTU POUR TOUS, a number of ragged Africans are chopping weeds. As we arrive, the airplane of the US embassy is coming in, and we wonder aloud why the United States maintains consulates in such out-of-the-way corners as Bukavu and Lubumbashi, in Shaba. "There is the CIA plane," Deschryver remarks, and I ask if he shares the popular opinion that Lumumba was murdered at the instigation of the CIA, that CIA agents are merely errand boys for international big business. Deschryver shrugs as if to say, What does it matter?

Deschryver is worried about the weather, which looks heavy toward the western mountains; in this season the good flying hours are in the morning. We are airborne a little after ten, circling slowly in the single-engine plane before climbing westward toward Kahuzi and Biega. The plane will cross between these peaks, which, unlike the Virungas, are not volcanic but granitic, a part of the great central rift of Africa. The highland forest of great trees, many of them now in flower, gives way with increasing altitude to the light feathery greens of the bamboo zone; somewhere below, hearing our motor, the gorillas may pause briefly in their chewing, though I doubt it. On the western slope, white torrents cascade steeply down into the Congo Basin, setting out on the long passage to the sea. To the north, leaning over at an extraordinary angle, a mass of granite rises out of the deep greens like a stone whale; otherwise the green extends unbroken as far out to the west as the eye can see. This is the Maniema Forest, a stronghold of cannibalism until after World War II, when measures such as execution may or may not have put the practice to a stop.

At lower altitudes a few Bantu huts appear; penetration of the forest here, Deschryver says, is very recent. He picks up the road that crosses the mountains and follows it north and west toward Walikale, less for purposes of navigation than because it is the only place to land in case of trouble. "Otherwise you are finished," he remarks, gazing out over the green expanse and making a cut-off motion with his hand. He points down at the small village of Hombo where several years ago, in the company of Lee Lyon, he had bought a snared *paon de Congo* for about two dollars. "They sold it to us like a chicken. I gave it to the international research station at Bukavu, but it died."

In 1949, as a young boy, Deschryver was brought by his Belgian parents to Bukavu. He was always interested in animals, he says, and after he completed school, he became a professional hunter – a very good one, it is said. But perhaps because of his training with James Chapin, he remained concerned with conservation, and in 1965 he requested that his hunting block at Kahuzi-Biega be made a national park; this was finally done in 1975. Though a few elephants still occur there, his main concern was for the gorillas, which were being killed by Africans for food. The gorilla's range extends into these lowlands, and in 1975, at Deschryver's urging, the boundaries of Kahuzi-Biega were considerably enlarged; the park now extends all the way west to Utu and to Uku, in a vast tract that includes much of the known range of the Congo peacock. Meanwhile, Deschryver has been featured in two television films on the gorillas, both widely distributed in the United States and Europe.

In 1967, at the time of the *Vita ya Schramm*, Deschryver was forced to leave the country. When he returned about six months later, his house and property had been destroyed. "I lost everything," he says, "everything," and as he speaks, that sad and bitter mask tightens his face.

Deschryver had been acquainted with Jacques Schramm, who had a coffee plantation in this region before he became a mercenary, but Schramm had never been a friend. "He wasn't doing what he did only for money," Deschryver remarked suddenly, after a silence; he made a forward pushing movement with his clenched fist. "No, he was *hard*!" He nodded. "He was too hard." Yes, he had heard that Schramm was still a mercenary in southern Africa – he shrugs again. "Who knows where that man is? He just disappeared."

*   *   *

The airplane crosses the brown Lua River. The lone road has degenerated to a thin brown track with a grass strip down the middle, a sign that vehicles are very few – we have not seen one. A brown scar in the forest to the north, surrounded by thin, isolated smokes, is Walikale. Here the Lua flows into the Loa, and the land is flat, for the white rapids of the highlands have disappeared. "The Loa is full of crocodiles," remarks Deschryver, coming as close as he ever comes to satisfaction. Not far to the west of Walikale the Loa will join the upper Lualaba, once called the Congo.

Under the plane the forest is primeval, without a sign of track or hut or smoke, green green green green as a green ocean, with here and there a glint of river under the islets of white cloud. The jungle stretches away under the leaden sky two thousand miles to the South Atlantic and beyond, along the Gulf of Guinea, to the westernmost African rain forest in Guinea.

The strip at Obaye is no more than a minute tear in this green fabric. It is already in view when Deschryver says, "I don't know whether my calculations are right or not, but Obaye should be just here." Soon he is circling the strip, and he makes a false landing to clear it of Africans, who are already running in from all directions. The roar scares up a number of big white-thighed hornbills that sail away among the strange umbrella trees, *musanga* (almost identical in appearance to a South American forest tree of an entirely different family and therefore a remarkable botanical example of the phenomenon called parallel evolution).

The smiling people at the airstrip are Banianga, who as recently as twenty years ago were famous cannibals, selling off their excess captives to like-minded tribes; they practice the shifting cultivation of those early Bantu who came down out of Cameroon in the first centuries AD. Standing tall among them is a big white man with glasses and neglected teeth who has been out here since the cannibal days as manager of the tin mines for Sominki. Victor Delcourt is surprised to hear of the quest for the *paon de Congo*. "Why, I have *eaten* it!" he exclaims. "Very good, too!" Yes, but has he seen it in the wild? "*B'en oui! Je l'ai tué moi-même!*" Twenty years ago he had seen one by the roadside, stopped his truck, and shot it. There seems no reason to doubt a man so innocent of his own accomplishment.

I leave Sarah and Alec in the hands of the only white man ever known to have seen, killed, and eaten *Afropavo*. We part with regret, for we have got on very well; there is talk already of another expedition, perhaps to one of the three avian regions left in Africa that Alec does not know. But since all three – Namibia, Angola, Ethiopia – are presently in a state of war, it is hard to imagine when this expedition might take place.

Deschryver is anxious about the weather; it is time to go. When the plane takes off again, the children run behind it, down the airstrip, and the big hornbills with white patches on their wings rise once again to flap and sail to far umbrella trees.

On the eastward flight Deschryver opens up a little and even speaks out once or twice of his own accord; when he chooses, he has a pleasant smile and a good laugh. But heavy weather is closing in behind us, and by midday, as Adrien had predicted, the weather has changed suddenly for the worse. Due to rising heat and moisture – the transpiration of this vast expanse of humid jungle – the rain clouds build up steadily all morning, and now they are bursting all around us, as rain comes in a hard patter on the windshield. Deschryver, frowning, forced off course, feels his way around the thunderheads, emerging finally well south of his intended route, at the northern boundary of the Kahuzi-Biega Park. A beautiful waterfall comes and goes in a mist of gray and green, and then we see that enormous rock, like a leaning tower, that we had passed on its south side on the trip west. "We are near Wagongo," Deschryver says, and he points to the heavy cloud mass not far south that shrouds Kahuzi. "If I flew there" – and once again he makes that cutting gesture with his hand – "then we are finished. When pilots get lost out here, that's it. So it's very good that I know just where I am." At Goma we would learn that due to weather his charter to the Ruwenzori had been canceled; we might as well have stayed there at Obaye.

The plane drifts along the western shore of Kivu, with its beautiful islets and sheltered coves hidden by the green steep walls of drowned volcanoes. The water turns in patterns of pure blues, deep, dark, and pale – whether cloud shadow or sign of depth it is hard to tell. Already wind streaks gather in the silver sheen that will form into gray chop this afternoon. At the north end of Kivu, where in 1912 broad coulees of lava boiled the lake, small craters guard the shore, and one of these is far out in the water, forming an emblematic U just off the mouth of a hidden harbor. Nyiragongo comes in view, a dim shadow in the heavy weather that is closing off the north, a specter of the fire mountains, quite unreal, and once again I am struck by the great beauty of this heartland of a continent, exclaiming aloud that it must be one of the loveliest regions in all Africa. Deschryver nods, as if this fact were tragic; despite his Zairian wife and children, he is not permitted to become a citizen. I ask if he intends to spend his life here. "Why not?" he says, turning to look me squarely in the face for the first time since I have known him. "What else am I to do?" (He died in 1989, still in his forties.)

A few weeks later I received a letter sent from Paris by Sarah Plimpton. George had joined them, and although they had not actually seen the Congo peacock, they believed they had heard the *gowé-gowah* that Chapin had recorded. According to Charles Cordier the cock calls loudly in the night – *ko-ko-wa!* – to which the hen responds – *hi-ho, hi-ho.*

Pygmies and Pygmy Elephants: The Congo Basin (1986)

On the last evening of 1985, the all-but-empty flight from Dakar-Monrovia-Lagos to Nairobi is crossing the lightless forests of the Congo Basin, passing at midnight over the Central African highlands of the Zaire–Rwanda border, where the earth's last bands of mountain gorillas sleep in their nests. Down there in the dark, the outraged Africans who are thought to have murdered the gorilla researcher Dian Fossey are still in hiding; Fossey is being buried there this very evening. On the screen is a South African movie, *The Gods Must Be Crazy*, a simple-hearted tale (though politically disingenuous, with its slapstick guerrilla squad of foolish blacks led by a caricatured Cuban). It's easy to follow without the sound track, and I especially enjoy the wistful grace of the Kung Bushman, whom I knew as Komsai seven years ago when his band was living in Botswana's Tsodilo Hills. Komsai had worked in South Africa's mines, he spoke the South African lingua franca called Funhalarou, and perhaps this is why he was chosen for this movie. When I crossed his path, he had gone back to the Kalahari and he was a hunter, with a newly killed eland in his camp, and the huge fresh lyre horns of a kudu bull, both taken with his bow and poison arrows. Somewhere I have heard that since participating in the film, Komsai has died; perhaps this is not true, perhaps the gods are not crazy after all.

At 2 a.m. in the new year, I am met in Nairobi by the savanna ecologist David Western, a husky, trim, and well-kept Kenyan citizen of forty-two. Dr Western is the resource ecologist for the New York Zoological Society, best known for its Bronx Zoo and New York Aquarium; he is also pilot of the NYZS aircraft in which we shall embark the day after tomorrow on a survey of the rain forests of Central Africa, paying special attention to the numbers and distribution of the small forest elephant, which may be seriously threatened by the ivory trade. As Dr Western – known since a small boy as Jonah – wrote me in a letter last September, "We still know remarkably little about either the forest elephant, which now accounts for sixty per cent of the ivory leaving Africa, or the Congo Basin, an area including about twenty per cent of the world's tropical equatorial forests. The forest elephant is something of an enigma, and reason enough for the entire trip."

The African elephant, *Loxodonta africana*, has been seriously imperiled by ivory hunters; recent analyses of market tusks show that the poaching gangs, having reduced the savanna or bush elephant, *Loxodonta africana africana*, to less than a half-million animals, are increasingly concentrating on the much smaller forest race, *L. a. cyclotis*. Unlike *L. a. africana*, which is easy to census by light plane, *cyclotis* spends most of the daylight hours hidden in the forest, and estimates of its numbers have been mainly speculative. Proponents of the ivory trade maintain that the forest canopy hides very large numbers of small elephants, while ecologists fear that in this inhospitable habitat the numbers have always been low. It is generally agreed that an African elephant population of two million or more animals could probably sustain the present slaughter for the ivory trade, which until very recently, at least, has produced about seven hundred and fifty tons each year. However, computer analyses indicate that if fewer than a million elephants are left, as many authorities believe, then the species is already in a precipitous decline in which half the remaining animals will be lost in the next decade. The future of *Loxodonta* may depend, in short, on an accurate estimate of the numbers of the forest race, which would lay the foundation for a strong international conservation effort on behalf of the species as a whole.

"There will be a large gap in our understanding of the forest elephant until we understand the forest better," Western's letter said. "That is one of the purposes of this survey. The truth is, we know very little about forest ecology. Only in recent years, with the realization of how rapidly the rain forests, with their great abundance and variety of life, are disappearing, especially in South America and southeast Asia, have we come to realize that the forest is a very important biome that cannot be ignored by anyone committed to conservation and the future of the earth. Because of its inaccessibility and low human population, the Congo Basin is still largely intact, but there is no reason for confidence that it will stay that way."

As for me, I am interested in both the forest and the forest elephant, and I enjoy the company of biologists, who teach me a great deal that I wish to know about the origins and structure and relationships of the natural world, which have filled me with awe and fascination all my life. Throughout our journey we shall be working with ecologists already in the field, and an elephant biologist will meet us in Central Africa and accompany us throughout the first part of the journey. Later we shall accompany okapi biologists and Mbuti Pygmy hunters into the Ituri Forest of Zaire.

Since our main destinations will be wilderness regions of the Central African Republic, Gabon, and Zaire, we will travel nearly seven thousand miles, from Nairobi, in Kenya, to Libreville, on Gabon's Atlantic coast, and back again. So far as Dr Western knows, this transcontinental forest journey has never before been made in a light plane, but the feat interests us much less than the discoveries we might make along the way. With luck, for example, we shall learn more about the mysterious "pygmy elephant" in C.A.R. and Gabon, widely reported for almost a hundred years. With the exception of the mokele mbembe, an elusive dinosaur-like denizen of the vast swamps of the Congo Basin, the pygmy elephant, *Loxodonta pumilio*, is regarded as the last large "unknown" animal in Africa. In a forest of such size and inaccessibility, it would be unwise to dismiss the pygmy elephant out of hand; the gorilla was reported for nearly a century before its existence was scientifically accepted, and the okapi, a large forest relative of the giraffe, eluded detection entirely until 1908.

Dr Western and his wife, Dr Shirley Strum, the distinguished social anthropologist and student of the baboon, have a new baby and a new house that faces across the Mbagathi River, which forms the boundary between the Nairobi National Park and the Kapiti Plain, in Maasai Land. Driving out the Langata Road, passing the demolished car of a New Year's celebrant, Jonah assured me that early in the morning I might see black rhino from his guest-room window.

Calls of the ring-neck and red-eyed doves reminded me as I awoke that I was once again in Africa. Now it is sunrise, and I see no rhino, but there are eland, impala, and giraffe, and a small herd of buffalo on the thorn landscape, still green and fresh after December's short rains.

The bureaucracy in the new Kenya is under stern instruction from President Daniel Arap Moi to serve the people rather than abuse them, as has been the popular custom on this continent, and preparations for our air safari go quite smoothly. But this morning the Directorate of Civil Aviation was down to a single airport clearance form, though six were needed, and all the copiers in the ministry were out of service, and by the time we filled out the long form and took it downtown to be copied, and completed the strict airport preparations and procedures, and passed through customs, it was already two in the afternoon, with a long flight across Kenya and Uganda into northern Zaire to be made by nightfall.

The New York Zoological Society's aircraft is a single-engine Cessna 206, which normally can go six hours without refueling. It has been specially fitted with a cargo pod and extra gas drums to give us a range of fourteen hours, very critical in the vast reaches of Central Africa where sources of fuel are few and undependable. This heavy-duty blue-and-silver plane is the sole survivor of a group of three that were formerly attached to the European Economic Community's Jonglei Canal Project, designed to bypass the Great Sudd of the south Sudan and carry Nile water more efficiently to the Moslem north. The southern tribesmen – Nilotic pastoralists of the Nuer and Dinka tribes – dispute what they see as continuing Moslem aggression at their expense. In recent years, the spear-carrying "rebels" have been supplied with modern arms by Ethiopia, and not long ago they blew up two of the Jonglei planes. The remaining one was sold to the NYZS. Its former pilot, a Kenyan citizen named Gwynn Morsen, was held hostage by the rebels for more than a year. "Spent most of my time thinking up ways to strike back," he told us this morning at Wilson airport, "and I think I've settled on a plague of rinderpest. Can't infect them with cholera or human plagues because they have all that already, so I'll hit them where it *really* hurts – their cattle!" Two years ago, when Jonah and I first discussed this journey, we planned to look at the great herds of kob antelope on Sudan's Boma Plateau, and the beautiful small park on the White Nile at Nimule where I first saw white rhino in 1961; but now one cannot land safely there, nor in Uganda, so pervasive are the civil wars on this sad continent.

"You're leaving too late," Shirley remarks when she comes to see us off, and we both know this, but by now we are frustrated, anxious to get going. Jonah, a bush pilot of thirteen years' experience, reckons that we will still reach the airstrip in Zaire's Garamba Park before dark. There we will refuel the aircraft from our spare fuel drums and spend a day with Kes and Fraser Smith, who are studying the last northern white rhinos. The following day we will head west to our first destination in the Central African Republic.

Leaving Nairobi, the plane turns northwest across Kikuyu Land and the Rift Escarpment, heading up the great Rift Valley between the Mau Range and the Aberdares. As it crosses Lake Naivasha, I peer down upon the bright white heads of fish eagles and a shimmering white string of pelicans; off the white soda shores of Lake Nakuru is a large pink crescent made by thousands upon thousands of flamingos. Then we are crossing the equator, droning northwestward over the Kakamega Forest, the easternmost outpost of the equatorial rain forests that extend all the way into West Africa. Off to the north rises Mt Elgon, on the Uganda border, as a great migratory flight of European storks passes south beneath the plane, on their way, perhaps, to winter range in the Serengeti.

The high winds of the new monsoon, blowing out of Chad and the Sudan, have shrouded the rich farmlands of Uganda in a haze of dust. The sun looms, disappears again, behind bruised clouds that are thickened by the smoke of fires in this burning land. The rebel forces of Yoweri Museveni might bring peace and stability to this bloodied country – in early January of 1986 still under the control of the violent soldiery of the beleaguered Milton Obote, who is now known to have presided over the tribal slaughter of even more thousands of his countrymen than did his predecessor, Idi Amin. (Even among African countries, Uganda seems unusually beset by bloody-minded tyrants, who were already ruling when the first explorers came up the Nile; in the days of Henry Morton Stanley, the despotic ruler was a man named Mwanga, for whom Idi Amin named his son.) The long red roads are strangely empty of all vehicles, for the countryside below, so green and peaceful in appearance, is in a state of utter anarchy and fear, with all communications broken down and the hated, vengeful army of the latest tyrant in retreat across the land, looting and killing.

The broad morass of lakes and swamps called Lake Kyoga, with its primitive island villages, is utterly roadless and indeterminate in configuration, like some labyrinthine swamp of ancient myth, there are no landmarks for calculating a precise heading, and the monsoon wind carries us just far enough off course so that we pass east of the Victoria Nile, which we had intended to follow down as far as Murchison Falls. By the time we correct our course, we must backtrack across the Albert Nile to the Victoria, following whitewater rapids to the extraordinary chute where the torrent hurtles through a narrow chasm and plunges into the broad hippo pool below. Twenty-five years ago, when I first came here, hitchhiking south from the Sudan into East Africa, this park (renamed Kabalega but now Murchison again) was famous all over the world for its legions of great-tusked elephants and other animals. Today most of the animals are gone, cut down by the automatic guns of marauding armies, including the Tanzanian forces that helped to depose Idi Amin. In February of 1961, this pool was fairly awash with hippopotami; now there is not a single hippo to be seen. The park's twelve thousand elephants are now three hundred. We see none. The only animals in view are a few kob antelope that scatter wildly at the coming of the plane. The booming white falls of the Victoria Nile, descending from Lake Kyoga, thunder undiminished in an empty and silent land.

From Murchison Falls, we take our final bearing for Garamba. The day is late, the skies in all directions dark with haze and smoke, as we set out across northeastern Zaire. Air charts of Zaire are out of date, therefore misleading, and Jonah, frustrated, must resort to my small relief map for his navigation. On this large-scale map, in the poor light, we confuse the town of Arua, on the Uganda side, with Aru in Zaire, so that none of the scarce roads and landmarks seem to fit, and the light fails nearly an hour earlier than expected as the sun sinks behind a dark shroud of smoke and desert haze off to the west. We are now disoriented, with only a very rough idea of our location. Small clusters of huts below, in the old fields and broken forest of rough hill country, are already dimming in the shadow of the night, and suddenly we know without discussion that we will not arrive this evening at Garamba, that even a forced landing in rough country is much better than finding ourselves in the pitch dark with no place to come down. (Not all pilots, as he told me later, feel confident about landing in the bush, and some tend to hesitate until the light is so far gone that *any* landing becomes very dangerous.)

The dirt roads are narrow and deeply rutted, and we must choose quickly among rough shrubby fields. Jonah banks for a quick approach, and slows the plane to stalling speed. Because coarse high grass hides the ground, and the field is small, he is forced to touch down quickly. Nose high, we settle into the stiff grass.

The plane strikes the brick-like laterite with a hard bounce and hurtles through bushes with a fearful whacking of stiff branches against metal. Missing the hidden termite hills and ditches, it suffers no worse than a few dents in the tail planes.

To make such a wild landing without mishap is exhilarating, and I congratulate Jonah on his skill, grateful to be wherever the hell we are still in one piece. All we have to do, I say to cheer him, is refuel the wing tanks, lay out our bed-rolls, and be off again at dawn. But this is the first time in thirteen years as a bush pilot that Jonah has been lost at nightfall and forced down, and though he is calm, with scarcely a blond hair out of place, he is not happy. As a man who neither drinks nor smokes and is before all orderly and neat, he takes pride in his preparations and efficiency, and he has not yet figured out where things went wrong. "Getting off again, Peter, may be quite another matter," he says stiffly, descending from the plane and staring about him, hands on hips.

From every direction, Africans come streaming across the country; we had seen some running toward the scene even before the airplane touched down. Within minutes, they surround the plane in a wide circle, and a few come forward, offering long, limp, cool, callused hands. They touch the wings, then turn to look at us again, eyes shining. Everyone is scared and friendly – the children run away each time we move, women smile and curtsy. "It is like an apparition to them," one young man tells me gently, in poor French, there by separating himself discreetly from these hill peasants who have never seen an airplane before.

Many of these Bantu folk of the northeastern region known as Haut-Zaïre (Upper Zaire) have some French or Swahili, and so we are able to converse freely, and a good thing, too. The first group of several dozen shy onlookers has swelled quickly to a noisy crowd of hundreds – at least seven or eight hundred, by the end – all of them growing more and more excited in that volatile African way that can lead very quickly to irredeemable gestures, and sometimes violence. Politely but firmly, our well-wishers warn us to move away into the dark, to let the people calm themselves a little. We are told that we have landed near the village of Dibwa, and soon the village headman, who is drunk, asserts his authority by demanding to see identification. An ad hoc committee, heads together, draws our passport numbers on a scrap of paper amidst random officious shouts and cries of suspicion and bewilderment.

In 1903, when the first Baptist missionaries penetrated this huge region west of the Nile – said to have been the last region without whites in the whole Dark Continent – it was known to other Africans as "the Land of the Flesh-Eaters", due to the rampant cannibalism of its inhabitants, and the reputation of these local Azande people (of northeast Zaire, southwest Sudan, and southeast Chad) has not improved much since that time. After the Belgian Congo achieved independence (became Zaire in 1960), there began a six-year struggle for power, and

Haut-Zaïre was pillaged by waves of undisciplined soldiery, guerrilla bands – the Simba rebels – and South African and Rhodesian mercenaries. Because of this recent memory of bloodshed and famine, and because Zaire is surrounded by unstable, often hostile African states, the Zairois are highly suspicious of unidentified white foreigners. But as in most Africans, their excitability is offset by a great courtesy and gentleness, and we were treated well by almost everyone in this remote community.

Now it is dark, but the people do not disperse. Increasingly it becomes clear that we will not be permitted to sleep here at the plane, that we are, in fact, to be taken into custody. "After all," my confidant explains, when I protest, "our people are very simple, they do not know why you have come here suddenly like this, or what you will do during the night." I look over at Jonah, who is getting the same message in Swahili. Having no choice, we agree to be escorted to the nearest hut, a quarter-mile away, where in a yard swept bare as a defense against night snakes, granary rodents, and mosquitoes, a fire is built and well-made chairs of wood and hide provided.

"We *have* to keep you here, we have to report you!" the headman explains, somewhat mollified now that we have decided to come peaceably. We sit surrounded by admirers, who wish to hear our story over and over. Soon we are shown inside the hut, where cane mats have been spread for us on the earth floor. "This is not what you are used to," one man suggests shyly, not quite sure of this, and eager to inquire about our customs. Two men ask to borrow my flashlight and have yet to bring it back when, still in good spirits, I close my eyes.

Toward midnight we were woken up and led outside. Someone had run across the country to fetch some sort of district secretary, and we gathered once more at the fire. Once again we produced our passports and told our story, which was duly recorded. The secretary had walked here from six miles away to gather this information. "I have done it for the security and welfare of my people," he informed us.

Another herald had been sent by bicycle to the town of Aru, almost twenty miles away, to notify the district commissioner, who arrived in a van with his aides and soldiery about 1.30 in the morning. This time a *gendarme* in green uniform banged into the hut, shouting abusively, shoving Jonah, and loosening his belt, as if in eagerness to whip us along faster. Outside, the calm, cold-faced commissioner had already been seated, and the foreigners were led to two chairs placed directly in front of him. Once again we showed our passports and accounted for ourselves, but this time the passports were not given back. Though we said we wished to stay nearby, to watch the plane, the commissioner informed us that a soldier would be assigned to guard it, and that we were to be taken back to Aru.

Under armed escort, we were marched across the fields toward the road. Without my flashlight, I could not see the hard-baked ground; I made a fatal misstep at the edge of a ditch, and tore my ankle. I fell to the hard earth with a mighty curse, aware that at the very outset of this trip, which would involve a lot of forest walking, I had resprained an ankle already injured in cross-country skiing. The pain was so violent that I did not notice the safari ants that everyone else was slapping: I simply hobbled ahead while I still could, gasping in anger and shock. Not until I was inside the van, seated opposite a sullen African with a machine pistol and another with two carbines, did I feel the *siafu* attacking me under my pants. I dealt with them all the way down the rough road to Aru.

Beside me, Jonah seemed as stunned as I, and we did not speak. Jolting along in the dead of night, with no idea what was coming next, there was little to say. With each new development, our predicament seemed to be worsening. We had no clearance for landing in this region, only at Kinshasa, where we were scheduled to arrive a few weeks later, and Zaire, with its reputation for violence and corruption (it is sometimes referred to as a "kleptocracy"), was no place to have one's papers not in order. Also, an investigation might identify me as the author of an article about a previous visit, a few years before, in which I was sharply critical of Zaire's puppet dictator – reason enough in this feverish climate to be arrested as an enemy of the state, if not a suspected mercenary or spy.

Twenty-five years ago to the very month, scarcely a hundred miles east of this place, on the Sudan border, I had also been in custody, under much worse circumstances (the murder of Zaire's prime minister, Patrice Lumumba, in January of 1961, had inflamed Africa, turning Sudanese friends into fierce enemies), and I had no wish to repeat any such experience.

In Aru, to our great astonishment we were not locked up – we could go nowhere, after all, without passports or airplane – but were dropped off almost casually at the quarters of a British pilot for the United Nations' High Commission for Refugees, which is kept very busy in this part of the world. Our host, routed out at 3 a.m., kindly showed us where we might lie down, observing in passing that Zaire was paranoid these days about "mercenaries," which has been a dread word in this country since the anarchy and massacres of the 1960s. Rumors had implicated Zairois soldiers when seven French whitewater boatmen who had entered the country without permission disappeared on the Zaire River a few months ago. The government revealed that they had perished in the rapids, though their boats were found intact and right side up, and the one body that turned up had been beheaded.

The pilot was flying to Nairobi at daylight, now two hours away, and Jonah, fearing that our friends at Garamba might radio an alarm when we failed to appear, sent off a message to his neighbor Philip Leakey to notify his wife that we were fine.

At 8 a.m., the pilot's Ugandan assistant drove us around to the district commissioner's house to inquire about our passports. We were referred to the chief of immigration, who referred us to the chief of police, who said he had reported our arrival to his superiors in the regional capital at Bunia and could not return our passports without their permission. Surely Bunia would decide to check our identities at Kinshasa, and, since it was Saturday, it now appeared that we might be detained here through the weekend.

Meanwhile, the authorities had no objection if Dr Western brought his airplane to Aru; they assumed that he would not vanish, leaving me and his passport behind. As Jonah wished to take off with an empty plane, the obliging police chief returned with him to Dibwa, where the people were ordered to chop brush, knock down termite hills, and fill up ditches while the plane's extra fuel and other cargo were unloaded for ground transport to the strip at Aru. As it turned out, the pair who had absconded with my flashlight the night before had used it to off-load all they could find in the unlocked cargo pod under the fuselage, including three jerry cans of fuel, a computer printer destined for Garamba, and a duffel containing all my clothes and personal belongings. The duffel, minus some of its original contents – toilet kit, malaria pills, spare flashlight, sneakers, sweater, hat, and every pair of socks and underwear – was retrieved eventually, but the fuel and the printer were gone for good.

Jonah made a skillful downhill takeoff and followed the road into Aru. By the time he arrived there, word had come to let us go. (Apparently Bunia had learned from Kinshasa that our visit was expected by the minister of national parks.) By early afternoon, we were in the air again, and headed north.

Nagero, on the Dungu River, forms the southern boundary of Garamba National Park. At its small airstrip, we were met by Alison (Kes) Smith, a pretty woman in her thirties with dark red hair. Dr Smith, born in England and now a Kenyan citizen, is the biologist on the Garamba Northern White Rhino Project, which is funded by various conservation groups and private donors. Her husband, Fraser Smith, is in charge of restoring to good operating order the logistical system of Garamba, which was the first of Zaire's parks, established by the colonial authorities in 1938. Accompanied by their infant daughter, the Smiths escorted us in the afternoon to the flat rocks by the hippo pool where they had been married just a year before in a roaring and blaring serenade from these hundred hippos. The silver limbs of the dead tree across the Dungu were decked with a winged red inflorescence made by companies of carmine bee-eaters, which, with their blue heads, cobalt rumps, and long streaming tails, are among the most splendid of African birds. With them were some smaller, only slightly less spectacular red-throated bee-eaters, and by its nest on a high tree sat a thickset white bird, the palm-nut vulture. Already we were far enough west so that endemic bird species of East and West Africa were overlapping; I had last seen this peculiar bird in Senegal.

Fraser Smith had constructed a small house on the banks of the Dungu, and the household presently included a large dog (a second dog had been taken by a crocodile), two cats, and a banded mongoose, which had enjoyed the run of the camp before taking up a habit of attacking people; its victims included its mistress, severely bitten twice. Since Dr Smith had mentioned its bad character, I was unpleasantly surprised to see the snout and beady eyes of this large weasel relative appear beneath the wood stockade of the outdoor shower into which I had limped just before dusk. There was no mistaking the intent of its opened mouth, which was to bite me as speedily as possible, and sure enough it whisked into the shower and nipped my heel before I could take defensive action.

As anyone knows who recalls Kipling's Rikki-tikki-tavi, a mongoose is much too quick for any cobra, let alone a crippled man in a cramped shower slippery with soap. With my inflamed and swollen ankle, I was already a bit rickety on the wet uneven bricks, and this evil-tempered viverrid, renewing its attack, had me at enormous disadvantage. Jonah and Fraser were away from camp, refueling the airplane, so I called to Dr Smith, more or less calmly, that she could find her mongoose near the shower. She had meant to take "Goose" for a walk, she said, and commenced to call it. The mongoose ignored her, darting in and out of sight under the stockade. I flicked hot water at it and made frightful growling noises, all to no avail; it backed out of view, came in swiftly from another angle, and sank its teeth into my toe, eliciting a sharp cry of vexation. "Is Goose biting you?" his mistress called. "So sorry!" It seemed that she was nursing her baby, but would come and fetch the mongoose in a minute.

For the nonce, I seized up a steel bucket and banged it down in front of my tormentor. This drove him back a little but did not deter him. Hopping mad, he dug furiously at the sandy earth – what field biologists call displacement activity, in which strong emotions are vented inappropriately. My toe was bleeding, my ankle hurt, and I, too, was full of strong emotion. Though loath to execute a house-hold pet by bashing its brains out with my bucket, I was considering this last resort when it darted out of sight, made a flanking maneuver, and shot in again from yet another angle, affixing itself to the top of my left foot with a terrific bite. There it remained until I kicked it free, emitting a wild oath of rage and pain.

Perhaps afraid for her pet's life, my hostess appeared almost at once, joining me in the shower without warning. On the soapy floor, her legs flew out from under her, and she landed on her bottom, careening into the stockade as the mongoose disappeared beneath. Looking up, soaked by the shower, she found herself confronted by the nudity of her amazed guest, covered a bit late by the bucket. "Sorry," she said, starting to laugh, and I laughed, too. "I have no secrets," I said, groping for a towel. "Just remove that mongoose." I pointed sternly at my bloody foot. And with suspicious speed, or so it seemed to me – as if, in this camp, an emergency mongoose-bite repair kit was ever at the ready – Dr. Smith was back at the shower door with bandages and disinfectants. "Sorry," she said. "Better take care of that. Might turn septic quickly in this climate."

The mongoose episode occurred exactly twenty-four hours after the forced landing at Dibwa, and considering all that had taken place so early in our journey, I felt the need of a stiff whiskey, in which Kes joined me. I asked her first of all to explain her nickname (it's from "Kesenyonye", or "Live in Peace", a name given her by Maasai tribesmen when she and her first husband, Chris Hillman, who was working on an eland study, lived in Maasai Land south of the Ngong Hills) and, second, for details of the white rhino project – specifically, why she felt so strongly that such a large international effort should be expended in a probably doomed attempt to save the last seventeen animals of the northern race, when the very similar southern race is well protected, and the species as a whole not currently in danger.

Among all land mammals on earth, white (from the German "*weit,*" or wide-mouthed) rhinos are second only to elephants in size. Dr Smith pointed out that the southern white rhino (the originally described race, *Cerathotherium simum simum*) was already endangered by the turn of the century and virtually exterminated in the 1920s by South African hunters; it was reduced to a remnant hundred animals before its protection was seriously begun. This number has now been increased to approximately three thousand, most of them in South Africa's national parks; white rhinos have also been reintroduced in Botswana, Zimbabwe, and Mozambique (though it seems unlikely that the Mozambique animals have survived that country's wars). This recovery lends at least faint hope for the recovery of the northern race, which is worth saving not only for itself but as a symbol of the conservation effort. (By spring 1989, the population has increased to twenty-two animals.)

The northern white rhinoceros was originally found in far northwest Uganda and northeast Zaire, the southern savannas of Sudan and Chad, and the Central African Republic, throughout suitable habitat north of the rain forest and west of the River Nile. In 1938, when Garamba was established, several hundred rhino were located by surveys, which until recent years have all been made on foot. By 1961, when I first saw these huge placid animals in the small park at Nimule, in the Sudan, an estimated one thousand to thirteen hundred white rhino were living in Garamba. Not long thereafter, the Simba rebels, protesting the murder of Lumumba and the ascendance of a pro-European regime, took control of most of Haut-Zaïre, including the Garamba Park. In the next few years the Simbas slaughtered ninety per cent of the white rhinos solely for their horn, the proceeds from which were used for the purchase of more weapons. In 1969, parks control was restored, but by 1977, when the rhino's numbers had increased to about five hundred, lack of government funding and logistical breakdown had removed all protection from the park's animals, which were now attacked more or less at will by organized poaching gangs from Uganda and Sudan, armed with automatic weapons from both countries' wars. By 1981, just thirty-six animals remained, and a survey two years later would locate less than twenty. The Garamba population has not increased in the years since, and everywhere else the northern race has probably been exterminated. The few lone animals that may still wander the empty eastern reaches of the Central African Republic will die without contributing to the population, since any meaningful increase in this remnant group would have to be achieved quickly, before the gene pool and breeding potential are further reduced by scattering, accident, or senility.

As the one certain defense against poaching, removal of these sixteen animals to a safer area has been considered, but there is no other safe, suitable habitat in Zaire, whose president-for-life Mobutu Sese Seko has decreed that these "Zairian" rhinos shall not leave his country. Instead he has promised help to the rhino project that has not been forthcoming. For the several months prior to our visit, Garamba's faithful guards and rangers had not been paid; they grew gardens by their huts in order to survive.

The Garamba rhinos might conceivably be protected in a small fenced area, but there are no funds for such confinement, which would introduce a whole new set of problems. As a last resort, they could be transferred to a zoo. Mark Stanley Price, a young biologist we spoke with in Nairobi, was involved in a successful program to restore a captive population of the white Arabian oryx to the Oman deserts. On the evidence of successful zoo propagation of the southern white rhino – there are now two hundred in world zoos – he does not doubt that these northern animals could also be raised successfully in captivity and thereby "saved". But reintroduction – a far more lengthy, expensive, and complicated process than mere release – is quite another matter. Even if a safe and suitable habitat still awaited them, the slow-breeding animals are huge and difficult to manage, and the ultimate irony might be that new veterinary regulations or new laws against international transport of wild animals might forbid the return of the saved species to its own environment.

Kes Smith, whose own plane was out of commission, was anxious to go on an air survey of Garamba, which she had been unable to make in several months. In the early morning, before breakfast, we flew north with Jonah across a vast plain of savanna grassland, already browning in the dry season, interspersed with shining, languid rivers. In the grassland stand large isolated trees – mostly the sausage tree, *Kigelia*. The more permanent water courses are enclosed by gallery forest – sometimes called "finger forest", because it penetrates deep into the savanna in long finger-like extensions of the rain forest that lies farther to the south. The rich green strands, which shelter many forest animals and birds, are set off by lovely lavender leaves of a combretum liana that here and there climbs to the canopy.

In comparison with the East African savanna, which has many medium-size animals, including zebra and antelopes, both large and small, this northern grassland has very few, a discrepancy mainly attributable to climate. Equatorial East Africa has two rainy seasons of about three months each, with corresponding dry seasons in which herbivores can crop back the new grasses, whereas in this northern savanna, with its mixed woodland, a single long rainy season produces and sustains a high, rank, thick-stemmed grass ten to fifteen feet tall. Such grass cannot support herds of small herbivores, being not only unpalatable but too coarse to be managed except by large browsers with big guts; there are no zebra, and the few antelope species resort to flood-plain grasses and burned ground.

Human beings and domestic animals, or the lack of them, are also factors. In East Africa, the pastoralists, with their diet of blood and milk, can encourage calving in the rainy season and still have milk throughout the dry, whereas in this region, calves born in the long rains are weaned off long before the dry season, which is harsh and long. Thus, the Sudanic pastoralists such as the Nuer and the Dinka must eke out their milk diet with sorghum and millet and savanna game, or "bush meat". Farther west, in these woodland savannas, the presence of tsetse is inimical to livestock, and the use of bush meat is much heavier, with a corresponding wildlife decline. Especially in West Africa, where the savanna belt between rain forest and the near-desert known as the Sahel is very narrow, and the human population very high, the need for animal protein has all but eliminated the wild animals.

On the flood plain are fair numbers of antelope – tiang, kob, and waterbuck – together with buffalo and wart hog and a few small herds of elephant. The Congo giraffe is also here though we do not see it. Kob and buffalo are by far the most common animals, and large black herds of buffalo may be seen along most of the many streams that flow south to the Garamba River.

The northern region of the park, which adjoins the meaningless Lantoto Park in Sudan, is rocky and hilly country, with only a small animal population, vulnerable to poachers. Unlike elephants, which are wide-ranging, rhinos are sedentary and are very easily tracked and killed, and the horn can be bashed off with a stone in a few minutes. Ivory poaching, on the other hand, is always risky and considerably more difficult and requires an efficient organization, since time is required to remove the tusks from a fresh carcass, and tusks are heavy to transport through roadless country. But the park rangers have not been provided with the means to patrol this remote area, with its poor roads, rivers, and precarious log bridges, and such animal protection as exists is concentrated on a thirty-two-square-mile area in this southern third of the park, entirely composed of savanna and slow water courses. This region contains almost all the remaining rhino, but even here they are threatened: a captured poacher recently admitted having killed two rhino in 1983 and another two in 1984, effectively eliminating, all by himself, any increase that the animals might have made.

In an hour's flying, we count ourselves lucky to spot three white rhino, a lone male and a cow with calf; seeing our plane, the calf moved closer to its mother, which raised her head toward the sky but did not run. The huge, calm, pale gray creatures with their primordial horned heads might have been standing on the plains of the Oligocene seventy million years ago, when they first evolved. Except for a lion rolling on its dusty mound, they were the only creatures at Garamba that did not flee at the airplane's approach. Kob scattered widely through the tall coarse grass, and the buffalo herds, panicking one another, rocked along aimlessly in all directions, and the big bush elephants of the savanna, wariest of all, hurried along through the high grass in their stiff-legged, ear-flapping run.

Toward mid-morning, Jonah and I head west across the Garamba River, on a four-hundred-mile flight to Bangassou, in the Central African Republic. We have left the rivers that flow toward the Nile; the Garamba is one of the many headwaters of the Congo (now the Zaire River). In the nineteenth century, when the Zanzibar slaver Tippu Tib sent his expeditions up the tributaries of the Congo, and Arab slavers came westward from the Nile, this savanna belt at the north edge of the rain forest was a great slaving region, and captured tribesmen carried ivory tusks back to the coast. Stanley's journals from his 1887 expedition – part of which was spent traveling with Tippu Tib – draw early attention to the devastating cost of the ivory trade:

> There is only one remedy for these wholesale devastations of African aborigines, and that is the solemn combination of England, Germany, France, Portugal, South and East Africa, and Congo [Free] State against the introduction of gunpowder into any part of the Continent . . . or seizing upon every tusk of ivory brought out, as there is not a single piece nowadays which has been gained lawfully. Every tusk, piece, and scrap in the possession of an Arab trader has been steeped and dyed in blood. Every pound weight has cost the life of a man, woman, or child, for every five pounds a hut has been burned, for every two tusks a whole village has been destroyed,

every twenty tusks have been obtained at the price of a district with all
its people, villages, and plantations. It is simply incredible that, because
ivory is required for ornaments or billiard games, the rich heart of Africa
should be laid waste ... that populations, tribes, and nations should be
utterly destroyed.

The region was all but emptied of human beings, and the few that were left,
infected with syphilis by the slavers, were beset by an infertility that has kept the
population low to the present day. More recently, the withdrawal of the colonial
administrations and their clinics has brought a resurgence of sleeping sickness
to both Sudan and C.A.R. For these reasons and others not well understood –
superstitious memories of the dark era and fear of Azande witchcraft as well as
cannibalism may have kept other groups from moving in – most of Haut-Zaïre
and eastern C.A.R., with its immense woodlands and savannas, swamps, and
rivers, shows no sign that man has ever been here.

In the great silence that settled on the land, the elephants prospered, and long
after King Léopold II's Congo Free State was taken over by the Belgian government,
this region remained the greatest ivory-hunting country in all Africa. Because it is
remote, without roads or towns, its herds were unmolested even when, in the late
1960s, the price of ivory escalated, and wholesale slaughter of elephants throughout East Africa began. The amount of ivory exported from Kenya rose eighty-six per
cent in a single year between 1970 and 1971, eighty-one per cent more the following
year; within five years, Kenya had lost half of its elephants, or about sixty thousand
animals, and by 1980 Uganda's elephants were all but gone. In Somalia, northern
Tanzania, Zambia, Mozambique, Angola, and throughout West Africa, the populations were reduced by fifty to ninety per cent. (Zimbabwe, Botswana, and South
Africa, which were farthest from organized poaching gangs and ivory depots, were
much less affected.) Inevitably the poachers turned to Sudan, in which the herds
were reduced from a hundred and thirty-five thousand animals in 1976 to fewer
than thirty thousand in 1983. In recent years, the pressure has intensified in Chad,
Zaire, and C.A.R., from which the bush elephant is rapidly disappearing. Here
as elsewhere, corrupt regimes have encouraged and controlled the trade in ivory.

The eastern two-thirds of the Central African Republic, like northern Haut-
Zaïre, is classified by ecologists as "Guinea savanna", after the broad belt of
grass and woodland extending eastward from northern Guinea, in West Africa,
all the way across the continent into south Sudan and Ethiopia. North of the
guinea savanna – a rolling plateau country up to three thousand feet high – lies
the Sahel, a dry grassland which, in the great drought that began about 1970,
has been steadily invaded by the Sahara Desert. To the south lies the tropical

rain forest, which extends from southern Guinea along the West African coast to Cameroon, widening out in the great Congo Basin and spreading eastward to the highlands of Central Africa.

This broad savanna with its sinuous reaches of riverain forest, stretching away north toward the Sahel, is entirely beautiful and awesome, and yet the great silence that resounds from a wild land without sign of human life, from which all of the great animals are gone, is something ominous. Mile after mile, we stare down in disbelief; we are not prepared for so much emptiness, for such pristine and undamaged desolation. Beyond Garamba we had encountered a few elephants, but these must have strayed out of the park, to judge from their great scarcity farther west. In hundreds of miles of unbroken wilderness, without so much as a distant smoke in sign of man, we see no elephant whatever, nor the elephant trails that give away the presence of these animals even from high in the air.

With its notably sparse population of human beings (the whole country has less than three million people, and a third of these, by present estimate, have crowded into the few cities and towns), C.A.R. would seem an ideal environment for elephants. Before 1970, there were thought to be well over a hundred thousand in this country, and as late as the mid-seventies, when elephants were disappearing almost everywhere else, it was hoped that this region in the heart of the African continent would survive as a last stronghold of the species. Instead, the animals were exposed to unrestricted slaughter, and official exports of ivory from C.A.R. jumped from four tons to a hundred and sixty-five tons in a single year. In just five years, here in the east part of the country, it is thought that four-fifths of the elephants were killed.

Jean-Bédel Bokassa, the "emperor" of what he called the "Central African Empire" until he was deposed in 1979, is said to have ordered the slaughter of thirty thousand elephants by helicopter gunships and other means. He wished to support his family enterprise, La Couronne, in its near-monopoly on ivory exports, which, according to the elephant biologist Dr Iain Douglas-Hamilton, who made a continental survey of African elephants in 1979, were largely based on ivory illegally imported from Zaire and the Sudan. (Zairian elephants, he discovered, were also being massacred by government troops.) In 1980, after Bokassa was deposed, bans on ivory exports were announced in both C.A.R. and Zaire, but neither was meant to be enforced, and the slaughter continued unabated. With official reopening of the ivory trade in 1981, as Douglas-Hamilton pointed out in a paper presented at a wildlife conference at Bangui in late 1985, C.A.R. was the only country left in Africa in which ivory hunting was "entirely legal, authorized, and operational".

In addition to the local people, the massacre attracted tough poaching gangs from Sudan and Chad that had run out of elephants in their own countries. The

Sudanese favored camel transport and automatic weapons scavenged from the wars all around the region, while Chad's wild desert horsemen stuck to traditional methods, riding up on the great beasts from behind and ramming their sides or crippling their legs with long sharp spears. (Out of thirty-two animals examined by a Peace Corps group in 1983, twenty-five had been cut down by spears.) Already "big ivory" was hard to find, and between 1982 and 1984, exports declined from two hundred tons to forty. In 1984, an air survey of C.A.R.'s northern parks sponsored by several international conservation organizations could locate no more than forty-three hundred elephants, indicating a decline of nearly ninety per cent in just four years. As Douglas-Hamilton observed at Bangui, "What happened in northern C.A.R. was caused by regional crises involving not only C.A.R. but Chad, Sudan, and Haut-Zaïre. Ten years ago this regional resource was beyond compare, five years ago it was in serious danger, today it is largely destroyed." In recent years, Sudan, Gabon, and C.A.R., responding to international pressure, have ordered an official ban on ivory export, but nobody thinks that this has slowed the killing.

Ivory hunters and others also killed every rhinoceros they came across, since the price of rhino horn had risen from thirty-five dollars a kilo in 1974 to five hundred dollars in 1979. In 1970, there were twenty thousand black rhino in Kenya; today there are five hundred and fifty, and figures are similar all over Africa; four of the black rhino's seven geographic races are as precarious as the northern white rhino. In 1982, it was supposed that three thousand black rhino roamed the C.A.R. – the only significant population left in all of West and Central Africa. Two years later, the air survey noted above was unable to locate a single one. A few black rhino in Cameroon are the last of their species in Central and West Africa.

A parallel drastic decline in buffalo and Derby eland is partly attributable to a rinderpest plague brought by the starving livestock herds from Chad and Sudan that overran the northern parks as a fifteen-year drought all across Africa moved the Sahara ever farther south. Whatever the reasons, a great silence has descended on one of the last redoubts of wildlife on the continent.

Already much of the recent harvest was coming from the smaller forest elephant, whose straight tusks are composed of a harder, whiter ivory that is easily detected in the shipments. Ian Parker, a wildlife entrepreneur based in Nairobi and a student of the world ivory trade, was maintaining that about sixty per cent of the ivory turning up in Hong Kong and Japan, much of it illegal ivory being exported through Burundi, came from the forest elephant. Yet Parker, a longtime participant in the trade, was also claiming that elephants were still so numerous that tusks harvested from natural mortality alone would adequately support the ivory commerce, which handled an annual average of seven hundred and fifty tons in the ten years between 1975 and 1985; except locally, he said, there was no such thing as an elephant crisis, since at least three million elephants were still at large in Africa. Douglas-Hamilton, on the other hand, had estimated a population of 1.3 million, and was convinced that *Loxodonta africana* was already endangered as a species.

Dr Western believes that even the smaller figure may be too high; the most recent analyses of ivory-trade records indicated that elephant numbers can no longer exceed one million, far less three. Between 1979 and the present, he says, the average weight of marketed tusks declined by one half, which meant that roughly twice the number of animals had to be killed to maintain that 750-ton harvest. It also meant that more than half the slaughtered animals were females, which in the old days were rarely shot at all. Analysis of ivory exports indicates that the average tusk weight is about three kilos, in an animal that formerly produced tusks of thirty-seven kilos each; computer analysis has shown that once average tusk weight falls below five kilos, a collapse of the entire population is at hand. The main source of these little tusks are juvenile males between five and ten years old – well below the age of reproduction – and mature females, twenty to twenty-five years old. Not a single tusk came from an animal over thirty-five years old, in a species which may attain four times that age. If there really were three million elephants, as Parker claimed, why was no one shooting mature males? And why did the tonnage drop off drastically in 1985 to four hundred and eighty tons, despite dedicated killing by ivory hunters all across Africa?

By using an arbitrary equation that correlates elephant density with average rainfall, Ian Parker concludes that very large numbers of forest elephant – about two per square kilometer – are hidden by the forest canopy, a figure higher than the highest density found anywhere in the savanna. Dr Western, whose own data Parker borrowed to construct his estimates, reminds me that elephants may eat three hundred pounds of fodder in a day, and defecate fifteen to eighteen times in the same period. "If you think of Parker's density figures in terms of a dung fight," he says wryly, "I can only say that you would never be out of reach of ammunition."

As Western had written to me in September, "The discrepancy hinges on the different estimates of forest elephants in Zaire, and to a lesser extent in Congo Republic and Gabon. There is very little disagreement elsewhere." If densities in primary forest are as low as he believes, then the African elephant as a species is in serious trouble.

The main hope of this expedition is to resolve that discrepancy once and for all. It is not that we are anxious to prove that the forest elephant is an uncommon animal – how much more exciting it would be to prove the reverse! – but that this proof, by dispelling self-serving data and wishful thinking, might lay the groundwork for a new era of responsible elephant conservation.

* * *

Bangassou, on the Mbomou River, described as a center of cotton, coffee, oil palm, lumber, and diamond production, is the only town in eastern C.A.R. (which together with Chad was known as Ubangi-Shari after their great rivers, in the days when both were still a part of French Equatorial Africa). We put down quickly to refuel at the Bangassou airstrip – we have no clearance – then take off again and continue west across savanna and forest to our next landmark, the Ubangi River. Below the Kouimba rapids, the Ubangi makes a great loop north. We do not follow it but maintain our course, crossing the river and flying three hundred miles over the jungles of northern Zaire in order to meet the Ubangi once again where it sweeps south on its last descent to the Zaire River. On this leg of the journey, like the one before it, there is scarcely a sign of human presence – no tracks, no huts, no smoke, near or far – though an artificial city has been built for Zaire's billionaire president somewhere off there to the south, at Gbadolite. Nor are there tracks of animals, nor visible life of any kind except huge black hornbills with broad white patches on their wings, flapping and sailing over the forest canopy and slow green rivers. Then the forest opens out on the great Ubangi, where a few pirogues hold more human beings than we have seen in the eight hundred miles since we left Garamba.

The river slides south to a great bend, and here rocks part it into rapids presided over by Bangui (the Rapids), the small capital of the erstwhile Empire of Central Africa. According to my trusty map, this pretty town inset in small steep hills lies just upriver from two villages, Bimbo and Zongo.

A French trading post established in 1889, Bangui, with its fine river prospect, is a typical colonial town turned capital city in the new Africa. Its decrepit villas, European cars, and more or less modern commercial buildings housing the remnants of colonial enterprises are set off by potholed red-earth streets, fragrant markets, head cargoes, traditional peasant dress, radio music and impromptu dancing, flowers and colors, and, everywhere, a restless proud humanity in bright clean clothes, streaming along under the trees to quarters that, for more people than not, will be tin-roofed shacks without electricity or plumbing.

The capital is set about with triumphal arches erected in his own honor some years ago by Emperor Bokassa, for whom the imperial boulevard into the city from the grandiose and empty airport was also named. It is now called the Avenue des Martyres, after the two hundred schoolchildren who were slaughtered on imperial whim, with the emperor's own wholehearted participation. Because Bokassa was a "charismatic" Francophile (he once presented a gift of diamonds to French premier Valéry Giscard d'Estaing), this by no means isolated episode disappointed his many French admirers, who for investment reasons had supported him long after his bloodthirsty predilections became known. When the schoolroom adventure drew international attention, the emperor and most of his country's money were hurried off to La Belle France, where he was living in the greatest comfort and "was very popular", or so we were told by his bewildered countrymen. (In October 1986, of his own accord, Bokassa returned to C.A.R., where he was tried for arthropophagy as well as multiple assassinations. The following June he was sentenced to death, but the sentence was commuted to life imprisonment, apparently in the basement of the presidential palace, where he lives today.)

At Bangui, where we spent two days conferring with wildlife officials, we resided at the Hotel Minerva, a more modest establishment than the Rock Hotel (which boasts a bar called "Scotch Club du Rock"), yet very lively, especially at noon when the offices close, most of them for the remainder of the day. The bar just inside the front door fairly swarms with elegant *poules de luxe* with high heels, long legs, liberated breasts, and sumptuous steatopygia, waving hard-puffed cigarettes in long cool hands. One young woman affects jeans and a T-shirt inscribed CHICAGO COSMIC, but most are attired in wide-open blouses and transparent skirts. The colorful ladies are well known to the *colons* and sullen-faced paratroopers in harsh haircuts who represent France's small "military presence" in its "special relationship" with its former colonies in Africa. These men squeeze the ladies' hands as they enter the bar – *Ça va bien! Et toi?* – and meanwhile the women are boisterously admired by their tattered young compatriots, who await the rare tourists outside in the street. The young men sell ethnic wood stools, dried forest butterflies, and bows and arrows said to come from the Babinga Pygmies in the south. *My fren? My fren? You wish a bow, a arrow?*

Perhaps in frustration, a young peddler teases a beer-bellied *colon* as he leaves the bar, and the big man whirls with a threatening gesture, causing the boy to back away. The white man waves contemptuously at the youth's wares, his poverty, his whole African being. "You think you are a somebody, is that it?" Offended, the other Africans crowd forward and the man retreats, slamming his car door – *Ça non, messieurs!* The youth appreciates my disgusted reaction, though his face is sad. "*Champion fistique,*" he explains. "He does not know how to laugh."

Our main business in Bangui is to urge the creation of a national forest park and promise the New York Zoological Society's cooperation to Raymond Mbitikon, minister of waters and forests, fishing and hunting, who asks us to prepare a survey and recommendation while we are down in the Bayanga region. The park was originally proposed last year by Richard Carroll, a former Peace Corps volunteer in C.A.R., now a doctoral student doing his thesis on lowland gorillas. Monsieur Mbitikon kindly dispatches a ministry vehicle for Bayanga with a week's provisions and drums of aviation fuel. The journey is about five hundred miles and fourteen hours over a rough road, and the truck will meet us there tomorrow.

To venture very far outside Bangui, according to a brochure of travel in these parts prepared some years ago by Air Afrique, "it is necessary to equip oneself seriously and be prepared for rather long delays." Since we are flying out tomorrow to Bayanga, in the far southern corner of C.A.R., we have seriously equipped ourselves with traveler's checks, to pay not only for provisions but for aviation fuel, for fuel comes very high indeed in what people living here believe to be the most expensive city in the world. We have lunch on the Ubangi River with the kind and helpful ambassador and officers of the American embassy, and the ambassador's wife, Katia de Jarnette, escorts me to a Peace Corps clinic, where my mongoose bites are thoroughly cleansed and a tetanus shot administered by a cheerful nurse appropriately christened Kandi Christian.

We are also "prepared for rather long delays", and a good thing, too. At the airport next morning we find that the compressor on the gas pump has broken down, and that gasoline in drums that cost three dollars a gallon yesterday will, for unmysterious reasons, cost five dollars today. We protest this piracy, and wait, and eventually the compressor is resuscitated. Before the plane can be refueled, however, a general failure of airport electricity knocks out the gas pump for a few more hours, and not until 3.30 in the afternoon, after flight clearance from the airport tower, customs, and immigration, do we clear the ground. We are accompanied on this flight by the British elephant biologist Richard Barnes, who made all the arrangements for us here in Bangui, and also by Gustave Doungoubey, director of management of wildlife, who is kindly escorting us to Bayanga.

Immediately southwest of Bangui, the plane crosses a huge palm-oil plantation and heads out across the rain forests of the Congo Basin. There is no savanna anymore, the rare patches of swamp are small, the scarce red tracks are narrow, shrouded by trees. Except for the rivers, which are not always in view, there is no place to come down in one piece. Some years ago in eastern Zaire I flew over this Congo Basin forest in a light plane, from Bukavu to Obaye, then north to Goma, and the sight of its monotone expanse of green, undulating in all directions to the green horizon, is just as disturbing now as it was then.

Even so, the rolling foliage is magnificent. Forest green and gray-green, jade, emerald, and turquoise, pond green, pea green – all the greens of the world unroll below our wings, set off by bright fire red leaves of the *azobe* (or *bois de fer* or "ironwood"). Here and there in the wet sloughs is a strand of raffia palms, said to be a favored haunt of pygmy elephants. Just once in the whole flight between the Ubangi and the Sangha do I see a sign of human habitation, two poor huts in a clearing near a forest stream.

The first glimpse of the Sangha River is a silver sliver among darkening hills in the late afternoon light. The plane swings south over slow rapids, the trees of the river islands mirrored in the silted water, and then the river opens out onto broad sand bars that in the dry season appear in front of the Bantu village called Bayanga.

Bayanga lies in the Lobaye Forest, in the farthest southern territory of C.A.R., surrounded by forests of the Congo Republic and Cameroon. Originally our plan had been to swing well east over the Congo Republic and count the elephants along the swamps and rivers, but M. Doungoubey received word this morning that Congo soldiers were crossing into C.A.R. in a border dispute, and might shoot at a small circling airplane, not realizing that elephants and not themselves were being studied. (Later we learn that the Congolese soldiers have withdrawn to their own border post, down the Sangha River, which flows due southward through that country to its confluence with the Zaire. "They put up their flag in our territory and we take it down again," said a C.A.R. soldier.)

Bayanga is named for the Sangha or Yanga fishing people ("Ba" – "Wa" in East Africa – is a Bantu prefix signifying plural man or "people") attracted here by Slovenia Bois, a Yugoslav lumber concession whose mill lies at the south end of the settlement, and whose acting manager, Janez Mikuz, is kind enough to meet us at the airstrip and refresh us with cold beer at the company mess overlooking the river before installing us at a comfortable guest house in the compound. But to our embarrassment our friend Gustave Doungoubey and his cousin, Monsieur Babisse, who has arrived with a soldier-driver in the truck, are installed separately in lesser quarters. Gustave, a bright, equable fellow who permits nothing so small as this to trouble him, seems not to mind; he has many friends here, all of whom come to embrace him. Next morning at breakfast, there is more discomfort when Monsieur Babisse and the local forestry official polish off a half-bottle each of Slovenia Bois's good Côtes du Rhône white wine, pouring it into man-sized tumblers and drinking it straight off like spring water. Our friends show no effects of their glad refreshment, then or later, but the Yugoslavs, who do not seem fond of Africans (Jonah remarks that this tends to be true of most Eastern Europeans), are irritated, plainly regretting that the natives of this country must be permitted at their European mess. However, they are civil to the Africans, and kind and hospitable to the whites throughout our stay.

From the settlement a bright red road runs southwest through the forest, crossing a bridge in a big thicket of bamboo and climbing a steep hill to a forest ridge. Manioc and long papaya fend for themselves in the thick weeds grown up around the unbranched columns of black skeletal trees a hundred and fifty feet in height. Like all forest Bantu, the Yanga practice the primitive slash-and-burn agriculture that has already destroyed most of the rain forest of West Africa. Often a forest garden is abandoned and a new one started even before the poor soil is depleted, since slashing and burning is easier than keeping up with the fierce weeds. In regions of dense population, such as West Africa, primitive agriculture leads inevitably to total degradation of the forest together with the disappearance of the animals, but in Central Africa, where the human population is so low, the random agriculture, by encouraging second growth, makes forage more accessible, and, where not intense, may actually increase wildlife populations.

The dust of the road is broken by the shifting soil prints of thick vipers, and the snake patterns are interspersed with tiny human prints of Babinga Pygmies (sometimes called Ba-Aka, after their Aka language). Lost in the weeds between road and field are the Pygmies' low leaf-thatched huts, which are woven of a strong latticework of saplings stuck into the earth to form the walls, then bent over and lashed together as the roof, giving great tensile strength to a light structure while obtaining the maximum space of a rounded dwelling. (Huts constructed on this principle are also made by the Turkana and Maasai and are in fact found all over the earth. Even the Inuit igloo is quite similar, including the long tubular entrance on one side, and so are the modern tents we carry with us.) Though the huts are scarcely four feet high, the tiny sleeping platforms of bamboo are often set one above another, in order to keep more people clear of the earth floor.

The middle-size descendants of those Babinga who have interbred with their Bantu neighbors have inherited few of the fine points of either race, seeming neither as handsome and husky as the Bantu nor as alert and merry as the forest people. By our rather narrow Western standards, most Babinga are unprepossessing, seeming stunted and bent rather than small, with scared, uncomprehending faces and the slightly averted gaze of uneasy animals. At a roadside camp, three naked little boys, feeling behind them with their hands, withdraw into the foliage in the slow way of wild things not wishing to be seen, and one drops to all fours before disappearing into the leaves, peering back at the huge white men over his shoulder.

Last night after dark we listened to Babinga drums, and this morning near the airstrip we hear raised voices, a simple wistful three-note descending chorus, *dee-do-do*, like a human echo of the sad sweet song of an emerald green bird, Klaas' cuckoo, which I watched this morning at the forest edge. According to the Bayanga people, the Babinga come here only in the dry season, to take advantage of old manioc plantations and perhaps work in the lumber mill. They erect their leaf huts outside the mill and the Yanga village. They are thought of as forest demons, not quite human, by the Bayanga. Like most Pygmy groups, they have a certain interdependence with their Bantu neighbors, who live mostly in rectangular wattle-and-daub huts, with tin roofs brought in by the lumber company, and are served by makeshift shops and a small bar. (Outside the Bar Patience is a decrepit jitney bus on which is painted SANGHA EAGLE. As a parting shot to those left in its dust, a message painted on the rear end reads GOOD WILL NEVER! It has been quite a while since the Sangha Eagle traveled anywhere. How it got here or where it used to go has been forgotten.)

Early in our visit to Bayanga, I accompany Drs Barnes and Western on a reconnaissance flight across the "Dzanga-Sangha Reserve" proposed by Richard Carroll, which would include an area of twenty-seven hundred square kilometers. We hope to persuade M. Mbitikon to enlarge Carroll's proposed reserve with the idea that in the future, when the timber leases have run out, it might be given the fully protected status of a national park.

After a few preliminary circles at high altitude, we descend again to a few hundred feet above the forest canopy; the trees flow down to the gallery forests along the Sangha River, bursting and shimmering with morning light. The ironwoods are burning bright in the sea of greens, and the strange semaphore of white-winged birds turn out to be groups of the huge brown-checked hornbills, crossing the cool glades of the forest.

To our surprise, not all these trees are evergreen, though there are many less deciduous species than one sees farther north. Even here near the Equator, the Congo Basin, unlike the upper Amazon and Borneo, has fleeting dry seasons, like faint echoes of the long dry seasons to the north and south, but what is probably more important to its ecology are the extended climatic changes, recorded in lake sediments as well as in fossil pollen and termitaria, that have occurred here ever since the Tertiary. These wet and dry periods were more extreme and of greater frequency than in Southeast Asia and South America, which have been largely undisturbed since the Cretaceous. The last great dry period, ten thousand years ago, entirely eliminated the forests of the central basin in what is now Zaire. The forest was limited to relict areas to east and west, known to ecologists as "Pleistocene refugia", from which fauna and flora spread out again as the rain returned. By comparison to the refugia, however, the central region remains "impoverished forest" to this day, although a pygmy chimpanzee is found there that does not occur anywhere else.

Our first forest elephant, a bull seen in a slough near the Dzanga Pan, shakes its head at the banking airplane as if in disapproval, but it does not run – a sign that ivory poachers must be rare here. Another good sign is the almost total absence of forestry scars other than narrow logging roads already overgrown. Later we learn from Slovenia employees that this advanced lumber operation, which exploits only four of the myriad tree species (three red hardwoods are cut for export, and a white wood is used in local construction), rarely removes more than one tree every few acres.

Selective logging, excellent in principle, often does great damage to the forest because of the network of forestry tracks and roads required to remove the trees, but, to judge from the minimal effects observable from the air, Slovenia Bois is taking unusual pains. By opening many small new clearings, this selective operation may have the same beneficial effect as the fall of ancient trees, which from the air look like giant skeletons on the forest floor. The sunlight streaming down through the tear in the forest permits a burst of second growth, providing accessible browse for many animals that cannot reach the nutrients high in the canopy.

Richard Barnes, who did his master's thesis on the bush elephant in Tanzania's Ruaha Park, is being sponsored by the NYZS in a study of techniques for censusing the forest elephant, which is very difficult to observe. Until now, the vague estimates of its numbers have been influenced by the bias of the guessers, and a much more accurate census will be needed before international conservation efforts can be mustered on its behalf. Dr Barnes's study area, which we shall visit, is in the Ivindo River region of northern Gabon, perhaps three hundred miles southwest of Bayanga, and before he is finished he will have made the first comprehensive census of forest elephants in Gabon, the methods of which can then be applied to the African rain forests as a whole. "We haven't worked out precise figures as yet," Barnes informs me in his usual precise tones. "There are certain anomalies in our dung-density data having to do with dung decomposition rates. But it is already safe to say that rain-forest populations will work out to less than one animal per acre, even in this region where elephants are reported to be common."

Dr Western nods. "And this is the region, southern C.A.R. and Congo, south Cameroon and north Gabon, where *cyclotis* populations are apparently highest. I'm told that elephants are already scarce in eastern Zaire, as I think we'll establish when we visit the Ituri, and it must be assumed that in large tracts of the Congo Basin there are scarcely any."

At Bayanga, Dr Barnes will use his techniques to arrive at some estimate of elephant densities in both primary and secondary forest, and after the reconnaissance flight on our first morning he and Dr. Western, with Monsieurs Doungoubey and Babisse and three Babinga trackers, set off on the first of his foot transects, in which elephant droppings over a predetermined distance provide the main basis of the count.

At Bangui the nurse had warned me that I must not walk more than absolutely necessary until my spectacular ankle swelling had gone down, and since I wish to be more or less fit by the time we arrive in the Ituri Forest, I decide to limit my forest walking to the afternoon. Slaus Sterculec, the man in charge of Slovenia's local construction, has kindly offered to accompany me to the Dzanga salt pan, a haunt of elephants perhaps two miles by forest path off an old logging track. Mr Sterculec, a lifelong bachelor and wiry jungle veteran of a breed less often seen these days in Africa, has been out here since the founding of Bayanga thirteen years ago, and he has not left the forest in the last five years. He turns up to fetch me with two Babinga hunters, Bisambe and Lalieh, who are markedly smaller than the three who have gone off with the other party. Bisambe, the elder of the two, is yellowish and hunched, with a big head, and both have incisors filed down to sharp points.

I am not displeased that Mr Sterculec has brought along his rifle. "It is not for hunting," he explains disarmingly. "It is for my fear."

At supper the night before we had discussed the pygmy elephant (*Loxodonta pumilio*), which is known to the native peoples throughout the tropical forest as a creature even smaller than the small forest race of the African elephant that we are here to study. Richard Barnes tells us that in Gabon nobody doubts the existence of this reputedly pugnacious little elephant, which is called *assala*. *A Field Guide to the Mammals of Africa*, published in 1977, provides a detailed description of this creature and cites its widespread reputation for aggressiveness. However, it notes that "the existence of a species of pygmy elephant is not generally recognized; the animals described are believed to be small members of the Forest Elephant."

The first description of a "pygmy elephant" appeared in 1906, based on a small animal (1.2 meters at the shoulder) taken in Gabon the previous year and shipped to the New York Zoological Society's Bronx Zoo. The would-be discoverer, Theodore Noack, a German professor, claimed it as a new subspecies of the African elephant *Elephas* [*Loxodonta*] *africanus pumilio*. Unfortunately it had doubled in size and was a normal forest elephant when it died nine years later – still an adolescent – but by that time it had been forgotten, its place in the scientific limelight having been usurped by a second "pygmy" of an allegedly separate subspecies, *E. a. fransseni*, collected in 1911. There was also a well-received report of a herd of five miniature elephants from the same locality on the north bank of Lake Leopold II, in the Congo, where the exciting new animal was known as the "water elephant", and was alleged to have amphibious habits, like the hippopotamus. Two more small elephants killed there in 1923 were identified as pygmies by no less an authority than the New York Zoological Society's celebrated director, Dr William Hornaday, and in 1936 another pair of "midget pachyderms", arriving alive in New York City, caused a great stir in the press and among the populace. One of these was still alive in 1947, by which time, like Dr Noack's specimen, it had grown remorselessly to full forest-elephant dimensions.

Nevertheless, reports by reputable observers continued, although the pygmy appeared to share almost the entire known range of the forest elephant, and did not seem to occur where the latter was absent. The local Africans in all equatorial rain-forest countries without exception agreed that there were two distinct elephants, the smaller of which was notoriously less wary and more aggressive than the larger. Furthermore, they said, it made a different sound, had more sedentary habits, and generally preferred swampy terrain, often in association with raffia palms, leading some authorities to speculate that even if it was not a separate geographic race, it was separate ecologically, and therefore entitled to subspecific status.

Those who doubted the existence of a separate race of "pygmy elephant" pointed not only to the tendency of captive specimens to grow up in captivity but to the absence of dependable sightings of juvenile animals in reports of pygmy herds. But if the existence of such a creature was unproved, so was the statement that it did not occur where the forest elephant was absent. Or so claimed its partisans, including a controversial Belgian zoologist, Dr Bernard Heuvelmans, author of *On the Trail of Unknown Animals*, in which he states that "to deny that the pygmy elephant exists, even as a subspecies of *Loxodonta cyclotis* [*sic*] is absurd." Also, the late W. D. (Karamoja) Bell, among the most celebrated of all African elephant hunters, described a herd of pygmies from Liberia. Bell made a drawing of these animals from memory, and the drawing revealed a female pygmy with a baby alongside. Others had also reported evidence of baby pygmies – the afterbirth of a killed female, a female in lactation – to which the naysayers retorted that evidence of sexual reproduction was no evidence of maturity, and that these reproducing females would continue growing and exceed the six-foot limit usually applied to the hypothetical adult *pumilio*.

On our trek into the forest, I ask Bisambe if he knows about the pygmy elephant, and he says he does. Asked if it was "plus méchant" – nastier, more aggressive – than the others, he murmurs, "*Ils sont tous méchants!*" at which both he and Lalieh burst out laughing.

The trackers wear ancient shorts and child-sized and decrepit red plastic sandals, but on entering the forest both go barefoot, carrying their sandals with great delicacy between their fingertips. Bisambe, who takes the lead, stops frequently to listen, poising right in the middle of a step, foot off the ground, turning his head to pick up some fleeting sound or smell amidst the raucous squawk and hooting of turacos and hornbills, the pungent dung and foliage aromas of the forest. "*Moku*" he whispers, or "*gandi*," with a slow mysterious smile, eyes dancing with delight. *Moku* is monkey (which monkey is the question; there are thirteen different species of diurnal primate in this forest, including the gorilla and the rare red colobus) and *gandi* – to judge from his deft mime – a species of duiker, a small forest antelope. Like many traditional hunters, the Babinga communicate in the bush with what seems to be a kind of soft ventriloquy; sometimes Bisambe, twenty yards ahead of me on the leafy path, murmurs something in his deep, soft voice without bothering to turn his head, and there comes an answering soft sound from Lalieh, twenty yards behind.

Dancing ahead of us along the narrow path are male diadem butterflies with big white dots on black wings (the female, very different, has her own name: yellow pansy) and big cobalt-and-black striped daneids. Smaller forms have cobalt spots or are entirely cobalt, and the same brilliant color – perhaps the one that shows up best in the forest darkness – flares again in the rump and tail of a green-breasted pitta, a secretive bird of the forest floor which I feel very fortunate to see.

Nearing the Dzanga Pan, Bisambe stops short again, and a moment later the snap of a heavy branch, like a pistol report, cracks the green silence, signaling the presence of a browsing elephant or a gorilla. Bisambe remains motionless for a little while, long fingers pointed like antennae. Then he moves on in dead quiet to a place where the thick canopy opens out, and afternoon sunlight pours into an open pan, perhaps four hundred yards in length and a hundred across. There he turns his big head with a smile to end all smiles, his hand pointing straight ahead between the trees.

From the west end comes a family group of elephants, a cow and three juveniles, and to the east a female with small calf and a large bull skirted each other. To my astonishment, the large bull has the high shoulders, huge ragged triangular ears, and heavy forward-curving tusks of the bush elephant. Another gathering of perhaps ten animals is far down at the west end of the pan. Directly in front of us, two very small male elephants with disproportionately big tusks are snuffling deep in a mudhole in the pan, which is broken by shallow pools of stagnant water.

I have scarcely focused on this odd pair with my binoculars when I see the faces of two Africans in the trees behind them. *Poachers!* I think, but a moment later I pick up a white face behind binoculars, and then another, observing the same two little elephants. Richard and Jonah, completing their transects through the forest, have been led into the Dzanga Pan from the far side. Just prior to my arrival, they tell me later, one of these feisty little tuskers had actually skirmished with the large savanna bull. Though there are other elephants in the pan, these small males with outsized tusks turn out to be the most intriguing of all the elephants we are to see throughout our journey.

In the near-windlessness, the female with three young has caught our scent and led her small group without hurrying into the forest, as Gustave Doungoubey and his armed men, spotting our Pygmies for the first time, come hurrying across the pan, suspecting poachers. Slaus and I step out into the open, eliciting sheepish grins from our African friends, and soon Jonah and Richard come across the pan to compare impressions of our first forest elephants, in particular the big "bush elephant" and the two small males.

Just as the forest elephant may follow the river trees into the savanna, and sometimes is observed in open country, the bush elephant penetrates deep into the forest. Richard Carroll had also seen "bush elephants", assuming that they were fugitives from the ivory trade slaughters to the north, but Jonah thinks it is the savanna genes that have penetrated so far south; this particular animal, in all likelihood, has never seen the open grasslands.

The other elephants, in varying degrees, display the characters of the forest race, *L. a. cyclotis*, in which the highest point of the body is behind the middle of the back, and the head tends to be held lower, so that the small rounded ears on the small head (which make them look like very young bush elephants) do not reach higher than the neck. In *cyclotis*, the tusks tend to be narrow, straight, and pointed straight downward. Presumably the low head and small ears are adaptations for forest travel, but the function of the vertical tusks, like so much else about *cyclotis*, is not yet known. (I speculate that straight tusks might be used for digging tubers, in the way that the walrus uses its straight tusks for digging clams, but Jonah appears unimpressed by this brilliant theory.) Nor is it known why the forest race lacks pronounced sexual dimorphism; in the bush elephant, a big male may be twice the size of an average female.

"I suspect," Jonah says, "that dimorphism in elephants, as in other polygamous species, is related to male competition for females. In the savannas, which are strongly seasonal, herds aggregate during the rains, females come into estrus fairly synchronously, and bigger males will of course win out. Here in the equatorial forest, the seasons are much less pronounced, and food and water are more evenly spread. Under these conditions, we suspect, female elephant herds are tiny and more evenly distributed, and probably breed all year round. If this is true, males would also be widely spread, and would not compete so strongly in one place and at one time, so that the advantage of size is less."

Richard, in his reserved, taciturn way, is discernibly elated by these interesting elephants, seen in the open, at close range. Never before has he had such a look at forest elephants, and this is only the second time he has been able to get photographs. "In Gabon," he had told me over breakfast, "they are always hidden, sometimes only a few yards away. We can be right on top of one and not know he's there. And even when we *are* aware of them, we make noise to drive them off, because" – and here he shrugged, as the relentless candor that is one of his likeable qualities overtook him – "because, well, I'm *afraid* of them.

I'm not prepared to take the risk of approaching strange elephants in the forest, and my fiancée has extracted a promise from me that I will not do so."

Unlike Jonah and I, who go about in shorts and sneakers, Richard spends every day out in the forest, and therefore feels he cannot afford our casual attitude toward such jungle afflictions as thorns and biting insects. In this very hot and humid climate (though the forest is much cooler than the clearings), he is fortified by a tight-buttoned and tight-belted dark green khaki field jacket, baggy trousers with large extra pockets, gaiters, and boots, together with a full complement of canvas bags, canteens, and compasses, bags of dust to test the wind, binoculars, camera, and other useful and less useful accoutrements. Peering out through owlish glasses from beneath his heavy-gauge rain-and-sun hat, he brings to mind old photos of nineteenth-century naturalists, with whom he shares an old-fashioned meticulousness and dedication that is most impressive.

If Drs Barnes and Western were surprised to see a "pure" bush elephant so deep in the forest, they were positively astonished by the tusk size of the two young males just in front of us, which, to judge from their height – no more than five feet at the shoulder – are probably about five years old. These creatures answered perfectly the description of the "pygmy elephant", even to an aggressive nature, displayed when the larger of the two had instigated that brief skirmish with the savanna bull, which was several times its size. But a few minutes later, the same little male had approached a female in the large group at the west end and engaged in unmistakable filial behavior. Thus in an instant he had demonstrated that he was not a mature elephant of pygmy dimensions and outsized tusks but an extraordinarily independent young forest elephant. The reason for that independence may well lie in the complete absence of lion, hyena, and wild dog, the only predators that might attack young elephants of this size in the savanna (the leopard is simply not large enough to bring one down). Freedom from predators permits a very early independence from the mother, and might account for the obstreperous groups of juvenile *cyclotis* that are reported as "pygmy elephants".

Though an adult male is only eight feet high while his counterpart in the savanna may be well over ten, forest elephants are thought to have a shorter life span than the bush form, and probably reach maturity much faster, tusks and all. "In the bush elephant," Jonah says, "you *expect* to find big tusks, because the male is so much bigger. But in the forest elephant, without dimorphism, such tusks are striking, even though male tusks grow much faster relative to age." If this animal and his companion are specimens of "pygmy elephants", as we suppose, there remains a certain enigma in those tusks, and their precocious development in at least some of young male *cyclotis*.

It is encouraging that these elephants are comparatively tame, a sign that they are

harassed little if at all – a point to be made in our recommendation of this place
as a national reserve. The foresters say that elephants are more plentiful farther
south, and that gorilla and bongo, though difficult to see, are common in the region.
What Dr. Western will probably recommend is a park far larger than the proposed
reserve, occupying the whole triangle of C.A.R. that lies between Congo and
Cameroon, with contiguous reserves or parks in those two countries – the first international forest park, preserving hundreds of square miles of undamaged habitat.

Since we have flashlights, Slaus and I, with Lalieh and Bisambe, decide to
remain here until dusk, when we might hope to see bush pig or bongo, or possibly
the giant forest hog. Our friends have scarcely disappeared when four more
elephants, golden yellow with caked clay from another bathing place, walk out
of the deepening evening greens onto the east end of the pan. Soon they are
joined by the big gray savanna bull, whose size, color, and configuration make
him look like a different species altogether. All five cross over to our side and re-
enter the forest, and we wonder if we will encounter them on the way back. Another
elephant comes and goes. Then, quite suddenly, the Babinga are gesturing.

The vanished five have reappeared at the edge of a grassy swale just to our right.
Not catching our scent, they keep on coming, passing too close as they head toward
the center of the pan, where they bathe and drink for a little while before the female
catches our scent in a subtle shift of wind. She lifts her trunk high, then directs it
straight at us like a blunderbuss. Silently, in unhurried hurry, the elephants move
out of the pan, and the sand plovers, the green sandpipers from Europe, and some
blue-winged, chestnut-colored ducks shift just enough in the wash of mud and
water to escape being flattened by the great round feet. I have never before seen this
beautiful forest duck (labeled Hartlaub's duck through no fault of its own), the nest
of which has never been located. "Faunistically", as Jonah says, in uncharacteristic
resort to eco-jargon, "the rain forest of the Congo Basin is very little known."

Two days later, while Richard continues with his transects, Jonah and I return to
Dzanga Pan, arriving at two in the afternoon so as to be ready when the elephants
come in; we are interested especially in large-tusked "pygmies". The day is hot,
the pan dead still: I watch a sun bird, a green shiny lizard, and a pair of chortling
gray parrots catching the sun in their red tails. (This species is the loquacious
favorite of caged-parrot fanciers and therefore threatened in the wild.) Not until
mid-afternoon does the first group of elephants appear, looming suddenly out
of deep green shadows in the forest wall across the pan, lifting their trunks to
sniff the air, swinging a forefoot several inches above the ground, ears uncoiling,
thin tails switching, in the constant "flowing" of the elephant, even a calm one.
"The first ones in are always suspicious," Jonah whispers.

This first group, which appear to be almost "pure" *cyclotis*, is scared away by two Babinga hunters who emerge from the forest to the southwest with big leaf-wrapped packets of fresh meat and whack a tree hard with a panga to clear out the elephants before crossing the pan. Twenty-two elephant come in once they are gone – mostly hybrids, with pronounced bush characters such as bulging brow, long back, and sharp-cornered ears. The sole young male is smaller than our "pygmy elephants" and lacks their heavy tusk development, yet he is even more independent in behavior, coming into the pan early, all by himself, traveling the length of it past other groups, and departing the pan, still entirely on his own, in another direction. "On the savannas," Jonah says, astounded, "elephants are eight years old before they leave their mothers. That one can't be more than three! In the savanna he wouldn't last one day!"

The forest west of the Sangha River is entirely roadless, stretching away across an unmarked boundary into Cameroon. Perhaps for want of first-hand knowledge, blacks and whites agree that the gorilla is most plentiful in that region, which is dense and treacherous, so Gustave says, and ridden with swamps aswarm with crocodiles. Its only inhabitants are Pygmies, but no local will accompany us, since they say that these Pygmies, who come in from Cameroon, are "*très mèchant*". (Cameroon is the westernmost territory of the Pygmies, who are thought to number about two hundred thousand altogether. The largest group – about twenty-five thousand – and the one most culturally intact, are the Mbuti, whom we shall meet in the Ituri Forest of Zaire.) International boundaries are of no concern to Pygmies anywhere, but possibly the Sangha River is a natural barrier between Pygmy nations. Or perhaps, being people of the forest, they are afraid to cross such a broad water at the mercy of the Yanga fishermen, who stand in the stern of their pirogues to paddle their narrow leaf-like craft up and down the currents in the shadow of the gallery trees.

Under the circumstances, Jonah and I will set off on a gorilla hunt alone. Since the pirogues are too delicate and leaky to carry two big passengers, Slaus Sterculec offers to take us across the Sangha in his riverboat, a decommissioned metal landing craft from World War II. Soon we are rounding the broad sand bars that appear in mid-river in the rainy season and crossing the heavy current to a break in the forest wall where elephants come occasionally to water.

Slaus is concerned that without a tracker we may lose ourselves in the dense forest, and on the far side he conscripts a young Yanga fisherman, Aliende, who agrees to guide us. Heading inland, Aliende skirts a broad and grassy marsh, perhaps an ancient oxbow of the river, and arrives at an overgrown, treacherous swamp perhaps a hundred yards across, all tussocks and tangled undergrowth, rotten footing and hidden holes, into which we sink well above the knee. On the far side, the rain forest has been much modified to their own advantage by the elephants, to judge not only from plentiful droppings but the numerous small clearings with abundant second growth that provides them fodder. This browse is also very useful to gorilla and the big forest antelope called the bongo, and before long we come upon gorilla sign – beds, feeding areas, old droppings. (There are thought to be several thousand gorilla in this southwestern forest of C.A.R.) Continuing westward perhaps two miles more, we find fresh green droppings and a sweet whiff in the air left behind from the night before. But the gorilla, who rarely shows himself until he wishes to have a look at his observers, remains hidden in the rank and heavy cover.

From the north, across the river, comes a shot; four more ring out in the next half-hour. Aliende stops and shakes his head; any animals nearby are sure to flee. He is not a Pygmy, and he grows unsure as he goes farther from the river, for there are no paths. He has marked our course rather casually with panga flicks, and two or three times on the way back, we see him misread his own signs even before he backtracks to pick up the trail. Near the river, there is a sudden burst of rufous animals out of a thicket in the grassy swale – Bohor reedbuck, an antelope we know well from East Africa.

At the river, Aliende slips away in his pirogue, and, waiting for Slaus, Jonah and I sit on the bank gazing out over the water. So far we have gotten on extremely well, perhaps a bit better than I had expected, though we have been friends for fourteen years. Increasingly we can laugh at each other and have fun, and since, on this journey, we share many interests and concerns, we are rarely short of conversation. There by the river, splitting an orange, we are full of wellbeing and contentment. Jonah tells me about his father, a British building surveyor and city planner who worked for the colonial administration in Dar es Salaam thirty years ago. In his spare time, Arthur Western was a hunter, but, like many hunters in East Africa, he was also a conservationist, and he was instrumental in the establishment of Mikumi National Park in what in those days was still Tanganyika. He was also an "honorary ranger" who was sometimes called upon to dispatch dangerous rogue elephants, and he was killed by such an animal in the Kilombero Valley, north of the Selous Game Reserve, in 1958, when Jonah was fourteen.

Jonah, who was born in England, returned there in 1961 to find work and complete his studies. "I was only anxious to get back to Africa," he says. In 1967, he took up residence in Amboseli Park, in Kenya, to complete his thesis ("The Structure, Dynamics, and Changes of the Amboseli Ecosystem"), and for the next ten years he lived mostly at Amboseli, under Mt Kilimanjaro, which he still considers home.

*   *   *

On a reconnaissance flight on our last afternoon, we are sorry to see no elephants whatever in the pans to the south near the Congo frontier, and only a single herd of forest buffalo. But once again there are elephants at Dzanga, which seems to attract most if not all of the local population.

During the flight over the forest, the plane develops a mysterious whine, as some sort of minor oil leak from the propeller films the windshield. I notice that on the return flight Jonah crosses over to the Sangha River and follows it back upstream to Bayanga. On the ground, as we refuel and prepare the plane for tomorrow's four-hour flight, I ask if coming back along the river had been a precaution, and he said it was. He tells me that that whine is nothing serious, the motor was overhauled completely before we started on this voyage, perhaps we will have it checked in Libreville.

Jonah seems preoccupied and even downcast; he says he is fighting off an achy flu. Walking down the twilight road toward the village, we discuss for the first time the fine points of a forced landing in these jungle rivers. "No margin for error out there, is there?" Jonah murmurs, managing a grin, and I nod, relieved that he realizes this, too, and feels relaxed enough to say so. He describes how Douglas-Hamilton once conked out over the forest, and, with the usual amazing luck that has rescued our friend from one scrape after another, peered down to see the only clearing in the region, which he glided into.

Since Jonah is nothing if not stiff-upper-lipped, he rarely mentions the awesome inhospitality of the equatorial forest from the perspective of a single-engine plane, perhaps because there is nothing to discuss: in the event of engine failure or forced landing, unless a swamp or river is within gliding range, a light plane would disappear into this greenness like a stone dropped from the air into the sea. (Even if by miracle the plane managed a pancake landing on the canopy without disintegrating or exploding, there are no low limbs on the forest trees, and the injured passengers might find themselves confronted with a jump of at least a hundred feet into the gloom below.) It would do no good to worry people by telling them our course, which is usually remote from radio contact, even if radio contact would be useful. One's best hope, all things considered, would be death on impact, since survivors could never be found, far less assisted. In short, why talk about it – the less said, the better.

The morning is hazy, and we do not take off until 9.30 a.m., after bidding adieu to our cheerful C.A.R. associates and kind Slavic hosts. Climbing above a lens of cloud, the plane heads southwest, crossing the invisible frontier and drifting out over Cameroon. An hour later, by rough estimate, Cameroon's border with northwestern Congo falls behind. Occasionally we glimpse the green snake of a slough or a dark gray-brown jungle river, the scar of a burned clearing, or even an overgrown red road with the glint of a tin roof at the end. (Later Jonah estimates that we were in sight of a swamp or river or some other such place to attempt a landing about a third of the time – optimistic in Richard's opinion and my own, and not heartwarming odds in any case, quite apart from one's prospects during and after such a desperate measure.)

In Congo, we peer down at Souanké, a human outpost perhaps an hour from the Karagoua River and two hours from the Gabon border, at the bitter end of the most remote road in all the world. We cross the northernmost province of Gabon, then the southeast corner of Rio Muni, a former Spanish colony currently known as Equatorial Guinea. Then we are back over Gabon again, crossing the steep green Monts de Cristal, from which fierce whitewater streams course down to the Atlantic. The Gulf of Guinea comes in sight within the hour, a dull streak on the gray tropical horizon. A rough crust on the sea edge is Libreville, the capital of Gabon, where we must seek permission to visit Makokou, in the tropical forests we have just flown over.

Makokou, on the Ivindo River of northeast Gabon, lies less than fifty miles north of the equator. The Makokou Institut de Recherche en Ecologie Tropicale, founded originally by the French, seems just the place for Richard Barnes to perfect the techniques for censusing the forest elephant, a task in which he is cheerfully assisted by his fiancée, Karen Jensen; Ms Jensen has trained herself carefully in analysis of dung, which provides forthright and honest evidence of elephant numbers. An easygoing and informal young American from Long Beach, California, where they are to be married in July, she appreciates Richard's rather formal personality (and vice versa) and suits herself up in full jungle regalia for their expeditions, just as he does.

Richard and Karen met a few years ago at Dian Fossey's gorilla camp at Karisoke, in Rwanda, where Richard was director of research and Karen was a research assistant. Both were impressed by Miss Fossey's fierce commitment to and thorough knowledge of gorillas, and both were alarmed by her misanthropic personality, which expressed itself most disagreeably in her violent prejudice against Africans, including her own cowed and frightened staff. "They lived in dread of her return," says Richard, "and when she arrived, the morale went all to pieces. She liked to abuse and humiliate African men, and because they had families, and jobs were scarce, they had to take it. We were told she would have poachers stripped, then thrash them head to toe with nettles; when she was drunk, she fired her pistol over people's heads."

One cannot question the veracity of Dr Barnes, who goes out of his way to be conservative in his opinions, and Miss Jensen supported him in all he said. "At the end," he told us, "she rarely went out into the field unless cameramen or reporters were in camp. She loved gorillas, perhaps, but she had no love for human beings. We were certain there was going to be violence, with which, on moral grounds, we didn't wish to be associated. It never occurred to us that she might be the victim until we spoke with the American ambassador, whose comment was, 'One of these days, they're going to come after her with pangas, as they did Joy Adamson.' Finally I went to the authorities and advised them strongly not to renew her visa. They had already heard how serious things were, but they said she attracted tourist income to Rwanda, which was badly needed, and they couldn't refuse her. Under the circumstances, we resigned; we felt we could not work there any longer."

Karen Jensen nodded her agreement; she has unpleasant memories of her own. That a colleague who started out so well (and won the admiration of such peers as George Schaller and Jane Goodall) should have come to such an ugly end was very upsetting, but their impressions of the last years of Dian Fossey are widely shared by others who had dealings with her. At a primate conference in 1985 in San Diego, Miss Fossey informed Dr Western that the only meaningful approach to conservation in Africa was to hand out condoms. "I thought I was talking to a crazy person," Jonah says. "I told her I didn't think we had much to talk about, and walked away. She was spitting mad."

In his years at Amboseli, Jonah worked continually with Africans, in particular the Maasai, whose cattle competed with the wild animals for the scarce grass, and he is convinced that conservation that does not cooperate with the local people is of limited value, confining the preservation of animals to the artificial limits imposed by the boundaries of a national park. "Putting a boundary around Amboseli did not protect it. If you work with the people, show them the benefits that may come to them, show them the compatibility of human use and conservation, they will support what you are doing, even help with anti-poaching. This way, wildlife conservation can extend beyond park boundaries." Jonah shrugged. "Things still go wrong, of course. The Maasai morani are forbidden to kill lions these days, and so last year, to prove themselves, they killed forty elephants instead. Nevertheless, cooperation with the other interests, with the farmers or pastoralists, or with the foresters, is far more effective in the long run than fighting everyone as Dian Fossey did. For one thing, the governments can support both interests instead of always having to choose."

One day we join Richard and Karen in a walk of ten kilometers through the forest, led by an old Ba-kota hunter named Bilombi. Though popularly supposed not to be a Pygmy, Bilombi is so small that much of the day is spent ducking under vines that the old tracker does not slash aside because he himself passes easily beneath them. This is not a failure of courtesy but of spatial apprehension, for he is an amiable old man. For a Bantu, he seems very easy in the forest, and familiar with all the nuts and fruits consumed by forest inhabitants, including man. One fruit the size and color of an orange comes from a liana called *mbolo*, which also produces a white sticky resin sometimes used in rubber manufacture. The *mbolo* climbs hundreds of feet to the top of some great tree in the canopy, where its bright fruits are consumed by monkeys. "Monkey candy," Bilombi says. Another small fruit, the *atanga*, is shiny purple-blue, and Bilombi stops to gather up a pocketful, which he wraps carefully for his family in the wide thin leaves that characterize the light-starved plants of the forest floor. "Everybody eats it!" Bilombi exclaims, with an utterly open smile of delight, as if in approval of all life. Then he says, "If you wait here, all the antelope will come!"

Bilombi is referring to the small forest duikers, but the sitatunga is also here, deep in the marshes, and so is the bongo of the elegant lyrate horn. Crossing a marshy stream, Bilombi points out the print of a larger antelope, which he says has been made by a sitatunga. Jonah shakes his head – "not long enough". And a swift green snake with a red belly which shoots from the leaf litter into a log Bilombi calls a mamba, though it is not. Probably Bilombi is mistaken in much of the information that he offers us, and tends to err on the side of what his white companions wish to see, but all the same his eye is sharp and his bushcraft expert. And so we learn about native medicines such as this tree sap which, when boiled, will deal with urinary mischief in all women, and this peculiar paste with thin white fibers, created somehow by a tortoise eating mushrooms; he draws our attention to a strangely swaying bush where a departing mandrill has not eluded his keen eye. At one place he whacks free a three-foot section of rattan that he calls "water liana", from one end of which, miraculously, a small but steady stream of pure good water flows into one's mouth. At another, the old man stops short and commences a weird nasal honking, used by the forest hunters to call duiker, and sure enough, a small blue duiker, large-eyed and delicate-limbed, hurries in across the narrow shafts of sun before whirling to flee with a great thump and scatter.

Today we are recording all elephant sign seen in each kilometer of our walk, footprints and scrape marks on trees as well as droppings, which Karen, compiling her "dung-density data", is very good at assessing as to age. Most of the droppings found today are old ones and well scattered, scarcely more than a round dark shadow of soft soil. "There are a lot of bush pig here," says Richard, "and they do a hell of a lot of rooting in this *tembo* dung. For that reason, our dung-density data" – and here he gives Karen an affectionate, sardonic glance – "may depend more on the density of bush pig than it does on the density of *tembo*." (Richard's use of the Swahili word for elephant, an echo of his days in Ruaha Park, is respectful and not an affectation; a man with fewer affectations would be hard to find.)

That elephants were here last month is borne out by the droppings, but there is no question that they are scarce here. "Soils and plants determine where an elephant *can* live," Richard says, as we pause to inspect the remains of a cooking fire near a stream where people have been fishing, "and man determines where an elephant *does* live." Elephant scarcity at Makokou is attributable to scarce fodder as well as to the occasional hunters from the Makokou settlement who make camp in these glades. (The men go hunting while the women fish the slow, dark forest brooks by constructing rough mud-and-log dams, braced with upright sticks, braced in their turn by long Y-sticks planted at an angle.)

Of all the countries in the Congo Basin, Gabon is thought to be the most intact, with the highest percentage of undisturbed forest and the least disrupted wildlife populations. Even so, wildlife seems scarce compared to the plentiful life in the savanna. "I'm not a forest man," Jonah says later, "but it seems to me that the available food produced here is much less than the food produced in the savanna, even if the mass is counted that is far out of reach of the elephants, up in the canopy. And much of the food that is within their reach is unpalatable, having developed secondary compounds – bad-tasting chemicals not related to the plant's growth – to keep elephants and other creatures from eating it. Richard is unwilling to give out premature figures, but from what I've seen, both here and in C.A.R., he's getting about one-point-five droppings per kilometer of walking, which – allowing time for decomposition – works out to a rough count of one elephant going by each month.

"I doubt if this will improve very much anywhere in the equatorial forest, whether the region is occupied by man or not. According to Ian Parker's figure of five elephants per square kilometer, there should have been two thousand animals in that area we investigated at Bayanga, which includes the high-density concentration around Dzanga Pan as well as a number of smaller pans and water courses. I very much doubt if there were two hundred altogether, and the average across the Congo Basin must be far less. Perhaps there were more originally, but I don't think forest elephant numbers were ever as high as people wished to think."

It is here near the equator that we thought a pure population of *cyclotis* would be found. We were mistaken. A young male shot yesterday by local authorities as an alleged crop raider was immediately butchered and eaten by the people, but enough was left to determine that it was a hybrid, with bush tusks extending well forward, and round, small cyclotiform ears.

*   *   *

In the dry season, when rocks emerge and its water is a clear dark tannin brown, the Ivindo reflects the huge pale-trunked trees of the gallery forest, the flowering lianas and fire red of the new leaves. It is very beautiful, especially among the rapids and rock islands down the river, where collared pratincoles and the exquisite white-throated blue swallows are the common birds. We see no crocodiles. A few years ago, a French hide trader gave rifles to the Ba-kota, who killed every crocodile in the Ivindo on his behalf, and the same pattern was repeated almost everywhere throughout Gabon, which has almost no crocodiles left. The rifles are still here and the Ba-kota still hunt the river in their delicate pirogues, with the result that the monkeys have withdrawn from the gallery forest where they are ordinarily most easily seen.

Away from the river, monkeys are still common; we see the talapoin, smallest of all African species, hurrying along low limbs from one tree into another, and the white-nosed guenon, making a wild twirling leap forty feet down onto the understory, and DeBrazza's monkey, a handsome creature that we saw earlier at Garamba, in Zaire, at the east end of its broken range. All three are of the great guenon tribe, the cercopithecines, which extends all the way across Africa, from the mona monkey in Senegal to the blue or Sykes's monkey of East Africa. (It also includes the vervet or green monkey, only known source of virus-free polio vaccine, and also the carrier of the viral source of the very dangerous "green monkey disease" which is a close relative of the AIDS virus.) Some authorities – Dr Western is one – regard the cercopithecines as mere geographic races of one great superspecies, despite their differences of size and color and their striking varieties of whiskers and beards.

Jonah's opinion would surely be anathema to Dr Jean-Pierre Gauthier, a friendly and expansive primatologist who has worked out of this research station for many years. Even at breakfast, Dr Gauthier is given to comical gorilla imitations, and also the fascinating coughs, moans, and long-distance shouts of the great guenon tribe that is his specialty. Sounds of aggression or warning may be shared by different species, he says, but the cries, the hooting of the males, the gathering calls and murmurings that keep the troop together in its travels through the forest, are so specific to each species that it is impossible for a juvenile of one species to successfully imitate the vocalizations of another. In fact, vocalization patterns in the five guenon species he has studied are directly related to the evolution of the various cercopithecine types.

Perhaps increasingly with the coming of man, forest monkeys have acquired new defenses, and many species in this brash and noisy group are largely silent. Others, such as DeBrazza's, are largely terrestrial, and when threatened, simply leap out of the trees (where they might be shot) and scamper off. The little talapoin may roost in low branches over water, and even a female carrying an infant will dive off the branch and swim away beneath the surface, a tactic that may have evolved first to frustrate the leopard. All such defenses demonstrate how difficult it is to capture these intelligent and wary creatures. Many hundreds of hours, Dr Gauthier says, are ordinarily devoted to every monkey darted or trapped and fitted out with a radio collar for further study.

Dr Gauthier, who lives in Paris, has returned to Gabon to investigate what he believes to be a new cercopithecine species. It was first described in 1985 by British primatologist Mike Harrison from the Région des Abeilles (Bee Country), about one hundred miles south of Makokou, where the strange monkey, known locally as *mbaya*, was first seen slung over a hunter's shoulder. The *mbaya* is most closely related to L'Hoest's monkey, and is said to be the wariest of a very wary lot, though this trait may be less significant in its avoidance of discovery than its limited range in a remote and largely uninhabited forest.

The rain-forest communities are the oldest on earth, with hundreds of insect species specific to each of the many species of its trees. Almost half of the earth's living things, many as yet undiscovered, live in this green world that is shrinking fast to a small patch on the earth's surface. Man has already destroyed half of the rain forests, which disappear at an ever-increasing speed, and a mostly unknown flora and fauna disappear with them.

Therefore, at every opportunity, we explore the forest, and often I go out alone, for walking in solitude through the dim glades, immersed in silence, one learns a lot that cannot be taught in any other way. The canopy of huge trees is closed, so that even at midday its atmosphere is cool and dark, too dark – too *mysterious*, it almost seems – for photographs. The forest silence is impermeable, entirely undisturbed by the soft bell notes of hidden birds, the tick of descending leaves and twigs or soft thump of falling fruit, or even the far caterwaul of monkeys. From far above come the unearthly squawks of great blue turacos, hopping and clambering along the highest limbs like *Archaeopteryx*.

Increasingly uneasy in one's own intrusion, moving ever more quietly so as not to wake things, one grows aware of immense harmony. The dust of the world spins in cathedral light in the long sun shafts falling from on high. The light touches a brilliant bird feather, an armored beetle, a mighty bean pod husk, silky and red, or hard and shiny as carved wood. The silent processions of the army ants, in their myriad species and deadly strength, glisten in dark ribbons on the forest floor; the taut webs of jungle spiders shine and vanish. High overhead, a bright orange *mbolo* fruit swells with sun in a chink of blue sky like a clerestory.

But this underworld is brown and green, and green is the color of the stifled air.

Man hunts in this forest, and few creatures are still left – monkeys, mandrills, squirrels, duikers, tree hyrax, several pangolins – to sustain the leopard whose scat I found yesterday near a forest pool. The scat was too old to attract butterflies, which lose all caution and are easily caught when feeding on the protein in carnivore dung. Like a beautiful lotus growing out of mud was the strange blossom of elusive life that we came upon one day on the forest path, cobalt and red and black and forest green. The blossom opens as the butterflies palpitate, drawing their life, their very color from their reeking feast. And they are hurrying, for in a climate that permits ceaseless reproduction, certain butterflies may begin and end their days in a single month.

All along, an enormous sound has resounded through the silence, and suddenly it transfixes one's awareness. It is the fierce wing shriek of cicadas, each shriek as painful to the ear as a blade sharpened on stone, yet joining with thousands of others in electric song and smoothing out in a wild ringing from the canopy high overhead. The thick-bodied, green cicadas are ventriloquial, Jonah says, and I wonder if this is not also true of those hidden forest birds whose beautiful voices seem impossible to trace. Most of the birds remain high in the canopy, but bird armies, or "ejaks", of mixed species – leafloves, wattle-eyes, malimbes, greenbuls – come flitting through the understory, and if one stands still long enough one of the hidden singers will appear.

Late one afternoon the yellow-cheeked trogon, a shy, uncommon forest dweller with emerald mantle and crimson breast and yellow spots behind the bill, flew from the shadows and perched dead still on a limb over the path. Like a spirit of the forest, it remained motionless even when we walked beneath it, and it did not turn its head to watch us go.

The Ivindo River, which flows south from the border region of Cameroon and Congo, drops off the high plateaus below Makokou in a series of white waterfalls and rapids to join eventually with the great Ogooué, which flows west past Lambarene to the sea. Like the Sangha, the Ivindo is one of many Congo Basin tributaries that are larger than any river in East Africa, or any river on the Indian Ocean except the great Zambezi and possibly the Ruvuma, on the Tanzania–Mozambique border. Nevertheless our attempts to follow it on our southward journey are thwarted by low clouds that almost turn us back. "That wasn't a good situation," David Western mutters, after making a tight circle back and gaining altitude before resuming his course. "The ceiling got lower and lower as we neared those mountains, and before you know it the aircraft could have been trapped down in some valley between hills, unable to see where it might climb out."

At the Ivindo's confluence with the Ogooué, we head west, making a landing at the Lope airstrip, between the Ogooué and the brave new Trans-Gabonais railroad designed to open up Gabon's unexploited interior to timber and mineral development. A few years ago, when the railroad up the Ogooué was being constructed, this Lope region was very hard hunted to provide meat for the crews. Today it is a wildlife reserve, and the animals are coming back, with buffalo and elephant now quite common. One day, perhaps, Lope-Okande, as it is known, will be a true national park, but for the moment it still issues timber leases. (Virtually the entire rain forest of Gabon, C.A.R., Congo, Cameroon, and much of Zaire has already been sold in logging units to European countries and the Japanese; already about one-fifth of Gabon's foreign income comes from wood.) And since the nation's oil, which financed the new railroad, is drying up, and since Gabon's mineral reserves are less extensive than was at first believed, the country's small population and its low rate of increase may prove to be a blessing. Even so, the people are officially exhorted to produce more children and occupy the wilderness regions to the east. Whether foreign investors or the Gabonais themselves will profit from this exploitation remains to be seen, but in view of the headlong scary rate at which the earth's rain forests are disappearing, there seems no doubt that humanity will be the loser.

Richard Barnes, who has accompanied us from Makokou, has kindly made arrangements for our various visits in Gabon, and we are picked up at the airstrip by Lope's warden. M. Sambouni drives us through the open savanna hills under Mt DeBrazza, named after the French explorer who discovered the Ogooué River and gave his name to the distinguished monkey as well as to Brazzaville, the present capital of Congo Republic. The extensive grassland in this region, in an odd pattern up and down the hills, seems to bear no relation to the ecological topography, and although M. Sambouni says that the savanna has always been here, he also says he must burn it each year to keep the forest from encroaching.

David Western is convinced that the savanna is "derived" – created, that is, by man's impact; in fact, he disputes the widespread notion that the great wildlife savannas of East Africa are a natural ecosystem, mysteriously unaffected by the presence of pastoral man for three thousand years. Since it has never been forested in present memory, the grassland must have been established in earlier centuries of Bantu settlement, perhaps as early as the first migrating waves of Bantu peoples, who are thought to have followed the rivers south perhaps fifteen hundred years ago in response to long-term drought or overpopulation in the savannas. Throughout this region, the patchwork grassland is so widespread that settlement must have been much more extensive than it is today, and only the depredations of the slave trade, and the fierce inter-tribal slaving wars that followed, seem to account for the great emptiness of this broken landscape.

In less than an hour, we arrive at the quarters of Dr Caroline Tutin, a young British primatologist whose airy camp on a savanna hilltop overlooks the Lope-Okande forest. For a year and a half in the early seventies, Dr Tutin, a small, trim young woman with green eyes and red hair, worked with Jane Goodall at Gombe Stream in Tanzania, after which, for a number of years, she pursued her own chimpanzee research at the Parc de Niokolo Koba, in Senegal. It was there that she first met her associate, Michel Fernandez, a genial French pilot, mechanic, and logistical expert who constructed and maintains their present camp. (Tutin and Fernandez remind me that we met in 1979, when I visited Niokolo Koba.) Dr Tutin says that she finds field work in Gabon exciting not only because most of its forest is intact but because this high western region of the equatorial rain forest was a Pleistocene refugia, where a very large, complex, and diverse flora and fauna survived the widespread cooling and drying on this continent that occurred during the Ice Age, ten thousand years ago, when most of the rain forest disappeared. Little is known as yet about this fauna, and even less about the flora, and she suspects that new species may yet be found. She agrees with her colleague Dr Gauthier that the *mbaya* is a distinct new species of cercopithecine, despite its very limited range of one hundred square kilometers across the Lolo River to the east.

At Lope, Dr Tutin is studying the behavior of chimpanzee and lowland gorilla, both of which, she says, were first reported from Gabon by American missionaries. Though she is still partial to the chimp – "Everything in its social organization encourages the development of high intelligence" – she is at present concentrating on the gorilla. In her first two years, she has located and censused five separate groups, not counting two or three lone males, but none of these animals are as yet habituated to human beings, and the big silver-back males (the French also like this term, saying "seelvairebok moll") are still given to roaring display charges that will cause even elephants to back up.

The great majority of gorilla threat displays stop well short of physical contact, but a year ago, on December 24 ("I remember the date well," says the victim), a lone silver-back rushed out of the thicket and bit Fernandez on the calf. The gorilla took him for another male, he thinks. "If he'd wished to kill me or seriously hurt me, he could have done so very easily," Fernandez told me, a surprised expression on his face, "but he didn't even bite me with full force."

Since male gorillas are equipped with large, sharp canines, this gentle bite left holes in his leg, the scars of which are still impressive. Similar bitings have occurred at Dian Fossey's camp at Karisoke, in Rwanda, and at Kahuzi-Biega, in eastern

Zaire, where I observed gorillas a few years ago, but none have been fatal despite the huge strength and fearsome aspect of what all authorities regard as a gentle vegetarian creature. "Imagine one of these great hunters shooting down a silverback!" Caroline Tutin says with quiet indignation. "It's hard to imagine a less sporting shot!"

The mountain gorilla of the Central Highlands, which is regularly shot by poachers for tourist "trophy heads" (the young are taken illegally for zoos, a process which usually involves shooting the adults), is now in serious danger, its population having been reduced to about four hundred, but, like the northern white rhino, it is regarded as a geographic race, not a true species, despite marked morphological differences in the two forms. (At present a third race is recognized – the eastern lowland gorilla, now reduced to a few small ranges in eastern Zaire. Between twenty-five hundred and forty-five hundred of this largest of the three gorillas, which include the animals at Kahuzi-Biega, are thought to remain.) Worldwide alarms of gorilla extinction that were sounded a few years ago were based on rough estimates that the combined populations of the mountain and the lowland races did not exceed five to seven thousand animals, but in a recent development – quite the opposite of what we now anticipate for forest elephant – Dr Tutin and other researchers have discovered an estimated thirty-five thousand gorilla in Gabon alone, and other healthy lowland populations as far west as Cameroon. (Richard Carroll's more conservative figure is thirty thousand to fifty thousand western lowland gorilla in all five countries of the western Congo Basin – Cameroon, C.A.R., Gabon, Congo, and Equatorial Guinea.) As in the case of the northern white rhino, this raises the question of whether so much conservation effort should be spent on a remnant and perhaps doomed geographic race – the mountain gorilla – when the species as a whole is not in danger.

With Jonah, I accompany Dr Tutin on an afternoon trek into her forest, which appears far more modified by elephants than the forest at Makokou. Because the gorillas are still shy, she thinks it unlikely that they will show themselves, and she turns out to be right, although we encounter a large number of fresh droppings. Dr Tutin deftly collects one in a polyethylene bag for food analysis. "Some of these smell quite nice," she says, and at this point she glances up at Dr Western, aware that his wife, Dr Strum, is a noted baboon authority. So gently that Jonah doesn't notice he is being teased, she whispers with a shy sly smile, "Better than baboons'!" (Remarkably, the best known primate researchers – Goodall, Fossey, Biruti-Galdikas [the orangutan researcher in Borneo], and more recently Drs Strum and Tutin – are women. The first three – known irreverently in primate circles as "the trimates" – were protégées of Louis Leakey, who felt that women had more patience for prolonged study, but this does not fully account for the phenomenon, for which no behavioural theory has been advanced.)

On a forest ridge, our coming provokes a crashing flight through the dense undergrowth. "Large duiker," Dr Tutin whispers. "Yellow-backed, I should think." We also startle a mustached monkey, one of three guenon species that share this forest with gorillas, chimpanzees, mandrills, gray-cheeked mangabeys, and black colobus. Dr Tutin says that primate species are even more numerous in south Cameroon, at the northern end of this Pleistocene refugia, which extends all the way down to the coast; she has seen gorillas on the seashore at Mayumba, in southwest Gabon.

The ridge opens out on one of the large rocks that jut up from the forest floor, and here we sit still for a little while, hoping to hear the chest thumping and other noises that might betray the whereabouts of the gorillas. What we hear instead is the strange "pant-hooting" of an approaching troop of chimpanzees, each animal's harsh cries joining with others in a wild ululation that rings and wanders through the trees. "They've found something good to eat, or they've run into another subgroup, perhaps both," Caroline murmurs, turning to listen with the same smile of unabashed wonder and approval that is so affecting in the hunting peoples. We cross the ridge to the far side, following the sound of the chimps feeding, but already the apes are falling quiet, all but hidden in the canopies of leaves. "They're settling down now for the night," Caroline says, smiling again. "I'll be here the first thing in the morning."

In the course of his African elephant survey in 1979, Dr Iain Douglas-Hamilton saw a troop of little elephants on the sea beach at Iguela Game Reserve, here in Gabon. Douglas-Hamilton's escort, Claude Pradel, the director of the hunting preserve of President Omar Bongo at Wonga-Wongue, and a veteran of thirty-three years in this country, told Iain that these elephant were *assala*, which is the local name for "pygmy elephant". If we wanted a look at the mysterious *assala*, the wild tract of thirty-five hundred square kilometers at Wonga-Wongue, extending inland from the coast, seemed very promising, since elephants were more protected there than anywhere else in this casual country.

Not without difficulties and delays, Richard Barnes and his friend Dr Aart Louis, the director of the national herbarium, have received permission for a brief visit to Wonga-Wongue, and on January 22, accompanied by Dr Louis and another Dutch botanist, Dr Jan Reitsma, and escorted by a soldier of the president's guard, we fly about seventy miles south of Libreville to a tranquil region of forest and meadows parted by clear streams that flow down from high grassy plateaus to the sea. Without much question, Wonga-Wongue, surrounded by vast marshes and lacking road access – one can only come by boat or plane – is one of the loveliest reserves in all of Africa.

Monsieur Pradel lives year-round at the president's camp on a wooded hill well inland from the coast, together with his wife, Nina, his nineteen-year-old son, Norbert, a German assistant, an African staff, four Bengal tigers, five puma from South America, a young chimpanzee, two zebras, and a very large monitor lizard, which resides in an empty swimming pool by the main house. Most of these creatures are the property of President Bongo, who is usually accompanied here on his rare visits by some other head of state who is anxious to shoot something. Thus Wonga-Wongue is exposed to hunting, as are Lope-Okande and Iguela, but the hunting here is as limited as it is infrequent. From the animals' point of view, at least, it comes closer to a true national park than any wild area in Gabon.

M. Pradel is away in Ivory Coast at the time of our visit, but Madame Pradel, a handsome redhead from Toulouse, is very hospitable in her husband's absence. She presides over an exotic living room lined with stuffed birds and monkeys, kudu and sable horns, a monkey-skull fetish, artificial flowers, photographs, amateur paintings, curios, and three saddles mounted on racks; one of the saddles is an ornate cowboy model acquired last year on a visit to Texas, where she also acquired the University of Texas T-shirt worn by young Norbert. The Pradels keep horses here but have not had much luck with them because of sleeping sickness and other, undiagnosed, ailments. "We've never kept a horse alive more than four years," she says. "It's very sad, watching them die."

All three Pradels pilot their own airplanes, but Madame Pradel, who sees to Wonga-Wongue's administration, has not left the reserve for the past two years. "What is there to do in Libreville?" she inquires, throwing her hands up in fine Gallic disdain. "I'm better off here. I don't wish to *die* here, but . . ." She shrugs. The first few years of her sixteen in Gabon were spent at Makokou; she describes to Richard the gigantic Makokou elephants that are now all gone. But what she remembers even better than the elephants are the huge Goliath and rhinoceros beetles in the forest.

Madame Pradel confirms the presence of *assala*; just the other day she has seen a troop with a tiny infant "no bigger than a toy". The presence of the infant does not fit our theory that pygmy elephants are nothing more than maverick young forest elephants, with or without precocious tusks, and neither does her account of a sick *assala* from Wonga-Wongue which after its death had been stuffed for display in President Bongo's palace back in Libreville. Judging from the worn condition of its tusks, everyone who saw this little animal, say the Pradels, agreed that it was at least sixty years old. But inspecting the photograph that Madame Pradel shows us, we see what looks like a four-year-old forest elephant, even to the body hair found on young animals. "The tusk wear doesn't mean a thing," Jonah says later. "Juvenile tusks often get chipped and worn, and look like tusks of older animals." What we wish to do as soon as possible is to inspect these *assala* in the field, and dispel the mystery once and for all.

Norbert Pradel offers to guide us around Wonga-Wongue during our stay. Dressed in camouflage fatigues and cap, packing a pistol, Norbert maneuvers the family's bush vehicle as rapidly as possible over the red sand roads. We flush one sitatunga, which has wandered up into the grasslands from the marshy lakes, but the only animals seen in abundance are red forest buffalo. Like the forest elephant, the forest buffalo is of the same species as its savanna kinsman, and it, too, is half the size of its savanna race and very different in appearance, carrying its much smaller horns as duikers do, swept back and tight for forest travel. Like their large relatives, the forest buffalo wheel to the four winds when panicked, nostrils high, ears wide and ragged, hummocking along on random courses that often carry them across the path of whatever it is that they are fleeing.

Some years ago, young Norbert's father was nearly demolished by a *bouffle* that rose and pursued him after his bullet dropped it, and gored him twice before plunging off into the forest. "And that one was *dead*," exclaims Madame Pradel later, ladling buffalo meat onto our plates; she tells us about a woman worker on the reserve plantation who recently survived a severe goring.

Because of its remote location and lack of access roads, Wonga-Wongue is virtually free of all but local poachers, who hunt for meat, and even these (from what Norbert views as a deplorable weakness in the tribal character) are betrayed by their fellow villagers at the first whisper of trouble. Only lately have commercially inclined outsiders started to appear. One such fellow was apprehended with forty-three decaying monkeys, which he hoped would still be pleasing to his customers in Libreville after a journey of seventy hot miles in his pirogue. Much more serious, Norbert relates, was an episode in which a white pilot in a military aircraft gunned down a troop of elephants with rockets. The carcasses were bulldozed under by a confederate on the Wonga-Wongue staff, to be exhumed again when the ivory had rotted free. These people were eventually traced and arrested, thanks to Claude Pradel, who has earned a reputation for enforcing game protection in this country where protection is, at best, a quaint idea.

Even on the highest plateaus, where the grass blows to the horizon, remnant isles of trees rise from the tawny land. The botanists agree with Western that all this country was once forest, and that this vast empty savanna, like the one at Lope, was originally cleared and farmed by Bantu peoples who later fled the pillage of the slave trade. The ancient soil, its minerals leached out by sixty million years of rain, was weakened further, Dr Louis believes, by erosion caused by primitive cultivation, so that the forests were unable to return. As in the savannas north of the forest, the impoverished grasses, which provide supplementary bulk to the large animals, are too coarse and poor to support the smaller herbivores; even the zebras of President Bongo seem to disdain them. These uplands have attracted some of the same bird life that one sees in the savannas of East Africa – eagles, larks, and swallows, the Senegal plover, the nightjars and spotted eagle-owls of the night roads – but by comparison, the birds are few, and of few species.

By the roadside I see the gleam of a large python, but unfortunately Norbert sees it, too. He yanks the vehicle onto the shoulder and runs it over, nearly losing control of the car in the jolt of the impact. Astonishingly the snake slides away. "Python," he says, disgusted. "Maybe three meters." I ask him rather sharply why he wished to kill it, and hearing no criticism, he answers cheerfully, "Because I do not like it. *Sont les sales bêtes.*"

In the late afternoon, a few elephants come carefully from the forest. Their usual habit is to feed all evening and through the night in the grasslands along the forest verges, returning into the green wall at break of day. Toward twilight, in a dusky sun, seven or eight are moving steadily through sand-colored grass along the distant trees. A solitary cow appears, then a young male, and, finally two cows accompanied by small young and a half-grown female.

Our young guide does not slow down when elephants are sighted, being of the opinion that the pesky things will head straight for the forest, no matter what, and that our one chance is to head them off with the speeding car. Given their chronic exposure to this technique, it was certainly likely that they would head straight for the forest, and all we see are baggy gray hindquarters being swallowed by the trees. But the last group is caught out in the open, and Norbert, cutting across country, rides right up alongside the fleeing animals. They wheel and scream, ears and tails lashing, and head back in the opposite direction, as we assure him we have seen enough. Unquestionably these are adult females with calves bouncing at their flanks, and they are by far the smallest elephants we've seen, not six feet high.

"*Assala,*" says Norbert Pradel, pleased he has shown us "*éléphant pygmée*" at such close range. I ask him if these little elephants were average size for the *assala*, and he says they are, reminding us that "big elephants" also occur here.

Next morning, in dense dry season mist, with chimpanzees howling from the forest, we approach on foot a lone adult male at least seven and a half or eight feet high, by Jonah's estimate. This elephant, too, has round small ears and lacks the protruding brow of male bush elephant, which would stand two or three feet taller at the shoulder, but his large ivory has the pronounced forward curve of the savanna race that we had noted even in one of the diminutive elephants seen up close the previous evening.

We had thought to encounter pure *cyclotis* rather quickly upon entering the equatorial forest, whether just north of the equator at Makokou or just south of it at Wonga-Wongue. What we had not expected was this very broad zone of hybridization in which large and small elephants coexist.

Traditionally paleontologists have believed that the bush elephant was the ancestral form, since its ancient bones have been found in the savanna. But bones don't last long in the damp forest (or researchers either), and since there were no savannas in pre-Miocene times, the African elephant must have evolved as a forest animal; either *cyclotis* is the original elephant or it evolved from the original, with the bush elephant appearing later. The non-adaptive and inappropriate bush habit of destroying trees while feeding was adaptive in the forest, where light must penetrate in order to produce second-growth browse, and this, too, suggests the forest ancestry of *Loxodonta*, on which most biologists now agree.

The Wonga-Wongue animals come as close to pure *cyclotis* as any we have seen, not only in morphological characters but in size. But somewhere, Jonah is convinced, there must exist a population with no trace of hybridization, to maintain the genetic characters identified with the forest race. He supposed that such elephants might be found in south Gabon, south Congo, or southwest Zaire.

Throughout our visit to Gabon, we had to return repeatedly to Libreville, not only because aviation gasoline was unobtainable anywhere else but because special clearances were necessary for light plane travel to what were termed "inhospitable regions". And it was at Libreville airport, on a dead, fetid morning, that we said good-bye to Richard Barnes, whose elephant expertise as well as taut logistical preparations and good company had made an important contribution to our journey.

Richard himself had no regrets about our parting, since he doesn't much care for light plane travel over long stretches of equatorial forest. "I'm awfully glad," he said to me with uncustomary fervor, "that I do not have to get back into that airplane." Had he known what awaited us over the next two days, he would have fallen to his bony knees in simple gratitude.

Heading southeast from Libreville to Kinshasa, in Zaire, on the first leg of our zigzag return across the continent, we cross the great Ogooué at Lambaréné, where Dr Alfred Schweitzer had his clinic, and continued southeast up the N'Gounié River. Two hundred miles out, the plane leaves the forest and crosses a broad country of marshlands and dwindling strands of trees. Here the forest ends. South Gabon, which we had envisioned as a last redoubt of the "pure" forest elephant, turns out to be a deforested land without visible life, only scarce and solitary huts with brown faded smudges of ancient gardens showing through pale weary greens. "Man-made," says Jonah of this wasteland, and when I wonder aloud about the fate of the men who made it, he says, not altogether seriously, "America."

According to our obsolete colonial air charts, the wandering red road that we are following runs all the way from Lambaréné to Brazzaville, capital of the Congo Republic, which lies across the Congo – now the Zaire River – from Kinshasa. (Like C.A.R. and Chad, Gabon and Congo were formerly a single administrative unit of French Equatorial Africa.) But not far beyond the Congo border the road diminishes into smaller tracks that scatter out among hill villages. These modern villages must differ little from those of former days, and they appear to be continuing the destruction of the land seen farther north, since the land around them is eroded, and their garden patches are miles distant across a worn-out earth.

The colonial road shown on the chart is gone entirely. We follow a southeastern course, picking up a landmark at the Niari River. Having no clearance for a landing in Congo, we must slip in and refill our wing tanks at a mission airstrip north of Dolisie, in open mining country, then take off speedily, following the new paved road toward Brazzaville.

Unaccountably this road swings off to the north, so once again we travel by dead reckoning, tending south across high barren country. The Zaire River cannot be very far, and in fact we cross a river soon thereafter, a swift narrow torrent through a gorge – too small, we agree, to be the great broad Congo with its famous steamers, largest river in all Africa. We forge on, southeast across a vast lonesome plateau. The empty land goes on and on and on, no end in sight, and no great river; more mystifying still, our maps show no roadless area of this extent in southern Congo. We stare at our watches and compass in disbelief. At mid-afternoon we see a small mission settlement with an airstrip; like it or not, we must land to refuel and find out where we are.

If the peasants who come rushing to the plane cannot read our map, they at least make it clear that they are citizens not of the Congo Republic but of Zaire. When I tell Jonah we are in Zaire, his jaw actually drops – one of the few times in my life that I have witnessed this comic phenomenon, though neither of us are in any mood to laugh. In fact, we are stunned by the realization that that narrow torrent in the gorge, so very different from our expectations, had been the mighty Congo after all.

When I ask for the general direction of Kinshasa, the people point at all points of the compass, and when I protest, one of them reproves me. "How are we to know? We are just here!" Feeling ashamed, I apologize and ask if they will lead me to the missionary. While Jonah refuels the plane, I set off quickly for the house of a kind Italian, Father Nicolo, who puts his finger on the map at a point more than a hundred miles southeast of our destination.

The Zairois, at first friendly and polite, are now comparing their suspicions. They begin to agitate and grow excited, for this place is just east of the Angola border, with its Cuban mercenaries (and its guerrilla war, largely financed, it is said, by the ivory from one hundred thousand slaughtered elephants). As it turns out, the people here are as paranoid about mercenaries as the peasants we met earlier in Haut-Zaïre. On my way back to the airstrip, they tug at my elbow, saying that it is too late in the day to reach Kinshasa. When I shake my head, they insist with increasing hostility that the people need to satisfy themselves that we are not spies; we must stay here until this "brusque" visit is investigated by the proper authorities. The spokesmen, more and more excited, start to shout, drawing attention to their own high sense of civic duty, and I realize with a pang of dread that unless we move fast, our history at Dibwa may repeat itself. I alert Jonah, who has refueled quickly. "We can just make it," he says, by which he means, There's just enough light to get us to Kinshasa, assuming we make no more mistakes. We have to chance it anyway, especially since, this very evening, we have an important meeting in Kinshasa that is the whole purpose of this leg of our journey.

We shoulder our way through the Africans and get into the plane and spin the prop to drive the shouters back. Father Nicolo stays well apart, wishing no trouble. Fortunately, in this mission settlement, there are no firearms. Jonah taxis to the far end of the strip as the spokesmen pursue us, and one tall screeching man in a red shirt holds his ground as the airplane comes at him, waving his arms wildly to flag us down, running aside only at the last minute. Having done his best to stop us, he is philosophical, no longer angry, and grins and waves with all the rest as we roar past.

The blue-and-silver plane crosses the upper Wamba River, then the Kwango, and returns north over the stark emptiness of the great plateau. As in so much of this country, the darkening villages appear abandoned, their starving inhabitants whirled away as if by wind into the human sink of Kinshasa. We watch the sun move down behind the clouds off to the west. Because the mission station was not on our map, and the missionary rather vague about locations, our heading can only be approximate. Over the great hollow of the river basin, there is mist, and with the last light failing fast, we are not sure if we are up or down the river from Kinshasa. Just as it appears that oncoming night may force us to make an emergency landing in a field, we see the broad expanse of Stanley Pool, then a city tower. As dusk comes, we are making our way in to the international airport called N'djili.

I am limp with strain and exhilaration and relief, and so is Jonah, to judge from the fact that he approaches the airport from the wrong direction and is on the runway when the man in the tower, peering through the descending dusk in the opposite direction, is still instructing him on his angle of approach. Jonah is embarrassed, but not very. He knows as I know that we are lucky to be here at all, that but for clear weather and good visibility, this day could have ended very badly. That we failed to recognize the river is my fault as much as his. Neither of us knew – and his chart failed to show it – that the great wide Congo, below Stanley Pool, narrows to a torrent that plunges down a canyon toward the sea.

Anyway, this is no longer the man who analyzed for days the reasons for the forced landing at Dibwa. Perhaps because light-plane flying in poorly charted jungle countries is so difficult, accounting for "mistakes" seems beside the point, and Jonah can now smile at our mishaps. "We must be the only travelers," he sighs later, "who ever missed both the Nile and the Congo on the same journey."

All is smoothed over at N'djili by M. Mankoto Mbele, the director of Zaire's national parks, whose staff sees us rapidly through customs and escorts us through Kinshasa's streets to our hotel. Later he meets us for a pleasant dinner at the house of Patrick Towers-Picton, a local representative of the European Economic Community who is interested in wildlife, proposed parks, and elephant projects. Jonah speaks persuasively on the importance of forest conservation in Zaire and of the possibility of creating an international forest park in the Sangha River region of C.A.R., Congo Republic, and Cameroon. We return to the hotel at 1 a.m., knowing we must rise at dawn to resume our journey.

Last night, our host referred to the wilderness between Kinshasa and Kisangani, our next destination, as "Zaire's Bermuda Triangle", because of the number of unlucky aircraft that have disappeared into that forest without a trace. As it turns out, special clearance is needed to fly a light plane into Zaire's immense forest interior. Also, we have not counted on the Kinshasa bureaucracy, which, even more than in Libreville and Bangui, is noisy and rude and inefficient on a heroic scale, so that even the simplest transaction requires at least ten times longer than is necessary. Questions are shouted and our answers scratched down on scraps of paper – snatched up, perhaps, from the floor or wastebasket – that may as well be instantly returned there, so certain does it seem that the information scrawled thereon will never be read again. The demanded passport or other document is waved about, picked up and dropped, or fanned in open incredulity and contempt for the lies and obfuscations it contains, when in fact the only thing amiss may be the bureaucrat's inability to read it.

The show is not intended for the traveler, who knows better, but for the swarm of lesser personages behind each desk – the relatives, the fetchers of soft drinks – who are desperately trying to justify their own niches in this system, and vie with each other in agreeing with the boss. Thus each must grab at and bang down the offending paper, expressing his professional dissatisfaction in the strongest terms, until finally everyone is shouting his own interpretation of the regulations. All this is conducted over the indecipherable static of the airport squawk boxes, which are invariably turned up to highest volume, and which, in conjunction with the senseless human din, make any significant communication out of the question.

Then suddenly the smell of money changing hands is in the air, and disputes collapse like froth in a boiled pot: the time has come to pay taxes and fees. However, the traveler's monies are rarely in the required currency, and no one behind the desk quite knows how to count, and anyway there is no change, and no one knows where change might be obtained. There are hints that the traveler might do well to forget the change, since gifts are in order for these worthy public servants who have cleared up the confusion that these mendacious documents have brought down upon them. To perceive such gifts as "bribes" is to fail to realize that they serve as salaries for these government workers who, in the corrupt anarchy of Zaire, may subsist unpaid for month after month, with no more prospect of a decent life than they had under Belgian rule.

Once customs is through with us, civil aviation refuses to clear our flight; the thousand miles over the forests to Kisangani is too dangerous for a single-engine plane. Eventually Jonah prevails, but it is past 11 a.m., after four hours at the airport, when the last official has satisfied himself that our documents and flight plan are in order. By this time, a large storm front to the north has appeared on the tower computers, but we are not notified of this until we have flown north for a half hour. We are warned to bear west of our course for the next hundred miles, after which we might locate a break in the front, and cross the river to Basankusu. Once again, we are fated to travel late, and will race the last light to Kisangani. In order not to waste time and precious fuel Jonah holds the plane as close as possible to the great storm front, a swirling mass of ugly grays with columns of rain and sudden lightning.

Our course is approximately northeast, but in the next hour and a half the storm forces us remorselessly to the northwest, over the burned and ruined plateaus of the Congo Republic. The storm shows no sign of diminishing, the airplane cannot find a way through. Trying to cut closer to gain time, the plane is caught by an immense wind and plunges drastically. The earth jumps up, causing the cargo to bang the cabin roof, as something breaks. The plane lurches and jolts as it veers away to westward, and a moment later the fuselage is struck by one of the black swifts that hurtle along the dark wall of the storm. The hard ping is like the ring of a hurled stone.

Suddenly all hell breaks loose; hurricane-force winds slam us up and down with terrifying violence; green forest races up toward us; and fuel barrels and gear fly loose in the rear of the cockpit. I grimly try to regain control of the plane while Peter grabs for the baggage. Twenty agonizing seconds later, the winds subside enough for me to veer northwest. Finally, after we're battered by two more screaming gusts, I turn south, defeated, for Kinshasa . . .

The storm is dangerous, we can see no end to it, and besides, we have used up too much fuel. We race the gray mass back toward the south, but it moves in over the river as the plane banks eastward below Brazzaville. Forced to low altitude by poor visibility, beating its way back up the river, the plane seems blocked by wild wind over the boiling rapids where the Zaire narrows into its gorge below Stanley Pool. Incredibly that gorge carries more volume than any river on earth except the Amazon, and so fierce is the torrent (we are later told) that no one has ever set foot on this forested island that looms through the blowing rain beneath the wing. Once across the rapids, the plane fights for headway among the small skyscrapers of Kinshasa.

By flying under the low scudding cloud base, over white-foamed rapids, between city skyscrapers where wind blasts hurl us up to the clouds one moment and almost down to the street the next, we reach N'dola Airport at the city's edge . . . *

Jonah requests clearance to land at the airfield called N'dola, which is much closer to the city than N'djili, but a medley of voices less calm than his own is haranguing him with irrelevant questions and issuing conflicting instructions, not only in two languages but from both towers. The plane is now in the black heart of the storm, with lashing rain and thick sinking clouds that keep it down among the buildings and a violent wind that tosses it from one building toward another with sickening jumps and drops and lurches. I pray that my partner is more confident than I that his airplane won't fly apart under such a beating.

I steal a look at him, with some idea that I might as well know the worst, and am relieved though not surprised by what I see. Jonah's face is grim and tense, just as my own must be, but there is no panic, only a twitch of exasperation at the instructions on the radio. When one of his tormentors orders him to proceed into N'djili and land toward the south – that is downwind – he answers tersely that he is proceeding to N'dola, after which he breaks off communication. In the tumult, he is holding the plane on its bounding course with sheer physical strength, and he has to concentrate on the approach. N'dola looms in the blurred windshield, and, maintaining his speed, he beats his way in very low over the sprawl of tin-roofed dwellings, lurching and tipping all the way onto the rainswept concrete.

* David Western, *Discover*, October 1986.

For a few minutes in the lashing rain, we sit in the plane in silence. We have lost a day, and will therefore miss tomorrow's contact at Mambasa, in the Ituri Forest, where people must make a five-hour round trip to fetch us. Also, we have wasted many gallons of expensive fuel. But, for the moment, none of this matters, so grateful are we to be on the ground. I am mightily impressed by the pilot's cool and skilled performance under stress, and saying so, I embarrass Dr Western by reaching out to shake his hand.

"I didn't care much for that experience," I say, a note of hysteria in my laugh, and Jonah shakes his head. The front, he says, was hundreds of miles long, far longer than any storm front he has ever encountered in East Africa, and the storm jolt that struck us over the Congo Republic he estimated at eighty miles an hour, the most severe he had ever experienced. Jonah had been told that such storms were not uncommon in the Congo Basin, especially in the rainy season, which has now begun, and we still have the whole of Africa ahead of us. Back there over the Congo Republic this afternoon, he says, he could have made an emergency landing on the burned plain, but such a storm would be very dangerous if it forced us off course over the forest, with no maps we could trust and no place to come down.

Silenced by these thoughts, we refuel the plane and complete most of the paperwork for tomorrow. By the time we return to the city through the raining streets, bitterly disappointed to be back, our relief has given way to intense depression. For the first and last time on the trip, we feel utterly disheartened, and we do not hide it. There have been bad patches before now – the descent of the Ivindo River into mist and mountains was one of the worst, so far as Jonah is concerned – but after two long days of stressful flying, racing the darkness, rarely certain where we were, after that scary approach into Kinshasa, and with the prospect of more bad storms to come, I feel tense and worried, dreading the days ahead.

Though he will not say so, Jonah is worried, too. After so many weeks spent with this man, day after day, meal after meal, under strain in the air and frustration in these cities, I know him a bit better than he imagines. He does not lose his head, rarely shows anger, and remains commendably sensible and decisive, but under stress, his voice goes a notch tighter, and he reverts to a rather stiff, officious manner, using my first name a lot, as if he were speaking to a child.

At supper Jonah is somber and withdrawn; he has done all the flying, borne all the responsibility, and he looks exhausted. Yesterday he was already suggesting that he should return home earlier than planned, that we should cut our stay in the Ituri Forest from ten days to five, that perhaps we should eliminate it entirely, although from the start we have regarded the Ituri as the main reward of a long, arduous journey.

In the depths of our gloom, we discuss our drastic choices, such as skirting

the tropical rainy-season storms by backtracking northward to Bangui before
returning eastward, or even, if storms trap us in Kinshasa, storing the aircraft
here until the rains are past, and flying home – he east, I west – by commercial
carrier. Either choice would eliminate the visit to the Ituri, and neither is an
acceptable defeat; we both know even as we speak that we will get up at dawn
tomorrow morning and try again.

Next morning we are at the airport at 6.30. The plane is fueled, our flight plan
is approved, the miasmal depression of the night before has vanished with the
rain. There are even patches of blue sky, and with any sort of luck, I think, we
shall escape Kinshasa, getting at least as far as Mbandaka, four hundred miles to
the northeast on the Zaire River. But whereas at N'djili our main delays were
caused by wholehearted incompetence, at N'dola we are subjected to a merciless
fleecing by every official who can lay his hands on us, each one discovering
something wrong with embarkation tax, flight plan, even dates on vaccination
cards, at least until some hard cash is forked over. The negotiation of so much graft
takes time, as we are waved into office after office, and increasingly we are aware
that once again the day is starting to get away from us, that even if good weather
holds it is nearly a thousand miles to Kisangani. Eventually we make a show of
temper, shouting threats to expose such greed to our friend, the minister Mankoto.
We bluff our way back to the airplane, but it is well past 9 a.m. when we take off.
    Early clouds over the swamps east of the river gradually burn away during
the morning. The plane cuts northeast across the Zaire's great wide bends, travers-
ing the plateaus of the Congo, then a vast swamp of raffia palms east of the river.
The map shows few roads in this great central region of Zaire, and anyway we
have learned not to depend upon these roads, since so many deteriorate and
disappear. For navigation we must count upon the rivers. On our left, where the
great flood sprawls out over the land in an archipelago of river islands, is the mouth
of the Sangha River, which we last saw at Bayanga. Farther on is the broad delta of
the great Ubangi, which has come south from Bangui. Then, once again, we are over
the Zaire, enjoying the steamers that push barges of cargo between river towns.
    The clouds are vanishing, the day is beautiful, and passing the airstrip at
Mbandaka (formerly Coquilhatville) I feel a great burst of exhilaration; we have
made our escape from Poubelleville, even if we should meet a storm in the next
half hour. I look over at Jonah, and he grins; he is happy, too. Already we feel sure
our luck has changed, that the long day we had anticipated as the hardest of
our journey will turn out to be the easiest and most enjoyable.
    Twenty minutes north of Mbandaka, we turn due eastward from the brown
Zaire up the Lulonga, a quiet and serene black river whose water is so clear that

sand bars are visible deep under the surface off the downstream end of river islets. Soon the water is a transparent tannin color, clear as red amber, and to my elated eye intensely beautiful. Along the river are lone pirogues and tiny villages, none of them more than a few huts under the shade trees on the bank. "This is Stanley's Africa," Jonah says, delighted. "Hasn't changed at all." At last we are flying over forest that could shelter elephants, and we discuss the one critical discovery we have made in the past few days: most if not all of the tropical forest of south Gabon, south Congo, and western Zaire, which we had thought must be the heartland of the forest elephant, and which is still included as viable habitat in charts and estimates of elephant population, has long since been destroyed or degraded. It is barren land where no elephant could exist.

The very wide hybridization zone extending deep into the Congo Basin, in which elephants of pronounced bush characters may be met with south of the equator and beyond, establishes beyond question that very dissimilar elephants live in the forest, and that widespread reports of a dwarf elephant have a basis in fact. The large hybrid form with its distinctive bush characters is the "big elephant" with which a much smaller animal is everywhere compared. The so-called *assala* is the forest elephant, *L. a. cyclotis*, which is very small by comparison to the bush race when not heavily endowed with the bush genes. Pygmy elephants – not everywhere distinguished from the *assala* – are not a distinct species or race but simply juvenile *cyclotis*, mostly young males, that separate early from the cow herds and may sometimes form small herds of their own. The two pygmies of outsize tusks and aggressive temperament at Dzanga Pan provided the first evidence, and the herd of little *assala* at Wonga-Wongue confirmed it.

Elephant authorities Iain Douglas-Hamilton and Cynthia Moss, who would separately inspect Jonah's photographs after our return, were fascinated by the discovery of the vast hybridization zone, which has never before been defined; until now, most observers had assumed that those "bush elephants" seen in the forest were wanderers or refugees from the dangerous open country to the north. Furthermore, both Moss and Douglas-Hamilton were fully persuaded by Jonah's explanation of the pygmy-elephant mystery provided by his photographs, which clearly show bush hybrids, forest elephants, and pygmies, all in the same picture. Of that five- or six-year-old that brandished big tusks at a hybrid male more than twice its size, then interacted in a filial manner with its mother, Moss remarked, "Without those tusks, I'd think that was a baby elephant. The tusks make it look sub-adult, at least fifteen years of age." Douglas-Hamilton agreed that on the basis of its tusks it might easily be called an adult "pygmy elephant".

In resolving one enigma, we appear to have stumbled upon another: where is the "pure" forest elephant, with its small head, low round ears, and vertical tusks?

We cannot be sure that such elephants don't persist in this vast trackless forest below, but I wonder aloud if in our time the pure *cyclotis* might have disappeared due to a mingling of the bush and forest races caused by the disruptive impact of mankind, not only in two centuries of ivory slaughter but in the accelerating destruction of the forest ever since. Jonah shrugs. Closer to the forest edge, he says, my theory might be sound, but it could not account for the hybrids much farther south. He speculates that the immense contraction of the forest caused by natural drying in recent millennia would account for the fact that the hybridization zone has spread so widely. Only two thousand years ago, conditions were so dry that woodland-savanna elephants were widespread throughout what is now rain forest, with the forest race confined to a few patches. Since this is only about thirty elephant generations, the bush genes are still apparent, perhaps throughout the forest populations.

At Basankusu, we land at the mission airstrip and refuel the wing tanks as people come out on foot and bicycle to greet us; this time we have a clearance paper, and nobody tries to detain us when we depart. Once in the air and headed east, we eat rolls scavenged from the hotel breakfast table, much amused by the realization that this is our first lunch in three days, not because we had no food along but because on both the previous days, the tense flight conditions and suspense had killed our appetite.

The broad flat wilderness of central Zaire is the bottom of the shallow Congo Basin. From here in the center of the continent the green monotone of forest spreads in a great circle to the far horizons. There is only the Lulonga, growing smaller, then its tributary, the Lopori, with scarce and diminishing hut clusters along the bank. Miles from the river, miles and miles and miles from the nearest voice, is the tiny scar of a crude slash-and-burn clearing, but the human being there stays out of sight. Who is this solitary *Homo sapiens*, so content to live so far off by himself, in a closed universe of hut and garden? No doubt he is down there staring up at his own small patch of sky, for not so many aircraft can have passed this way; we are many miles off to the north of the air routes of Zaire. Perhaps there are forest elephants down there, but we do not know.

Some three hundred miles east of its confluence with the Zaire, the Lulonga-Lopori makes a great bend toward the south, and here we forge straight on over the rain forest, sixty miles or so, to complete the crossing of the great north bend and return to the Zaire River. In a sun-filled, windless afternoon, enjoying the peaceful sweep of the upper river, we continue upstream a hundred and fifty miles to Kisangani, where the Tshopo and the Lualaba come together below Stanley Falls as the Zaire River, the great Congo.

If Kinshasa is one of the saddest cities in all Africa, Kisangani (formerly

Stanleyville) is among the loveliest, despite the testimony of its bullet-scarred façades and the bleak aspect of the Place des Martyres; this main square commemorates the victims of the execution that took place here in the violent civil wars of the early sixties, when Kisangani was the headquarters of the rebel government. The happy spirit of the place, in its pretty location on the river, is reflected in the harmony and order of even the humblest wattle-and-daub hut in the clean-swept yards, the absence of litter, the neat bundles of charcoal and vegetable produce set out unguarded by the wayside, and, most important, in the unfrowning demeanor of the people seen on the evening road in from the airport. Along the riverfront, in fire light of setting sun, large pirogues tend the gaunt fish weirs, and a fish eagle crosses the broad, slow expanse of the silver current that carries the weight of the Central Highlands rains toward the sea.

Flying east from Kisangani, the Cessna follows the Bunia road, a rough red section of the trans-African track that winds across Africa from the Gulf of Guinea to the Kenya coast. This forest region still shows the effects of the anarchic period that followed Zaire's independence in 1960, when many people, villages, and gardens were destroyed by the successive waves of soldiers, rebels, and white South African and Rhodesian mercenaries that swept in and out of Kisangani. In the quarter-century since, with the region depopulated and communications broken down, the colonial airstrips and many of the side roads still indicated on the charts are little more than shadows in the trees, having been subsumed by the surrounding forest. Excepting the rivers, the trans-African itself, barely maintained, is the only landmark, a welcome thread of human presence in this dark green sea.

On all sides, to the shrouded green horizons, lies the unbroken Ituri Forest, in the region perceived by Henry Morton Stanley as the very heart of "darkest Africa". The Ituri extends north to the savannas and east to the foothills of the Central Highlands, with contiguous regions of wild forest to the south and west. In the nineteenth century, the region was a famous source of ivory, which was carried back to the coast at Zanzibar by the slave caravans of Tippu Tib, and by all accounts was a great redoubt of elephants throughout the decades of the Congo Free State and the Belgian Congo. Even today the Ituri remains largely intact, since it lies on the rim of the Congo Basin, above the waterfalls of smaller and less navigable rivers. In Western's opinion, any estimates we make of the Ituri's present population of forest elephants may be used as a fair gauge for the rest of Zaire's forests. In so much wilderness, in the absence of good information, it is tempting to imagine large companies of elephants passing unseen beneath these silent canopies, but past estimates are probably much too high.

*   *   *

In the 1920s, the colonial authorities moved the scattered Bantu villages onto the new road, where the people could be more easily taxed, conscripted for labor, and otherwise administered. This concentration, and the road itself, attracted ambitious new immigrants – the shopkeepers, hotel owners, gold panners, truck drivers, and the like. The newcomers who make up what anthropologists refer to as "the road culture", with its dependence on the big cargo trucks that comprise most of the scarce vehicles on the trans-African. On the fringes of the road culture live twenty thousand to forty thousand Mbuti (no one quite knows), the largest and most culturally intact of the Pygmy groups that are scattered here and there across the rain forest, from the Central Highlands west into Cameroon; the Pygmies are one of the most ancient of African peoples, and among the continent's last groups of hunter-gatherers.

At the Epulu River, Dr Western buzzed the camp of American biologists John and Terese Hart, and a number of people ran outside to wave. With the help of the Mbuti, the Harts – John is an okapi biologist and Terese is a forest ecologist – have begun the first serious study of the elusive forest relative of the giraffe called the okapi, which is found only in this region of Zaire.

Due to our difficulties in western Zaire, we are already a day late, and at the airstrip at Mambasa, about forty miles east of Epulu, the missionaries tell us in reproving tones that the Harts had made the five-hour round trip yesterday for nothing, that we must go to the center of town and hitch a ride on one of the trading trucks that also serve as buses in this area. And so, at noon, we find ourselves set down in the shade of a big mango, with plenty of time to observe the village life of these Babila Bantu. The soft-voiced courtesy of village people is the other side of the insecure loud rudeness in the towns, and we have hardly arrived when two little boys are sent out with wood chairs for the visitors; our benefactor never appears.

From across the way drifts the smell of cooking fires. Pale maize in sheaves is drying on the thatch of rectangular small huts of daub-and-wattle. To the sound of chickens, and yellow weavers in the palms, two young women with upright hair in sprigs, using hardwood pestles and an old wood mortar, pound bitter manioc into white flour with alternating thumps, thrusting out colorful kanga-clad behinds on every stroke. Nearby, the men chop new bamboo for a hut with a bamboo frame, lashing the cross-pieces to the uprights with green palm fronds. The panga chop and pestle thump fall into rhythmic counterpoint of bursts of laughter, hoots, and noonday squalling. The cheerful faces belie the depredations of both Simba rebels and government soldiery, some twenty years ago, when most of the priests and missionaries of this region fled or were massacred, and the starving people went into hiding in the bush. The last Simba war chief, with his Mbuti guide, was captured in the forest in 1970, and both were shot here in Mambasa's street.

Along the road trundle big bicycles with heavy cargoes; on their head the women tote big shallow bowls of aluminum or tin filled with food or washing. Umbrellas, popular all year round as shelter from cascading rains and equatorial sun, set off a bright new *kikwembe*, the all-purpose wrap-around cloth used as a garment throughout eastern Africa.

A red truck does not stop for us. Two hours pass. High sun and soaring cumulus, bright clothes spread to dry on the fresh grass.

From the well, in single file, comes a line of little girls, each with a container on her head. "*Nyayo Polo*," they sing in wistful harmony as the child bringing up the rear chants in hard counterpart, "*Nyayo Polo!*" The tallest girl, who leads, is Polo. Follow Polo!

In early afternoon, a trucker agrees to carry us westward to Epulu. He is a strong man, bare to the waist, and he wears a towel prizefighter-style around his neck. When Jonah inquires in Swahili how long it will take to reach Epulu, he answers shortly, "It takes time." He is intent on a flirtatious young woman passenger, but his interest is not romantic. "*Citoyenne*," he insists in a low voice, hard hand extended, and she flounces a little in contempt before she comes up with the fare. Most of these traders on the road, and the shopkeepers, too, are of the Nande, an energetic Sudanic tribe of the foothills to the east who moved down into this depopulated region after the Simba Rebellion to prey upon the mission-softened natives.

I climb onto the cargo and arrange myself to enjoy the journey, much as I did twenty-five years ago, traveling south through Sudan. My *compagnons de voyage* are a noisy band of local people, and the cargo consists of oil drums, shovels, sacks of maize flour and manioc, plantains, a wood peanut huller, and a tethered cockerel, bill gaped wide in fear and thirst. The truck jolts forward to a roadblock set up by the Zairois soldiery for the main purpose of extracting some sort of livelihood from all who pass.

Jolting and trundling through potholed hill country, the truck comes up behind a funeral procession. The driver nudges into the procession, which is led by a chanting semi-naked shaman in a long-tailed fur cap, waving a long fur strip to the beat of drums, and dancing in a continuous slow circle in front of a coffin draped in new blue *kikwembes*. When the crowd will not part for it, the truck takes its place in the procession, grinding along for fifteen minutes in low gear. The mourners turn off on a path into the forest as the sky behind us darkens, with first gusts of a wind that will bring rain.

A man steps from the forest, holding a dead guenon by the tail; the passengers shout and bargain with him, but nobody buys his monkey meat. When the rain comes, a tarp is lashed across the frame over cargo and passengers, and we lurch on, along the deeply rutted road. The truck stops again when a Land-Rover headed eastward turns around; John Hart and a friend, Rick Peterson, have come to meet us. The truck passengers help unload our gear, which includes provisions for the Harts, and we continue westward on this rain-filled main road across Africa that is all but impassable in the rainy season.

Outside the village of Epulu, two small figures carrying spears trot along ahead of us. They jump sideways into the roadside grass and smile and wave hard as we pass. John Hart, an ebullient redhead, thirty-five years old, yells out to them in greeting, and I see that they aren't boys at all but short-legged little men of the Mbuti, called Bambuti by the Bantu cultivators.

Until recently it was supposed that the Mbuti were driven south from the savannas by the expansion of those Bantu peoples who followed the rivers into the forests, probably as a consequence of population pressure or because of prolonged drought; today it is thought by the Harts and others that the two peoples arrived together. The Bantu probably brought agriculture here about four thousand years ago, perhaps in a dry period when this region was not forest but savanna woodland; very likely the Ituri was uninhabited before that time. But unlike the Mbuti, the so-called forest Bantu have never become acclimated to the forest. They maintain their clearings and their bare swept village yards as a defense not only against snakes but against the overwhelming trees, with their darkness and malevolent night spirits. Even a sophisticated Zairois writer dreads the forest: "Anyone venturesome enough to try to blaze a trail through it would soon beat a hasty retreat. Everyone who knows it well – hunters, medicine men – never strays more than a short distance beyond the clearings . . . Whatever the legends may say, hunting expeditions and incantations of witchcraft never take place very far from settled areas . . . Even to its most intimate acquaintances, the proud forest reveals itself only through a few clearings scattered along its periphery."*

We stop at Bosco's Okapi Sport Hotel and Bar for some cold beer, then head downriver to the Hart camp, where we are met by Terese Hart – called Terry – John's sister Nina, the young Hart daughters, Sarah and Rebekah, and a crowd of friendly and enthusiastic Pygmies. Glad to be in the Ituri at last, we sit down happily to a warm supper of plantains, rice, and manioc greens cooked with bits of fish from the Epulu River. In this dry season, collared pratincoles fly like terns along the river and African cormorants sit like sentinels on the dark rocks.

The camp is preparing to set off for five days in the forest to the north, where the Harts hope to find a promising location for okapi study. With Rick Peterson, a

---

* S. Diallo, *Zaire Today* (Paris: Editions j.a., 1977).

young anthropology student born in Zaire and raised by missionary parents in Equateur Province to the west, Nina Hart and seven-year-old Sarah will start out a day early, in order to cut Sarah's long trek in half. Because I am still a little lame and because I am anxious to get into the forest, and because Rick Peterson, who is fluent in the Zairian lingua franca called Lingala, can translate for me with the Mbuti, I shall accompany the advance party. Led by a young Mbuti hunter named Atoka, we will join a large group of his tribesmen at their hunting camp on the Lelo River, meeting Jonah Western and the Harts at the Ekare River camp the following day.

Before it slips away into the forest, our path traverses slash-and-burn farm plots dominated by lone trees. By the path is an old calabash wrapped in rotten netting under a shelter of banana leaves, beside which hang a hippo tooth, a piece of wood with a crucifix scratched on it, and a strange wrinkled black fruit. I wonder what the local missionaries would make of this Christianized *dawa*, or medicine, concocted to keep thieves out of the garden; the netting will carry the corpse of the transgressor who does not take warning, says Atoka.

Like the other Mbuti men, Atoka carries little besides the hunting net draped in hanks across his shoulders. With quick small steps, his wife, Masumba, humps along beneath a cargo basket braced by a bark tumpline, an infant riding on her shoulders. The other diminutive women are similarly equipped, for the head cargoes borne with such elegance by the village women are not practicable here on forest paths. Once in the trees, away from judgmental Bantu eyes, the women go bare-breasted; a few wear only a small loin string in order to move more freely in the humid heat.

The path, though ancient and well worn, is narrow and overgrown, and the people keep in touch with one another with loud whoops and hootings, which also serve to push elephants and buffalo and leopards from their path. So close to Epulu, there is little sign of elephant or other creatures, and the whooping is mostly an expression of sheer exuberance and joy at the return into the forest.

At a slow, clear stream, Atoka fashions a fresh green-leaf cup, and we drink gratefully. A monkey hurtles through the branches. There are three species of colobus here, six guenon species, two mangabeys, the chimpanzee, and the olive baboon, but so close to the road they are all heavily hunted. We will see more tomorrow, Atoka says. Soon we come across the first footprint of an elephant, which he believes passed about three weeks ago, to judge from dried mud scraped on a sapling. "This is our soap," he says of the gritty river clay. Farther on, he finds the first hoofprint of okapi, though this print, too, is more than a week old.

In his lyrical and elegiac book *The Forest People* (which is dedicated to Atoka's father, Kenge), the anthropologist Colin Turnbull, who worked here at Epulu in the fifties, perceived the Mbuti as hunter-gatherers who could survive entirely on forest products and whose independent culture was threatened by the demands of the agricultural Bantu, "a rather shifty lazy lot who survived the ravages of Tippu Tib's slave-traders by treachery and deceit." But John Hart, who did a master's thesis on Mbuti hunting and economy based on research done in the Ituri from 1973 to 1975, no longer believes that the Mbuti survived on hunting and gathering in the forest, since for most of the year primary forest cannot supply them with sufficient calories. (He points out that during the sixties, when waves of invading soldiery stripped Bantu gardens, many Mbuti also starved to death.) What he found was a complex symbiotic situation of "cultural reciprocity", in which the Mbuti were in close economic and cultural relation with the forest Bantu. The government encourages them to put in gardens, but as Turnbull remarks of any Mbuti project undertaken outside the forest, it rarely amounts to more than "a lot of noise and big ideas". Terry Hart says, "They realize the value of a garden, and they have the strength and enthusiasm to chop down trees, but they very rarely follow through. They work hard in the Bantu gardens, slashing and burning and at harvest time, but rarely keep up the few gardens of their own."

Both Harts believe that the Mbuti have always led a nomadic rural life in community with the agricultural peoples, who provide them with iron tools, tobacco, and vegetables in exchange for day labor in the fields, hunted meat and honey, mushrooms, forest medicines, thatching, and firewood. The Mbuti are also depended on for sacred songs and dances, propitiary sacrifices, and ceremonies at funerals, marriages, and other rites of passage, being thought of as closer than the Bantu to the old ancestral roots and still in touch with forest spirits that the Bantu – but not the Mbuti – fear. The Mbuti, in turn, depend upon the Bantu to organize their own weddings and funerals, and regulate quarrels. Their relations are mainly amiable, even though the Bantu dismiss the Mbuti as inferiors – undisciplined and undependable wild flighty creatures, woefully lacking in social or political structure. (Unlike the traditional villagers, the new "road culture" Bantu have few dealings with the Mbuti, whom they disdain as "barbarians" and "wild animals".) Among themselves, the irreverent Mbuti use similar terms for the superstitious Bantu, at whom they have a tendency to laugh.

"The Mbuti like money like everybody else," John Hart says, "but when they want to go back to the forest, no amount of money can stop them. That's what I like about them – that devil-may-care quality, so rarely seen among the Bantu. They are happy to sell you their good spear even though they may need it the next day. But if they are capricious, they are also free; they swoop in and out like birds, they never worry about tomorrow. That lack of forethought and dependability can make dealing with them pretty exasperating, but they make up for it in many other ways. Without them, in fact, it would be impossible to work here in the forest."

The Harts are both bright, cheerful people with pragmatic determination to make things work, despite the logistical frustrations of operating in Zaire. John came here originally with the encouragement of Colin Turnbull, and Terry as a Peace Corps volunteer. After they married, in 1977, she became a student of forest ecology with emphasis on botany, and John turned to wildlife biology; both received their PhDs last year. They communicate with the Mbuti in *ki-ngwana*, a breezy version of Swahili used in Haut-Zaïre (and not always comprehensible to Jonah Western, who speaks the classical Swahili of the Tanzania coast), and they share a sincere affection for Africans in general and the Mbuti people in particular. In return, they have won the approval of the Mbuti, who help them gladly whenever helping suits them.

In his years in the Ituri Forest in the mid-seventies and again in the early eighties, John Hart had only a few glimpses of the okapi, about whose natural history almost nothing is known, and Jonah and I have no serious hopes of seeing one. The animal is wary and elusive, despite its large size and boldly patterned legs and high striped haunches – a very odd creature altogether, with its long hyenoid head and a long pink giraffe tongue it uses to pluck leaves at the stem rather than browse them. Probably the one okapi we shall see is the young captive female at the government's Okapi Station at Epulu, where holding pens for zoo-bound animals were set up originally back in the twenties by an eccentric Harvard man named Patrick Putnam – the original settlement here was called "Camp Putnam" – and are now being refitted for a capture project by the Miami Zoo.

What the Harts hope to do after finding a good location is to capture a few okapi in leaf-covered pit traps, fit them with radio collars, then release and follow them, in the hope that eventually they will become tolerant of human proximity if not human company and reveal some of their habits in the wild.

Understandably the Harts are eager to get their study under way before the Ituri is overrun by local gold panners and ivory poachers, and by the inevitable European interests to which Zaire's compliant president has already granted huge timber leases in the forests to the west. At the moment, John says, there are still very few guns in this remote region, and the disruption caused by gold panners may be more serious than the occasional incursion by armed poachers, though the increasing scarcity of local elephants would tend to belie this. What they would like to see – and intend to promote – is a national park in the Epulu region. The Maiko Park in the Maniema Forest to the south is supposed to shelter the okapi and the elusive Congo peacock, but it exists mostly on paper and has no funds for anti-poaching measures, nor even much evidence that the two creatures it is set up to protect are there.

The Lelo camp of sixteen or seventeen leaf huts is set in a rough circle in a forest glade near the Lelo River. The round or oval bun-shaped huts, which are made in a few hours, are higher and more open than the huts of the Babinga Pygmies that we saw west of the Ubangi, which were oven-shaped and closed except for the tubular entrance on one side. No fresh leaves have been added since the last hunting trip, two months before, but one woman weaves big round arrowroot leaves into a new latticework of saplings stuck into the ground, then bent and lashed together over her head, deftly locking each leaf by pinning it with its own stem. Leaves of another arrowroot are used for plates and wrapping food packets, and both species are gathered into the women's baskets as the people move along the forest paths, together with wild fruits and tubers, medicines, and the lianas used for netting twine and basket weaving.

In mid-afternoon, the hunters have not yet returned. There are only naked infants and old women, puppies, a few chickens, a soft murmuring in the fire smoke and sun shafts. Every little while the oldest woman calls out in a deep resonant voice "*UAO-ba-hey!*" She is summoning the hunters home. "This is the forest," Atoka explains. "We must be together." And soon small men appear out of the trees, two here, three there, nets folded like great hoods on their heads. Some carry the spears once used for killing elephants, others have tiny two-foot bows with poisoned arrows, used for birds and monkeys. Each man comes to us quietly, extending a shy hand; some make a little bow. Soon there are a dozen men in camp, and more will come.

"*Tata akumi, nzala esili, esili,*" sing the women. The father has come, hunger has ended.

The hunting has been poor, just two blue duiker, pretty little blue-gray forest antelope with big dark eyes gone glassy in death. The duikers are dressed, singed on the fire, cut up and cooked in bent-rimmed blackened pots. Besides metal blades and cheap Chinese flashlights with dead batteries, the pots are the only road-culture implements in camp. The women scrape manioc and forest tubers, including a wild yam. *Etaba*, they call it, "the potato of our Ancestors", known long before the true potato (and manioc, plantains, and maize) were brought to Africa from the New World during the centuries of the great slave trade. Rick Peterson asks if the people ever planted this "potato" (I had noticed taro planted outside the clearing) and Atoka shakes his head. "*Ye moko aloni yanga,*" he answers in Lingala. *Ye* – "He Himself," meaning the Forest – grew it. The Mbuti speak pidgin Swahili and Lingala, but among themselves they use ki-Mbira, the tongue of the Bambira people east of Epulu. "Ki-Mbuti and ki-Mbira are the same," they say, unaware that their own language was lost long ago.

Each household cooks separately, over a separate fire; some fires have a rack built over them, for drying meat. All are in easy speaking distance of one another, and the older hunters sit with their wives by the opening of their huts, close as two birds. The men fashion chairs of four stout sticks bound in a bundle with vine thongs, then spread in a four-legged seat platform. The younger men gather in the center of the glade, laughing and talking as the children and small hunting dogs wander through. The dogs glean a meager living from the human leavings, and are struck almost every time they come in reach.

The sun is falling now, only the treetops all around are still in sunlight, and the fire smoke that drifts toward the blue sky. The noisy camp, well fed, fills with wellbeing. This is the Mbutis' world; no Bantu come here.

Men and women alike, in their spare moments, work at the manufacture of the nets that are the foundation of the hunting life. (Hunting with nets is not confined to the Mbuti, nor do all Pygmy groups resort to it; it is practiced by a Bantu group in Equateur Province, says Rick Peterson, but not by the Babinga Pygmies who were our trackers in Central African Republic.) The inner bark of a euphorbia liana is stripped off in lengths, dried in the fire smoke, then rolled hard on the thigh, after which it is spliced to greater lengths and rolled again into a hard green twine, gathered in hanks. "One can climb into the trees with it," the people say admiringly, though in fact even large duikers break through the nets. The twine is manufactured by both sexes, and the hunters weave it into mesh, then string it with shiny amber seeds from another euphorbia favored by duikers, the better to attract them.

This is the first return to Lelo and the first hunt in two months; therefore offerings and propitiation must be made to the Mangese ya Pori – the Ancients of the Forest, the Ancestors, or "Those Who Were Here Before Us" – to ensure the success of the hunt. At dark, the hunters erect an altar table of fresh saplings in the forest, laying their hunting nets before the altar on the forest floor. An elder, Asumani, chants the names of the Ancestors, tossing cooked rice furnished by the white people in the four directions; after each name, the hunters, seventeen or more, grunt in deep soft voices, "*Nyama!*" which in both Swahili and Lingala means wild animal, or meat. Chanting the names of Ancestors and spirits will summon up the beneficence of the forest.

Asumani has given us his hut; he and his old wife will sleep beside the fire. We protest that there is no need, that we are happy to sleep outside, but Atoka tells us that to refuse him would be rude.

Though the night is clear, there is thunder from the north; rain comes and goes. Cheerfully the people blame the rain on the thoughtless children who slapped the water while playing in the river. Tomorrow, they say, we shall all go to better hunting grounds on the Ekare River. Exhilarated, the men hoot and whoop, bursting out loudly and spontaneously throughout the evening; often they make a loud hollow report by cupping one hand and smiting an air pocket made by holding the elbow to the chest. Rain, embers, stars. A man gets up and dances joyfully from fire to fire, to make the people laugh, and women are singing brief, wistful songs that seem to echo the haunting birdcalls from the forest.

Before daybreak arises a great shift and murmur, some loud spitting. Infants are restless, somebody whoops, another person takes advantage of the quiet to vent a grievance, the whole camp is laughing at some shouted joke. Laughter is constant; at one fire or another it springs up and ripples around the circle of leaf huts. Soon the women, tending the plantains laid into the embers, are splicing into twine the shredded bark dried at the fire overnight, while the hunters mend and weave new mesh into their nets before folding them neatly for the journey.

We start off early, led by the elder Omudi, a tiny man who looks surprised and worried at the same time; Omudi wears his net in two drapes over his shoulders and a loop in front, like a churchman's cowl. Vines have overgrown the path, which is very old, the people say; perhaps it was made by elephants, since it was here even before the Ancestors. Omudi opens up the path with little neat clips of his panga, making low tunnels through the undergrowth at just the right head height for a man scarcely more than four feet tall. In other places the understory is open, revealing the trunks of the great trees that forge upward toward the glints of sky above. By comparison to the lowland forests in Gabon and C.A.R., this part of the Ituri Forest seems smaller, drier, more like an immense woodland than tropical jungle. The dominant plants, besides the euphorbias, are the leguminous *Caesalpiniaceae* and the milky-sapped sapotes, which include the gutta percha rubber trees sought by the Belgians.

Within the hour the others overtake us, for the Mbuti have few possessions and travel light. All but the youngest are self-propelled, running to keep up with the quick pace, and most will lug something, if only a leaf packet of food. The men carry their nets and weapons, and the women bear embers wrapped in heavy leaves and food-filled fire-blackened pots, mortars and pestles, and leg-trussed chickens on broad basket tops.

Everyone goes barefoot but two lepers; these men wear old European street shoes not because they are ashamed of their diseased feet but because their soles hurt. In recent years, the traditional bark-cloth aprons of the hunters have been replaced by hand-me-down boys' shirts and shorts from the bales of old clothes sent by church groups to the Third World, and bought from the depots by Zairois entrepreneurs who resell them at a great profit to the Pygmies. A hunter known as Avion wears the black remnant of an Apple Computer

T-shirt; another has a kid's gray sweatshirt that reads PITTSBURGH STEELERS.

The Mbuti delight in Sarah Hart, a fair-haired child of seven in lemon T-shirt and sky blue pack who flits along the path like a forest butterfly. Where we cross a log over a stream, the Mbuti women, wading the ford above, call out to her "Salah! Salah!" and she runs off to catch up with them. Sarah, who returned here with her parents a few weeks ago, is not at home yet, and I wonder how long it will be before she realizes that her own kind are nowhere to be seen, that she is alone in the dark forest with little folk whose tongue she cannot speak. Soon I hear her voice raised in apprehension, and I come upon her around a corner of the path, mouth wide, eyes round, not far from tears. "I was a little scared," she says. I bend to give her a reassuring hug, and she puts her arms around my neck. Later I come upon another little girl, this one leaf brown, scarcely three. She has run her small nude body to a standstill and now waits, thumb in mouth, beside the leafy trail, calm in the knowledge that she is safe here in the forest, that someone will be along who will gather her up.

In an overgrown camp by the Bougpa spring, an hour north of Lelo, are big marijuana plants ready for harvest. A hunter walks over, plucks some sticky leaves and smiles, murmuring "*bangi*". Soon women appear, fires are started, the old huts swept out with leaf brooms, the dooryard weeds chopped down to the red earth. From somewhere comes an immense pipe, a hollowed plantain stem longer than the reclining men, who tamp the resinous leaves and inflorescence into the clay bowl. Embers are laid upon the top, and the pipe moves slowly around the circle.

One of the Bougpa huts has been demolished by an elephant, and nearby there is fresh elephant sign, perhaps seven or eight prints and a few droppings. I am inspecting the first one when a hunter overtakes me. "*Tembo*," I say, and he says, "*Bongo*." Excited, I peer all about for tracks of the beautiful big forest antelope, and the hunter laughs. Both words mean elephant. "Ki-Swahili *tembo*," he explains, "ki-Mbuti *bongo*" (pronounced *bawn-go*). When he says ki-Mbuti, he means ki-Mbira, though the Pygmies speak this Bantu tongue in the singsong Mbuti way.

Soon the hunters decide that Ekare is too far, it will be too late to make a hunt after arriving, we must hunt here at Bougpa and continue on to Ekare tomorrow. When I suggest that our own small party proceed to Ekare, from where the Harts hope to begin a reconnaissance tomorrow, Omudi says no, the people must stay together. Quickly, without discord, everyone rises to go. Ekare is not far after all, the people say, it has good hunting, the men can make a quick hunt there this afternoon.

Even when nearing the Ekare region, the hunters maintain a continual hooting and shouting, slipping along in swift single file on the shadowed path. "Come on! Let's go! It's a long way to the camp! There we can rest!" – these are the sort of things that they are calling. Sometimes they imitate birds and animals – chimpanzees, hornbills, duikers. They say that this din does not scare away the animals, not even elephants, which only withdraw from the smoke of human fires. Like all else, fire comes from the great forest, to cook the forest food and provide warmth, and to warn the leopard.

The Ekare camp, in a glade on the ridge above the river, is hidden from the sky by the high canopy. There has been rain here. The huts are rotten but soon they are swept out, and transparent fire smoke drifts on the sunlit air. Everything is done swiftly, and easily, yet these easygoing people are never idle even when sitting by the fire but are always working something with their hands.

In early afternoon, the Harts and Western arrive from Epulu with a new group of Mbuti led by Kenge. The people call Jonah Piloto and they call me Mangese, meaning Venerable One, as in Mangese ya Pori, the Ancients of the Forest. Though not yet sixty, I am an elder by African standards. I feel honored by my title and approximately as pleased as I was when a withered old Bandaka woman came out of her hut as we left Epulu, pointing at me and crying out, "Take care of him, for he is old like me!"

In the five-hour walk north from Epulu Jonah reports, all they have seen are a few monkeys, high in the canopy. As an East African ecologist Jonah is accustomed to large numbers of large mammals, readily studied; in the forest, as we have learned throughout this journey, large mammals are uncommon and elusive, and difficult to observe even when found. "I'm glad to have come to Central Africa, glad to have seen the rain forest," he says, "because it's one of the most neglected biomes, and one of the most important. But I could never work in forest. So much time is necessary to gather so little information!"

Jonah is particularly disheartened by the relative scarcity of elephant sign in an undamaged habitat where poaching has apparently been minimal: "We must assume, contrary to our hopes, that in large regions of the Congo Basin there are scarcely any." The elephant's decline must be partly attributable to hunting, but John Hart says there are few guns in the villages. As for the Mbuti, they take what they need in the way of food and medicines but affect the forest life scarcely at all.

More and more it seems apparent that unbroken rain forest is inhospitable habitat for large mammals. Except along the water courses, or in clearings made by the fall of a giant tree, the available food is mostly in the canopy, far out of reach of okapi and gorilla as well as elephant. In the absence of elephants, which modify the forest by creating and perpetuating second growth, other animals are bound to be scarce as well. Jonah concludes that, while high human impact will impoverish the forest, moderate impact in the form of shifting cultivation – that is, slash and burn – creates a good deal of secondary forest that is accessible to animals, and that a patchwork of primary and secondary forest is the optimum condition for prosperity as well as diversity in animal populations. ("Low human population is essential if this is to work," John Hart observes. "Higher populations assure impoverished forest no matter which farming technique is used.")

Increasingly Jonah is fascinated by the impact of man on the environment, which in his view is not always destructive to its wildlife and can, in fact, be very beneficial. In the sixties, he says, European and American biologists turned to the African savannas as the last great natural bastion of primeval life, unchanged since the Pleistocene; they held to the traditional view that this stability, providing time for evolution, was a condition for speciation and diversity, which accounted for the great variety of savanna life. Jonah concludes that, on the contrary, the savanna is a patchwork of different habitats, and is always changing, having been modified for thousands of years not only by fires and elephants but by man. John Hart has learned that a layer of charcoal two thousand years old underlies much of this region – good evidence of a dry savanna period, and of fires set by human hunters. In South America, there is evidence of fires twenty to thirty thousand years old, and comparable evidence may yet turn up in Africa. Dr Jan Reitsma, the botanist who accompanied us to Wonga-Wongue, in Gabon, had pointed out that, structurally, tropical rain forests in South America and Africa are very similar, but that while undisturbed forest in South America is still plentiful, Africa has scarcely any. Not only man but the large herbivores have modified African forests, and the greatest modifier is the elephant.

In Dr. Western's view, man has always had a profound impact on savanna systems, ever since he burned off the first grassland to improve hunting. "Remember that savanna woodland between Garamba and Bangassou? Hundreds of miles of what looked like wonderful wildlife habitat, without any sign of human impact – where were the animals? I very much doubt if the complete absence of wildlife was entirely attributable to overhunting. When man and his fires disappeared, the wildlife declined, too. One can't say that man's activities are 'good' for wildlife, but neither are they always bad, and this is particularly apparent in the forest."

Tree burning restores minerals to the old soils for a few years, but it destroys the specialized fungi known as mycorrhizae that are critical to forest growth. Where large populations of primitive agriculturalists burn down the forests, as in the derived savannas seen in Gabon and western Zaire (and also throughout West Africa), the destruction must lead to flood, erosion, and degraded land on which only a few pest species can survive. (This is a necessary consequence, not of intense settlement but of poor land use; large populations have lived off certain Asian lands for thousands of years.)

But where humans are few, and the burning moderate, gorillas as well as elephants are drawn to second growth; abandoned clearings, which the elephants maintain, sustain many other birds and animals. Similarly, disruption and change through fires, floods, and landslides, the silting of deltas, the meanderings of rivers, even big trees crashing down and creating clearings – all these produce a patchwork of habitats that increases diversity of life, since it prevents dominance by a few species. This is why life in the open light of river margins, with thick growth accessible from the ground, is so much richer than in primary forests between rivers, which are almost empty.

The following day, while Rick and I go hunting with the Mbuti, Jonah accompanies the Harts on a reconnaissance of the Itoro River to the north, where elephant sign is more abundant and a good deal fresher, not only in secondary forest but along the drainage lines. But even here, "as far from humanity and habitat destruction as one could get", poachers had left their slash marks in the undergrowth, and Kenge told him that the elephants were far less numerous than they were ten years ago. Even so, he does not feel that enough elephants remain here to create habitat that would support a larger population. If the Ituri may be taken as a rough gauge of elephant numbers in wilderness regions of Zaire, then, as in Gabon and C.A.R., that number cannot significantly exceed one animal every two square kilometers, in a rain forest already more reduced in size than we had anticipated. If anything, Douglas-Hamilton's rough estimates of forest elephant numbers – the most conservative in general circulation, and the ones we expected to corroborate – are much too high.

The Mbuti were once famous elephant hunters, popularly supposed to run under an elephant and drive spears into it from beneath. "They had to work close, using jabbing spears, but I doubt if they did that very often," John Hart says. "They're the ultimate opportunists; they would bring it down any way they could." Elephant hunting died out in the early seventies, with the decline of the elephant itself, and the only Mbuti who go after them today are those who serve poachers as gun bearers and trackers. ("We hunt neither elephant nor okapi," Kenge says, trying not to laugh, "because that is against the law." However, an okapi slowed down by the nets would almost certainly be killed and eaten. "Very good, too," says Terry Hart, with a charming smile.)

The hunters return in late afternoon with four blue duiker, not enough to feed our growing camp. There are twenty-six huts at Ekare, most of them occupied; there must be sixty people here in all. Sibani the Leper, one of several Pygmies more yellow in skin color than brown, can no longer tend his net due to sore feet, but he has a big bright yellow-green-and-black monitor lizard that he shot with his bow and arrow. With glee, he describes the fury of the finish: "I jumped right into the water with my pants on!" At supper I accept his offer of fresh lizard meat, only to be told, once I had started, that I could not have antelope as well, since mixing the two might jinx tomorrow's hunt.

Toward dark, Omudi makes a lengthy speech about how the people have come back to Ekare thanks to John Hart. "We're here in the forest to be happy!" he cries. "No anger! We're here to be happy! Anybody who has a bad spirit, keep it in town!" And the people seem happy, even those who had wished to linger at the Bougpa camp.

Slowly, as the evening passes, the men begin to sing, keeping time with fire-hardened sticks and an old plastic oil container as a drum. The simple harmonies, rising and falling away like strong quiet fire, are intensified by choruses and clapping and the counterpoint of solo voices, in an effect intensely subtle and sophisticated, despite the repetition of the simple lyrics. "Let us all sing this song" – or, better, put ourselves into this song, be one with this song. Or "I didn't eat; other people ate." Or "The food we put out for the Ancestors got eaten by the dogs." For often there is humorous intent, especially in the love songs: "If you can't climb the buo tree [a tall, straight-trunked relative of the elms without lower limbs], forget my daughter." There are also hunting songs, and honey songs and dances, especially in August, when the brachystegia trees come into blossom and honey becomes the most sought-after item of diet. "Go out with your lover and spend the day beneath the honey tree" is a song of explicit and joyful sexuality, with vivid gestures of a honeyed arm thrusting in and out of the hive.

All songs are implicitly sacred. "The forest gives us this song," the people say, meaning, "The forest *is* this song."

Another night, a man named Gabi dances slowly with a bow, tapping the bowstring with a stick, using his mouth at one end of the string to achieve resonance. Later he dances as Dekoude the Trickster, a masked green figure bound head to toe in leaves who gets people lost in the deep forest. Soon the girls and women rise to dance, in an intricate pattern in and out of a half-hoop of stiff liana that one of their number, seated on the ground, raises and lowers on the waves of music. Before each culminating leap, each woman holds her hand out over the ground and sings, "Before I am given another child, this one must be as tall as this!" Each time this is said, the women laugh loudly at the men.

The best dancer and best singer in the camp is Atoka's sister Musilanji, who is lighthearted and bursting with life. According to John, she is much in demand among the truckers and other Bantu in the villages, and, not being possessed of a grudging character that might permit her to say no, she has contracted syphilis along the way. As a strong and beautiful solo voice in both the women's group and men's, Musilanji sings with all her heart, and later, after everyone has crawled into their huts, she laughs with the same all-out spirit at the dirty jokes of old Sibani, laughing until she rolls upon the ground, gasping for breath, laughing until she hurts and squeals for mercy, her passionate abandon so infectious that, stretched out in our leaf hut across the circle, unable to understand a single word, I laugh hard, too.

Before daybreak, the cries of forest animals awake the camp, and the din intensifies, with staccato arm claps, as the men make ready to set off on the hunt. Over the breakfast fire, Kenge says, "It is all joy, it is making the *mangese* of the forest happy," and his sister-in-law Asha nods agreement. Kenge, a handsome, serious man, now gives a speech, reminding the hunters that they must no longer kill okapi or elephant, that any outsider found in the forest with a snare must be arrested, that nets are all right because the People come and go and do not harm the forest life.

There is something chastened about Kenge, who is no longer the lighthearted young hunter to whom Colin Turnbull's book was dedicated a quarter-century ago. He is now an elder, and he takes himself seriously, and is taken seriously, for everyone knows that his picture appeared in a book. In camp, though he laughs at us with all the others, he sits in a chair with his arms folded, talking mostly to Asha, who cooks for the whites, and keeping himself subtly aloof, as if, at ease in neither world, he was fated to mediate between the groups. "Kenge knows he is somebody," says John Hart sympathetically, "but he doesn't quite know who."

Atoka is all nerved up for the hunt. With great finesse and delicacy, and sounds to match, he mimes the approach, the rush at the net, the finish of the big yellow-backed duiker he intends to kill. His arms and pointed fingers dart in imitation of the antelope's quick legs and sharp hooves, he claps his arm with a loud hollow report to alert the others that his duiker has been netted, he squats, he leaps, grabbing one leg of the animal and twisting it over on its back, screeching in triumph even as he demonstrates how the others will come running with their spears.

Dodging driver ants, Rick Peterson and I cross the Ekare on a dead tree and follow the path into the forest, where we come upon a small unattended fire that one of the hunters had gone out earlier to prepare. Here Atoka drops his net and summons the Ancestors to witness this offering of precious fire to the forest and the purification of the hunters in its smoke; if the forest is contented, all will go well in the hunt. One by one the hunters come, squat down, let the smoke bathe them. Tambo holds a leaf over the smoke, then rubs his chest with it. The men smoke bangi, "to give them strength and get them ready," says Atoka. We rise and go.

Moving off the path into the forest, the hunters are quiet and keep signals to a minimum; in the thick cover, each man seems to know just where to go. Already some are stringing out their nets, unwinding the long coils from their shoulders as they run deftly through the understory, then returning along the line to raise the net and hang it firmly on shrub branches and saplings, taking pains to see that the bottom edge is firm against the earth. Atoka's net, overlapping others at each end, is three to four feet high, seventy-five yards long, and by no means the longest. With twelve hunters, the entire set will be a half kilometer around, enclosing about twenty acres in a semicircle.

Atoka's net overlaps that of Asumani, who nods as we go by. "*Merci*" is a word he has learned to say, and he tries it out quietly in greeting. Already the women are appearing, following around outside the nets to the narrow entrance. A signal comes, they enter and fan out, whooping and calling, each one headed for her husband's sector.

We wait just inside the net, on a log that overlooks a forest gorge. It is Atoka's turn for a poor spot, close to one end; he does not expect much. We listen to a great blue turaco, green pigeons, an unknown cuckoo; a scrub robin flits briefly into view, cocking its head in the thrush manner. Off in the distance, a great tree topples of its own accord – a crack of thunder and an avalanche of matter as a hundred and fifty feet of timber, dragging down vines and lianas, snapping limbs and saplings, tears a long slash in the canopy and thumps the waiting earth. A wave of silence follows, like a forest echo.

The silence is broken by a loud arm clap, for game has been seen near the nets. From the shouts that follow, Atoka learns that a big red duiker, *nge*, has pierced Gabi's net.

Quickly we rise and make another set, not far away. This time an *nge* is entangled. There comes a wild yell from the west, two nets away, and we follow Atoka on a dead run through the trees toward the strange sheep-like bleats of this forest antelope that the hunters imitate so skillfully. The men there ahead of us at Mayai's net have seized the legs of what turns out to be a Peter's red duiker, a species I have never seen. The mesh is freed roughly from its long head and neck as it flops and thrashes, staring up at us with strange blue-filmed night eyes. Without ceremony, Asumani hacks its throat, and at the rush of blood, everyone laughs. Though the forest has given them this food, the hunters are no more reverent toward it than they are to their camp dogs; this irreverence, rare among traditional peoples, seems curious in the light of the earlier propitiation of the forest. "*Ekoki*," they say to us, and "*malamu*". Both words mean "good".

Returning to fetch Atoka's net, we pass the deaf man, Poos-Poos, who has the narrow shoulders of a woman and often wears his *kikwembe* tied around his neck, the way a Pygmy woman wears it near the road. Poos-Poos is grieving. A *seke* – a white-bellied duiker – approached his net, then ran away. But later, when the men have gathered after an unsuccessful set, Poos-Poos cheers everyone with a very comic imitation of his drunken self leaving the truck-stop bar, trying to find his way back to the forest, putting twigs in his eyes, butting his head into the tree trunks. The hunters laugh, and laugh still harder when they see that Rick and I are laughing, too. They feel protective about Poos-Poos, who cannot articulate, and often emits weird hoots, shrill cackles; Mayai accounts for him by tapping his ear and then his temple, to indicate why Poos-Poos is incomplete, and when he does this, Poos-Poos, his soft brown eyes wide and round as a lemur's, smiles an enchanted smile, as if blessing us all.

Yet Poos-Poos, able in every chore, has his own net and spear and travels as an equal with the hunters except in rainstorms, when he loses his bearings and has to be led by the hand. He is very kind and popular with the small children, and he is alert, as he has to be, to keep up with the rest in an existence so dependent on good hearing. Poos-Poos is chronically in a high state of tension, and his strange face, slightly askew, is scarred by grievous marks of concentration, pinching his forehead, that are lacking in his lighthearted companions. Perhaps he is not retarded as I had imagined, but on the contrary, atremble with trapped intelligence, wild with frustration.

Slipping through the forest, the hunters see bees moving back and forth, and the hunt is suspended while they search without success for the hive. We cross a pretty tributary brook known as Ekare's Daughter. An elephant has crossed ahead of us, and okapi sign is everywhere. Then the set is made, we wait again, watching a bird party of leafloves and greenbuls that glean the understory foliage, in shafts of sun. Another *nge* and also a blue duiker, *mboloko*, are taken, to great whoops of triumph that drown out the hoots and yelling of the beaters.

In the next set, a blue duiker escapes, nothing is caught. Rain comes. The Mbuti seek out a big tree with heavy lianas, which thicken the canopy above with their own leaves, providing shelter. With his hands idle, Atoka is restless. "This is the work of the Forest," he says. "We hunt, we wait, we get up and go again." So far today he has caught nothing, but he knows that in the partition of the antelopes his family will be given meat. "The first thing we learn is *kosalisa* – to take care of others. We Mbuti do no one any harm. If I sleep hungry, you sleep hungry; if I get something from the forest, you will have it, too."

In the next surround, a heavy animal wheels and crashes away through the thickets just in front of us, and a woman who has seen the creature comes running down the line of nets shouting, "*Moimbo!*" This is the yellow-back, largest of all duikers, up to a hundred and forty pounds. But the rarely caught *moimbo* slips past the line of nets and flees; only a blue duiker is caught. Another blue duiker, on the final hunt, comes to Atoka but pierces his net in an explosive jump at the last second. Atoka does not complain or appear disheartened, and on the way home he remains behind to gather up wood for the fires. This evening we will eat antelope with the others.

The following day three animals are caught. One is a *moimbo* and another is a water chevrotain, not an antelope at all but a relation of the primitive tusked deer of Asia. The *moimbo* was speared by old Pita, and Atoka, with wild snorts and cries, acts out each second of its final moments, to show how the big yellow-back, pierced between the ribs, twisted frantically on Pita's spear, heart pumping.

Even dressed out and cut in pieces, the *moimbo* was too big to fit in Pita's old wife's basket, and Tambo's young wife, asked to help carry the meat, threw a tantrum in the forest, relieving the tensions that build up in an Mbuti camp. She worked herself into a frenzy, screeching and rolling on the ground to insure attention, hurling wild insults at the people in general and her husband in particular. Gentle Tambo, one of the few unexuberant Mbuti, tries to ignore her like everybody else, but after a half-hour, when her drama threatened to disrupt the hunt, he felt obliged to come and beat her. Returning to camp, she started in again, accounting for her behavior with a tearful and aggrieved oration that the people heard out with intense discomfort, after which she took shelter in another hut, among one of the households which, while not rejected, seem subtly excluded from the group that leads the hunting and the singing. (The small family in the hut beside my own, I notice, rarely join in the jokes and banter, which for all I know may be at their expense.) A long, tense silence was broken by some ribald observation that collapsed the whole circle of huts in grateful laughter, after which camp life proceeded in the same gay and offhand way as it had before.

On the first of February we left Ekare, walking straight south to Epulu, about fifteen kilometers away. At the Bougpa spring, black colobus monkeys were making their deep rolling racket; near Lelo two big red colobus, long tails hanging like question marks, sprang into the bare limbs of a high tree to watch us pass. Kenge, who helps Terry Hart with her botanical collections, identified various fruits and medicines along the way, including an orange shelf fungus used by the Mbuti to cure diarrhea. He pointed out odd termite nests like huge gray mushrooms in the tree roots, and the orange paste spat out by fruit bats, and a place where the forest hid the People from the successive waves of soldiers, rebels, and mercenaries who pillaged and murdered in this region in the first years after independence.

On the night of our return there was an *elima*, or girl's initiation ceremony, and the sound of drums and chanting came from the Mbuti camp along the road east of Epulu. Later we heard shouting from the Babila village that could only mean trouble, and next morning the local *gendarme* turned up in his crisp green beret and green uniform with red shoulder tabs and made a complaint to Terry Hart, who was talking with me on a terrace overlooking the river. Kenge had got drunk and stirred up trouble, and his family had led in a drunken brawl that had ended with the destruction of a Bantu house, and Atoka and the spirited Asha had been jailed, the *gendarme* said. He suggested that their American friends pay for the damages, having brought them back out of the forest where they belonged. The Harts were mistaken in treating the Pygmies like real people, he continued; they should simply be given food and a few rags to wear. As for Atoka, he should be "tortured", said this new African, by which he meant – to judge from prior episodes – beaten bloody with clubs, since there was no other way for him to repay his debts. It turned out that the victim had provoked Atoka by denouncing the Mbuti as "*nyama*", or "wild animals", an opinion in which the *gendarme* fully concurred. The Pygmies had to be treated like the animals they were, he assured Terese Hart, who winced but said nothing. We stared away over the striking rocks that emerge in the dry season from the Epulu River, which winds southwest to the Ituri, the Nepoko, the Arumimi, and a final confluence with the great Congo west of Kisangani.

In Mambasa at daybreak, old Father Louis, who was away in Italy on leave when the Simba rebels killed the other Catholic missionaries at this station, is already up and about, and says good-bye. He has red cheeks and a saintly smile. "I must go to the church," he explains vaguely, waving both hands. From the evangelist mission, we pick up mail to be posted in Nairobi, and at 6:30 a.m. leave the mission strip and fly southeast along the overgrown red road toward Beni, where the huge forest ends at last in a populous agricultural region of small hills. The hills open out over the valley of the Semliki, and from here we can see for a brief time the Ruwenzori peaks, in equatorial snows seventeen thousand feet high, named by Ptolemy the Mountains of the Moon.

Where the Semliki River winds down through Zaire's Virunga Park into Lake Edward, the silver-and-blue plane passes through the Central Highlands. A soft bed of clouds lies on the land between the Virungas and Ruwenzori, but everywhere else the clouds have burned away. Coming out of the dark forest and mountains into the sun of the savanna, the silver plane bursts free into the open air.

In fresh morning light, the plane drifts out across Lake Edward, forty miles wide, with a lone fishing boat far out on the broad shine, and halfway across Jonah turns to look at me. "We are leaving Zaire," he says with a big grin, as relieved as I am to be back in East Africa. (Not long after our return to Nairobi, Kes Smith notified Jonah from Garamba that the Zairian authorities had come hunting for us twice, intending to arrest us on our return journey.)

Until the most recent despot in Uganda restored the old colonial names to lakes and parks in the hope of reassuring frightened tourists, Lake Edward was Lake Idi Amin Dada. (Lake Albert, farther north, is at present Lake Mobutu Sese Seko, though this, too, must pass.) The far shore is the southern part of Ruwenzori National Park, in southwest Uganda, and here we see herds of hippo at the water's edge. The destruction of Uganda's wildlife under Idi Amin was continued by the unpaid and lawless Tanzanian soldiery who helped depose him, but when the Tanzanians left at last, in 1980, an attempt was made to control any further slaughter, and the animals have started to come back. In the past weeks, the latest tyrant had been deposed by the latest reformer, Yoweri Museveni, in whom the desperate Ugandans have great hope, but Uganda was still in a state of anarchy, and we would not land here to refuel.

Like most of the Ugandan landscape that is not under marsh or open water, the land beyond the national park has been cleared of its last trees, and because this soil, the product of volcanoes, is richer than the ancient, leached-out soils beneath the rain forest, it can support a dense agricultural population. (However, it is the rural population in this region of Uganda that more than any other in the world is beset by AIDS.) Farther south, toward the border with Rwanda, the soil pales out into savanna, and the farmers are replaced by a semi-pastoral people with large herds of cattle. Their Maasai-type oven huts and large corrals are enclosed by thornbush to discourage lions.

The savanna land flows on into Rwanda, and Jonah, more and more content, remarks, "It's nice to have the freedom to fly and know that you can land anywhere if you have to." I have the same sense of wellbeing, understanding why he was reluctant to say such things over the forests. To acknowledge the strain would not have helped and might have harmed us.

The plane crosses the soft hills and lakes of Rwanda's Akagera National Park, where a group of young elephants released in 1974 have increased to more than forty. The twenty-sixth and largest of this group was killed after it charged and killed Adrien Deschryver's friend, the photographer Lee Lyon. Jonah descends to a low altitude, and we fly for fun for the first time in weeks; though we see no elephant, we enjoy the hippo and buffalo, eland, topi, and impala, and also a few sitatunga in the papyrus swamps and lakes that stretch away east of the park into Tanzania.

An hour beyond the Tanzania border, boat sails rise from the fishing villages in the archipelago of islands in the southern end of Lake Victoria. White pelicans glide along the shores, and a flock of avocets slides beneath the plane over the silver shimmer of the open water. The inland sea stretches away one hundred and fifty miles into Speke Gulf and the mouth of the Mbalageti River, in the Serengeti

Park, where we can put down almost anywhere to refuel. "From Lake Victoria," Jonah says, "it will be wildlife country all the way into Nairobi."

Over Speke Gulf, Jonah reflects a little on our journey. He feels it was "tough but fantastic", and I agree. In regard to the forest elephant, he has no doubt that both natural densities and the extent of forest habitat are less than the most pessimistic estimates. "We just don't have the reservoir of forest elephants that we were counting on," he says, "which puts even more pressure on the bush elephant to sustain an ivory trade. The bush elephant is already in serious trouble, and because of its role in creating habitat, its disappearance will be followed by a substantial collapse of all of the large mammal fauna, which has already happened in West Africa." These are the findings he will document for presentation to world wildlife authorities to lend weight to conservation arguments, including a campaign to ban the worldwide trade in ivory. Though not good news, it will help end the ivory trade and protect the future of the elephant in Africa.

The Serengeti Plain is a hundred miles across. Flying low over its western reaches, the plane dodges the vultures that attend the endless herds of wildebeest and zebra that scatter away across green grass below. Hyenas in a ditch, a lone male lion. Thousands of wildebeest are streaming across the plain south of the high rock island known as Simba Kopje, near the long road that comes into the park from Ngorongoro and Olduvai Gorge. Nowhere on the Serengeti, in this high tourist season between rains, do we see dust raised by a vehicle, not even one. More ominous still, on a hundred-mile west–east traverse of the whole park, not one elephant is seen where years ago I saw five hundred in a single herd. "Poachers," Jonah said. "The Serengeti elephants are down seventy-five per cent. What's left of them are mostly in the north, toward the Maasai Mara."

In 1961, the Serengeti was my ultimate destination in East Africa; in the winter of 1969, it was my home. We land and refuel at Barafu Kopjes, a beautiful garden of huge pale granite boulders and dry trees, in the clear light, where years ago I accompanied George Schaller on long walks across the plain to learn how primitive humans might have fared in scavenging young, dead, or dying animals. The wind is strong in the black thorn of the acacia, and a band of kestrels, migrated from Europe, fill their rufous wings with sun as they lift from the bare limbs and hold like heralds against the wind on the fierce blue sky.

Then we are aloft again, on a course northeast toward the Gol Mountains, in a dry country of giraffes and gazelles. Olduvai is a pale scar down to the south, in the shadow of the clouds of the Crater Highlands, and soon the sacred volcano called Ol Doinyo Lengai rises ahead, and the deep hollow in the land that is Lake Natron, on the Kenya border. We will fly across Natron and the Athi Plain and be in Nairobi in an hour.

Acknowledgements

In addition to Dr David Western, I am grateful for help and hospitality, instruction, and good company, to almost all those people, black and white, who are mentioned in the book. Dr Richard Carroll and also Drs William Conway and William Weber of the New York Zoological Society provided helpful information and support. Finally my thanks to Mr William Shawn of *The New Yorker*, which paid my share of the considerable expenses of the forest elephant survey made in 1986.

PART 3

Sand Rivers

For Eck and Donnie Eckhart
and
For John Owen

On an early African morning, Brian Nicholson and I set off for the south, wading across the Mbarangandu not far above its confluence with the Luwegu. Climbing the ridges between rivers, we shall follow the game trails for about eight miles, then descend to the Luwegu and continue south for perhaps three days before turning east to explore a high plateau with its own extensive swamp or pan. From the plateau, we shall descend a tributary river that comes down off the west escarpment of the plateau and turns northeast, arriving eventually at the Mbarangandu. There is no good map of this region, and neither the plateau nor the river has a name. As for the pan, Nicholson is the only white man who has ever seen it. Excepting C. P. J. Ionides and Alan Rees, the warden of the western Selous, he is the only white who has ever walked through the vast southern reaches of the Reserve. "This is the heart of the Selous," Brian told me, "and you and I will be the first into most of the country that we're going to cross." if the water has subsided enough in the next fortnight to permit Land Rovers to come upriver, bringing supplies, we shall explore still further south, up the Mbarangandu; otherwise we shall head back downriver, returning to Mkangira in about ten days.

At this place the river is edged by high elephant grass where big animals might be hidden, and as we pass into it and our friends disappear, the laughing young porters fall silent in an instant, as if entering the unknown. For the next hour, as the sun rises and the file of men climbs to the open woodland of the ridge, there is no sound but the tentative duets of barbets and boubous, and the soft whisper of our passage through dry grass.

In crossing the Mbarangandu, leaving behind the tracks and Land Rovers, the tin-roofed game post, the green tents of our camp at Mkangira, we have also left behind all roads, all sign of man, and in doing so, we seem to have entered a new Africa, or rather, "the Old Africa", as Brian calls it: behind the heat and the still trees resounds the ringing that I hear when I am watched by something that I cannot see. "You're getting the feel of it now," he mutters, peering about him, for he, too, has sensed the power and the waiting in the air. "Only people to come this way in years, I reckon; I don't think the bloody poachers have got this far." Years ago, he had laid out a track for patrolling this part of the Mbarangandu, but all that was left was the pathway made by the round wrinkled pads of elephants, in the silent years without sound or smell of man when the huge gray apparitions had followed the abandoned road. The shadow of the road is only visible to the eyes of Goa, and soon it vanishes in the sun and dust.

As tracker and gun bearer, Goa is in the lead, a rifle over his small shoulder with the butt extended toward Brian Nicholson. The gun is a heavy-bore .458 of Belgian make, an "elephant gun", very useful for stopping large charging animals. Goa holds his free hand far out in front of him, as if extending it to be kissed, fingers pointed down as if to dowse the ground before him for the slightest sign or sound or scent of danger; he moves so lightly that he seems to rise ever so slightly off the ground, at the same time craning his head as if to see over tall grasses that, much of the time, are well above his head.

There are six porters, young Ngindo who were recruited from Ngarambe village, just outside the eastern boundary at Kingupira, and behind the porters, making sure that none falls by the wayside, is the young Giriama camp assistant named Kazungu, who will serve as cook. Kazungu did not wish to accompany this foot safari because he thought he would have to carry a load upon his head, like these unsophisticated young Tanzanians; as late as yesterday, he was complaining of an excruciating pain in his right foot, screwing up his lively face for emphasis. But when informed that he would only have to carry his own gear, together with a panga for cutting firewood and brush, he was happy enough to come along; in fact, as I discovered later, he kept an enthusiastic journal of the safari which he and his friend, the Taita mechanic John Matano, translated from Swahili into English and were kind enough to let me use:

> We began our safari at the junction of two rivers, the Luwegu and the Mbarangandu, and the date that I left was the 2nd September 1979. We were eight of us and two Europeans, one as our guide, whose name was Bwana Niki, and the other a book writer from America whose name is Mister Peter. And I was the tenth one, as the cook. One of us was an askari of the bush [the game scout, Goa] so we had no doubt with wild animals. We walked for a number of kilometers until we came to the Luwegu ...

The porters take turns carrying the old-fashioned tent that Brian wished to bring along, despite my feeling that we did not need it. Since I am carrying nothing but binoculars and notebooks, I feel slightly ashamed, whereas Brian is not sheepish in the least. "If I had to carry one of those loads in this sort of heat," he admits cheerfully, "I wouldn't last out the first hour. I've never carried a thing on trek in forty years, and I never shall." What I was hearing wasn't laziness – Nicholson is anything but lazy – but a principle left over from the reign of Ionides, who liked to say, "I never do anything that can be done for me by somebody else."* Brian is proud that all his old safaris were elaborate – far more elaborate, as he says, than this one. "Always had my own tent, of course, with tent fly and camp table and chair, and my gun bearer and cook and a hell of a lot of porters. Sometimes I'd be out five months at a time, so I needed a lot of equipment, but also it was important to be comfortable. Took along whatever I wanted, as a matter of fact. I had one man who just carried books, another who carried a coin chest for buying food in the settlements; the rest carried my personal gear and the food for all the others. On short safaris through settled areas, I had fifteen porters; on long ones through the bush, I would have forty. But once the food started to go, I couldn't have all those people sitting around eating up what was left, so I'd send them back in lots of six; they couldn't be sent off in ones and twos, not in *this* country."

On the ridge between the rivers, the file moves rapidly, in ant-like silence, as if in flight from the accumulating heat. Since leaving the Mbarangandu, we have encountered no animals at all, only the pale rump of a kongoni, vanishing like a ghostly face into high grass. Other animals have come and gone – we see a rhino scrape, the elegant prints of greater kudu, old droppings of elephant and buffalo – but as the day grows, so does the sense of emptiness in the still woodland, which is not a closed canopy but open to the sun, and everywhere overgrown with high bronze grass. "All dead, dry stuff," Nicholson mutters. "No good to animals at all. In my time, the whole Reserve would be burned over every year, two at the most; I had over four hundred game scouts who spent most of their time out in the field, and burning was their main job." He murmurs to Goa in Swahili, then stalks on, and Goa steps off the elephant path and sets fire to the tinder grass, which ignites with a hollow rush of the dry air. The fire leaps up with a hungry crackling, and a dark pall of smoke rises in our wake as we move southward.

This thin, tall man walking ahead of me in his big floppy hat, old shirt and shorts, and worn red sneakers looks more like old Iodine must have looked than the conventional idea of the East African professional hunter, or the crisp old-style warden in regimental khaki: I like this "Mister Meat" for his lack of vanity. In his angular, stoop-shouldered gait, he keeps up a long easy pace, remaining close to the swift, effortless Goa, yet every little while he turns and casts a hard, bald eye back along the line, noticing quickly when the porters fail to keep close ranks in river thickets and karongos, or when one or more tends to fall too far behind. "*Wanakuja?*" he calls. "Are they coming?" And with the barrel tips of the shotgun that he carries he moves a thorn branch off the thin trail, anticipating the bare feet of the young porters. His concern is professional – foot injuries

* Wykes, *Snake Man.*

will cripple our safari – but it isn't unfeeling, whatever he might have one believe.

Ahead, three young bull elephants are standing beneath a large and dark muyombo tree, which at this season, in anticipation of the rains, is covered with a red canopy of seed pods. Getting our scent, the elephants move away in no great haste as we come down into a grassy open glade. The blue acanth flowers of dry ground give way to blue commelina and lavender morning glory, and there are meadow springs and frogs and singing scrub robins. "At this season, most miombo is pretty dry from one end of Africa to the other, but here in the Selous it's so well watered that these little paradises occur everywhere in the dry woods," Nicholson says, as the porters set down their loads beneath a tree. "That's why we didn't bother to bring water bottles." But Goa is out putting the torch to the dry grass all around, and over this paradise black smoke is rising; within minutes, the racquet-tailed rollers appear, filling the crackling heat with strident cries as they hawk the insects that whir up before the flames.

We head southwest across the river bends to the Luwegu. Unlike the Mbarangandu, the Luwegu still carries a swift flood of brown-gray water that in most places fills the river bed from one side to the other. This high water, unusual at this time of the year, must account in part for the scarcity of animals along the margins, since there is more water than they need in the pools and springs back in the woods. Where we come out on the banks of the Luwegu we see no elephant at all, only a large crocodile which lies out on a bar along the bank, its jaws transfixed in the strangled gape with which these animals confront their universe. In the mile between bends of the river two large herds of hippopotami are visible; it seems likely that there are too many, that one of these long, slow years there will come a great dying-off of the huge water pigs, to bring their numbers back into balance with the wild pastures that they have pushed further and further from the banks. According to Brian, such dying-off occurs in the Selous about once every seven years, in separate places; he remembers it once in the Ruaha, and another time on the Kilombero. But today they steam and puff and honk in great contentment, though two get at each other every little while in a great blare and thrash, to banish the monotony of river life.

Everywhere as we walk upriver the animals are starting to appear; it seems to be true, as Brian claims, that here in the Selous the animals are not especially active early in the day, as they are elsewhere, and do not move about until mid-morning, though *why* this might be true is not clear. Among the smaller animals that cross our path are ground squirrels and the green monitor lizards, small relatives of the great Komodo "dragons" of the East Indies, and a black-tipped mongoose, scampering along the bank, that is red as fire; the banded and pygmy mongoose are common in the Selous but this is the first of this weasel-like species

I have seen. Impala are numerous and remarkably tame, and a band of waterbuck under a tamarind beside the river lets man walk up within a few yards before prancing off in a pretty canter into the woods; further north these animals would take off at a dead run at the sight of vehicles, which ordinarily disturb them less than a man on foot. Wart hog and wildebeest are also rather tame, though not confiding. Under a big tree by the corner of the river, from where the Mahoko Mountains can be seen off to the west, stands a placid group of elephants; not until we move a little uphill to the east of them, to let the breeze carry down our scent, do they give way. Kazungu described the scene in his journal:

> We saw elephants where we wanted to pass. We went upwind of them to give them our smell, and this make me understand that no matter how dangerous an animal is, if he is not familiar with a smell, he will run.
> We went up and down the hills and met some different animals.

Behind the elephants is a large grove of borassus palms, with their graceful swellings high up on the pale boles; from each palm, or so it seems, a pair of huge griffons violently depart, their heavy wing beats buffeting the clack of wind-tossed fronds. At this season, the borassus carries strings of fruit like orange coconuts, which are sought out by the elephants; here and there in the dry hills, far from the nearest palms, lie piles of dried gray borassus kernels, digested and deposited, from which the last loose dung has blown away. The mango-like kernels remind Brian of the elephant habit of gorging on the fallen fruits of the marula tree. "Used to ferment in their stomachs, make them drunk or sleepy; they'd just lie down on their sides and snore. Ever hear an elephant snore? Oh, you can hear that a *hell* of a long way!"

Keeping the porters close, we push through thickets to a shady grove beside the river. This first day we shall quit early, while the sun is high, to give the Africans a chance to dry the strings of dark red meat jerked from the buffalo killed yesterday near Mkangira; the biltong will be their main food for the journey. Goa and Kazungu string a line between high bushes on the bank to hang the meat, which is brought up in big handfuls by the porters; once dry, the biltong is very hard and tough and may be slung around amongst the luggage.

Abdallah spreads green canvas in the shade, and the sahibs lie down upon it to take tea. Since Brian's red sneakers are blistering his toes, the decision to stop early is a good one; also, the Ngindo are not trained porters and will collapse quickly in this heat – it must be a hundred degrees or more – unless they are given a day or two to get broken in. The remarkable Abdallah of the squint eye and sweet laugh is now doing headstands in the sun – actually jumping on his elbows in a small circle on the thorny ground – but two of his companions are laid out like corpses. One of these is Kalambo, who wears huge blue boxer shorts with a white stripe that extend below his knobby knees, and the other is a heavy boy with the name "Davvid" who wears a bright red shirt. Then there is Amede – short for Muhammed – who walks with the sway of a giraffe, and Shamu, whose face is wide-eyed, innocent, faintly alarmed, like the face of a small antelope; his small size and slight body, his expression, make him look too young to be carrying loads that might bend his bones, but on closer inspection I see that Shamu is a full-grown man who has retained a child-like air of innocence. Most of the time he sits quietly to one side, smiling delightedly at the witty sallies of his friends.

Finally there is Mata, small-faced as a vervet and given to harsh yapping barks; Mata likes to walk apart from the file of porters, and once or twice he dared walk on ahead when Goa and Brian had paused to light their fires. Bwana Niki had murmured something in Swahili which brought a bad look to Mata's face; he seemed to consider a spry remark, but then thought better of it.

"You'll have trouble with that one," Rick Bonham[*] had said, but the Warden knew better. "Once you put a bit of distance between them and the camp, and they have to depend on you for their protection, they're quite anxious to please," Brian had said, and he was right; after the first encounter with the elephants Mata fell back into line, and gave no more trouble after that first day. "Oh, there are exceptions to the rule of course," Nicholson reflected later. "Once had to kick a porter in the balls and give him a good clout to go with it. No choice, really." When he says these things, old Mister Meat fixes me with that bald eye and gives a faint clack of his false teeth, and I can't make out whether he intends this as a literal account of makeshift discipline in the bush, or if he is teasing my "American" notions about Africans, or whether he is feeling nostalgic about the grand old days when Ionides could have a whole Ngindo village flogged and get away with it. But as it turned out, he meant just what he said: the offending porter, Brian told me later, "was using blackmail in a very remote place, threatening to dump all the loads and abscond with his fellow porters unless I doubled the agreed pay. He was a huge man, who could have torn me apart easily if I hadn't disabled him."

By early afternoon the clouds have gone, and the day is dry and hot. Drinking gratefully from the brown river, I realize how rare now are the places left in Africa where one can drink the water without risking bilharzia or worse; in the Selous, one can sip with impunity from pools and puddles and even from big footprints in the mud. Later I find a safe bathing place behind a silvered log, and lie back for a long time in the warm flood, watching the western sky turn red behind a gigantic

[*] Richard Bonham; director of Nomad Safaris in Mombasa; who accompanied us to the Selous; but not on foot safari.

baobab across the river. Behind me in the forest, an elephant's stomach rumbles – or perhaps the elephant is pondering my scent, for Brian says that what is usually called stomach-rumbling in elephants is actually a low growl of apprehension and perhaps warning. Trumpeter hornbills gather in the mahoganies over my head, and I am attended by a small dragonfly, fire red in hue, that might have flown out of the sunset. I am extremely content to be here, yet I do not look forward to the evening; Brian and I have got on well enough, all things considered, but other people have always been around to smooth over the rough edges. I don't know this man as yet. We have been thrown together by fate, not by affinity, and doubtless he regards our enforced companionship as warily as I do.

When I get back to camp the Warden is lying on his cot before his tent, head raised on his elbow, watching me come. I am not surprised that he and I have been having the same thoughts, or when he says, coming straight out with it, "You know, Peter, when this idea came up that you and I should go off together on a long foot safari, I was dead set against it. As late as Kingupira, I was telling Tom Arnold, Absolutely not! You can't just go bashing off into the bush with some fella you've never set eyes on; had to have a good look at you first." Especially, I thought, after having read my book on Africa – and once again, Brian anticipates me. Although we have been together for two weeks, he mentions the book for the first time, and actually says, "I thoroughly enjoyed it." Together we laugh about that first night in Dar-es-Salaam; en route to the Selous. "Didn't know how to act!" Brian said. "Didn't know what was wanted of me, really."

Not only his words but his whole manner confirm what I thought I had already noticed, that he has left his mask behind at the main camp in Mkangira. He seems happy and relaxed, eager to talk, and the talk is almost entirely free of that cynicism and intolerance that I thought would cause trouble between us. Over our simple supper of beans and rice, he speaks with real affection and respect of some of the Africans on his old staff, such as a scout named James Abdallah who as a youth had been conscripted to help haul that steam engine up there to Madaba. "Terrible work. After three months, I think, James ran away and hid out in the forest."

In those early days, Brian says, he spent most of his time on elephant control, which was often a bit risky. I lost a very good man once to an elephant, one of my head game scouts, like old Saidi – you might think of a head game scout as a sort of regimental sergeant-major. Today they call them game assistants: I suppose they think it's less demeaning to be an assistant than to be a scout! But anyway, this other Saidi – Saidi Nasora Kibanda – was a first-class shot, which is very rare among Africans; he was also a superb hunter, and very knowledgeable, one of my best men. One day about 1965 Kibanda was out with a trainee on elephant control, and the trainee wounded an elephant which Kibanda had him follow up. I'll never really know what happened; when these things occur, the survivor always puts things in the best light for himself. But apparently the elephant attacked, and the trainee ran, and for some reason, Kibanda failed to stop that elephant, although they were in open country and it should have been a routine shot. That elephant destroyed him." Brian paused as if granting Kibanda a moment of silence. "Old Kibanda was a hell of a good fellow, and his death came as a hell of a shock to me, I don't mind telling you – that man was my right arm. Very loyal, very intelligent – a very nice man altogether."

Brian clears his throat, frowning a little. "I suppose I lost one or two game scouts every year, out on control work, but I can't think what could have happened to Kibanda. These large-bore precision weapons stop an elephant pretty easily, although most Africans have a hard time believing it; perhaps that's why they don't aim properly. Usually the animal will come at you with his head low, and you shoot at the forehead, above the eyes, to hit the brain; if the head is raised, of course, you shoot just at the base of it. Either way he goes right over, no problem at all.

"Of course there are times when nothing seems to go right, and probably it was one of those times that caught up with poor old Kibanda. I had a day like that myself. I was stationed on Mahenge at the time. We had been asked to deal with three bull elephants that were getting into the shambas, then becoming aggressive with whoever tried to drive them out, and running around knocking over houses, too. The people had these flimsy sort of *kilindos*, or huts-on-poles, that they would put up to keep watch on the crops; when elephants came, they would try to drive them off by beating on tins and the like. One day there was an old woman in one of these huts, and when three bulls turned up in the gardens, she started beating on her tins, and the elephants came for her, knocked over the hut and trampled her and tore her to pieces – made a real mess of her.

"When I arrived and finally had them located, I had to stalk them through very high grass, over my head, and when I came up with them, they were all together in a kind of opening they had beaten down in the high grass under a sausage tree. Two were broadside to me, one completely screening the other, and the third was looking off in another direction. When you shoot an elephant in the brain, it always sits back on its haunches, and I reckoned that the near one, falling back that way, would give me a fair shot at the one behind it. Then my gun bearer would give me the other gun, and I'd have two barrels to use on the third animal.

"Well, the first part of the plan worked well enough; the first sat backward, I dropped the second, and grabbed the other gun. But the third animal was already taking off, and I got off two quick shots aimed at the pelvis, because a pelvis shot will cripple an elephant and stop him so that you can finish him off properly.

However, I had shot too fast, and he kept going. Because I wasn't absolutely sure the second elephant was dead, I told the gunbearer to load up the first gun, showed him just where he should point the barrel, and then I took off after number three. He was only about sixty yards away, and badly hurt, but my third shot didn't drop him, I still don't know why, just set him running again, and a fourth shot intended for the pelvis didn't stop him either; all it did was turn him right around. I realized that the gun was empty and I had no more cartridges, hadn't thought I'd need them, you see, and I did the only thing I could do: I ran like hell back down that path that the elephant had made through the tall grass. After about five yards, I tripped and fell, and he was on me.

"This elephant was badly hurt, and his trunk was full of blood, spraying all over me, but he couldn't smell me, you see, and after he missed me with his tusks, he somehow lost me, and I was able to roll away. Luckily, he decided to take off again, and I ran back to my gun bearer. I didn't have Goa at that time; this man was only a trainee who never did make it as a gun bearer, and when he saw me all covered with blood, he panicked; he thought the elephant had got me, and because I was running, he imagined it was still hot after me, and so he departed in the opposite direction. When I caught up with him, I gave him a hell of a clout to calm him down, and grabbed a handful of cartridges out of his pouch and went back and finished off that elephant. That was the closest call I ever had with a wild animal."

A half moon rests in the borassus fronds over our heads, and a tiny bat detaches itself, flits to and fro, and returns into the black frond silhouette. We lie peacefully upon our cots and watch the stars. From the forest comes the hideous squalling of frightened baboons trying to bluff a leopard, or so we suppose, since there is plentiful leopard sign around the camp.

In the moonlight the bull hippos of the herd move in close to the bank to bellow at our fire; in trying to frighten us away, they panic one another and porpoise heavily away over the shallows, causing great waves that carry all the way across the river and slap on to the mud of the far bank. Man does not belong here, and the hippopotami cannot seem to accept us; we have disrupted their whole sense of how the night-time world unfolds in the Old Africa. They do not go ashore to feed but remain out there just beyond the fire light, keeping watch on the intruders and banishing our sleep with outraged bellows.

This is how Brian has arranged the day. We shall rise at six, have tea, and be off at seven; at about nine, we are to break for tea and porridge. At mid-morning, we shall walk again for two more hours, then rest in the hot part of the day; in mid-afternoon, we shall walk for two hours more, tending toward the river, where we shall make camp at the first good site.

Leaving the river forest in the early morning, we emerge on to an open plain and head south again over low hills between broad bends of the Luwegu. The bright green grass around a pan has attracted an early morning convocation of impala and wart hog, baboons and geese, and the pan is full of baby crocodiles; storks and herons stand about, minding their own narrow-brained business, and a pair of skimmers, feeding together, draw fine lines up and down on the still surface.

This morning everyone is silent. The porters speak just once, murmuring softly amongst themselves, and instantly Goa stops and turns and, after a moment, says almost inaudibly, "*Nani ani ongea?*" "Who is talking?" When nobody speaks, he takes this for an answer and goes on. Over his shoulder, Brian murmurs, "I always have it as a rule: no one talks on trek except me and the tracker." I nod in approval, not bothering to answer. Talking almost invariably detracts from the real pleasure of walking, in which one finally enters the surroundings. And in the wilderness the human voice is disturbing to animals we might otherwise see, quite apart from the fact that nothing must intrude upon Goa's apprehension of his surroundings.

Now Goa has stopped again, raising one hand. Shadows deep in the scrub ahead have shifted, and soon a bull elephant moves out into the open, in no hurry, since Goa has left him time and space in which to take his leave. There are more elephants during the morning, in twos and threes and fives; although on foot, we are rarely out of sight of them.

A solitary eland bull, a glimpse of kudu. Huge ground hornbills fly away with the slow, ghostly beats of their white primaries that seem incapable of keeping such large birds aloft; like vultures, which are also huge and without enemies, the *batutu* seem exceptionally shy. Yellow hyacinths shine in the grassland, and a bush of daisy-like composites, with a solitary red-stemmed lily unlike any flower we have seen. The country is more open here than it is to the north of Mkangira; the white-crowned black chat of the miombo woodland is no longer common, and the racquet-tailed roller has been replaced by the lilac-breasted species of the savanna. Even the tsetse seem to have lost the appetite they show in the closed woods; I watch them alight on the shirt of the man ahead, but they do not bite.

Against the blue hills to the west stands a cow-calf herd of elephant. Getting our scent, a young cow leads the juveniles away while the old matriarch stands guard, trunk high, as if in warning; and soon we see the young toto hastening away after the others, the top of his small earnest head scarcely visible in the high grass. Not far off there is a wildebeest, then a mixed band of impala, waterbuck, and eland; the antelope move calmly to the wood edge, unafraid. For a long time the big gray eland bull stands watching us, attended by three soft brown cows with calves. Like other striped animals – kudu, bushbuck, zebra – eland are taboo animals to the tribesmen to the east of the Reserve, who know that eating striped beasts may bring on leprosy. (This view is shared by tribesmen of the Sudan–Zaire border, who will not eat bongo.)

On the far side of the wood, we find ourselves among a herd of waterbuck almost before a long calm look persuades them that it might be best to take their leave. In numbers of animals seen this morning the far south of the Selous compares with the great parks, but the tameness of almost every creature in this country south of Mkangira has nothing to do with the aplomb of sophisticated parks animals which, being resigned to the human presence, are not tame so much as half-domesticated. Here the confiding curiosity appears to stem from a trusting innocence of man, unlike anything I have seen elsewhere in Africa.

Once again the Luwegu comes into view, set off by broad white sand bars and tall palm trees, the surface broken here and there by clumps of rocks that turn out to be hippos. We descend to the bank at the end of a sand bar where a giant kingfisher, night blue and chestnut, has seized a fish too big for it to manage; it squats on the sand belaboring the fish, then gives this up and lugs its catch away across the river, which at this bend must be three hundred yards across.

As Goa sets his fires we head south, trying to cut across the river bends. Since the river bears west, we are soon inland and higher than we intended, emerging at last on the cliff of an escarpment. Five buffalo lying down under black boulders heave to their feet and hump away into high grass, and from the rocks, a black eagle takes wing across a hidden valley of baobab plains and grassy glades and palm and water pans, cut off from the world by the steep cliffs and hills east of the river. Brian had never known that this place existed; in his years here, he had always found a way around these rough escarpments. "If I'd known about it, I would have come here and made camp; a place like this is bound to be crawling with game. It's likely that the tribesmen who once lived here knew it, but we must be the first white people ever to come here."

Beyond the escarpments, the Luwegu crosses a flat plain, but in the southern distance can be seen the sudden mountains where the river descends from a steep-sided gorge. The Wandewewe Hills beyond are part of the Luwegu watershed, but most of its tributaries descend from the Matengo Highlands west of Songea. These elevations on the great inland plateau are drained by the long rivers that flow northward, following the tilt of the plateau toward the Rufiji. The Luwegu and the Mbarangandu run almost parallel, and both are characterized by broad canyon valleys between steep cliffs of reddish sandstone that rise on both sides to long flat-topped plateaus.

We follow a steep buffalo trail down the escarpment, crossing the plain of baobab and pushing more buffalo out of the dense shade of a karongo. Then we climb again, still too far to the east, working our way around more hidden buffalo; in the very steep, hot, thorny going the Ngindo are exhausted, but on account of the buffalo their nerves give them the energy to keep up. Over the centuries the elephants have found all the paths of least resistance, and Goa follows their clear trails up and down the broken country, but by midday two of the porters are "pretty well knocked-up", as Brian puts it. Because there is no shade where we strike the river, we continue along the hot slow sand, enter the bush again and find ourselves between an agitated hippo and the river.

For all one reads about lion and elephant, buffalo and rhinoceros, it is probably this vast water pig of other ages, with its immense jaws and long shearing teeth and unexpected speed, that kills more people than any other animal in Africa, and it does so most often when, as now, it finds itself cut off from sanctuary in the water. We stand a moment, at a loss, listening to this beast's companions disporting in the river, and then Goa leads in a polite circling maneuver, working inland to give the hippo a clear path. Misinterpreting this move, the hippo retreats inland a little, too, then stops to glare again, coming fully about to face us as it does so. Because we are all hot and tired, and no solution is in sight, we cross quickly between the hippo and the river as Goa calls to the young porters to keep up.

In the dense river thickets once again, the porters keep up smartly without being told. Brian kicks at fresh manure and mutters, "Liable to turn up a buffalo just now . . ." He has scarcely spoken when the porters yell and scatter, dropping their loads. Goa whirls and raises the rifle; we had passed the buffalo, which then burst from a thicket by the river only a few yards from the line of men. It does not charge but runs off in the direction we have come, as all the porters squeal with nervous laughter.

Never having been on safari before the young porters are inexperienced with big animals, but this has not always been true of the Ngindo. Though they practice a subsistence agriculture – growing mostly maize, millet, and cassava – and keep a few goats and chickens, the Ngindo were essentially hunter-gatherers until this century and to this day have retained the small, slight stature of bush hunters. Probably they made small impact on the wildlife populations, since apparently they were always few in number, living in small, semi-nomadic groups along the rivers. A Portuguese document of 1616 mentions the sparsity of the inland population in this region, referring to it as a "terra deserta", and human numbers were maintained at a low level by the constant attrition of the Arab slavers, the Ngoni Zulu, and the Germans. Though some Ngindo must have been taken as porters and slaves, they offered no resistance to the caravans of the eighteenth and nineteenth centuries that passed through on the way to the interior from

Kilwa; where chance offered, in fact, they stole one another's children and bartered them for salt, cloth, and the primitive firearms that still serve in out-of-the-way places as items of prestige, and thus made at least a minor contribution to the desolation and disruption of the countryside, the pillage and burning and inter-tribal raiding, and the destruction of wildlife that the slavers and ivory traders left in their wake almost everywhere throughout the country.

Though local tradition says that the Ngindo people were always forest hunters, it may be that this was a consequence of chronic disruption and flight. "We do not stay long enough to eat our own mangoes", is an Ngindo proverb. The original Ngindo homeland is thought to have been further south, extending across the Ruvumu River into what is now Mozambique; apparently they were pushed northward by the Ngoni Zulu who swept up from southern Africa in the nineteenth century. Eventually the fierce Ngoni, with their well-organized militia, came into bitter conflict with the Germans who were settling this region from the north, and the hapless Ngindo were caught in between. Having gone to the Germans for protection against the Ngoni, they found that these white men were still worse. *Wanatoka wafako, wanakwenda waziwako*, they said, in mourning for themselves: They go from where there is death to where there is burial.* The Germans needed slave labor to make cash crops out of their cotton, and malingerers were given twenty lashes. These beatings inspired such resentment that finally, in 1905, the Ngindo people at Kabata, not far east of the Selous Reserve boundary, rebelled against an order to pick cotton. The revolt spread to the Lung'onyo River region, where a witch doctor produced a magic water to protect Africans from European bullets, and soon five Germans, including a bishop and a nun, were destroyed by Ngindo at a place called Mukukuyumbu, near Liwale; others were killed by Pogoro people near Madaba, and it was at Madaba that there commenced, in November of that year, the efficient and thorough suppression of what came to be known as the Maji-Maji Rebellion. The Germans are said to have made a point of executing the eldest son of every family in the region, and at least 100,000 Africans were slaughtered. (In this same period, the Germans were carrying out repressions of a comparable brutality among the Herero of what is now Namibia.) Everywhere villages and crops were put to the torch, with no respite for the planting of new gardens, and in the next three years as many thousands – hundreds of thousands, some authorities have said – died of starvation, the humid skies were dark with vultures and a shroud of fire, and lions prospered. In 1908, an old man named Sulila at Masasi made a song recounting the dark years of his people:

---

* See R. M. Bell, 'The Maji-Maji Rebellion in Liwale District', *Tanganyika Notes and Records*, 1950.

Then comes the war of the Mazitu [Ngoni]; guns are fired by the Germans; then they ran away. But the Germans came; it was dangerous to see. The bush was burnt; the goats were burnt; the fowls were burnt – the people were finished altogether. The tax came up . . . still they were not satisfied. Mr Sulila telegraphed to the District Commissioner, "He may skin me to make a bag for his money. Now I am tired." *

An historian wrote, in a paraphrase of Tacitus, "The Germans in East Africa made solitude, and called it peace." †

Just after five, we make camp beneath a big tamarind at the river's edge, opposite a grove of high borassus. Upstream, a solitary bull elephant wanders the bank; farther on an eland emerges from the trees, very pale against the dark greens of the river forest, and a cow elephant and calf stand at rest in the late afternoon sun, as if lost in some long twilight meditation. A harsh racketing downriver is made by a pair of huge Goliath herons, performing a courtship ritual in the shallow water: it seems appropriate that the largest members of their worldwide families, the Goliath heron and the giant kingfisher, are still abundant on these big wild rivers, though no longer common elsewhere in East Africa. The herons display to each other with broad wings and nervous dancing as a third heron, to all appearances an injured party, turns its back on them and sits in a hunched position on a sand bar, staring toward the north.

Kazungu. brings us mushroom soup, and Brian gives his bowl to me; he cannot eat it. In 1959, he says, he came down with serious stomach pains, which he did nothing about for four years. "Had knotted guts whenever I ate anything; couldn't eat fresh fruit or vegetables at all. Finally got down to about one hundred pounds." Not until it seemed that he might starve to death was he persuaded to go to the tropical disease hospital in London, where his ailment was eventually diagnosed as *Histoplasma Duboisiei*, the first recorded case in Africa of a rare gut fungus that is not uncommon in the Persian Gulf. "All they had were some experimental drugs, which they did not hesitate to recommend since otherwise I would be dead within six months. And the drugs worked, because here I am, but I really couldn't eat properly until 1973, when a friend of ours up in Nairobi recommended yogurt. Cleared me right up in two weeks – the only thing I can't eat now is mushrooms."

In fact Brian still eats very little, and seems to prefer the gray oatmeal gruel and

---

* K. Weule, 'Native Life in East Africa', London 1909, quoted in Kjekshus, *Ecology Control and Economic Development in East African History*.

† J. P. Moffett, *Handbook of Tanganyika*, 1958.

rice that tided him over his long illness. Not being the sort to concern himself about other people's preferences, he discarded almost everything with taste in it that Karen Ross* had set aside for our safari, saying that we must travel light. ("I tried to slip in a few goodies for you," Karen warned me, "but he tossed them right out again.") Brian sees no reason why I should not adjust my habits to having two meals a day. "People worry too much about food," he says. "Afraid of going without, so they eat too much, women especially – their main occupation, I suppose. Especially here in the tropics, where habits are apt to be sedentary, it is better to eat less." And so the single bowl of gray *porrigi* at mid-morning represents the midday meal as well as breakfast, and the rice with beans at supper is the one full meal of the day. I don't bother to protest that his bloody tent weighs a lot more than the discarded food: two meals suit me in this heat, and eaten outside under the trees and stars, the simple fare tastes very good indeed.

I ask Brian what the tropical disease hospital said about the yogurt cure for *Histoplasma Duboisiei*, and he says that he did not bother to report it. Taken aback, I ask – not entirely insincerely – if he does not wish to help his fellow man. "Not really," he said, not entirely insincere himself, and again I hear that echo of Ionides: "The convenience or profit of others is a matter of supreme indifference to me unless it happens to coincide with my own."

In our camp tonight, Kazungu writes:

> In the morning I made tea while other people packed up the camp – a tent for the two white people and a ground sheet for the rest of us. Then we began our safari. As usual we take our breakfast after two hours. We came across six elephant with calf and had to pass far away; as usual, an animal with baby is very fierce. We saw four buffalo, which are bad animals; he doesn't care about anything or anybody, but does what he likes, you cannot trust him. I fear the buffalo more than anyone . . .
>
> We made a big fire because of wild animals like elephants and hippo so they would not come near. Most of riverside is path of wild animals to come and drink water. I didn't get good sleep because I have never slept outside without a tent.

It is always Goa who puts up the tent, assisted by one of the young Ngindo, and it bothers me slightly every time they do it, probably because the Africans do not have one. It is true, of course, that they could erect the canvas kitchen fly brought for that purpose, but they prefer to use this as a ground cover, sleeping in a tight row on top of it and keeping the fire going all night long. They are uneasy

---

* Karen Ross, camp manager for the Safaris, who accompanied us to the Selous, but not on the foot safari.

about elephants as well as lions, but elephants rarely wander into camp except in parks. As Brian says, "The elephant is very considerate, really. Rhinos blunder in sometimes, and lions come about, but a round from the shotgun usually sees them off. Now a man-eater, of course ..."

In the distance rises the early morning sound of the ground hornbill, the remote dim hooting of a woodland spirit – *poo-too, po-to* – a lugubrious ghostly reverbera-tion that seems to emanate from a cavern under the earth. In West Africa this bird is considered sacred, and Kazungu and Goa say that if you kill one, the young ones will appear by your house and make this sound – *poo-too, po-to* – and very soon you will take sick and die. The Ngindo say that Kazungu and Goa are mistaken: if you should be foolish enough to kill the *nditi*, as the bird is called in this part of Tanzania, you will die without further ado.

We make good time over the river plains – we are now well south of the black rock escarpments – passing large tame herds of wildebeest and impala, slowing only to make our way around the many elephants, not less than six groups in the first few miles, although there are never more than five together. None seem bothered by the file of men, there is no threat display whatever, and most of them do not move away as we go past. Buffalo sign is copious, but the buffalo remain hidden, as do the rhinoceros and the lion: last night I heard a lion roar toward dawn – I have heard lion almost every night since coming to the Selous – but in this long-grass country they remain unseen.

A wood of "silver trees" (*Terminalia sericea*), as Selous called them in his journals, descends to broad pans of black cotton clay twisted up into hard ruts and potholes by huge megafaunal feet – a quagmire during the rains, now petrified into near-stone that is very hard on the bare feet of the porters. Then we are in river forest once again, and here Goa slows a little, feeling his way into the gloom with hand held out in front like a moth's antennae, leading the file in a winding course to avoid a confrontation with the depositors of all this fresh and shining dung. In pockets of sun, I find myself alert to the white butterflies, cat musk, thick blood-red kigelia blossoms with long yellow stamens, and the somber hum of bees.

In mid-morning we come to an area that has been burned over. The fire is recent; there are no sprouts of green tussock, only white remnants on the blackened ground – the bone-white shells of millipedes and giant land snails unable to escape the sweep of fire. Antelope droppings are baked a strange bluish gray. Goa locates a simple cooking fire in the thicket on a mound, and we find the place, scraped bare of stones, where men have slept – the first and last sign of man's presence that we would come across in this country south of Mkangira.

After a silence Brian says, "Looks like they were here about a week ago." Perhaps he, too, is thinking that the animals seem very tame for a country in which poachers have been operating, for now he says, "It's possible, of course, that it's *tambika* – that's ancestor worship, from the days when people lived along these rivers. They come out here sometimes to *tambika*, or at least they did. On the other hand, poachers will use that as an excuse: 'We're just a few ancestor-worshippers who stumbled upon all this ivory we're carrying.'"

Over mid-morning *porrigi* and tea, Brian talks about the footpath that crossed the Selous Reserve between Liwale and Mahenge, beyond the western boundary. The Ngindo of Liwale have relatives at Mahenge who were cut off when Ionides' expanding elephant reserve was joined to the original Selous, and to visit them without trespassing in the Reserve meant a journey on foot and by jitney of at least eight hundred miles. Since even those who could afford the time could not afford so many jitney buses, it was inevitable that people would cross illegally, and rather than have them scattered through the bush and perhaps remaining there, Ionides had made it legal to use this footpath, which was about one hundred and twenty miles in length. In Brian's opinion, this path a few miles to the south was probably the access route for whoever had made that camp fire.

"When they come in this far," he said, "they're after ivory and rhino horn; they can get meat much closer to home, most of it legally, because the country here in southern Tanzania is still wild. This isn't Kenya. In most of Kenya, until recently at least, almost the only game that people could find in most areas outside the parks was a few small antelope. Of course the poachers will shoot game, too, to live on, the way we're doing ourselves on this safari, but that's not why they're here."

The Ngindo hunters are leaders in their villages, as is the case among Goa's people; they are "poachers" only to the white men, whose demand for rhino horn and ivory is what has put the animals in danger. "Often a village will have one great hunter," Brian relates. "The people chip in and buy him a rifle and arrange for his bearers and assistants; others may also buy a gun and have him do their legal killing for them. He's not somebody out of work, or outside the law in any way; invariably, he's a respected member of the community, with wives and children and shambas and all sorts of prestige, which he deserves, because he takes risks and he knows his business. That's why it's hard to get people to testify against him. When I sent a man like that to jail, I used to go and pick him out again in about six months and have him come work for me; he would always be capable, and would know his region of the bush in great detail.

"Of course, people coming in this far have the rivers to contend with. In the dry season, they can wade across if they want to risk the crocodiles, but in the old days, at least when there was patrolling, they came mostly in the rains, when they knew that the tracks would all be mired and our machines unable to move. In a river as large as this, they'd use a *kungwa*, which is essentially a section of muyombo bark about nine feet long, the half-round of a big tree or all of a small one split along one side, with ends plugged up with bark and mud. Pretty rickety affair, but it usually got them over. Up on the Kilombero, of course, the poachers coming in from outside would come down in canoes, especially when the crocodile trade was in full swing." Brian grinned a little to himself, remembering. "Once we were trekking up the Kilombero – we'd heard there was poaching up that way – and we saw that the poachers had their camp out on an island, and we had no boats. So we sent one of the game scouts up the river, pretending to be a poacher himself, and yelling across that a hippo had overturned one of his canoes and a man had drowned, and to please send help. When the canoes came from the island, we arrested the rescuers, then used the canoes to go back to the island and arrest the others, though not without a fight."

Until 1958, when Alan Rees became warden of the western Selous, the poaching there had been almost as rampant as it was in the north, near the towns and the main road; in fact, the Reserve was overrun by meat-hunters, often outfitted by local traders, and the slaughter of game was so widespread that certain regions have not fully recovered to this day. Not until 1961, when the Selous Reserve administration was coordinated under a new chief warden, Major B. G. Kinlock, was poaching brought under control in the north and west: between mid-1962 and the end of 1963 some sixteen hundred people were convicted for offences in the Game Reserve; many tons of wire snares and miles of fencing were seized and destroyed, and more than two hundred firearms were confiscated, together with an enormous collection of spears and bows and arrows. From that time until Nicholson's own departure in 1973, organized poaching was no longer a problem in the Selous.

On the river beach at the next bend, where two hippos stand facing each other as if made of stone, a line of *siafu*, or soldier ants, is moving along a narrow tunnel just under the surface of the sand; the tunnel is roofed with a sand crust, but here and there the crust has fallen, exposing the glistening nerve of ants as they hasten away into the thicket.

"I remember the old days on the farm," Brian said. "We'd have to camp out when the ants came, because there were no insecticides or anything. But as soon as everything was eaten, they would go away, having cleaned the place out down to the last cockroach; wouldn't see a rat or a mouse for the next six months. There's nowhere to hide from them – swarm over everything." Recalling how back at Madaba the *siafu* had driven Tom Arnold from his tent one night, Brian grinned. The only thing that could stop these *siafu* was another ant, the *sangara*, a very swift yellow-brown species which he had pointed out at Kingupira; they appeared to run nimbly over the backs of the slower *siafu* and spray the line with some sort of formic acid.

On the first day of our journey Brian had mentioned that his red sneakers were giving his toes hell and cramping his feet too, but he ignores my suggestion that he put on socks or plasters – "No room", he says – and he has no other boots or shoes to take their place. I have no spares either; in the cause of traveling light, we are sharing one small duffle that contains everything we have brought, including flashlights, Brian's cigarettes, and my notebooks. Yesterday Brian was obliged to bandage his little toes, and this morning, after the first two hours, he borrowed my knife and cut holes in his sneakers to keep them from doing him any further damage. As it is, we shall have to quit in the early afternoon, and tomorrow – a day early – we shall leave the Luwegu and head east toward the Mbarangandu, before the distance between rivers grows any wider. This isn't because of Brian's feet, or because we have not seen animals – the plains game were all there this morning as well as a number of elephant and buffalo – but because of that burning, which we have assumed was done by poachers. With the sight of that fire-blackened land, of that transgression, a sense of the vast silent Africa, "the Old Africa", was dissipated, and the Mbarangandu will be our last chance to restore it.

This afternoon we take shelter from the sun in a bush orange grove by the Luwegu, drinking our tea and chewing on the long hard strips of buffalo biltong. Eventually the biltong proves too tough for the false front tooth I had installed eighteen years ago to replace one broken on an expedition in New Guinea. The damned tooth shatters to pieces in my mouth, and I spit it out in consternation; as in New Guinea, I am pretty far from help if the thing acts up. Brian is not the least bit sympathetic; in fact he laughs. "Makes you look tough," he observes, "like you really mean business." And he removes his own false teeth, leaving gaps on both sides of his incisors that give him the aspect, as he says himself, of a huge rodent. Turning his back, he suddenly whirls and stares at me over his shoulder, letting the two rodent teeth emerge on his lower lip. "This is your captain," he says, and bursts out laughing, claiming that he does this sometimes with strange passengers in his airplane. Though I doubt this story, it doesn't matter, since he has me laughing, too. "If you hadn't been going at the bloody biltong like a hyena, instead of chewing it off in delicate bits like me, it would never have happened," Brian says, and we laugh anew.

A light unseasonal rain that fell last night is attributed by the Warden to the bush fires that in these months are set all across Africa in the miombo belt, from southern Tanzania and northern Mozambique to the coastal forests of Zaire and

Angola. The morning is heavy and humid after the rain, and two of the porters, complaining of headaches, are given aspirin. Behind their round dark aching heads, a flight of egrets passes down the early river.

During the night, a small leopard made off with one of Kazungu's sneakers, which on this foot safari have replaced the green Wellingtons he was wearing for a while as a precaution against cobras. As the only staff member with shoes (although Goa uses rubber sandals that make a faint snick-snick as he goes along) Kazungu is understandably upset, but the cat prints are clear in the damp sand, and he soon locates the spat-out sneaker a short distance back in the thickets.

This morning we abandon the Luwegu in order to cross the ridges toward the east and explore an unnamed sand river that comes down off a high plateau. On the north end of that plateau, high above the dry savanna woodlands all around, is the large pan that the Warden remembers as "crawling with elephant" and other animals. He is eager to revisit the nameless plateau and its pan, which he discovered in his last years in the Selous.

An hour is needed to cross the flat river plain of the Luwegu, on the east side of which a pair of Bohor reedbuck start up from high grass along the wood. The going is mostly very fast, but because of large animals we travel no more than a few miles in an hour. Buffalo tracks and buffalo manure are copious, and so are the attendant flies that do not sting but alight damply on the eyes and mouth. Then we are in thickets and karongos once again, and Goa, squatting to see beneath the bushes, craning, listening, picking out the big and silent shapes that watch us pass, must move circuitously and with more care. Brian, too, is wary and alert, kicking apart a fresh elephant mound, then stooping without breaking stride to judge the proximity of its maker by the degree of warmth that rises to his fingers.

In a sand river – and he thinks this is the one that has no name – we meet a cow elephant with half-grown calf. The cow goes off into the thicket to our left and the calf dawdles, then blunders toward the right, starting to bawl. Unaccountably, Brian and Goa move between the animals, and a moment later the cow, no longer visible, is bellowing from a short distance away; reverberations from the thicket make it clear that other agitated pachyderms are behind her. Goa turns quickly, taking the shotgun and giving Brian his own Game Department rifle. ("He knows I am more skillful with it," Brian explained later, "so he doesn't mind.") The porters rush forward in a covey to take up positions behind the guns. After a mild demonstration charge that brings the guns up, the cow wheels and goes trumpeting off with the others; probably it was not that dawdler that had concerned her but a much younger one too low down in the bush for us to see.

A mile away, vultures spiral upward from a kill, and we have gone less than a few hundred yards when Goa's deep and urgent voice says, "*Simba!*" Two

lionesses, then two more, shoot out from beneath an enormous tree fallen into
the river bed perhaps thirty yards away; they are followed by a big growling
male with a fine mane which accelerates as it sees the file of men, its big paws
scattering hot sand. The lion bounds across the river bed and up the bank. The
whole bend of the river stinks of lion, and there are print patterns of the litter
of small cubs, which must be lying hidden just close by. Brian says, "I seriously
doubt if those lions have ever seen a man before; even the poachers stick to the
main rivers. Yet look at how fast they shot away! What makes them run off like
that? Quite interesting, really. If we'd come up on them in a Land Rover, chances
are that these wild lion would be just as tame as those lion in the parks. It's the
cars that fool them; they can't seem to identify men in cars. If you're up in a tree,
a lion will recognize you straight away, even though that's not the way he's
accustomed to seeing you."

A lone African hare crosses our path in its age-old silence, and in the thicket,
banded mongoose skirl and squabble, in furor over some edible find. Every little
while we pass the dung-spattered double scar on the dry ground that marks a
rhino scrape; although we have seen many fresh scrapes in the past few days,
the great primordial beast itself has remained hidden. Soon the porters take
their rest in a grove of the sand river, which twists and turns back and forth across
our course toward the south, and Goa and Kazungu dig down in the dry sand until
the hole fills with the clear water that will be used for morning tea and porridge.

In the early afternoon, blue water glints in the eastern distance; at this time of
year, when all but the main rivers have gone dry, this can only be the Mbarangandu,
which we had not expected to see until tomorrow. If the two rivers are so close –
not much more than twelve miles – then we are further north than we imagined,
which means that we have struck almost due east, instead of east by south as
we intended; we have no compass, and throughout the morning the sun that
would have given us a bearing has been hidden in the fire-shrouded sky. We
turn due south. I am glad of the miscalculation, which brought us to this place at
the right moment: we have hardly seen the glint of river when Goa points out
two rhinoceros, a mile away down a long slope of the savanna; one fades quickly
into the high grass but the other lingers a few moments, turning broadside, before
barging off into the bush.

I yip with pleasure, and Goa is delighted. To Brian he says, "The only thing we
must show him is leopard!" Goa has a sudden fine full smile that sends wrinkles
back on his tight hide across the high cheekbones to the small tight ears: the
old hunter looks like a hominid designed for passing through bush quickly and
quietly, catching nothing on the thorns. Never watching the ground for vines
and holes and sharp grass-hidden stones but seeming to drift over the earth, he

scans the terrain with those yellowed eyes that see so much, on all sides and far away.

Old elephant paths of other seasons cross the rolling hills of high bronze grass, but there is no sign of animals whatever except for two pretty klipspringer, tawny and gray, which prance along the black granite rim of a low escarpment; from this black rock, in the white sun, so very hot that it bakes our feet, a dark thing flutters up like a great moth – the freckled nightjar, which makes its home on the black outcroppings of stone.

Here and there on these black platforms, emerging like low domes out of the grass, lie shards of quartz, agate, chert and other stones, apparently brought here to be worked by stone tool cultures, for many are distinctly flaked, with the characteristic hump that betrays the method; occasionally I pause long enough to stuff one or two of these ancient tools into my pockets, including round tortoise cores flaked all the way around the edge, like those Hugo van Lawick* and I had found on the ridges north of Mkangira. The heat of the tools, and the feel of their great age, is somehow satisfying and profoundly reassuring, as if we had passed into another age, as if those Stone Age men had paused here yesterday, taking the sun god's name in vain as they cursed their sharp, obdurate stones, scowling in the heat.

Cutting across a series of wide bends, still heading south, we come down to the river. Two waterbuck, two wart hog, and two buffalo wait on the bar, like creatures left behind by Noah's Ark; the buffalo refuse to give ground at our approach, although we shout. We have circled wide and now stand in the shallow water, trying to ease them up into the thicket so that we may proceed along the sand. "Don't want to make them think they're trapped," says Brian. We can go no closer to the lowering brutes, which have backed up with their spattered rumps against the bank. Before the wrong move can be made, the buffalo wheel suddenly and plunge off up the bank into the thicket, agitating a group of elephants that we had not seen.

In the shade of a big butterfly-leafed piliostigma we stretch out on the cool sand, and I listen to the young Africans behind me; they are still excited by our encounters with the *tembo* and the *simba*, and describe to each other in dramatic tones and with nervous squeals how Mzee Goa and the Bwana Mkubwa (for they are too young to have known Brian as "Bwana Niki" and refer to him as the Head Bwana, the "Big Bwana") raised their *bunduki* to protect our lives.

While Kazungu. busies himself over his pots, Goa walks inland and sets fire to the bush, then wades across the shallow Mbarangandu and fires the high grass on the far bank; in a few minutes, the clear African day beside the river is despoiled

---

* Hugo van Lawick, the photographer who took photographs for the original edition of *Sand Rivers*.

by a crackling roar and columns of black smoke, which stings the eyes, and stinks, and dirties the sky. A pair of hawks are circling a tree where the accumulated grass and deadwood is feeding fire that booms and reverberates as it moves away; perhaps their nestlings have been singed of their feathers, and even now nod just a little, blackening in death.

Brian, sensing my disgust, insists once more that early-season burning is essential to wildlife management in the Selous. There are moderate rains in the months of December, less in January; the heavy rain that renews the vegetation is concentrated between late February and early May, when twenty-five to thirty inches may fall here in the south and twice that amount in the Kilombero region and the west. The two rainy seasons tend to merge into one long one, in which the grass grows very high, coarse, and unpalatable, and smothers the wild pasture for the remainder of the year; the use of fire as much as the removal of the inhabitants is responsible for the fact that the game population of the Selous is many times greater than it was when the first Europeans came into this country.

No doubt Brian is right in terms of game management; it is the necessity of all this "management" that I resist. One day I ask him if any of these fires ever occur accidentally, through lightning or other random events, and he says that he thinks it very unlikely; even if they did, they would not travel far. This poses a question that neither of us can answer: since it is thought that this "dry forest" is a recent habitat type, created, perhaps, by the fires of those early hunters who left their flaked tools on almost every high place and granite outcrop in this landscape, and spread and maintained by human activity ever since, how is it that such creatures as Lichtenstein's hartebeest are endemic to the miombo, since they must have evolved many thousands of years before mankind had fire at all?

As we talk, Brian makes an odd drumming with his fingers on a log, two soft beats followed by two hard, and noticing that I notice, he says "*Mgalumtwe.* That's the local dialect for 'A man has been eaten.'" They drum this message on a hollowed-out log with a bit of hide stretched over one end: M-ga-LUM-TWE! The villagers come to the call of the drums, armed with spears and bows and arrows. Sometimes they harass the lion but they rarely kill it; it just goes off, more dangerous than before. That man-eater might be raiding in an area of a hundred square miles, which makes it very difficult to come up with, especially when you're traveling on foot. It might take two people in two nights in the same place, then disappear entirely for two weeks, presumably taking animals instead. Often man-eating is seasonal, during the rains; in the dry season, when animals are concentrated near the water points, these lion seem to prefer animals, returning to human beings in the rains when the animals scatter. But man-eating was certainly most prevalent where game was scarce because of human development; the lion that were unable to catch what game was left – especially lion that were old or crippled – turned to human beings. I remember one I shot, still on the man whom it had killed outside his hut and dragged into the bamboo. That lion was in terrible condition, half-starved really, due to porcupine quills and an infection in its throat that kept it from swallowing. It could only take little bits at a time, which was why it was still feeding on that man when I arrived.

"But most man-eaters I saw were in good condition, and they were wary. Baits rarely worked on them, they were too clever. You had to wait until the next person was taken, doing your best to persuade the villagers not to drive it off the kill but to let it gorge itself. After that, it wouldn't go too far before it fell into a heavy sleep, and I'd have a chance to reach the place before it woke up again and moved away. Tracking it, you'd find places it had lain down and then got up again, until it found the place where things felt right. Usually that was in deep thicket, and sometimes all you could see when you crept up was a patch of hide. Finally you had to shoot at that and hope the bullet would disable it. Otherwise, you might have it right on top of you."

One problem was the superstition among villagers that a man-eater must be a *mtu-ana-geuka-simba*, literally, "a man-turned-into-a-lion", a witch with whom it was dreadfully dangerous to interfere. This superstition was often shared by the local game scout stationed in that village or sent out to dispatch the lion – including the mighty Nonga Pelekamoyo, or Take Your Heart, uncle of old Saidi (and also uncle of Rashidi Kawawa, Tanzania's first Prime Minister after Independence, and currently Minister of Defense). This two-hundred-pound Ngoni – the one who had set fire to all the Ngindo settlements on Brian's first tour through the region of Ngarambe – was sleeping in a bamboo stockade in a village beset by a man-eater when the lion burst straight through the bamboo in order to get at him. Miraculously the lion seized, not Nonga, but the wooden bed that the villagers had provided for their savior. The lion actually dragged the bed clean out of the stockade, and Nonga Pelekamoyo, managing to roll off, escaped unharmed. But afterward Nonga refused to consider any further dealings with this *mtu-ana-geuka-simba*, and turned the whole case over to Bwana Nyama.

Brian reckons he has killed about fifty lions, of which perhaps nineteen or twenty were man-eaters; the rest were stock-raiders, which usually got that habit from feeding on dead cattle after drought or plague. Asked if fear had ever been a problem, he thinks a moment, as if such an idea had never occurred to him before. Frowning, he says, "One is bound to be tensed up, of course, but if it was *really* fear, you wouldn't bloody well do it, especially after you've put a bullet in some dangerous creature only to have him go thrashing off into the thicket. Then you've got to start all over again, and it's a lot worse than before." He shook his head, and changed the subject. "I recall one lioness over here on the Mbarangandu that jumped out and scattered the porters, then came towards me. I knew she was not a man-eater, in a place so remote from human habitation; I thought she must have cubs, so I didn't shoot, just held the rifle on her, backing up slowly. She kept on coming, keeping the same fifteen yards between us, snarling and thrashing her tail. And then, when she figured that her cubs were safe, she turned suddenly and bolted for the long grass. Quite interesting, really."

"In the north," Brian says, "man-eaters are rarely a problem, but here in the south they still occur regularly. Not so many in the settled areas any more, because the lions themselves are dying out, and there is still enough game around to feed those that are left. But two or three people have been taken along that footpath" – and he pointed south – "between Liwale and Mahenge. Except for that porter at Kichwa Cha Pembe, I've never lost any of my people to a lion, but you have to be careful."

By nightfall the humidity has lifted, and the flying clouds part on a cold full moon. All around the horizon, as the wind chases them, the flames of Goa's fires leap and fall in the black tracery of trees like a demonic breathing from within the earth.

Lying out under the stars, we reminisce about friends we have in common. When first approached about joining this safari, I had been told that Brian Nicholson had invited along Myles Turner, now a game warden in Malawi, who had befriended me in the Serengeti in 1969 and 1970; this evening I expressed regret that Myles was unable to join us after all. Brian stares at me. "I thought it was you who had invited Myles!" he said. I shake my head: I had been told that Myles was an old friend of Brian, and the suggestion was made that I could get a lot of good material sitting around the campfire at night listening to the two wardens talk about the late great days when the native knew his place. Although Brian knows that I am teasing him, he grins.

"Well, I've known Myles for a long time, that's true; I've known him since about 1948. Good hunter, too – very patient and painstaking. And as I recall, the first gun I possessed, some sort of air gun, once belonged to Myles. But I can't imagine what Myles and I would have reminisced about; never did one thing together that I can recall. Last year Myles was in Nairobi, and I asked him to stop by the house, talk over this safari. He said he was very busy, had to go to Nyeri and so forth, and as it turned out, he had no time for me when he got back. Can't say I was surprised when the news came that he couldn't get leave after all. In the old days, when he was a warden in the Serengeti, he used to say, 'I'd give anything to get down there and see that bit of Africa of yours.' I invited him, and more than once, but he never came."

Another friend of Brian in the early days was a young Provincial Forest officer named John Blower, a wanderer whom I crossed paths with many years later, in

Ethiopia, and again, years after that, in Nepal. Blower had been fascinated by the possibilities of the Selous and thought that the Lung'onyo River region might be best protected by making it part of the Forest Reserve. At one point, he made what Brian calls "a hell of a trek" from the Kingupira region west to the Ulanga River, then south to Shuguli Falls, then up the Luwegu River to Mkangira, and from there back to Liwale. "Half-killed his porters. He'd set out in the morning and never look back, and some of these chaps were still turning up weeks later. Couldn't hire a porter around the Liwale area for six months afterward." Hearing of this, Ionides had been furious that a walk through the Selous should have been made without his permission, and subsequently, at some sort of Game Department function in Arusha, he asked a young man if he had ever come across "this bastard Blower". It was Blower himself, of course, whom he addressed, and after a decent interval, they became great friends.

In 1953 Nicholson was summoned to Kenya to serve with the Kenya Police Reserve, patrolling against Mau-Mau terrorists around Nanyuki. By 1954, when he was called a second time, the hard-core Mau-Mau had retreated up into the Aberdares, and Brian served with the Kenya Regiment in field intelligence operations about twenty miles northwest of Nairobi, where he participated in the "pseudo-gang" operations. "We'd black our faces and go out at night, wearing old clothes, and an African whom the Mau-Mau did not know had turned against them would lead us straight into their camp. He'd do the talking to get us past the guard, and once we got into the middle of them, we'd shoot the place to pieces. That's what really won the war; it completely confused them, they never knew who was for them and who wasn't, and there were cases toward the end in which two genuine Mau-Mau gangs were shooting up each other. John Blower was sent up there on the same thing, though I didn't see him. I was with Billy Woodley and several others; we were very close friends in school, Billy and me, and we still are." Remembering something, Brian smiles. "When we were kids, we used to go hunting out on the Aathi Plain, where Embakasi Airport is today. One day we were trying to stalk some tommies, using cattle to cover our approach – no luck at all. Then more cattle came along led by a prize white heifer, and damned if I didn't forget that gun was loaded. I said to Billy, If that was a buffalo, this is how I'd shoot it – BLAM! Down it went! That must have been thirty-five years ago!" As Brian says this, he sits straight up, more startled by the passage of time than by the trouble he had brought upon himself with that fatal shot.

At dawn, the smoke of Goa's fires has gone, the air is clean and cool, with the wind from the southeast; the prevailing weathers all across East Africa derive from these easterly trades off the Indian Ocean. Until today, it has been hot an hour after sunrise, reaching a hundred degrees, or so we estimate, late in the morning and maintaining that temperature until mid-afternoon. For those who must carry loads through thorn and tall dry grass, over black granite and the lava-like black cotton of the *mbugas*, it is just as well that on most days we travel for no more than five hours. Since the porters are well rested every afternoon, their spirits are high – so high, in fact, that occasionally it is necessary to damp them down. "*Usi piga kilele!*" Goa whispers at them, turning on the trail. And they do not mimic him or mutter, only smile a little, walking along under the awkward loads with the swaying elegance of the women in their villages, arms close to their sides but hands curved out, fingers extended, the loads clinging somehow to their heads. Only after moments with big animals do they hoot and chatter, letting off steam, and if this makes me smile, and I cannot hide it, they then have the excuse they need to squeal with laughter.

Although Brian is fond of saying that these porters can't compare with those on his old staff, who were "trained up to it", they win his grudging respect as the days go by. "They're a very good lot," he acknowledges. "Out five days, and not a single complaint yet." Even the saucy and single-minded Mata, from whom at least impertinence had been expected, has decided to comport himself as a professional porter on the basis of his one previous safari, and sets a stern example for the others. (Only at Mkangira, in the *ngoma* put on by the staff, did Mata display his cynical opinion of the hospitality, greetings, and thanks to the white visitors that the songs were intended to convey. In woman's costume, Goa's straw hat pulled down rakishly over one eye, he went swanking in and out of the line of porters as they danced and chanted, mimicking their thanks to the White Bwanas with squirming hips and raised prayerful hands and eye rollings of burlesqued gratitude – *Asante sa-a-na!* – in a parody so wild and deadly in its execution that whites and blacks alike giggled uneasily, not knowing where to turn. Mata himself had laughed openly into our faces, and his revenge was the artistic high point of the *ngoma*, surpassing even the strange dance of Abdallah, who kept time to the tom-tom while hopping on his head and elbows all the way around the fire circle.)

Leaving behind the smoldering black land of Goa's fires, we wade the river and head south through long, rolling savanna hills between the Mbarangandu and Njenji rivers. The morning remains cool and pleasant, with no trace of humidity, and the high grass, bronze and shining, flows in the south wind and early light. A flight of the large trumpeter hornbills lilts along the dark lines of big trees where a karongo descends toward the river, and a solitary white egret stands immobile in the rank green margins of a spring; this is the common egret, a cosmopolitan species, the only bird in the Selous that is also common in North America.

Coming up swiftly over a rise, we run into an old bull buffalo perhaps thirty yards away. As Brian seizes Goa's rifle, the bull rears his snout, seeming to glare at us past flared wet nostrils, big horns shining; the depthless black eyes never blink in the long moment that it takes for nose and ears and eyes and modest brain to weigh the choice between attack or flight. We hold quite still. Given enough time and space, the buffalo will almost always take the most prudent course, and after a few seconds of suspense this one, too, gives the heave and snort that accompany these bovine decisions and goes crashing off downhill into the thicket.

Apart from this buffalo and a few small groups of elephant, animals in this long-grass country have been scarce, as if all the waning energy in the coppered hills and yellowed trees and sinking rivers of September had been distilled in the fierce greens of the parrots and the paradisal blues of the brilliant rollers. But on the far side of a rise, in an open hollow, the missing animals have taken shelter from the silent landscape – impala, wildebeest, wart hog, zebra, and elephant, with a flock of the huge *batutu* in attendance. Led by the hornbills, all but the elephant stream away uphill toward the blue sky, striped horses shining in the high bronze grass.

Goa follows the old paths of the elephants, which follow the ridge lines and avoid the stony depths and thorn of the karongos; it is pleasant to sense that most of these neat trails, two feet across, from which all grass has been worn away, have never been seen or walked by human beings. Eventually a path descends toward the river, and from a bluff we contemplate an elephant with calf, at rest on a clear shoal in the middle of the glittering Mbarangandu; in the new light of the river morning, they seem to dream, lulled to forgetfulness of where they might be going by the clear torrent from the southern mountains that casts sparkling reflections up the gray columns of their legs. We wait. Others have crossed ahead of them, feeding calmly in rank canebrake by the river, and when the cow and calf move on, we wade out into the sun-filled flow and continue southward.

Before long we are stalled by another elephant, this one a young bull standing in the grass of the river margin. Since more elephants are visible in the dense thickets, Goa leads the file on to the sand bar, passing in front of the elephant, and a bit close. When the bull begins to flap its ears and paw the ground, Brian and Goa, exchanging guns, also exchange an old-days grin of recognition; they have met this situation many times before. Brian says later that they must have killed three hundred elephants together (of the estimated thirteen hundred he has executed in his lifetime), almost all of them on control work in Tanzania; it has been many years since he took one on license. Between one and three thousand elephants were destroyed annually in control operations throughout his twenty-three years in the Game Department, and this was only a fraction of the total number taken here in the southeast.

The bull does not yet have our scent, nor does he see what makes him nervous, although Brian claims that elephants' sight is better than people imagine; perhaps he has heard us, or perhaps what has come to him is some subtle shift in atmosphere that affects his sense of elephant wellbeing. Testing the air with lifted trunk, he steps down on to the river bed, then swings around to dig a hole under the bank. When the water wells up, he picks up a trunkful and hurls it overhead, so that it falls with a fine *splat* upon his back; he sprays himself behind his ears and under his belly. In the process he develops an erection, but the lumbering penis is gingerly, first lowering a little like a boom, then bobbing upward in alarm as its owner moves out over hot sand. Nearing the river at a point downwind of us, the elephant stops short, then turns toward us, trunk held high; the gland takes cover as he wheels away and hurries into the bush.

A big pan not far away up the east bank of the river has always been a famous place for elephant and game; in other days, this pan held a large pool that was permanent home to crocodiles and hippos, but the hippos eventually wore their runway to the river so deep that at last the whole marsh emptied out, obliging these two species to gain a living elsewhere. It was here at Likale, Brian says – and he points to an open wooded hill on the south side – that he saw the greatest and most splendid kudu of his life. On the north side, sixteen elephants feed on the green carpet of an *mbuga*, and a number of others are in sight, including two that cross the river to join those on the western bank. In the dry pan, one hundred buffalo stand in a compact herd, with nearly that number of impala, thirty wart hog, a band of kongoni with a new calf, a zebra herd at the far wood edge where had been seen the great kudu of yore, and a quorum of the elongated birds that stand about at the water's edge the world over. Brian looks about him, saying, "I feel as if I was just here the other day. Nothing seems to have changed very much." I couldn't make out whether he was glad or sorry.

Having always been wary of returning to any wild place that has meant a lot to me in case it might have changed, and not for the better, I ask him why he has been so anxious to return to the Selous. At this, he glares at me, defensive. "Who said *I* was anxious to return here? Tom Arnold tell you that?" When I say nothing, but just meet his gaze, he comes off it with a sheepish smile. "No," he says quietly. "I get a lot of pleasure out of being here. See how the game is doing. Visit the old places. See my old staff." He glances at Goa, then blurts out, "The Selous is home to me, you see; it's the only place on earth where I feel I belong." Asked if he wanted to be buried here, as Ionides had been, he answers stiffly, "Don't give it much thought. Doesn't pay to be morbid. Don't expect I care very much what they do with me after I'm dead."

We wade the river and make camp just opposite the pan. To the east, the land rises to steep red escarpments; these broad valleys with steep cliffs may well be indications of ancient fault lines of the Great Rift that runs south from the Red Sea to the blue Zambezi. On all sides is an airy view of the Old Africa, and I am delighted that Brian wished to camp here and sorry to see the look of discouragement upon his face. "I'd been looking forward to this place," he says, "and it's the best we've seen, yet it just doesn't compare with the way it was. That buffalo herd used to be three or four times that size! And we have yet to see a single elephant with decent ivory!" It was just about this time last year that he and Arnold had flown up the Mbarangandu on a reconnaissance for this safari, "and there was a *lot* of game here, a lot of game, and all the way along: I don't believe we were ever out of sight of elephant." I protest that even a poaching epidemic, of which we have found no sign at all, could not have wiped out so many elephants in a single year, and at this he brightens; we should not forget, he reminds me, that the rains were very late this year, while last year they were normal. "We're well into September, and the Mbarangandu still looks as it normally does by late June or early July! The dry season is two months behind schedule, and the animals are still scattered. There's no need for them to concentrate along the rivers. There's water everywhere out in the bush, you've seen it for yourself!" For a moment Brian's voice is elated again, as if this familiar litany has cleared his doubts, yet, as I am beginning to perceive, a part of him has no wish to be consoled, for a moment later he is glum again. "I suppose it's a mistake to revisit a place you loved, to make this sort of sentimental journey. I haven't made a foot safari since 1963 – everything was Land Rovers after that – and a place can change a lot in sixteen years."

I repeat my arguments, to reassure myself as well as him: the scarcity of big bulls with large tusks is bothersome, of course, but it is simply not possible that the thousands of elephants observed from the air in 1976 and 1978 could have been killed off by poachers or even by plague, since on this trek we have found not one dead elephant. Also, the fact that the groups were so small was strong evidence that they were not being harassed. And wasn't there also a certain negative reassurance in the case of the rhino? Regularly along our way we have come upon fresh rhino scrapes, and since the rhinoceros regularly returns to the same place to defecate, almost all of these scrapes must represent different animals: yet the pair this morning were the first ones we have actually seen on our safari.

In the 1960s a number of rhino were killed because of a notion among Orientals that the compacted erect hair of the rhino "horn" was a cure for impotence and certain fevers: the accelerated rhino slaughter of today has come about because rich Arabs of the Middle East have made a fashion of daggers with rhino horn handles, for which they are willing to pay over six thousand dollars apiece. The fad or fetish for these phallic daggers has jumped the already very high price of horn up to five thousand dollars per kilo in Hong Kong – the worthless stuff commands more than pure gold – and unless drastic measures are enforced, and soon, an ancient species may vanish from the earth millions of years before its time because of sexual insecurity in *Homo sapiens*.

Even ten years ago one could take for granted encounters with a few rhinoceros; these days it is a stroke of luck to see one. So far as it is known, black rhinos have been all but eliminated from Uganda. Kenya's recent population of fifteen to twenty thousand rhino has been reduced to between twelve and fifteen hundred. Since the early 1970s, the rhino in the Tsavo parks have declined from seven or eight thousand to one hundred and eighty; in the small Amboseli park, the decline is from fifty to ten. Rhino poaching has crossed the border from the Mara into the Serengeti, and the other important Tanzania parks – Ngorongoro, Manyara, Tarangire, Ruaha – have already lost at least three-quarters of their populations. In the Selous the most recent estimate of rhino numbers, made during the air survey of 1976, arrived at the figure of four to five thousand, which must be the last large healthy population of this species in the world.

In the late afternoon, I wade the river to observe the large impala herd, which is mostly engaged in group activity that seems to anticipate the rut; while the does amble back and forth, uninterested, the bucks all run about, tail flags held high and barking like sick baboons, pausing here and there for a quick skirmish, running on. A few elephant and buffalo still linger at the edges of the plain, and the thirty wart hogs are still present, avoiding one another's company, moving about on their front knees and snuffling into the earth.

Dark clouds and wind. At dusk, under the eastern bluffs where an elephant is throwing trunkfuls of fine dust into the air, a ghostly puff of light explodes, another, then another. I cannot see the elephant, only the dust that rises out of the shadow into the sunlight withdrawing up the hill. At dark a hyena whoops and another answers, for the clan is gathering, but their ululations are soon lost in a vast staccato racket, an unearthly din that sweeps in rhythmic waves up and down the river bars, rising and falling like the breath of earth – then silence, a shocked ringing silence, as if the night hunters have all turned to hear this noise. Somewhere out there on the strand, I think, a frog has been taken by a heron; my mind's eye sees the long bill glint in the dim starlight, the pallor of the sticky kicking legs, the gulp and shudder of the feathered throat. The frog's squeak pierces the racket of its neighbors, which go mute. But soon an unwary one, perhaps newly emerged from its niche under the bank, tries out its overwhelming need to sing out in ratcheting chirp; another answers, then millions hurl their voices at the stars. The world resounds until the frogs' own ears are ringing, until all identity is lost in a bug-eyed cosmic ecstasy of frog song. In an hour or two, as the night deepens, the singing impulse dies, leaving the singers limp, perhaps dimly bewildered; remembering danger, they push slowly at the earth with long damp toes and fingers, edging backward into their clefts and crannies, pale chins pulsing.

Toward midnight I am awakened by a bellow, a single long agonized groan; a buffalo has cried out, then fallen silent. Perhaps something is killing it, perhaps a lion's jaws have closed over its muzzle, but I hear no lion, now or later. At daybreak a bird call strange to me rings out three times and then is gone, a bird I shall never identify, not on this safari or in this life. As a tropic sun rolls up on to the red cliffs across the river, setting fire to a high, solitary tree, the moon still shines through the winged piliostigma leaves behind the tent.

Kibaoni, or "Signboard", is a location on the Mbarangandu River where Ionides had caused a sign to be put up on the footpath between Liwale and Mahenge, reminding the Ngindo that they were in a game reserve and that it was forbidden to stray off the trail. A few miles short of Kibaoni we head west from the river, climbing gradually toward the red cliffs of a plateau. Though our destination is right there before us, Goa seems oddly disoriented and indecisive, wandering back and forth and tending into the wrong paths, until finally Brian stops him and explains the route. To me he says, "He knew where he was going, but never having been there before he had no sense of it. That's why he was wandering like that."

On a grassy hillside of small trees, a burst of terminalia saplings has sprouted out of a rhino scatter on the path, and there is lion spoor. Then Goa's hand is up: he points. A large dark animal stands in the high grass below the ridge line. With binoculars I pick out four more sable, lying in the copper-colored grass of the ridge summit; they do not look at us but face eastward, over a broad sweep of the river, two miles away. Then another big male, long horns taut, is standing up and staring at us, his shiny black hide set off by the white belly, chestnut brow abristle with morning light above the twin blazes of his face. Apparently he gives the alarm, for now another bull jumps up, and then another. The bulls regard us for a little while before leading the herd away along the ridge line and down on the far side. A dozen animals cross the sky, including a very young calf, and probably as many more never emerged from the high grass but simply withdrew down the north side of the ridge. The two lead bulls watch the others go before moving up through a small glade of silver trees at a slow canter, turning against the sky to stare again, then vanishing from view.

"They're incredibly tame up here," Brian remarks. "Don't know why this herd pushed off so soon. I've walked up to within twenty yards of sable down in this part of the country."

At the foot of the plateau, heart-shaped prints of sable ascend a slide where elephants have broken down the small steep cliff to make a pathway up and down the escarpment; in precipitous places, an elephant may sit back on its haunches and brace all four feet out in front to slow down its descent, but sometimes it is killed or injured anyway, and I wonder if the first one to try it in this place might not be buried deep beneath all this red rubble.

On the flat tableland above the cliff is a stand of closed miombo woodland, and we have not penetrated it very far before we pass twin gouges of a rhino. Before long, light appears beyond the brachystegia, and the graceful dark trees open out upon an elliptical pan nearly a mile in length, ringed all the way round by the closed woods. "Goa has never been here," Brian murmurs, "and the Ngindo in this country don't seem to know about it, either. Even my esteemed predecessor never knew about this place. So far as I know, you're the only white man besides myself ever to see it." But as he speaks, he is scanning the lost pan: despite all the sign that we have seen, the well-worn paths that have beaten flat the woodland edges, the good clear water, there are no rhino, elephant, or sable, not a single animal of any kind. In a way, the emptiness makes the great pan more impressive – the stillness of the glittering water, the yellow water lilies and the tawny marsh grass, the circle of still trees that hide this lovely place from the outside world, the resounding silence and expectancy, as if the creatures of the earth's first morning might come two by two between the trees at any moment. A pair of jacanas stand in wait where the east wind stirs the floating vegetation, and a few swallows loop and flicker in eternal arabesques.

"*Pumzika*," Brian says, and the porters, sullen, dump their loads; they seem to wonder why we have come all the way up here. Even Kazungu, who was mildly rebuked early this morning for letting the porters eat up all the food, has curdled a little in his attitude for the first time on our safari. Not wishing to talk, Brian goes off a little way and sits down with his back against a tree. Soon the wind dies. A scaly-throated honey guide comes to the gray limbs overhead, calling out to us to follow; otherwise the woodland is dead still. Kazungu, who knows perfectly well that tea and porridge are expected after the first trek of the morning, is sitting himself down, doing nothing about a fire, until finally Brian must call out to him, "Is our tea ready?" To cheer him up, Brian adds, "*Tu na tupa macho yetu kambini*," "We are throwing our eyes toward our camp" – in other words, From here we are starting home. Kazungu grins, and the porters look pleased, too; they have enjoyed themselves despite their labor, but now they are ready to return. Only Goa shows no elation; he is content with whatever Bwana Niki decides.

Before leaving Mkangira the Africans were given enough biltong to last eight days, or even ten if they took a little care; after five days the biltong is all gone. To carry loads, the porters say, they need something stronger than rice and porridge, and as the beans are already in short supply, another animal will have to be shot. Brian dislikes the idea very much. "For one thing," he says, indicating the waiting trees, "I would hate to break all this silence with a bloody great noise." We can take guinea fowl, wart hog, buffalo, or impala, and the first choice is impala: most of the Ngindo are Moslems, which eliminates wart hog, one or two guinea fowl would not suffice, and to kill buffalo would be very wasteful. "Anyway," Brian says, "I don't want to shoot at a dangerous animal with that Game Department .458 that I've never fired; I doubt very much that it has ever been zeroed in. If somebody got gored out here by a wounded animal, we'd be in serious trouble. The nearest settlement where we might send for help is at Liwale, at least four days away across rough country. Probably send us back a couple of aspirin."

From this nameless pan on this nameless plateau we shall head back north to the sand river where two days ago we surprised the resting lions, then follow it north and east to the Mbarangandu, which we shall descend to Mkangira. We realize now that this pan has been our outward destination, that today we are turning back to the New Africa, to an orderly life, to "civilization". At this prospect, Brian's expression, so clear and youthful in recent days, visibly sours. He wonders aloud if our companions have been fighting. "Always women who do the fighting on safari, usually against one another. Probably get back and find some of them camped on the far side of the river!" He is joking, of course, and starts to smile as a sly, bad expression comes across his face. "Who knows what they've been up to back there!" he exclaims, warming to his fantasy. "Buggery and lesbianism, probably! I tell you, the human animal when he gets despondent is bloody bad news!" And this bad old bush rat, Mister Meat, with his unshaven jaw and bad smile and loose teeth, removes his cigarette holder and laughs himself red in the face, and I laugh with him, not so much at what he has said but because of the infectious gusto of his cynicism.

Brian sighs, gazing about him. "In Africa, out in the bush, man is still a part of nature, and what he does is mostly for the better. It is only where the bloody Western civilization has come in that everything is spoiled." Brian has a poor opinion of *Homo sapiens* and his ambitions, but in the main he is amused by human folly, not made gloomy. Now he grins. "I told Melva* once that human beings were the dirtiest and most destructive animals on the face of the earth, and she took it personally, Women aren't really very logical in these matters.

---

* Nicholson's wife

But now she understands my point of view." He heaves to his feet, and sets off into the woods without a backward glance at the hidden pan.

On an elephant slide on the north end of the plateau lies an old cracked tusk that has been there for many years – mute evidence that no man comes this way. Descending, we head north through rough and unburned country. Goa is setting his fires again; columns of thick smoke rise up behind us as we head north to Mto Bila Jina, the River Without Name.

Coming down off the Luwegu side of the high plateau, this big stream that becomes a sand river in the dry season tends to the northward, bending close to the Luwegu. Eventually it curves away toward the northeast as a tributary to the Mbarangandu, an avenue of sand perhaps forty feet across, under steep banks lined on both sides by big trees; even now, deep in the dry season, there is clear water not two feet beneath its hot white surface. Because of the river's serpentine course, we do not walk along its bed but cut cross-country between bends, holding to our northerly direction, and in the early afternoon we break the journey at a rank meadow spring on an open hillside. When the day cools a little, we continue onward, skirting an occasional elephant, hearing the bark of an occasional Sykes' monkey or baboon, crossing and recrossing the River Without Name. All the while, Brian is looking for impala, but there is no sign of impala, or of wart hog, or of guineas, only the baked savannas and dry hillsides and open woodlands of high grass.

Toward sunset, where the river rounds a bend, three buffalo bulls stand together at the end of a long stretch of clean white sand. Brian is footsore and discouraged and irritable, and he knows that for the first time on our safari, the morale of the Africans is precarious due to the real or imagined need of meat. Earlier he had said that in shooting a buffalo too much of the meat would be wasted, even if two porters gave their loads to the others in order to lug all the meat that they could carry, but now he decides without further ado to execute one of the bulls. Leaving the rest of us behind, he stalks with Goa to a point on the stream bank not twenty yards from the three buffalo below, a point-blank range from which he is sure to drop the animal with the first bullet. At the crack of the rifle, the buffalo sags down upon the sand with the windy groan of death, and in the echo of the shot, the Africans laugh and clap their hands together. No second shot is needed, and when we come up, I congratulate Nicholson on killing the buffalo with such dispatch; he refuses the small comfort I have offered. "I hate doing that, it really depresses me," he says. "But we were getting into a serious food situation with these porters. Karen and Rick have never been on a real foot safari, where beans are the staple; they gave us twelve kilos when what was required was a whole bloody sack." He swears to himself, restless, unable to make his peace with it; I had not suspected that he would be so upset. After all, this man has killed thousands of animals, and no doubt hundreds of buffalo among them; the buffalo is not an endangered species, and these three bulls may have passed the reproductive age since they had wandered off from the large herds. Even the "waste" will not be seen as such by the carnivores and vultures that will reduce this buffalo to bones in a few days. It is not the waste that bothers him, but the intrusion by man into the "heart of the Selous" which was symbolized by that isolated shot.

Already Goa is preparing for the butchering, cutting dense branches of the dark green adina trees to lay as a meat rack on the white sand beside the carcass. Despite the hard day they have had in the dry hills, the Africans are inspired with new resolve by the dead buffalo. "We'll have to camp here through tomorrow so they can smoke that meat; they'll start tonight. And they need the rest. That's one reason I decided to shoot that buffalo and have done with the food problem; there's good water right here, we can camp next to the animal, they don't have to lug all that wet meat out of the woods."

The inert dark mass lies sprawled on the white sand, tongue lolling, as ticks and flies crawl over its thin belly hair and testes. In sunset light, Abdallah cuts its throat, and the thick blood pours away into the sand, and still Brian Nicholson does not stop talking. "These buggers can gorge themselves on meat tonight, and with my blessing, and all day tomorrow, too. And the next day, one man, maybe two, is going to carry nothing but meat; the rest will have to manage the extra loads. Because I'm not shooting anything again." I have the feeling he may still be talking to himself as he goes off down the stream bed for a wash.

On the damp sand just beneath the adina and tamarind grove where we will camp, Kazungu has paused a moment in his digging, as if hypnotized by the upwelling of clear water. Beside him are fresh tracks of both leopard and lion, and as a yellow moon rises in the east to shine through the tamarind's feather branches, a leopard makes its coughing grunt not far downriver. Soon lions are roaring, no more than a mile away. Brian says that because of their poor sense of smell, lions usually depend on vultures to locate carrion for them, and that he'd seen hyena using vultures the same way, going along for a few hundred yards before cocking their heads to locate the spiral of dark birds, then trotting on again. Though he doubts that lion would find the carcass, hyena or leopard might come in this evening, under the big moon.

That evening I ask Brian if he would ever consider returning to the Selous were he given a free hand to reconstitute it. "You never know," he says, after a long moment. "Don't want to burn all my bridges behind me. But I worked for next to nothing all those years; they can't expect me to do that again. Don't want to wind up on the dole in some little charity hole in the UK." – and here he looks up at me, genuinely horrified. "Oh God, how I'd hate *that*!" he says, and I believe him. There is nothing inauthentic about Brian Nicholson's self-sufficiency and independence, evolved out of hard circumstance very early in his life and reinforced at the age of nineteen when he banished himself to the wilds of Tanganyika. Unlike Rick Bonham (and unlike Philip Nicholson, the only son of a legendary warden of the great Selous) Brian has no romantic heritage in East Africa, or even a strong family to fall back on; neither did he ever have the celebrity enjoyed by the wardens of the great tourist parks, such as Bill Woodley and David Sheldrick and Myles Turner, the ones taken up by the shiny people who made East Africa so fashionable throughout the sixties. Not that he has complained of this, or even mentioned it; he has no self-pity, although here and there one comes upon a hair of bitterness. One day when he lost a filling, I told him he'd get no sympathy from me, not after his hard-hearted response to my shattered tooth back there on the Luwegu. This teasing was meant as the only sort of concern he could permit, but Brian failed to smile, saying coolly instead, "Unlike you, I *expect* no sympathy." There was a certain truth in this, but perhaps the remark revealed more truth than he had intended.

"The Selous ought to be set up under its own authority," Brian is saying, "financing itself and administering itself, not vulnerable to people who aren't really interested. That was the trouble down here when I left – lack of real interest. Now Costy Mlay, he was sent down here from Mweka, and he quickly understood the problems and saw the potential. Costy's the exception; he was interested, and he's *still* interested, even though he is no longer with the Game Department. Costy's very bright, and he's not a politician.

"To lose the Selous now would be such a dreadful waste, and especially when you realize that everything is present that is needed to administer it efficiently, all of the groundwork has already been done! For example, all the road alignment – when I was here, we were operating over three thousand miles of dry season tracks. And the placement and grading of the airstrips – that's done, too. They just have to be cleaned up again. There's even the nucleus of a good staff – the old game scouts who still know the country, who could train up a new corps of men, set up patrol posts. That's the first thing I would do if I ever came back here, get my old staff together to train up good new people, like some of these young porters we have here now. I'd try to persuade Damien Madogo to come back, and I'd get hold of Alan Rees. Rees was my right-hand man all the way through, he was principal game warden for the Western Selous – held the same official rank as I did. No story of the Selous would be complete without mentioning Alan; he was a fine hunter and a fine warden, conscientious and patient and very good with his staff, and in addition, he's a first-class naturalist; he just loves being out in the bush, rains and all, and his wife is the same way.

"The senior warden up there in Dar, Fred Lwezaula – he's all right, too. He's doing the best he can, considering the fact that nobody up there in Dar appreciates what they've got down here. There aren't many people in the government who even know where the place is! I don't think it's ever been brought home to them that the Selous is unique. It is not just a big empty part of the ordinary monotonous miombo country that takes up most of southern Tanzania; it's well watered, it's vast, it's almost entirely surrounded by sparsely populated country, it's an ecological unit – or several ecological units, as Alan Rodgers says – and there's nothing like it in East Africa. But the Selous has to be self-supporting if it is going to withstand all the demands for land and timber and the like that are bound to come; we proved it could support itself very easily, and build up the country's foreign reserves as well, and still remain the greatest game area in the world." The Warden paused for breath, then concluded quietly, "If only for economic reasons, they owe it to the future of their country to see to it that this place doesn't disappear, because it's very precious, and it is *unique* – I can't say it too often! There's nothing like it in East Africa!"

Both lion and leopard cough and roar intermittently throughout the night, but at daybreak there are no fresh tracks around the puddle of congealed blood, the pile of half-digested grass stripped from the gut, the sprawl of entrails, the mat-haired head with the thick twisted white tongue. Overhead, the moon is still high in the west, and shimmering green parrots, sweeping like blowing leaves through the river trees, chatter and squeal in the strange moonset of the African sunrise.

By the time the buffalo was butchered it was late last night, and the Africans were exhausted; the meat was heaped in a big pile by the kitchen fire to discourage theft by passing carnivores, and this morning, under Goa's direction, Mata and Abdallah are cutting heavy Y-shaped posts and setting them into the ground. The posts will support a rack of strong green saplings, and under the rack a slow fire will be tended that will keep the meat enveloped in thick smoke. "This is a day they will always remember," Brian comments. "Down here in southern Tanzania, they have no livestock at all except a few goats and chickens; the poorer ones get hardly any meat. So this is a unique experience for most of them, perhaps the one time they will ever have it – the day on which they were actually paid to sit around and eat all the meat they could hold. Of course that used to happen with the elephants I had to shoot, but those people weren't paid for it, as these are." He describes how in the old days, traveling light on elephant control, he would camp next to the killed animal in this same way, living exclusively on elephant kidney and sweet tea and rice cooked in advance and packed tight into a sock – a clean sock, mind, he adds, with the trace of a smile.

I take advantage of a day in camp to go off by myself and look for birds, walking alone up the sand river. By the dead buffalo, a vague cold smell of turning meat is mixed in a repellent way with fleeting sweet whiffs of bush orange, but soon there is only the faint mildew smell of the haze of algaes on the damp sand, which everywhere is cut by the tracks of animals; criss-crossing the marks of eland, kongoni, bushbuck, hippo, buffalo, and elephant are myriad patterns of unknown small creatures, and also the round pugs of lion and leopard. Since I am barefoot, it would be difficult to circle through the bush if something came down into the river bed and cut me off from camp: I listen for the crack of limbs, the buffalo puff, the rhino *chuff*. Brian had recommended the services of Goa and his .458, but Brian himself has a poor opinion of Goa's marksmanship, and to observe birds with an armed escort – ! Anyway, I wanted to get off by myself.

Walking alone is not the same as trudging behind guns; one stays alert. And although this is not the first time on this foot safari that I hear the wind thrash in the borassus palms, the moaning of wild bees, it is perhaps the first time that I listen. Walking upstream, I am shadowed for a while by a violet-crested turaco which moves with red flares of big silent wings from tree to tree, then hurries squirrel-like along the limbs, the better to peer out at me, all the while imagining itself unseen; occasionally it utters a loud hollow laugh that trails off finally into gloomy silence, as if to say, "Man, if you only knew ..." A large patch of blue acanth flowers on the bank is shared by the variable sunbird and the little bee-eater, and when I pause to watch the sunbird, a tropical boubou climbs out of a nearby bush and utters its startling bell notes at close range as its mate duets it from a nearby tree, then unravels the beauty it has just created with a whole run of froggish croaks that cause an ecstatic pumping of its black-and-cream-colored boubou being. Brown-headed parrots and a beautiful green pigeon climb about in a kigelia, which has also attracted a scarlet-chested sunbird. Cinnamon-breasted and golden buntings flit in separate small flocks across the river, and a pair of golden orioles skulks in a bush; ordinarily these shy birds frequent the treetops. At a rock pool, perhaps a mile upstream, I watch striped kingfishers and a white-breasted cuckoo-shrike, and listen to a bird high in the canopy that I have never heard before and cannot see; its single note is a loud and clear sad *paow!* Circling it, waiting, listening, I am rewarded at last with the sight of a lifetime species, the pied barbet.

At camp, toward noon, the vultures are already gathering: fifteen griffons have sighted the buffalo carcass and are circling high overhead. But soon they have dispersed again, after swooping in low for a hard look; though nothing threatens vultures, they are wary birds, and too many humans for their liking come and go around our camp less than fifty yards away. There is a lion kill not far downriver, to judge from the resounding noise heard in the night; perhaps the vultures have gone there to clean things up.

In early afternoon, over the river trees, heavy rain clouds loom on the east wind. Then a light rain falls, and the returning griffons, accumulating in dead silence, fill bare limbs back in the forest with dark bird-like growths; at some silent signal, half a hundred come in boldly on long glides, feet extended; they strip the buffalo dry and clean within an hour.

By late afternoon the smoked meat is shrunk down to black curled twists of leather. The Africans take turns tending it, and the others sit upright in a circle under the tamarind: the small-faced Mata, and tall Amede, and the small man with the child's wide-eyed face who is called Shamu, and the squealing Abdallah with the squint, and Saidi Kalambo in his big hair and huge blue boxer shorts, and the heavy boy in the red shirt who is called "Davvid" although he is a Mohammedan – "*Davvid* Endo Nitu", he insists firmly. And Kazungu says, "I also have a foreign name of 'Stephen', but now I am proud of using my African name."

Only Goa does not join in as the others laugh and tell one another stories. Mzee Goa, as the Ngindo call him, Old Man Goa, lies flat out on a piece of canvas, making the most of his day of rest, staring up through the dark green leaves of adina and tamarind at the blue sky. On the tamarind bark over his head, a large agama lizard is pressing up and down in agitation, and not far away, on a broken elbow of a piliostigma, a tree squirrel sits calmly, observing the human camp. Across the sandy soil near my own feet, where I sit on my campaign cot before our tent, a blue-black hornet, hard tail flickering, is dragging a dying spider twice its size toward some dank hole where it can be sealed in with the hornet's eggs.

At dark, the Africans move up close to the kitchen fire, which dances and flickers on the naked skin of dark chests and arms; behind them rises a stand of tall pale grass, higher than their heads, and beside them, on a bed of adina fronds, lies the big pile of dried meat. In more places than one, I think, along the northern borders of the Game Reserve, groups of young Africans such as these must be smoking their poached meat around bush fires very much like this one.

Since his Swahili is excellent and since he enjoys the jokes as much as they do, Brian teases the Africans a lot, and the younger ones joke back at him, as much for their own amusement as for his. Like Kazungu, they are good-natured, never impertinent, there is no air of aggression in their merriment. Yet I notice that Goa, though he laughs sometimes at Bwana Niki's jokes, never volunteers a sally of his own; his is the last of the colonial generation. And the Warden retains the colonial manner with the Africans, giving orders in short and peremptory tones. Except in calling out a name – Kazungu! Goa! (he doesn't know the porters' names – they are all "Bwana") – he never raises his voice; intentionally or otherwise, he usually speaks in such low tones that Kazungu or Goa must come up very close to hear him, seating themselves on the ground before his feet. On the other hand – unlike Ionides – he is never abusive or sarcastic, never shows anger even when exasperated, and takes the time to chat with them and make them laugh, though he is embarrassed when I ask him to translate one of the jokes. "Got to keep them simple, you know," he says, reverting to his old White Highlands manner. This time he has told the porters that if they keep on eating up the white man's food, they will grow very pale and their hair will straighten, and though a Mombasa Kenyan like Kazungu is too sophisticated for this jest, the Tanzanian country boys enjoy it.

I suspect Brian Nicholson of liking Africans, despite all the conventional prejudices he displays. If I had any doubts about this, most of them would be resolved by the evidence of my own eyes and ears that Africans, from the simplest of these porters to an urbane, well-educated man such as Costy Mlay, seem fond of Brian, whose fluent Swahili must convey subtleties of understanding and even concern that are absent in most whites. Unlike Ionides, Brian was born in East Africa and has known and worked with Africans since he was a child. It is true that he has usually been in a superior's position with these people, which goes a long way to explain his preference for country Africans over those in the city, and no doubt he would agree with Ionides that Western civilization has reduced many first-rate Africans to third-rate Europeans; I no longer bother to point out that, forced to adapt suddenly to an African culture, a first-rate European would certainly be thought of as a third-rate African, at least for the first few hundred years.

Kazungu, who can speak some English, is teaching me a little Swahili, and Brian teases him, saying that Kenyans don't really know how to speak it. "The Brits have really buggered up the Swahili language. Say *Jambo* instead of *Hujambu* just for a start. And then they answer '*Jambo*', which is all wrong, too. Once asked an African up there, '*Ume elewa?*' which means, Do you understand? and he became frightfully offended – thought I was accusing him of being drunk. To be drunk is *kulewa* – not the same sound at all." And Kazungu laughs, nodding his head; he freely admits that these young Tanzanians speak better Swahili than he does, since for them it is not a lingua franca but a local tongue.

As camp cook and a man with a bit of English, not to mention experience of such cities as Nairobi and Mombasa, Kazungu has prestige among the porters. But he never abuses his position, in part because he is outnumbered six to one. This evening, in the only unpleasant tone I have heard in the past fortnight, Davvid Endo Nitu is informing Stephen Kazungu Joma that if the arrogant Kenyans don't behave themselves, the Tanzanian Army will march through their country as it did through Uganda, to teach them a lesson once and for all.

Brian doesn't think much of my argument that the temporary anarchy in Uganda is probably worth it to get Idi Amin out of power, although I back up my position by relating a story told to me by Maria's* brother, now a doctor in Australia, who had done his colonial service in Kampala. One of Peter Eckhart's teammates on the rugby team was a young African giant who was already heavyweight boxing champion of Uganda and a marvelous athlete, Peter said, immensely powerful and very fast for his great size; what struck Peter, who is not liberal in any way and doubtless shares the political outlook of Brian Nicholson, was this man's gentleness and consideration toward all the white players and absolute ferocity toward other blacks – "murderous", to use Dr Eckhart's word, and a good word, too, in the light of later events. And then there was the warning that the British left the new leaders of Uganda when Independence came, concerning a young lieutenant named Idi Amin who was ruthlessly extermi-nating recalcitrant tribesmen up in Karamojong, how they were sure to have trouble with this fellow if they didn't bring him under control immediately ...

And Brian shrugs, not because what I am saying is not true but because such excess is only to be expected on this continent: the bloody display of power is an African tradition. "Why was Amin any worse than that emperor up in Central African Republic, or the one in Guinea? Butchering people right and left, and nobody paid any attention." I cannot deny this. Who had concerned themselves about the deaths of the thousands massacred in Guinea by President Macias Nguema Biyogo? What could his Belgian friends reveal about political oppression under Colonel Seso Seke Mobutu, the western puppet still catering to European interests in Zaire? And hadn't the French cynically supported the "Emperor" Jean-Bédel Bokassa of the Central African Republic despite the well-documented knowledge that he had personally taken part in the massacre of two hundred schoolchildren?

We are edgy on this subject, and I am considering how to change it when I notice the bottle of whiskey that sits like a reproach beside my cot. Since wine and beer were too bulky and heavy, this bottle has been brought along for me instead, but in the wellbeing and exhilaration of the foot safari, I have felt no need for it; on the other hand I am mildly embarrassed, since it has been an extra

* My friend Maria Eckhart, who was born at Moshi, at the foot of Kilimanjaro

weight in someone's load. Thoughtlessly I suggest that it be given to the staff, to celebrate when we reach the Mbarangandu, and Brian snaps, "Absolutely not! You Americans ruined your own natives with alcohol; leave ours alone!" I know he has taken advantage of an opening, and I know why, but I manage to repress a sharp retort about the echo of colonialism in that "your" and "ours"; his choice of words does not change the fact that he is right.

Tonight we have buffalo kidney to go with our rice and beans, and while we eat Brian describes how he had once been hurt by a buffalo that had been wounded by a "big-game hunter" from Dayton, Ohio. "That was in the Maasai Mara, about 1949, when I was learning the hunting safari business as assistant to a chap named Geoff Lawrence-Brown. We had followed up this fellow's wounded buffalo and it jumped out of my side of the thicket, right on top of me. I got two rounds off into this dark blur, and it went down, but not before it caught me with the outside of its horn and sent me flying. I was pretty badly banged up."

I ask his opinion of these "big-game hunters", and the Warden grunts. "Don't know much about these people, really. Only stayed in that business long enough to qualify for my professional hunter's license. I always had my eye on the Game Department, you see. But I will say that most of the professional hunters I knew had contempt for a lot of their clients. Some tried to find nice things to say, and were loyal to their clients whether they liked them or not, but there aren't many professionals of that caliber any more. And a number of clients simply weren't physically fit enough to track their animals, even if they had nerve enough to leave their Land Rovers. Sometimes they shot from the windows, or rested their rifles on the bonnet of the car; many animals are unafraid of cars, so they had them at point-blank range. Sometimes the hunter and his client got out of the car on the far side from the animal, using the car as a hide; as soon as the car moved out of the way, they shot, and later it was claimed that they hunted the animal on foot. The client forgets what he wants to forget by the time he gets back home.

"A lot of these clients are first-class people, of course, but others are just big drinkers and big talkers, very childish men. What amazes me is how they worship their professional hunters, look at them like gods. I've seen grown men who seem to have good sense in every other way – must be good businessmen, at least, if they can afford that kind of safari – go all to pieces over one of these professionals who might just be a bloody idiot, and often is. Some of them are good men, good hunters and good conservationists, but too many are in it part-time, looking for quick money, or perhaps they're farmers who've shot a buffalo or two – short on experience and long on bullshit.

"One damned fella shot a rare cheetah down here, mistook it for a leopard – how could you mistake a cheetah for a leopard? The way they look, the way they move – why, they're not alike in any way! Another one told me he'd seen lesser kudu here, and dik-dik. Well, he hadn't.

"One hunter had trouble qualifying; there was no one who would vouch for him. He claimed to be a friend of mine, and used me as a reference when he applied for his license; probably thought they wouldn't check, since I was so far from Nairobi. I wrote back to say I'd never heard of him, which was the truth, but somehow he got his license anyway. And there was another one who claimed he knew me, too, one of these birds with a leopard-skin hat band and so many elephant-hair bracelets he could hardly lift his arms, you know the type. Told Billy Woodley he'd worked with me on elephant control down along the Ruvuma. Well, one day Billy and I were going through Namanga, and Billy introduced us, or rather, he said, 'I don't have to introduce you two, since you already know each other.' For some reason, the subject of our days together down on the Ruvuma never came up.

"Here in the Selous, we didn't care much how these people got their animals; if the professional did most of the killing for his client, as was sometimes the case – the client fires, and he never hears that second shot – it was more efficient and a lot more merciful. The point was that the Game Department needed the revenues, and every animal was paid for; a game scout went along with each safari to record any animals lost when wounded, since those counted on their limit, and to see that the limit was never exceeded. Each year we established a quota for each hunting block, according to what it could easily support, and we were very strict. I caught one German hunter who'd killed a rhino, although he had none on his quota, then tried to bribe one of my game scouts to keep him quiet; the scout came straight in and reported it, bringing the money. This German had also let an unqualified assistant take people out after buffalo, which was forbidden. I confiscated his license and told him he had forty-eight hours to get out of the Selous. The clients begged me, of course, but I just told them that they'd have to find themselves another hunter."

A cold clear morning. Well before daybreak, voices murmur and human figures move about, building up the fire to keep warm. A smell of carrion hangs heavy on the air, but the leopard, heard again last night, has not visited the buffalo, nor did the lions follow up our circling vultures. As for hyena, none have been heard since we left the Mbarangandu, nor are there hyena tracks in the sand river.

The sun-dried meat is packed into the loads; every man must help to carry it, since they mean to take it all. In the cold sunrise, the porters are quickly ready. As we depart, a stream of parrots in careening flight recaptures the sausage tree across the river; the fleeting human presence will lose significance with the last figure that passes out of sight in the dawn trees.

We are headed north again, into burned country, and the spurts of green grass in the black dust are sign that these fires preceded those we made on the way south; if this is the eastern edge of the large burn that we struck in the first days of our safari, then we are closer than we think to the Luwegu. In the bright grass the animals are everywhere, making outlandish sounds as we approach; the kongoni emit their nasal puffing snort, the zebra yap and whine like dogs, the impala make that peculiar sneezing bark. But the two buffalo that canter across our path are silent, the early red sun in the palm fronds glistening on their upraised nostrils, on the thick boss of the horns, the guard hairs down their spines, the flat bovine planes of their hindquarters.

At the edge of the plain, between thickets and karongos, Goa rounds a high bush and stops short; without turning around he hands the rifle back, as Brian and I stop short behind him.

In a growth of thin saplings, at extreme close quarters, stands a rhinoceros with a small calf at her side. The immense and ancient animal remains motionless and silent, even when the unwarned porters, coming up behind, gasp audibly and scatter backward to the nearest trees. Goa, Brian and I are also in retreat, backing off carefully and quietly, without quick motion: I am dead certain that the rhino is going to charge, it is only a matter of reaction time and selection of one dimly seen shadow, for we are much too deep into her space, too close to the small calf, to get away with it. But almost immediately a feeling comes, a knowing, rather, that the moment of danger, if it ever existed, is already past, and I stop where I am, in pure breathless awe of this protean life form, six hundred thousand centuries on earth.

In the morning sun, reflecting the soft light of shining leaves, this huge gray creature carved of stone is a thing magnificent, the ugliest and most beautiful life imaginable, and her sheep-sized calf, which stands backed up into her flank, staring with fierce intensity in the wrong direction, is of a truly marvelous young foolishness. Brian's voice comes softly, "Better back up, before she makes up her mind to rush at us," but I sense that he, too, knows that the danger has evaporated, and I linger a little longer where I am. There is no sound. Though her ears are high, the rhinoceros makes no move at all, there is no twitch of her loose hide, no swell or raising of the ribs, which are outlined in darker gray on the barrel flanks, as if holding her breath might render her invisible. The tiny eyes are hidden in the bags of skin, and though her head is high, extended toward us, the great hump of the shoulders rises higher still, higher even than the tips of those coarse dusty horns that are worth more than their weight in gold in the Levant. Just once, the big ears give a twitch; otherwise she remains motionless, as the two oxpeckers attending her squall uneasily, and a zebra yaps nervously back in the trees.

Then heavy blows of canvas wings dissolve the spell: an unseen griffon in the palm above flees the clacking fronds and, flying straight into the sun, goes up in fire. I rejoin the others. As we watch, the serene great beast settles backward inelegantly on her hind quarters, then lies down in the filtered shade to resume her rest, her young beside her.

We walk along a little way before I find my voice. "That was worth the whole safari," I say at last.

Brian nods. "Had to shoot one once that tossed a porter into a thornbush and wouldn't give up, kept trying to get at him. But by and large, the rhino down in this part of the country have never given me much trouble." He turns his head and looks back at me over his shoulder. "Still, that's a lot closer than you want to get, especially with a gang of porters. If this was Tsavo – !" He rolls his eyes toward heaven. In an easing of the nerves, we burst out laughing, and the Africans, awe-struck until this moment, laugh as well: *kali* ("hot-tempered", dangerous) or not, a rhinoceros with new calf ten yards away was serious business!

Yet seeing the innocent beast lie down again, it was clear how simple it would be to shoot this near-blind creature that keeps so close to its home thickets, that has no enemies except this upright, evil-smelling shadow, so recent in its ancient world, against which it has evolved no defense. Its rough prong of compacted hair would be hacked off with a panga and shoved into a gunny sack as the triumphant voice of man moved onward, leaving behind in the African silence the dead weight of the carcass, the end-product of millions of browsing, sun-filled mornings, as the dependent calf emerges from the thicket, and stands by dumbly to await the lion.

We head northeast into dry grassy hills. Big pink-lavender grasshoppers rise and sail away on the hot wind, the burring of their flight as dry and scratchy as the long grass and the baked black rock, the hard red lateritic earth, the crust of Africa. To the west rise rough black escarpments, and beyond the escarpments an emptiness in the air, arising from the depression of the Luwegu's valley. Toward the southwest border of the Reserve shrouds of dull smoke ascend to the full fire clouds, all across the Mbarika Mountains.

The path descends into inland valleys of dry thorn scrub and long clinging strands of shrub combretum, then small sand rivers of sweet musky smells and cat-mint stink where crested guinea fowl, a shy forest species, run away cackling under the thickets. But there is no water, and because of their extra loads of meat and the strain caused by the encounter with the rhino, the porters are already tired before noon. To Brian's annoyance, they keep falling far behind. "It's very easy to get lost in bush like this," he mutters. "They must stay together."

Beneath borassus palms a small trickle of good water runs along the bed of a karongo, but under the red banks a juvenile elephant is swatting its legs with a fan of fresh-broken branches, and across the ditch at the wood's edge a cow moves back and forth in agitation; then a second cow with a smaller calf moves into view and disappears again. It is hard to tell how many elephants are here, or where they are, but the nearest among them are a lot too close. Uneasily, the porters set their loads down, all but the small wide-eyed Shamu, who stares astonished at the elephants like a little boy. Goa says sharply, "*Tua!*" (literally, "to land") – "Put your load down!" And Shamu does so as the second cow emerges part-way from the nearest thicket, ears flared out, and drives us back with a loud blare of warning. The confused calf in the karongo tries clumsily to climb the bank, and a third elephant, until now unseen – doubtless the mother of a calf we have not seen either – comes for us across the karongo. "*Kimbiya!*" Goa tells the porters. "Run!" The Ngindo scatter off into the bush, and the rest of us back up rapidly for the second time today. But the cow has stopped behind that wall of vines; we wait and listen while a boubou, startled out of its bush by the elephant, flies across the karongo and resumes its duet without a care.

The calf in the karongo is safely away, and the other calves are, too; we do not see the elephants again. Those in the bush right in front of us have simply vanished, so silently and so magically that even Brian can't quite believe it, and goes poking about in the bush in a gingerly way, just to make sure. Meanwhile, the porters have traveled so fast and so far that we have trouble reassembling them. "We lost track of ourselves," Mata admits, in the wonderful translation of Kazungu. We cross the karongo, drink warm water, and rest in the cool green shadow of an afzelia. Brian is pensive. "Have to be very careful with these animals, more careful than usual. I don't want to provoke a charge if I can help it. We're a long way from help, you know, if somebody gets hurt, and there's no track for bringing in a Land Rover. These emergencies can happen very fast, even when you see the animals and take pains with them, as we did here." He shakes his head. "What you don't want is to have one elephant cut off from the others. You try to make certain that they're all gone past before you push ahead, but sometimes in dense thicket like this, there's one that's slow or old that you don't see, and then there's trouble."

I am content that the Warden is being careful, and after all these encounters I have complete confidence in his nerve and expertise.

"One time, up on the Ruaha River – and by the way, we have more of the Ruaha right here in the Selous, about seventy miles of it, than they have in the Ruaha National Park – I had an elephant get in among my porters after I'd gone past. Chased one poor devil way off into the *bundu*, hot after him, you know, squealing like hell. Usually an elephant is quiet when it comes for you, at least until it's right on top of you; that's when it starts to yell. But this old cow yelled all the way, so we knew just where to follow. Kept coming on scraps of the porter's clothes – the turban he wrapped up on his head to cushion his load, then his shirt, his shuka – everything! He was running naked! But there was no sign of the body, so we kept on calling. After half an hour we reckoned that the poor chap must be a goner. We kept on calling, *Hoo!* – and suddenly, from a great distance, we heard, *Hoo!* The chap returned on his own two feet, all scratched and scared, but he was in one piece. Those clothes had saved him. Hadn't thought to shed them, they were just ripped off by the thorns, because with that elephant behind him he wasn't fussy about his route, he just went *moja kwa moja*, straight on through. But the clothes distracted that old cow just enough to slow her down. He never knew whether he'd outrun her or eluded her; he'd just kept running flat out, he said, until he realized that there was no more noise behind him."

We have hardly started out, toward three, when we run into more trouble. From a deep thicket comes a profound ominous mutter. Exasperated by the failure of the porters to keep up despite their hard experience this morning, the Warden begins a low muttering of his own. "What are these old cows so cross about?" he frets, cautioning the oncoming porters to be quiet. At that moment, the hidden elephant gives a loud and scary blare of warning close at hand – too close for the shot nerves of the Ngindo, who drop their loads and flee without further ado. As Goa and Brian exchange guns, and Brian jams cartridges into the chamber, a Sykes' monkey gives its loud *yowp* of alarm, and there comes a single sharp loud crack of breaking wood, then a dead silence. After a few minutes, when nothing happens, the porters are whistled for, and come in very quietly, one by one, grab up their loads, and flee again, loads to their chest. Not one was smiling. The porters are *choka sana*, very tired, from carrying the extra loads of meat and from the strain of all these encounters with big animals, and for the first time on the safari feel free to say so. "These elephants really made a pest of themselves today," Abdallah sighs as we pause to sip water from a ditch.

Our recent adventures with animals have broken down some of the formality between blacks and whites, the separation between their safari and ours. Kazungu tells me that he has never been on a foot safari before, nor have any of the young porters except Mata. Through the big voice of Kazungu I try to explain to the young Ngindo how precious this wild country is, where the water is clean and the game plentiful and even the dread rhinoceros is so peaceful. All the young porters nod fervently, saying "*Ndio, ndio, ndio,*" and Abdallah says, "It is good to see our country, and where the animals are staying," at which they all murmur "*Ndio!*" once again. It turns out that Abdallah is not an Ngindo but a

Makonde, the coastal tribe now famous for wood sculpture. Although he seems no older than the rest, Abdallah is married and has one child, and Kazungu says that he himself has plans to marry, possibly next year. Kazungu has kept up his journal:

About 9 a.m. we suddenly met a rhino ... To avoid being attacked by this rhino, we had to go slowly backward. I was very frightened. For a few minutes, nobody knew which way to go ... This was the first time I saw a rhino face-to-face.

After leaving the rhino we went right down to the river to make the porridge, then resumed our safari. The people were behaving very well, there was no trouble, they were more attentive now to what they were told, they were polite ... The safari was hard for people carrying loads on their heads and shoulders, but through good cooperation in a tough position, everybody was happy. They were tired, but still they were enjoying themselves. The only trouble they had was getting adjusted to hunger before the morning meal.

As we were proceeding with our safari, we met some elephants resting. When they realized we were around they started screaming, and we were shocked, and ran away and climbed on the trees, leaving our belongings behind. I knew I would be all right because I stayed close to the person carrying the gun. Everybody ran away except Goa, Bwana Niki, Bwana Peter, and me.

Of the afternoon's encounter, Kazungu wrote:

We could not see this elephant, could not see or hear anything with our ears and everyone was trembling. The elephant started screaming very highly, and this time the belongings were scattered around, and even I dropped my luggage and ran away. Later we started calling to see if we could find each other.

After all this, we went down to the Mbarangandu.

Sand rivers, river thickets, green *mbuga* and dry black cotton marsh, grassy ridges and airy open woods, yellow and copper, red and bronze under blue sky – the miombo woods are bursting into multicolored leaf, well before the onset of the rains.

In mid-afternoon, along the edge of the wood, a female kudu steps out into bright sunlight. She is crossing one of the black granite platforms inset like monuments in the pale grass, so that even her delicate hoofs are clearly visible. A second doe, already off the rock, awaits her. Then a magnificent bull kudu – all adult males of the greater kudu may be called "magnificent" – moves in the same slow dreamlike step over the rock. The kudu are upwind and do not scent us, nor have they heard the sound of our approach. They fade into the woodland. But where the elephant path tends uphill toward the woods, the bull awaits us; this time he raises big pink ears as if to listen to the oriole in the canopy, then stops and turns and gazes at man for the length of a held breath, displaying all the white points of his face – the white muzzle and cheek stripe, the white chevron beneath the eyes, the ivory tips of the great lyrate horns. Then he wheels and canters up the ridge, disappearing in seconds, although a kongoni that pronks along behind him is visible for a long way into the woods.

It is late afternoon when white sand bars and the blue gleam of the Mbarangandu appear like a mirage in the parched valley, and near sunset when we reach the river plain. Near the river, Goa's sharp eye picks out an elephant skull deep in the thicket; he emerges carrying two tusks, which he will deliver to the Game Department. But the gun bearer cannot be expected to carry, and Abdallah and Mata take them away from Goa without grumbling and strap them on to their own loads, although each tusk weighs at least twenty-five pounds.

East of the river a dust devil arises, and one of the porters murmurs "*Moto*" – "Fire". Brian explains that the dust devil is actually a kind of thermal, upon which Goa, who almost never speaks except when spoken to, makes one of his rare utterances. As the younger Africans stare at the white men, wondering how we will take it, Mzee Goa says forcefully, "*No!*" Brian awaits him. "No!" Goa repeats in his deep voice. "That wind is made by a very big kind of snake. This snake lives in the Taita Hills, under the hill called Kasigan; this snake looks after the wellbeing of our hills. When it stirs, there are rock slides, and when it emerges, the spirits take it up into the sky in one of these spiral winds. The big snake is not visible, but if you listen carefully you can hear a kind of ringing."

Impala go bounding off in all directions, as if to spread the bad news of man's arrival, and in an harmonious broad bend of the river a group of kongoni on an evening outing walk sedately on the sand, escorting with ceremony a new and pretty calf, as if they could scarcely believe that it was theirs. Seeing the oncoming men they bounce away upriver, and because the calf still runs like an antelope, it keeps up with their odd progress, making long ground-gaining leaps like a small impala. But neither impala nor kongoni have run far before the flight impulse forsakes them and they turn their big eyes and big ears to take us in.

Beyond the kongoni five elephants, dusted the red color of the Tsavo elephants of Goa's youth, stand peacefully in the sun-bloodied water, and downriver a solitary bull feeds in a meadow just behind the bank. Like all the bulls that we have seen this is a young one, with small ivory, and reading my thoughts Brian says, "Where are the big bulls, Peter? I can't pretend to myself much longer that all those elephants seen from the air are back up in the thickets, or the big herds of buffalo, either; we've been back in the thickets, and they're just not there." I remind him that we had been lucky to see rhino, despite the abundant sign of rhino presence everywhere; it would have been simple to miss these enormous beasts entirely in a country as huge and wild as the Selous. Brian nods; he is not really upset. "Upriver from Kibaoni, now, where this river opens out in great flat plains, there's a lot of wild cane that elephants seek out in the dry season; perhaps *that's* where they all are. Perhaps they've all gone further south."

On the river sand, the footprints of ten men obscure the sinuous tail trace of a large crocodile, set off by hieroglyphs of odd long-toed feet. September sandpipers sweep up and down the bars, and a sand plover flutters forth in injury display from a nest depression somewhere near our path; the sandpipers are autumn migrants from the northern continents, but for the sand plover of austral Africa, it is now spring.

An open point set off by borassus palms, with a prospect of open plains and hills and broad bends of the river, and animals in sight in all directions – here was a camp site of the Old Africa that would have been chosen by those men of unknown color who left stone tools on the black granite, more than a thousand centuries ago. We bathe in the river, and afterward I fix myself a whiskey with fresh river water and sit propped up on my cot, on a low open bluff under borassus, gazing out across the sweep of sunset water to the green plain of Africa beyond; I feel tired, warm and easy, and awash with content. Kazungu brings good buffalo stew, and as the stars appear we listen to a leopard just over the river – big deep coughs, well-spaced and strangely violent in a way that the lion roar is not, followed by that rough cadence so like the sound of a ripsaw cutting wood. Perhaps the leopard is disturbed by the unfamiliar light of a fire across the river; perhaps, like that gentle rhino, like the tame antelopes of the southern Selous, it is only vaguely troubled by our intrusion, having had no experience of man.

"I reckon the leopard is about the wildest animal there is. He's keen in eyesight and hearing as well as sense of smell, and he can hide so well that you can't see him when he's right there next to you; that's why following up a wounded one is bloody dangerous. Back on the old farm in Subukia, when I was a kid, there were still a lot of leopard about, raiding the stock; I had a big skin on the wall of my room that scared me, I used to imagine awful encounters with leopards." In his disreputable green shuka and red sneakers Brian lies back on his cot, fresh-shaven, towel around his neck. "My stepfather was mauled by one. This leopard had been taking his pigs, and he got a shot at it and wounded it. Perhaps half the time a wounded elephant or buffalo, even a lion, will push off again when you follow it up, but not a leopard. A wounded leopard is going to come for you the very first time you bother him, every time; sometimes he doesn't run for the thicket at all but comes straight for you after the first shot. He's so bloody fast that you don't realize he's coming until he's already covered half the ground between, and he isn't a big target, either – if you manage to stop him before he's on you, you're bloody lucky. Anyway, my stepfather was a farmer, he hadn't much experience of the bush. When he went after that leopard he was torn apart, and later they had to amputate his leg. No antibiotics then, of course; he was lucky he survived the septicemia."

When I ask Brian if he liked his stepfather, he frowns. "My stepfather was a steady sort of chap, but I never knew him well enough to know how much I liked him," Brian says, slightly uncomfortable. "They send you away to school pretty early in East Africa; I was only about eight, and even when I managed to get home, he was always out on the farm all day." Brian raises his eyes and looks me over, as if considering whether to say what he says next. "Didn't know my real father at all. Had a farm at Eldoret where I was born, but lost it during the Depression. My parents divorced when I was three, and I was given my stepfather's name when my mother remarried and we moved down to Nakuru. My dad came down here to this country, it was Tanganyika then; his name was Dickinson. He died in South Africa in 1967, and the rest of them were scattered to South Africa and Australia and Rhodesia, all but my half-brother Mike, who's a first-class wildlife painter in Nairobi. Can't say I know Mike, really. My mother's in Johannesburg with my full brother; haven't seen her in the last twelve years. My brother's in business there. I can't say I know him, either; never did." After another pause, he shrugs. "Ionides was sort of a father, I suppose, though I was already nineteen when I first met him."

Considering his history, one can quite understand the susceptibility of this young recruit to the fierce Ionides, who was not only a legendary hunter but the despotic ruler of a vast, unknown domain. And the impression made was a profound one, to judge from apparent similarities in attitudes and statements, even style: a certain odd smile, a cocking of the head, an indifference to food, alcohol, and dress are all traits that were noticed in his mentor, and so is the defensive habit of trying to conceal enthusiasm or excitement in order to be prepared for disappointment. But Brian Nicholson, for all his self-imposed isolation, needs a woman and perhaps he needs children, and try as he may, he cannot achieve the coldness of Ionides or even his notorious "eccentricity", which by all accounts consisted mainly of cranky self-absorption and a rather childish defiance of conventional restraints such as might have been imposed at Rugby School. For example, Ionides felt constricted by socks, underwear, and neckties, and dispensed with these even on his rare visits to London.

"Iodine was thought 'eccentric' because he liked living alone off in the bush. He didn't need people. He had all those books he left to me, and he could quote from every one of them, and I reckon that was all the company he needed. They also decided he was 'eccentric' because he didn't bother much about his clothes, and because he liked snakes, and because he visited a witch doctor and let himself get bit by a young cobra, to try to establish antibodies in case of snake bite. Not the least bit eccentric, really. I'd have been thought eccentric, too, if I hadn't been more conventional and got married.

"Iodine warned me about getting married, but I didn't listen; I had been out in the bush too long. Having small children, Melva rarely came out on safari in those early years; she scarcely set foot in the Reserve until after we moved up to Morogoro. She keeps the house beautifully, she's a lovely cook, she's good at gardens, and of course she saw to the three children. She helped me in many ways, of course, but she never became part of the work out here, she saw the Selous as a visitor might see it.

"You know, Peter, it's a funny thing," Brian continues, after a pause. "We saw so few people all those years, and now that we're back there in Nairobi, we don't see many people either; I don't even see very much of Billy Woodley. Mind you," he says, "I've been out of the Kenya wildlife scene since I came down here, and I've just been flying bloody airplanes since I went back." He grunts. "Tried to get Billy down here more than once. He always said the same damned thing that Myles Turner used to say: 'You've got a great bit of Africa down there, I'll have to come and have a look at it!'" The Warden shakes his head. "Neither of them ever came. It always amazes me how few people interested in wildlife have taken the trouble to come to the Selous."

Brian sighs. "It used to be that the day I left for overseas, I was already pining for Africa, not just the animals, you know, but the whole way of life out here. But since I've been up in Nairobi, I don't feel like that any more; the way Nairobi is today, being there is like being overseas, and I don't mind leaving it at all."

Rick Bonham had once mentioned to me having seen some fine bronzes and old books of Africana that Ionides had given Nicholson; to Rick's surprise, Brian had said more than once that he wished to sell them and tonight, in fact, Brian asks me what I know about the prices of old books and bronzes, describing those he had been given by Ionides. He had long since got rid of a pair of vast tusks, 101 and 103 pounds, from a great trophy elephant that he had shot on license, long ago up on the Kilombero, and he had already sold off all but one of his fine guns, a Rigby .275 that he had kept aside for Philip. The guns had been sold quickly in the bitter year that he had quit the Game Department and returned to Kenya, and perhaps, I thought, he would sell Ionides' books in the same spirit; possibly this was a way to put behind him his bitterness about what was happening to the great kingdom of the elephants that he and Ionides had created.

Brian recalls that one of his old hunting rifles had gone to an assistant warden named Johnnie Hornstead, "one of the most generous fellas you would ever meet, and a fine mechanic, too. Old Johnnie was a hell of a mess – great big stout fellow with a big beard, used to go around barefoot all the time. One time there was someone out here, taping a television show, and this TV man said, 'Well, Mr Hornstead, you must have a lot of time on your hands out here in the bush, may I ask what you do in your spare time?' 'Just mess around,' Johnnie informed him. 'Well, that's very interesting, Mr Hornstead, but would you mind amplifying that a little? Can you tell us what it means to mess around?' 'Why, certainly,' says Johnnie, 'what I do, you see, what I do is, well, I just bugger about!'" Brian whooped with laughter at this memory of old Johnnie, shaking his head. "One day when Johnnie was drunk, he was just sitting there sprawled out, barefoot as usual, a lot of food dribbled down on to his beard, and his drink, too, and the hair on his head all standing up and filthy dirty, and all upset about something or other that I'd said to him on the subject of evolution. And finally he opens up one bleary eye, belching, you know, and he says, 'I don't care if you are my superior, I don't care if you give me the sack for it, I'm going to tell you something, Nicholson – you're socially unacceptable!'" And telling this story, Brian laughs so hard that tears fall from his eyes, and we set each other off, making such a noise that even the Africans stop talking, and in that instant I realize that for better or for worse this socially unacceptable man and I have become friends.

When we stop laughing, we are quiet for a while, listening to the passing of the river. Asked if he thinks our foot safari has been worth while, he nods, saying, "Frankly, Peter, I've enjoyed your company." I have certainly enjoyed his, and say so; I am pleased that both of us can acknowledge this without embarrassment, however anxious we might be to change the subject as rapidly as possible. "I think this is the prettiest place we've made camp yet," Brian says finally, looking out over the gold-red of the river. "You know, I reckon I'm one of the very last people left who's done the real old African foot safari, staying out sometimes for months on end. Trekking with porters through remote, wild, wild bush like this, that hasn't changed a bit in three hundred years – that's not done in Africa any more. In Kenya, people just jump into their Land Rovers and minibuses and combis and away they go, but there really isn't any place left to go to. I saw the last of it up there twenty or thirty years ago, and the Selous is the last of it down here, make no mistake. That's why Rick Bonham is so excited. He's too young to have seen how Kenya was; this is the first time in his life that he's had a look at the real

Africa. Wants to move right down here, set up a safari camp. Philip, too," he said. "When I was his age, I was already down here on elephant control, and of course he wants to do what I did, and he can't; for one thing, Philip, I keep telling him, you're the wrong color. And for a second thing, you can't be me." No more, I thought later, than Brian Nicholson could be C. J. P. Ionides, or than Ionides could be Frederick Courtenay Selous. Yet, different though they were, there was a certain continuity between these three unsocial animals, who had strayed out of the herd existence into a hunter's life that, as someone has written, was lonely, poor, and great."

As he sits there barefoot in his shuka, freshly washed and his hair combed, and fit again after a fortnight in the bush, I have a glimpse of the young Bwana Kijana, come down to the Tanganyika Territories to join the Game Department on elephant control; in the strange half-light of sunset, the lines gone from his face and the gaze softened, he appears much as Ionides must have first seen him, as he must have appeared to the pretty Australian girl named Melva Peal, now sitting by the mess tent back at Mkangira, smoking her cigarettes and drinking her tea, and gazing with mild bafflement at the darkening river, winding down across that part of Africa where she has spent most of her life.

Over Brian's shoulder I watch Goa; he has gone down to wash, and now sits on his heels by the river's gleam like a driftwood stump. Each evening Goa comes to receive the instructions for the next day from Bwana Niki, and now he approaches and hunches down at a little distance, a mute, dark silhouette on the river bluff. Brian has not noticed him, but when I point, says, "Goa."

"This man here was always interested in the animals," Brian murmurs, as Goa comes and sits down on the ground nearby. "He really cares." In these days on foot safari Brian has spoken with affection and respect not only of Goa but of many Africans he has known and worked with in the bush, granting them status as companions, as real people he could like and trust. When I mention this, he frowns. "If you find someone you can work with, out in the bush," he says, "someone you can trust, you're bound to become friends."

In recent years, Goa Mwakangaru has married a Taita woman sent down to him by their families, and he has two children. Now he wishes to return to Kenya, although he knows that if he does so there is almost no chance the Tanzanian authorities will send him his Game Department pension. Squatting on his heels near Bwana Niki, as content as ourselves to gaze out on the river, Goa says quietly, "All the good work that we did here in the old days is being ruined. There is nothing for me here in the Selous. I am discouraged, and I would like to return to my own people in the Taita Hills."

During the night, hyenas draw near to vent their desolate opinions, and toward daybreak the lions are resounding. "Never heard them at all," the Warden grumps, sipping his tea in the gray-pink light of the dawn sky; he has slept badly on the narrow camp cots that in recent years have replaced the sturdy safari cots of other days. "Don't like to miss the lions in the night. Never get sick of that sound, no matter how often I hear it."

In the red sunrise, a pair of pied kingfishers cross the path of light on the shallow river to the palm fronds overhead, and mate in a brief flurry in the sun's rays. With the light, the ground hornbills are still, and doves and thrushes rush to fill the silence.

A cool wind out of the south; we head downstream. A herd of impala, the emblematic antelope of Africa, springs away over the green savanna, and as we pass, the great milky-lidded eagle owl eases out of a thick kigelia and flops softly a short distance to another tree, pursued by the harsh racket of a roller. Already tending north-northwest toward its confluence with the Luwegu, the river unwinds around broad sand bars and rock bends, and wherever it winds away toward the east, the man called Goa cuts across the bends, following the river plains, the hills, the open woods, and descending once again to the westward river.

Acknowledgements

Especially I wish to thank Tom Arnold MP and David Paterson for inviting me to join the Selous expedition, and Brian Nicholson, who put aside a healthy distrust of writers in order to share his unique store of information and experience. All members of the expedition, African as well as European, made invaluable contributions that are identified within the text, and in addition, Hugo van Lawick made many helpful comments on the first draft of the manuscript.

Dr Alan Rogers of the University of Dar-es-Salaam provided a considerable amount of important information on the ecology of the Selous, and Drs Iain Douglas-Hamilton, John S. Owen, George B. Schaller, Thomas Struhsaker, and David Western were all helpful on critical points.

P. M.